ISRAELIS SPEAK

The Mideast, 1977 Showing Locations Mentioned During the Discussion

TERRITORY OCCUPIED BY ISRAEL SINCE JUNE 1967

APPROXIMATE AREA CONTAINING ISRAELI ARAB VILLAGES OF THE SO-CALLED "LITTLE TRIANGLE."

LEBANON

SYRIA

Golan Heights

- Maalot
- Safed
- Acre

Lake Tiberias

Galilee

- Haifa

- Nazareth

ISRAEL

- Umm el Fahm

- Jenin

Samaria

- Tulkarm
- Taybeh
- Tira
- Qalqilya

Kadum

- Nablus (Shechem)

Jordan River

Damiya Bridge

MEDITERRANEAN SEA

WEST BANK

Tel Aviv
Jaffa

- Lod
- Ramle

- Ramallah

- Ramat Eshkol
- Jericho

Allenby Bridge

Amman

JORDAN

- Ashdod

Latrun

- Jerusalem

- Bethlehem

- Gush Etzion

Dead Sea

- Hebron
- Kiryat Arba

- Gaza

Judea

- Samu

Gaza Strip

- El Arish

Negev

EGYPT

MILES

0   25

SINAI PENINSULA

ISRAELIS
SPEAK

About Themselves and the Palestinians

Edited by Larry L. Fabian and Ze'ev Schiff

Carnegie Endowment for International Peace
New York   Washington, D.C.

I.S.B.N. cloth 0-87003-007-8; paperback 0-87003-008-6.
Library of Congress Catalog Card Number: 75-51150

Printed in the United States of America.

Contents

Appendices

Preface

In 1976, the Carnegie Endowment for International Peace, a private and non-profit American foundation, invited a group of Israelis to spend a week discussing Israel and the Palestinian Arabs, and the prospects for peace between them. Neither the Israeli government nor the American government had a hand in initiating the meeting, in shaping its agenda, or in selecting the participants. The meeting took place only because the Endowment and these Israelis believed it is important for Americans to know more about how Israelis themselves think, feel, and speak about a problem so significant for Israel and the Palestinians, for the Israeli-American relationship, and for the course of Middle East diplomacy.

This book, ultimately, is the collective product of thirteen Israelis who are speaking only for themselves. They do not pretend, nor were they expected by the Endowment, to represent something called "Israeli public opinion." No group of thirteen Israelis could—as anyone who understands Israel knows. Although they do not reflect the full spectrum of views and variations in the extraordinarily complex Israeli political scene, they are politically and professionally diverse, and in the aggregate they provide a fair sample of the country's main currents of thinking in the internal debate on the Palestinian issue.

Theirs is a human document, as well as a discussion about politics. They grapple with national and personal dilemmas; they are not just searching for diplomatic options. They enter what turns out to be, in the end, a maze of ambivalence and disagreement and contradictions. At the center of the maze, however, is a core of consensus, a common denominator that defines what it means today to be an Israeli determined to assure the future of his nation. On the final day of the conference, Yair said it simply: "We now have a place under the sun, our place. And we are not going to relinquish this right, this privilege. After a long period, we don't have to ask anybody permission to live there."

As these Israelis searched for the right answers, it became evident that they also were searching for the right questions. In their unfolding discussion, the questions multiplied, while the answers remained elusive. Indeed, for the complicated and interconnected issues that pit Israelis and Palestinians against one another, perhaps no conclusive answers exist. Despite the richness of the dialogue, the discussion displays many gaps that were never narrowed, many ambiguities never clarified. The reader will find no collective predictions about Israel's probable diplomatic strategy, and no group declaration of objectives for

_y. What will be found—or can be found—are insights into the ways
_re likely to articulate their national interests vis-à-vis the Palestinians.
_ participants reviewed trends in Israeli public opinion and policy thinking
_ut the Palestinians. They appraised developments within the Palestine Libera-
tion Organization, and among the Palestinians in the West Bank, the Gaza Strip,
and Jordan. They assessed the Israeli-Palestinian-Jordanian triangle, and the
United States-Israeli-Palestinian one. Various participants led off each topic of
discussion with informal prepared remarks. At the conclusion of the meeting,
each participant had equal time to sum up his overall impressions, to offer prescriptions or prognoses for the future—and then to be questioned by his
colleagues.

The result was 800 pages of transcripts, all in English, the conference's working language. Prior to the meeting, the Endowment suggested that the resulting
transcripts be the basis for a published report, that all participants be identified in
the report as having taken part in the conference, and that the report would not
attribute expressed views to particular individuals. These understandings were
agreed on as the basis for the project. The participants also had understood that
one of them would be responsible for co-editing the report. At the end of the conference the Endowment asked Ze'ev Schiff to undertake this task with Larry L.
Fabian, director of the Endowment's Middle East Program. Fabian acted as
procedural chairman of the meeting, but neither he nor I participated substan-
tively; in the spirit of a dialogue designed to be exclusively Israeli, we remained
essentially observers. The participants had understood beforehand that only the
co-editors would exercise final judgment about what portions of the transcripts
(which were not distributed to the participants) would be used, and how. The
editors chose to draw heavily on the transcripts, for reasons they explain in their
overview. Each participant had an opportunity to offer reactions and suggestions on the draft of this book. None possessed or sought a veto over its
contents.

The Endowment owes special appreciation to the Rockefeller Foundation,
which made available for this meeting the Foundation's Villa Serbelloni Conference Center in Bellagio, Italy. By assisting with logistical preparations for the
meeting, and by providing an atmosphere conducive to intensive and uninter-
rupted discussion, the Foundation contributed importantly to this project's
realization.

What the discussants and the editors have produced is in some ways a unique
document—certainly for American audiences. Some participants themselves
even felt that such an exchange of views, structured according to the ground
rules of this conference, would have been an unusual event in Israel. The Endowment is grateful to them, and we believe their dialogue merits attention by all who
care about the connection between peace in the Middle East and the deeply
rooted issues dividing Israel and the Palestinians.

Thomas L. Hughes
President
Carnegie Endowment for International Peace

ISRAELIS
SPEAK

Anyone wishing really to comprehend Israeli perspectives on this problem needs not a simple picture of reality, but an accurate one.

1

Editors' Overview

When we read the meeting's transcript for the first time together, our reactions were unexpectedly similar. Despite our different backgrounds—one an Israeli who for decades has lived with the conflict and written about it as a journalist, the other an American distant from the conflict personally and only recently exposed to it professionally—we found ourselves agreeing basically that the dialogue contained much that might interest a diverse readership. We also saw a kind of coherence in the transcript. It reflected faithfully the nuances of the participants' different political views, their expert and non-expert perspectives, and the rhythm of their reactions and counterreactions to the discussion's main themes. In all, it exposed what they regard as the essential problems between Israel and the Palestinians. We therefore decided to make maximum possible use in this book of the transcript itself, and to leave our own language and interpretations comparatively inconspicuous.

We think the result does the fullest justice to all the participants' own opinions. A neat, tight synopsis written by the editors would no doubt have been easier for the reader to digest. But then it would have been us and not them speaking.

This overview offers a glimpse of certain recurring trends in the discussion—without necessarily giving them any particular weight or implying that all or even most participants addressed all topics. Our introductions to Chapters 4 and 5 supply some brief background, and we have inserted explanatory information where needed in the dialogue. Beyond these interventions on our part, the discussants are on center-stage, and their own concluding statements and exchanges seem to us an appropriate finale for this volume. Throughout, we have only rarely, and for editorial reasons, changed the sequence of presentations, comments, and questions.

Each participant has been given a fictitious name, which he keeps for the entire proceedings. The meeting was candid. The participants spoke freely and often unselfconsciously. We decided not to dilute remarks simply because they were frank. The participants challenge each other vigorously. They probe deeply into Israel's predicament on the Palestinian question. They trace its impact on some of

Israel's most sensitive internal and external interests. They acknowledge their country's choices to be at once risky, uncertain, profoundly controversial, and probably unavoidable.

Anyone who is interested in doing so could easily take this or that fragment of the discussion out of context. Others might misinterpret the participants' spirit of constructive self-examination and self-criticism. These are liabilities of our lighthanded editorial approach, and we are not unmindful of them. Yet we sensed from this meeting that its content deserves no less than the maximum possible exposure. To read it in its totality is to see that for the participants, the dialogue reflects their affirmation that the Palestinian issue must be tackled within the context of Israel's fundamental interests, and not at the expense of those interests. And it reflects a belief that anyone wishing really to comprehend Israeli perspectives on this problem needs not a simple picture of reality, but an accurate one. The discussion, however imperfect and inconclusive it is, paints this reality as Israelis see it and as they want others to understand it.

To view the Israeli-Palestinian question through Israeli eyes, the reader must be sensitive to two undercurrents in these discussions. First: 1967 matters more than 1973. The consequences of Israel's victory in the Six Day War greatly heightened the country's dilemma about the Palestinians, and qualitatively altered for the first time since 1948 the practical implications of that dilemma. Second: for Israelis, there are no precise boundaries around "the Israeli-Palestinian question." It is enmeshed with the entire Jewish-Israeli experience in historic Palestine and with all important dimensions of Israel's present-day diplomatic situation.

The Israeli-Palestinian imbroglio has preoccupied Israel longer than many outside observers realize, even though the Palestinians did not attract world headlines until the late sixties and early seventies. But the 1967 war had already thrust the Palestinian question into prominence as a national problem virtually overnight, engaging all main elements in the Israeli political establishment. And the 1973 war turned the question into a foreign policy issue again with a suddenness that most Israelis did not anticipate.

After 1967, no longer could the 1948 war be seen to have resolved the underlying conflict that had escalated between the Jewish and Arab communities in Palestine during the period of British rule under a League of Nations Mandate in the twenties and thirties.* If the conflict had appeared to dissolve after 1948 into an international refugee question or into a domestic Israeli matter of policy towards the Israeli-Arab minority, the appearance was shattered in 1967. Physical barriers were once again down between the peoples who had been insulated from each other since the days of the mandate, only this time in the uneasy and uncertain circumstances of Israeli occupation.

After 1967, too, many Israelis were exposed at a personal level for the first time. They visited the West Bank out of curiosity and religious attachment—indeed, during the first year or so after the war, these visits became something of a national pastime. Israelis served in the army there. They engaged in commercial transactions. They saw a growing proportion of Israel's manual jobs filled by workers coming into Israel daily from the West Bank and the Gaza Strip. They

*Appendix XI contains a series of historical maps depicting the evolution of the conflict from the mandate period to the present time.

saw Jewish-Arab contact on a daily basis in the city of Jerusalem, the formerly Jordanian sector of which was annexed by Israel during the summer of 1967.

Controversy over the future of the territories and their Palestinian inhabitants became a more or less permanent feature of the political landscape in Israel during the years that followed. Prominent leaders and major political parties could not avoid the issue. The military occupation produced a subtle and complex adjustment between ruler and ruled, neither party finding it completely satisfactory or absolutely intolerable, and neither forgetting that the bedrock reality was the Arab wish to see the Israeli dominion come to an end. And the general Israeli population, once the novelty of visits to the West Bank and the Gaza Strip wore off, paid less personal attention to them, despite continued official and commercial contacts.

Of the participants only Amir characterized the impact of 1967 as bluntly as this: "It may very well be that in retrospect—it still seems premature to draw conclusions—the war of 1967 will appear as the greatest disaster in the history of the state of Israel." The context for this observation on the final day of the conference was his judgment, which was contested sharply by some colleagues, that Israeli acquisition of Arab lands during the Six Day War marked the beginning not only of a more dangerous and exhausting cycle of military mobilzation in the Middle East but also of a heightened Arab determination to carry on its struggle against Israel, and an intensification of the Palestinian problem.

The discussions amply show other reasons why 1967 is regarded as a major turning point in Israel's relationships to the Palestinians. "We have to remember," Dror urged, "that most of the Israeli public was, at first, indifferent about the Palestinian question because hundreds of thousands of immigrants came to Israel between 1948 and 1967, and, for them, the Palestinian question was just an abstract question. Their indifference was evident in the almost complete absence of the subject from educational curricula and even from press articles."

Not only did Israel in 1967 acquire dominion over more than a million Palestinians in the newly-annexed Arab sector of East Jerusalem and in the West Bank and Gaza Strip territories that were placed under military administration. Not only was Israel then confronted with dramatic change in the country's demographic balance, potentially threatening to erode the state's essential Jewish majority and posing practical and moral problems for the Israeli community. More important were the more subtle political aftereffects of the 1967 war that were felt throughout the Palestinian population, and that gradually altered Israeli perceptions about the meaning of the Palestinian question.

Closest to home, 1967 increased the self-awareness and nationalism of the 470,000 Arab citizens of Israel, an incompletely assimilated minority who remained there after the 1948-49 war and who now comprise 13 percent of Israel's population. Eitan's assessment was that "the direction of the changes in public opinion among Israeli Arabs since 1967—certainly after 1973—was towards Arab nationalism as the Palestinian Arabs present it." And in the West Bank, a comparable process of change was discerned by Oren after 1967: "The Palestinian issue in the Gaza Strip and in Lebanon, but not in the West Bank, was acute for twenty years, from 1948 to 1967. But after 1967, the Palestinians in the West Bank began to feel the issue acutely too." As expressed in various ways during the meeting, this assertion boiled down to a belief that had Israel not taken the West Bank in 1967, the Palestinians who had for twenty years lived there under Jordanian rule might have become progressively more Jordanianized and less likely to assert an independent Palestinian identity. As Oren continued: "But after 1967 this process of Jordanianization in the West Bank stopped, and the West Bankers became more and more Palestinian. I think that the same process occurred in the Israeli-Arab population."

Since 1967, the growing debate in Israel on the Palestinian question produced divisions within major political parties, between the Left and the Right, and within the ruling coalition led by the Labour Party. Political party allegiance and simple labels do not serve to categorize Israeli views on the Palestinian issue. Nor can the opinions of the public at-large be discerned with much precision by polls or by the results of national elections. Polls are too impressionistic or too insensitive to the volatility of Israeli opinion on the subject. And the Palestinian question did not figure as an election issue in either 1969 or 1973—the only two national election years since the Six Day War.

Furthermore, after 1967 the Palestine Liberation Organization (PLO) intensified its military and political campaign against Israel, attracted new identification from the Palestinians under Israel's control, and acquired greater Arab recognition and international recognition after the 1973 war gave new diplomatic prominence to the Palestinian question.

The dialogue leaves the reader with an impression that the internal and external developments have brought Israel closer perhaps than it has been since 1948 to a crossroad on the Palestinian question. Many Israeli concerns intersect at that crossroad. These thirteen individuals, in order to discuss the Palestinians and Israel, felt compelled to draw into their discussion questions ranging from the meaning of Zionism for Jews and Judaism, to the Palestinian nationalist reaction against Zionism in the twenties and thirties, to the implications of the September, 1975, Sinai II Pact between Israel and Egypt. In ways more complicated than this dialogue can convey, the Palestinian question reaches to the very essence of Israel. To treat it only as a question of military or diplomatic strategy, or of whether to talk or not with the PLO—however important these questions are in their own right—would be to misread what is perhaps the most important message of these discussions.

That the Palestinian question is so fundamental becomes evident, first, as the dialogue exposes participants' views about the relevance of Zionism for their main subject. These were among the assertions about the legacy of Zionist history: That the Zionist experience and indeed the entire history of the Jewish people validates the supremacy of Zionist rights as against those of the Arabs of Palestine, even if their national and political identity is now regarded as authentic. And that injustices committed against the Palestinians during the course of fulfilling Zionist aspirations impose a moral obligation on Israelis to strive for a solution of their conflict with the Palestinians, not in spite of Zionist imperatives but because of a commitment to justice that gives meaning to Zionism in its contemporary setting. These were among the assertions about the choices of Zionism today: That the continuation of a vital, Zionist Israel can be assured only through some kind of accommodation between Israel and the Arabs. And that Israel's future not only can, but must be secured independently of such an accommodation, even assuming it to be feasible. These were among the assertions

Dialogue Fragments

"Had I taken part in this forum eight or ten years ago I might have expressed completely different views on the scope of the Palestinian problem. Yet, as much as I would like to escape it, I feel we can't escape admitting that recently the problem once known as 'the refugee problem' has passed a substantial transformation and is now an issue on a national level. I do accept the fact that a process has started which can very well result in the creation of a new people within the broad sense of this word—the Palestinian people. And believe me it wasn't simple for me to finally arrive at this conclusion. Without diminishing the importance of the conflict with the Palestinians, I believe that the whole conflict in the Middle East did not originate with the Palestinians and its solution does not depend solely on some agreement with them. Yet I do believe, at the same time, that without some progress on the Palestinian issue, no progress towards final true peace is possible because of the commitment of the whole Arab world to the Palestinians."

"In my own home, my daughter speaks about the right of the Palestinians."

"In my pessimistic mood, an image often plagues me; it was used by a Jewish philosopher in the 1930s. He spoke of the angel of history. He said that the angel of history is an angel who goes backwards into the future. He looks toward the past, and he is pushed by a big wind backwards into the future. And I'm afraid sometimes in my pessimistic mood that in Israel, if we cannot take the really courageous decisions, we shall be like the angel of history—with our faces turned toward the past, but with the wind really pushing us backwards into the future, without our knowing or seeing where we are going."

"It is impossible to discuss any political questions without a broader historical outlook. And this is especially true in relation to the Jewish people whose consciousness of the historical dimension is essential and central—more than for any other people. I have to return to the past because I have only the past. What do I have? I don't have the future."

Dialogue Fragments

"The possibilities are only two: either to reach an agreement or to be demolished."

"We all have only two options: either submission or, as I think, we should try to find our own way in this very dangerous world."

"I myself don't remember from the age of six one peaceful year."

"We are polarized today in Israel on this question because we are not only discussing the Palestinians, but also how we see Zionism. How do we see Zionism in the context of Judaism? In my view the Palestinian question makes no sense if we do not speak on that level."

"I believe that in a way this symposium was actually about Zionism. It was about whether we believe or not anymore in Zionism, and about how hard we are ready to fight or how much we are ready to sacrifice for Zionism."

"Zionism has only begun."

"The Zionist movement has already passed its peak."

"I value peace above anything."

"I will answer the Arabs, 'I want your peace more than anything— well, almost more than anything. Zionism is more important to me.'"

"The Arabs, the people in the street, they want peace. They don't want to kill and to be killed, to destroy and to be destroyed."

"The first Arab is still to be born who will say to himself and to his brethren, 'this war is bad for me.'"

about the future of Zionism: That it will be nourished by massive Jewish immigration—*aliyah*—from the Diaspora to Israel, guaranteeing a large Jewish majority there even if Israel does not return territories and the Palestinian population won in 1967. And that prospects for *aliyah* in such numbers are illusory or uncertain enough that only an Israel without the one million Palestinians of the West Bank and the Gaza Strip can be assured of a substantial Jewish majority for the foreseeable future.

Underlying these portions of the dialogue were participants' convictions about the character of Zionism and democracy in an Israel with a significant minority whose natural rate of increase greatly exceeds that of the state's Jewish citizens. Does Israel face one day a painful choice between remaining an essentially Jewish state with a decisive Zionist majority or remaining a genuinely democratic one with full political rights granted to a large minority that is neither Jewish nor Zionist? How, if at all, is the moral and political complexion of such a choice different for an Israel comprising the Israeli-Arab minority now citizens of Israel, or for an Israel that governs also the Palestinians of the West Bank and the Gaza Strip? In terms of Zionist values, is there a political solution to these dilemmas? And is there a moral solution?

Second, the Palestinian question reopens the issue of the legitimacy of Israel's borders. Many participants assume that the most deeply rooted opposition in the Arab world to Israel's legitimacy comes from the Palestinian Arabs who began the fight against Zionism in the twenties, and who refused to accept the UN Partition Plan of 1947 because it sanctioned Israel within internationally recognized boundaries—even more limited than Israel's borders between 1949 and 1967.

Is the maximum conceivable Palestinian compromise now an acceptance of Israel within those 1947 borders? Would movement back toward the 1967 borders defuse or merely intensify pressures for a 1947 solution? Would the Soviet Union, Europeans, and others in the international community support such a solution? How reliable are indicators that the 1967 borders would be recognized given certain conditions? If Israel retains territories acquired in 1967, will Palestinian nationalism in those territories deepen or recede, and with what consequences? Is future Israeli Arab separatism an added threat to the integrity of the 1967 borders, since the Israeli Arabs live mostly in areas not part of Israel according to the partition map of 1947? And would such irredentism inevitably result from the emergence of a Palestinian state in the West Bank and Gaza Strip? That these questions were pursued as often as they were underlines how problematic they are for Israelis and how troubling are some of the possible answers.

Third, the Palestinian question connects at many points with vital issues in Israeli diplomacy. Not all these issues receive attention in the dialogue, but among them, three are featured prominently.

One is the connection between fundamental, long-term Arab intentions toward Israel and Israel's opportunities for diplomatic maneuver, about which a pointed exchange took place during the first hours of the conference. Feeling that expert assessment by Israelis leaves "very little to the imagination about what are the real intentions of the Arabs—Palestinians and the Arab countries—and how deep these intentions go and how seriously one should take them," Yair said, "What I am going to say might be a simplification, but nevertheless true: the Arabs and the Palestinians are not going to rest before the state of Israel is abolished. In my view, this is the major fact. All the rest is beside the point." And Amir responded, "Experts ... do not differ on the basic interpretation of Arab attitudes and intentions, [but].... all the rest is not beside the point. Precisely the opposite.... Once we have established the Arab intentions toward Israel, then the question arises: what do you do under such circumstances? ... Do you indulge in despair? Or in hopes linked to the possible use of nuclear weapons? Or do you continue to search for any possible arrangements which can be worked out ...?" The group's answers varied, as did their views on whether Israel's immediate diplomatic objective should be peace, some transitional steps to reduce the level of conflict, or some form of coexistence short of peace. They differed on how much leeway Israel possesses to negotiate and on how much Israel can do to influence Palestinians to move toward peace with Israel. The participants found themselves confronted with one of their clearest dilemmas: most of them proposed policy directions that they themselves admit are likely to be unacceptable either to the Arabs or to the Israeli public—or to both. Little else in the dialogue so vividly underlines the elusiveness of solutions mutually acceptable to the Middle East protagonists.

The Palestinian question also connects pervasively with Israel's strategy toward Jordan. None of the participants argued—as some Israelis have since 1967—that a separate peace with the Palestinians on the West Bank and the Gaza Strip is any longer possible. Some think it never has been. Some argued that the local Palestinian leaders still might be able to play an active role in future diplomatic processes—and that Israel ought to encourage that role—even if they cannot reach a separate agreement with Israel. No one in the group challenged the proposition that since 1973 the PLO has achieved a position, in practical terms, as the pre-eminent representative of the Palestinian people—although, as we explain in our introduction to Chapter 4, they accepted this proposition for different reasons and drew from it widely differing political conclusions. With all of these considerations contributing to their thinking, the group asked: Is Jordanian moderation a thing of the past, or does it persist? Was Israel right to have positioned itself to save King Hussein in 1970—and in doing so, to protect American interests as well—if he had not been able to handle on his own the Palestinian Fedayeen challenge to his throne during the Jordan civil war that year? If Israel were to return the West Bank to King Hussein could he continue to hold it? Is Jordan, with its East Bank Palestinian majority, eventually going to become a state led by the Palestinians and possibly the PLO—no matter what Israel does? And should Israel promote this outcome?

The Palestinian question, finally, connects inevitably with the triangular relationship between Israel, the United States, and the Palestinians. Because the participants felt that this triangular connection cannot be separated from the US position on the overall conflict as such, the broader contours of the Israeli-American relationships received considerable attention. The American attitude towards the Palestinians and the PLO was said to have undergone marked shifts in recent years, with the United States no longer treating the Palestinian question as a humanitarian-refugee issue, no longer deeply estranged from the Palestinians as it was a decade ago, and no longer willing to believe that a negotiated settlement in the Middle East is possible without taking account of the Palestinians. Some in the group believe that Washington has already decided to

Dialogue Fragments

"I daresay that the American attitude toward the conflict is our central problem."

"It doesn't seem to me that there is a serious strategic American interest in Israel."

"For a moment we must forget our wonderful atmosphere. In twenty-four hours we'll be on our way home. There are the famous homing pigeons, homing doves, and even the hawks are homing. We are on our way home, and let us be now home. And let us ask ourselves, 'What is going to happen in the near future?' There is one simple answer to it. What you call the conflict—I call it the war—is going on. It is not going to be discontinued. I don't see when, not in the near future. And we have to survive this war day by day and hour by hour."

"It makes all the difference in the world if you know that you have absolutely no choice in something. Take the kids now in their last year of high school and their first year in the army. Among them I see this deterioration of principles. It is coming out of sheer confusion and despair—not knowing where they are going, what they are doing. If my son asks me: 'Did we really do everything to try to make peace with the Arabs?' Or, when he goes to the army, if he says: 'I have to stand in [the West Bank] and hit some of the school children over the head there—did we do everything to avoid this?' If I tell him we really did everything we could for peace, but they didn't want it, then he will know that he has to hit them over the head, that it is necessary."

"We used to say that there is a leadership crisis in Israel. I don't think it's a leadership crisis. It's more a confusion crisis. It's the first time since the establishment of the state that we have to find exact answers to a new challenge. Maybe Israel is confused about the alternatives she is facing. But we are in complete agreement on one issue: the issue of our survival."

opt for a Palestinian state, others that Washington still prefers to see Jordan as primarily responsible for the West Bank and will maintain this posture until the Jordan option no longer seems feasible.

Some participants acknowledged that their own preferred solutions to the Palestinian question would guarantee a serious conflict of interest with the United States, but on balance they believe Israel should be prepared to accept this consequence—though within the group there were diverse views about how such a conflict of interests could be managed, and how detrimental it might be to the basic fabric of Israeli-American relations.

The participants' judgments about these relations are shaped importantly, of course, by their perception of Israeli dependence on America as well as by their strong reaction against the post-1973 thrust of American Middle East diplomacy. Pinhas, a participant for whom American strategy has meant Israeli territorial withdrawals without satisfactory concessions from the Arabs, believes that in a future conflict of interest between Israel and the United States, Israel will have "to force a serious reassessment of American policies." He urges that "instead of trying to maneuver within the limited official community," Israel will have to see if American public opinion and the Congress will agree with its positions. To a colleague who had warned of adverse results for Israel from this strategy he said, "I'm not sure ... that the outcome will be unfavorable for Israel."

Had this meeting been convened in 1967 or any time soon after the Six Day War, it would not have produced a dialogue like the one that unfolds in the following pages. Israel's military victory had given the society a buoyant self-confidence, a pervasive belief that the defeated Arabs were left with no choice but to make peace, a conviction that captured Arab lands and the people inhabiting them were the ultimate bargaining cards that Israel would lay on the table when the Arabs finally came to negotiate. They did not come. They said at the Khartoum Arab Summit in 1967—no peace, no negotiation, and no recognition. As the Palestinian question evolved in the intervening years, and as it became one of the most divisive issues in Israeli politics, another even more destructive war in 1973 prefigured a shift in the balance of power between the Arabs and Israel. This war's ambiguous political outcome generated some hope that the very ambiguity could provide the impetus towards peace that Israel's earlier victory could not.

Whether this hope is still alive is a topic on which the participants hold different views. Yet what is evident is that this group does not indulge in illusions about the importance of the Palestinian question for Israel's national interests. For them it is crucially important. They acknowledge that for Israel, as well as for the Palestinians and the Arab states, some political satisfaction for the Palestinians is now essential. Some readers will believe that their dialogue points to possible paths toward that satisfaction; others will not.

The specific rationales advanced during this meeting for some kind of a resolution of the Israeli-Palestinian conflict also would not have been voiced immediately after the 1967 war. Then, most Israelis did not tend to say that they needed to find a solution because they owed it to themselves—to their sense of morality about Palestinian rights, or to future generations of Israelis, or to an Israeli public confused about whether peace with the Palestinians is possible. Then, most Israelis did not tend to say that a Palestinian solution was required because without one the Arab-Israeli conflict would go on, would lead to more

destructive wars and possibly to nuclearization of the Middle East, and would encourage demoralization and extremism within Israel itself. During the meeting,
not all of the participants accepted these rationales, but they heard them, they
reacted to them, and they gave one or the other of them a credence that would not
have been possible a decade ago.

The multiple perspectives that make up the Israeli posture toward themselves
and the Palestinians begin to emerge from the very outset of the dialogue. Amir's
opening portrayal of the Israeli political scene evoked immediate challenge and
refinement from participants with different intellectual orientations, different
descriptions of the problem, and different judgments about policy choices. He and
several other participants focus primarily on the diplomatic-political and security
ingredients of Israel's situation—particularly the internal and international
changes since 1967 that have pushed the Palestinian question higher on the foreign policy agenda, the motivations behind Israeli policy positions, the appraisal
of Arab intentions and capabilities, and the dynamics of interacting Israeli and
Palestinian policies. A second broad approach among the participants, while not
disregarding these pragmatic considerations, places relatively greater weight on
the historical, ideological, and moral factors in the Israel-Palestinian equation.
And some participants saw these factors more influential for the Israeli public at
large than the arguments and counter-arguments dominating the debate among
the policymaking elites. A third approach divides Israeli attitudes on the basis of
whether or not they entail different interpretations of Zionism and its implications for the Palestinian question. These several postures are not necessarily
mutually exclusive. Some participants drew on each of them; others did not. It
was a matter of priority, emphasis, and proportion.

Since Amir's attempt to summarize the broad trends in Israeli thinking served
throughout the conference as a touchstone for those participants who agreed
with him as well as for those who did not, we present it separately as Chapter 2,
the backdrop for the dialogue that begins in Chapter 3.

*The debate has been our bread and butter for
so many years.*

2

Ourselves: One View

AMIR: A change has been taking place since 1973 in Israeli political thinking about the Palestinians. The Palestinian question has become more concrete and tangible, compared to its earlier status in the internal Israeli debate. I am not saying that before the Yom Kippur war the Palestinian issue was completely abstract or ideological, or concerned only with historical rights and principles; it did have some concrete aspects even then. And I am not saying that after 1973 the ideological dimension became unimportant; it still looms quite large. But certainly, as a result of a number of developments, the Palestinian problem for the Israelis is now a problem which relates to practical politics. The Israeli government and people now are confronted with a need to answer specific questions about the Palestinians.

Before 1973, we should remember, the basis for all efforts to seek some sort of arrangement to settle the Middle Eastern crisis was Security Council Resolution 242. It does not mention the Palestinians directly, only the refugee problem, implying that the Palestinian issue is a humanitarian one within the framework of a conflict basically between the Israeli state and the neighboring Arab states. Before 1973,

there was no pressure from the United States on Israel to include a Palestinian element in its positions. Nor was there any significant pressure in this direction from other powers.

Within the context of practical diplomacy, the Palestinian issue was not really central, and the Palestinians themselves were not a very significant element among the major political factors in this conflict. The Fedayeen were crushed in Jordan in "Black September," and they never constituted a real military threat to Israel.

Finally, Israeli positions were formulated by the government of Golda Meir. That government did not recognize, or the leading trio of that government—Golda Meir, [former Defense Minister] Moshe Dayan, and [Minister-without-Portfolio] Israel Galili—did not recognize, the need to deal with the Palestinians or even with the Palestinian issue. We all remember that famous interview in which Golda Meir said, in effect, that there was no Palestinian political problem, in fact there were no Palestinians at all.

The implication was that somehow it is a non-problem, that to the extent the issue exists, it should be attributed to misguided Israelis and others who accepted a basically false version of the nature of the conflict.

However, after 1973 three major changes appeared. The first was a change within Israeli politics. The authoritarian style of Golda Meir was replaced by the compromise style of Rabin's cabinet. As a result of the Yom Kippur war, there was a need to reformulate the platform of the Labour Party. Elements within the party which had not been allowed to make their voices heard effectively during the years of Golda Meir now managed to force a compromise on the party. This resulted in the famous fourteen points of the Labour Party platform at the end of 1973, which for the first time recognized the existence of the Palestinian problem.*

The second change was the initiation of a new diplomatic process, starting with Resolution 338, and the Geneva conference and leading to the US-sponsored step-by-step diplomacy. Within this diplomatic process, the need for a position on the Palestinian issue could no longer be avoided. The United States, perhaps, has not changed formally its position on the Palestinian component of the problem, but there were indirect hints to this effect, coming from the President himself, or from such State Department aides as Saunders.

These were signals to the Israelis that a position on the Palestinian issue would have to be formulated.

In the context of these diplomatic efforts the Arabs also clarified to some extent their concept of how the Palestinian element fits into their solutions. The Egyptians, particularly, made it much clearer than before 1967 that they wanted to see, in addition to a complete Israeli withdrawal from the territories, the establishment of a Palestinian state in the West Bank and the Gaza Strip. The need to relate to these Arab demands, which were supported also by some outside the Arab world, produced—for the first time on record—an Israeli cabinet discussion of the Palestinian problem, in July of 1974.**

The third change was the growing recognition of the PLO as "the sole representative of Palestinian rights." First the Arab world itself formalized its commitment to the PLO in the 1974 Rabat Resolution. Then the United Nations accepted Yasser Arafat, and is at present in the process of accepting the PLO into a growing number of UN bodies. Subsequently, a growing number of nations allowed the PLO to open offices in their capitals. There has been an increasing conviction in Europe and elsewhere in the world, including nations friendly to Israel, that the PLO

*"The peace agreement with Jordan will be between two sovereign states—Israel and with its capital a united Jerusalem and an Arab state to the east of Israel. Israel rejects the setting up of another, separate, Arab-Palestinian state west of Jordan. The independent identity of the Palestinian and Jordanian Arabs can find expression in a Jordanian-Palestinian state bordering Israel, under conditions of peace and good relations with Israel."

**At a meeting on July 21, 1974, a draft statement was presented to the cabinet, saying "efforts must be made to attain a solution to the problems of the Palestinians, if genuine peace negotiations with the Arabs are to ensue." And, "Israel will conduct negotiations with Jordan and the Palestinian factors which recognize Israel and its independence, and which are ready to reach agreements for lasting peace with Israel, on the basis of agreed and secure borders." Five ministers voted for this statement; thirteen voted against. The majority statement that was adopted read: "the government will work towards peace negotiations with Jordan [but] will not conduct negotiations with the terrorist organizations whose aim is the destruction of Israel."

"Golda Meir: 'Who Can Blame I.

Question: It seems to me that the heart of the Middle Eas
to be found in the plight of the Palestinians with their sense o
admit a measure of responsibility?

No, no responsibility whatsoever. If you say, is I
cooperate in the solution of their plight, the answ   ˷s. But we
are not responsible for their plight.

This is a humanitarian problem. But the Arabs who created this
refugee problem by their war against us and against the 1948 UN
resolution have turned this into a political problem. After all, there
are millions and millions of refugees in the world and I have not yet
heard anybody that said the three million Sudeten Germans should
go back to Czechoslovakia—nobody. I do not know why the Arab
refugees are a particular problem in the world.

Question: Do you think the emergence of the Palestinian fighting forces, the
Fedayeen, is an important new factor in the Middle East?

Important, no. A new factor, yes. There was no such thing as Palestinians. When was there an independent Palestinian people with a
Palestinian state? It was either southern Syria before the First
World War, and then it was a Palestine including Jordan. It was not
as though there was a Palestinian people in Palestine considering
itself as a Palestinian people and we came and threw them out and
took their country away from them. They did not exist.

There is really no such thing as a representative body speaking
for so-called Palestinians. Perhaps there was a possibility of coming
to some understanding with people of the Western Bank. After two
years, everybody has come to the conclusion there is no such thing.

Nor do I favour a separate, Palestinian Arab state. There are
fourteen Arab states with immense territories, with natural resources. What would this tiny state of the Western Bank really
mean as to its viability, as to the possibility of existence? It would
have to be part either of Israel or of Jordan.

An interview in the *Sunday Times* (London), June 15, 1969.

...esentative of Palestinian ...herefore must be recognized. ...uced, in Israeli politics, attempts ...pond to this challenge with such posi- ...ns as those of the Yariv formula.*

Let me try to outline schematically the spectrum of views within the Israeli public. The various facets of the debate, which has been our bread and butter for so many years, are all represented here, all the shades of opinion and styles of polemics.

To outline this spectrum, we shall obviously need some terminology. I suggest we use simply the terms "Left" and "Right." I propose to use them not in their traditional connotations, but simply as code words—using the term "Left" to indicate the Palestinian orientation in Israeli thinking and Israeli politics, and the term "Right" to indicate exactly the opposite.

For the purposes of the discussion, I will submit that those who are more Palestinian-oriented than Prime Minister Rabin—whose views I shall outline in a moment—will be described as being on the Left. And those who are less Palestinian-oriented than the prime minister will be described as being on the Right.

I shall have, of course, to use generalizations: the number of opinions in Israel on this subject is almost as great as the number of Israeli citizens—perhaps even greater.... I divide the various schools of thought into seven categories: Extreme Left, Left, Tactical Left, Center, Liberal Right, Right and Extreme Right.

I shall identify in this spectrum only political groups and political ideas within the framework of the Zionist consensus, and not outside it.

I include in the Extreme Left—and I stress that the word "extreme" does not connote "extremism," only an extreme position on this spectrum—groups like the new Council for Israeli-Palestinian Peace.** I include all those elements in the Israeli political public which maintain that there is a Palestinian people, and that the land of

Israel, Eretz Israel, is in fact the homeland of two peoples—the Jewish-Israeli people and the Arab-Palestinian people. They maintain that the conflict between Israeli society and the Palestinians is really the crux of the problem, the heart of the Arab-Israeli conflict. They maintain, therefore, that a solution should be sought in a partition of the land between these two peoples and the creation of a Palestinian state more or less behind the 1967 borders, with special arrangements for Jerusalem. This group accepts the creation of a third state between Israel and Jordan. It also is ready for negotiations with the PLO.

The Extreme Left, of course, is criticized by the Right, which usually suspects

*Aharon Yariv, former minister and head of military intelligence, described his formula in this way in a 1976 interview in *The Jerusalem Post Magazine*, June 18, 1976, p. 9.
"What I have said, again and again, is that I am prepared to talk to the PLO, or any other Palestinians, subject to three conditions: they have to repudiate the clause in their Covenant which calls for the elimination of Israel; they have to recognize the right of Israel to exist as a state; they have to give up terrorism."

**The Council is a private Israeli group established in 1975, whose program declares: "We affirm: That this land is the homeland of its two peoples—the people of Israel and the Palestinian Arab people.... That the establishment of a Palestinian Arab state alongside the state of Israel should be the outcome of negotiations between the government of Israel and a recognized and authoritative representative body of the Palestinian Arab people, without refusing negotiation with the Palestine Liberation Organization, on the basis of mutual recognition."
"The Israel Council for Israeli-Palestinian Peace: Manifesto," *New Outlook*: 19 (February/March 1976), p. 69.

United Nations Security Council Resolution 242
November 22, 1967

1. *Affirms* that the fulfillment of Charter principles requires the establishment of a just and lasting peace in the Middle East which should include the application of both the following principles:

(i) Withdrawal of Israeli armed forces from territories occupied in the recent conflict;

(ii) Termination of all claims or states of belligerency and respect for and acknowledgement of the sovereignty, territorial integrity and political independence of every State in the area and their right to live in peace within secure and recognized boundaries free from threats or acts of force.

2. *Affirms further* the necessity

(a) For guaranteeing freedom of navigation through international waterways in the area;

(b) For achieving a just settlement of the refugee problem;

(c) For guaranteeing the territorial inviolability and political independence of every State in the area, through measures including the establishment of demilitarized zones;

United Nations Security Council Resolution 338
October 22, 1973

2. *Calls upon* the parties concerned to start immediately after the cease-fire the implementation of Security Council Resolution 242 (1967) in all of its parts;

3. *Decides* that, immediately and concurrently with the cease-fire, negotiations start between the parties concerned under appropriate auspices aimed at establishing a just and durable peace in the Middle East.

it of being essentially non-Zionist. But criticism against it also comes from groups to the left of Center. They argue that the Extreme Left does not read the PLO correctly, that it overstates some vague indications within the PLO of readiness to recognize the state of Israel, indications which in fact have not been formalized and do not represent any concrete political trends within the PLO. They argue that this group belittles the security problems of Israel and the great risks involved in the creation of a Palestinian state along the vulnerable 1967 borders. They argue that the group does not realize that the Palestinians in the West Bank are part of a greater society which lives today on both sides of the Jordan River and that it is unrealistic—not only in terms of Israeli interests, but also in terms of Palestinian realities—to sever that link.

The second group, which I call Left proper, would include some persons in the ruling Labour Party's heirarchy and a good part of Mapam [a left-wing partner in the Labour Alignment] and the Independent Liberal Party [a centrist party in the governing coalition]. I would say it might also include Yigal Allon, although as a foreign minister, I suspect, he doesn't always have the latitude to air his views freely in public. The Left also maintains that the Palestinian issue occupies a central position—albeit not exclusively—in the Arab-Israeli conflict. For them this recognition is not a matter of yielding to external pressure but a reflection of a basic, historic Israeli interest. As Allon puts it, it is the Israelis who should insist that a comprehensive agreement should be reached with Palestinian participation.

This school of thought also recognizes the existence of a Palestinian people. It tends to regard the problem of the West Bank in terms of the people and not only in terms of territory. They warn that the

---

The Saunders Statement

Harold H. Saunders, a ranking State Department official, gave on November 12, 1975, congressional testimony that later received wide publicity in the Middle East.

"We have also repeatedly stated that the legitimate interests of the Palestinian Arabs must be taken into account in the negotiation of an Arab-Israeli peace. In many ways, the Palestinian dimension of the Arab-Israeli conflict is the heart of that conflict."

"What is needed as a first step is a diplomatic process which will help bring forth a reasonable definition of Palestinian interests—a position from which negotiations on a solution of the Palestinian aspects of the problem might begin."

"It is obvious that thinking on the Palestinian aspects of the problem must evolve on all sides."

The full text of this statement is reprinted in Appendix I.

annexation of the West Bank would not only jeopardize the Jewish character of the state of Israel, but might also undermine the moral fiber of Israeli society.

The Left differs from the Extreme Left, I believe, mainly on two issues. First, they are not ready to negotiate with the PLO in its present form. They argue that by expressing such readiness Israel not only would contradict its own principles and interests but also diminish the chances of any genuine changes taking place within the PLO itself in the future. And, second, this school of thought doubts the feasibility and advisability of a third state. It stresses the need for a solution linking both banks of the Jordan, either in the form of a federation—a Palestinian-Jordanian federation—or by some other arrangement. Some say that the Palestinians and Jordanians themselves should settle this issue and the Israelis should not try to think it out for them. Others say that within the larger Jordanian state, genuine Palestinian participation could materialize, for the Palestinians would constitute a majority. There are many variations on these themes, but the common denominator is that a future settlement must be made with genuine participation of the Palestinians—not a token participation and not one invited only for propaganda value.

The Left proper is definitely within the mainstream of the Israeli and the Zionist public and has strong representation within the Israeli cabinet itself. The Right challenges it on three accounts. First, the Right says that the whole program of the Left proper unrealistically assumes that the Palestinians and Jordanians will be ready to implement it, something which is very difficult to envisage. Ideas like the Allon Plan,* they argue, have been proposed and rejected by both Palestinians and Jordanians in the past. In addition, a solution linking both banks of the Jordan is strategically risky for the future existence of the state of Israel. And, finally, such a solution contradicts the basic Zionist aspiration of having a homeland for the Jewish people in Eretz Israel—not merely in a part of Eretz Israel.

I call the third group tactical because its members basically do not believe in a solution worked out between Palestinians and Israelis. The Tactical Left does not hold that any substantial, significant Palestinian participation in the diplomatic processes would serve a purpose. Nevertheless, they feel that—considering the pressures on Israel, the problems Israel has in world public opinion, the problems that Israel may have in its future relations with the United States—it would be advisable for the Israelis to present a more positive verbal position on this issue. Instead of repeating the classical negative formulas of Israeli leaders, they say, a positive formula can be submitted: The Israelis would negotiate with the Palestinians, or even the PLO, and would be ready to regard them as a partner to a solution if they fulfilled certain conditions—like readiness to recognize the state of Israel, to abolish the National Covenant,** and to terminate terrorist warfare. The chances of their accepting these conditions, they maintain, are negligible anyhow.

This formula is usually associated with Aharon Yariv. By the way, Navon, who suggested a similar formula, apparently does not belong to this school, for he advocates the evacuation of substantial parts of the West Bank in order to make meaningful progress toward a historic solution of the Israeli-Palestinian conflict. †

What is typical to the Tactical Left is that it seeks to change the image of Israel's

*Documents describing the Allon Plan are reprinted in Appendix III.

**The full text of the Covenant is reproduced in Appendix II.

†Yitzhak Navon is chairman of the Defense and Foreign Affairs Committee of the Knesset.

position, to make it more innovative, more dynamic, more flexible, more sophisticated—but, at the same time, it does not wish to concede any major points.

The Left proper says that this position, being merely tactical, does not belong to the Left at all. For the Right, and for the Center as well, this position is not acceptable—they sometimes describe it as a "half-pregnancy." Their argument is that one cannot really expect to use such tactics without being ready to face a situation in which the bluff will be called. It is self-defeating to set conditions for something which one does not want to materialize in the first place. If the conditions are met in some formal and vague way, there will be negotiations with the PLO, and then the materialization of the third state will become an almost inevitable development. Therefore this approach, according to the Center and the Right, may have some merit in the short range; but in the long range it is hazardous and should be avoided.

This brings us to the Center, which is also, by the definition being used for our purpose here, the position of Prime Minister Rabin. It maintains that the problem of the Palestinians should be recognized—but the solution of the problem as it has been stipulated in the platform of the Labour Party should be left to the framework of negotiations with Jordan. In discussions of the solution, Prime Minister Rabin often uses a phrase which is rather ambiguous. He states that the Palestinian problem should be solved "in the context of the East Bank and Jordan." This is open to two interpretations. It may mean either that the Palestinian problem should be solved exclusively within the framework of the East Bank and Jordan, or that it should be solved while maintaining the West Bankers' link to the East Bank and to Jordan. This ambiguity is intentional, not accidental, for while Prime Minister Rabin accepts the principle of a territorial com-

promise in the West Bank (conditional upon the voters' acceptance), he also regards it as undesirable and a great risk to the security of the country.

The Center strongly opposes any negotiations with the PLO or, actually, with any other independent Palestinian faction. It accepts, however, the participation of Palestinians within the framework of a Jordanian delegation.

This position draws fire from both wings. The Left is unhappy with it because it suspects that the Center is basically reluctant to accept any withdrawal from the West Bank, and that it regards withdrawal at best as the lesser evil in comparison to prospects within the framework of an imposed settlement. The Left feels that the Center—even if its attitude is somewhat more flexible on the question of the West Bank and the question of Palestinian participation—does not accept what the Left considers as the positive element in such a settlement, namely its value as a historic compromise between the two peoples. On the other hand, the Right rejects the principle of compromise in the West Bank, and the recognition of the Palestinian problem as such.

I would define the Liberal Right group as those Rightists—I shall elaborate shortly on what "Right" means in this context—whose thinking focuses not only on the territory, the land of Israel, but also—to a large extent—on the Arab society living on it. They seek a positive solution to the problem of the status of Arabs of the administered territories which will remain under Israeli government.

This school of thought has produced such ideas as the Federation Plan of Defense Minister Shimon Peres. He speaks of a federal arrangement for the whole territory of Eretz Israel: Samaria, Judea, [biblical names for the present-day West Bank] and the Gaza Strip would constitute three regions, while Israel behind the 1967 borders—the "Green Line"—would also form a number of such regions. The Arabs beyond the Green Line would be allowed either to accept Israeli citizenship or to retain their Jordanian citizenship (the assumption being that most Arabs would retain their Jordanian citizenship). Government would function on three levels. There would be the municipal level, with local forums in which every inhabitant could participate. The regional level would have a parliament of its own, in which, again, all local inhabitants would participate; it would deal with such domestic problems as education and health. Finally, there would be the national level, in which only Israeli citizens and those Arabs who wished to have Israeli citizenship would participate. Foreign policy, security, and defense would be dealt with on this higher level only.

Others in the Liberal Right speak of forming one state in which all Arabs would enjoy equal rights as Israeli citizens. They argue that theirs is a basically liberal solution for the social aspect of the problem which is ignored by a good many members of the Right Wing; they also argue that their solution, in reality, would not threaten the Zionist nature of Israel.

The Left feels that this school of thought doesn't differ from the Right, except in its awareness of the need to formulate rightist concepts in terms which may be more acceptable to the enlightened public within and outside Israel. It is, therefore, basically tactical—just as is the Tactical Left. The Right does not challenge this trend too sharply, probably because it assumes that the two trends share the same premises.

Then there is the Right, which has as its common denominator two basic tenets. First: the whole area of Eretz Israel is the homeland of the Jewish people, and of the Jewish people only. Arabs may live in this territory with basic civil rights ensured to them, as in any enlightened state, but they do not have any legitimate claim on this land, as a collective, to equal the historical rights of the Jewish people on Eretz Israel. Second: the Right rejects the notion of the existence of a Palestinian people. This notion they regard as an Arab invention designed to harass Israel and gain the support of public opinion. Basically there are only Arabs, and they are united in their animosity to the state of Israel and determination to destroy it.

The Right argues that the conflict between the Palestinians and the Israelis is a zero-sum conflict: any concession given to the Palestinians would be at the expense of Israel's existence. The demands of the Palestinians and the Israelis are mutually exclusive and cannot be reconciled. It is an historical clash which must be decided in a very clear way. Any move toward giving a Palestinian political group a viable existence would produce an irredentist entity, which would be committed to the continuation of the struggle and the destruction of Israel. Compromise is self-defeating. A give-and-take process with the Arab world in general, and with the Palestinians in particular, is an illusion. Substantial Israeli concessions will simply tempt the Arabs to increase their pressure.

The Right stresses that the strategic needs of Israel require full Israeli control of the West Bank. The Yom Kippur war has demonstrated, the Right says, that Israel may be more vulnerable than previously thought, and therefore no strategic position may be given up without compromising Israel's viability.

The Left feels that the rightist attitude ignores the realities of the situation. It ignores the genuine and authentic aspiration of Palestinian Arabs to have a political community they can call their own. It ignores the centrality of the Palestinian issue in the Arab-Israeli conflict. The Left rejects the argument that a Palestinian state, or a state in which Palestinians are partners, would necessarily produce an irredenta greater than the present one. A society which does not have any political expression, they argue, is likely to produce greater militancy than a society whose national aspirations are partly satisfied.

The Extreme Right comprises, according to my categorization, people—like the Gush Emunim*—whose basic ideas are not very much different from the Right in general, but they are distinguishable because of their spirit and readiness for activism. The Gush Emunim people, especially after 1973, feel that their political activities are implementing religious, or nationalist, visions which supersede any pragmatic considerations. They feel they are fulfilling an historical mission of far greater magnitude than any of the practical considerations brought up in the debate between the Right and the Left. They attempt to establish settlements in the West Bank—because they feel that settlement throughout Eretz Israel is the crux of Jewish revival. The settlements are patently intended to prevent the emergence of any Palestinian entity, recognized by Israel or otherwise.

Those who sympathize with the Gush Emunim point out that this movement is perhaps the most authentic expression in our generation of the original Zionist vision. It reflects the same spirit which motivated the early *aliyah*.** In a society which has become very pragmatic and motivated by materialistic self-interest, Gush Emunim is said to represent the old spirit of dedication and idealism, which to some extent has diminished in Israeli society.

Some of those who do not accept the ideology of Gush Emunim nevertheless accept the authenticity of this phenomenon in terms of the Jewish historical experience. The critics of Gush Emunim believe this movement, ignoring the realities of international politics, is basically irrational and millenarian. These critics say the spirit of this movement goes back to what they regard perhaps as a streak of self-destructiveness which has emerged in

Jewish history in various periods of crisis. These critics warn that yielding to this Messianic spirit completely disregards realities and leads inevitably to disastrous results.

In closing, I would like to list what I see as the five main issues of the Israeli debate. I will pose them as questions.

The first is whether Israel *should* evacuate any territories in Eretz Israel. Is there any legitimate claim by any Arab group to parts of the country? Does the state of Israel, as the embodiment of the Zionist vision, have the right to evacuate territories of its historical homeland to other nations? This is the ideological dimension of the issue, and one facet of it is the question of Jerusalem.

If the answer is affirmative, then the next issue will be: *Can* Israel evacuate any territories in the present circumstances? Considering the fact that the Arab armies, especially after 1967, have grown in quantitative and qualitative terms so much that the defense of Israel becomes more and more difficult and strategic depth becomes increasingly important for defense—is it still possible to give up territories in the West Bank where Israel is most vulnerable? Which territories, if any at all, can be evacuated and under what conditions? Can Israel abandon the defense strip along the Jordan River or the central ridge of Judea

*Gush Emunim is a political movement composed of mostly religious, highly nationalistic, and primarily youthful Israelis committed to retaining the West Bank. Their attempts to settle in the territory have brought them into confrontation with the government, which opposes settlements not authorized by the cabinet.

**The first *aliyah*—Jewish settlers in Palestine—started in the early 1880s; members of the second *aliyah*—who were motivated more by Zionist-Socialist ideals—spanned the years 1904-1914.

and Samaria? This is the strategic dimension of the issue.

The third issue—if an affirmative answer is given to the second question—is perhaps the most central to our discussion. *With whom* should the Israelis negotiate if they are ready for a territorial compromise? Which Arabs have a legitimate claim? Should the Israelis deal with Jordan only? With the Palestinians only? With a combination of both? And if the Israelis are ready to negotiate with the Palestinians, with which representative body and under what conditions? This is the predominantly political dimension.

If the evacuation of the territories is seriously discussed, then the fourth issue arises: *What links* would remain between those territories evacuated by the Israelis and the state of Israel proper? This leads to the discussion of open borders, the right of Israelis to settle in those territories, economic dealings, confederative or other ties between the two states, and the solution of at least part of the refugee problem within such a framework. This is perhaps a basically constitutional dimension.

The fifth issue is on a different level because it must be faced mainly by people who give a negative answer to the first and second questions. What would be the status of the Palestinian Arabs in the territories that would not be given up? Would the Arabs in the West Bank and the Gaza Strip receive Israeli citizenship? Would they be allowed participation in the Israeli political framework? What kind of self-rule or local autonomy, administrative or political, would be granted to them?

If my analysis so far is correct, then the two issues that are central in Israeli thinking are the ideological and the strategic. The ideological commitment often determines the strategic arguments. Usually, people who are ideologically committed to retaining the whole of the land in Israeli hands also evolve the strategic considerations which go with this position. Conversely, Israelis ideologically committed to a position seeking a compromise with the Palestinians usually accompany it with strategic arguments which would make that appear feasible. It rarely works the other way round, with strategic arguments shaping ideological ones.

The image of Palestinian society held by various Israeli groups is often determined by their basic attitude to the problem. If the basic attitude is rightist, then "the Palestinians" are identified with the terrorist organizations. Thus, when the Right says "Palestinians" it usually means Yasser Arafat and the PLO. On the other hand, the Left equates "Palestinians" with Palestinian society, focusing on the population of the West Bank and Gaza.

Within the Israeli public since 1973, a shift towards the two extremes can be discerned. On the one hand there has been some conspicuous movement towards the Left. The government itself, which according to this division had been before 1973 in the Right, today constitutes the Center. Also, some people in the Israeli elite who were in the Right, or perhaps in the Center, now would be classified in the Tactical Left. On the other hand, there has been also a substantial movement to the Extreme Right, as shown by the fact that Gush Emunim managed to mobilize popular support after 1973 far beyond anything it had managed to mobilize before that.

Let us be very clear here. We are trying to find out our attitude towards political statehood for the Palestinians.

3

Ourselves: The Reactions

BITAN: The change after 1973 is not a real change; it is only a change in the emphasis on the Palestinians in foreign policy and at the official political level—where it has become central and unavoidable. This has happened as the result of stronger world public opinion against Israel, the strengthening of certain groups in Israeli politics that earlier had already been more Palestinian-oriented, and the impacts of the Yom Kippur war.

Moreover, I don't fully agree with the spectrum Amir has described. Because when it comes to the centrality of the Palestinian problem, I think from the Extreme Left to the Extreme Right, everybody knows that the Palestinian problem is the central problem in the conflict.

DROR: Everybody except Mr. Rabin.

BITAN: All right. I think that everyone *should* know. And some people on the Right—I'm sure Begin* —would agree that the Palestinian problem is the central problem.

EITAN: That's only semantics.

BITAN: No, it isn't. From the historical, as well as the humanistic or the moral point of view, of course it's the central problem.

The concrete conflict Zionism had the moment it came to Eretz Israel was with the Arabs living in Palestine. Recently, the change is in the Palestinian problem as a political issue—you now have to take decisions. Everybody agrees that without a solution of the Palestinian problem there will not be a solution of the conflict in the Middle East. This is a consensus. The difference of opinion is about what kind of pragmatic-political solution is desirable, not about how central the Palestinian problem is.

I wouldn't say that the Extreme Right or Gush Emunim are motivated only by irrational, religious, nationalistic, non-pragmatic drives. What you called the Extreme Right have some very good rational, non-mystical arguments. True, they have some higher values, which I hope all of us have. The Extreme Left no less than the Extreme Right have certain moral values that must sometimes be given priority over political considerations.

*Menachem Begin is leader of the right-wing Herut Party, as well as of the Likud Bloc composed of Herut and other opposition parties.

Public opinion and the policy thinking of experts don't necessarily agree, and don't have to overlap. The question is who represents the man in the street. Public opinion is mostly that of the so-called silent majority. In this silent majority—and even in the Extreme Left—there is strong suspicion of the Arabs, the Palestinians. You can divide the degree of suspicion according to generations, not just in age but also in mentality. What characterizes this position is a good memory. Either personally or indirectly, this generation remembers the very bloody history of our lives with the Arabs in Palestine, or in Eretz Israel.

You don't have to remember personally anti-Jewish riots in 1921 or 1929. It's enough to talk about my generation; we remember personally 1936 to 1939, [the period of the Arab revolt against British Mandatory authorities and hostilities against the Jewish community in Palestine]. This generation, this kind of mentality, rejects the very glorious terms and names and cliches now used to designate the Palestinians—"liberation army" or "commando groups" or "guerrilla" or "resistance." When I talk about the Palestinians, I can only talk about those who have officially been recognized—I don't know what's going on in the hearts of the Palestinians of the West Bank or elsewhere. Officially, in the view of the Arab world and world public opinion, the Palestinians are represented by what is called the PLO.

This generation tends to identify the Palestinians—the militant Palestinians who are fighting for the Palestinian cause—with the Palestinian Arabs in the twenties and thirties. The same phenomenon. The same methods. But different weapons—they now have fewer knives and more machine guns. The principle is the same: killing Jews—not just Israelis—including unarmed men, women, and children. Israelis and Jews are attacked *because* they are Jews. For a very large part of Israeli public opinion—much larger than

is expressed in policy-thinking or policy-making—this is the view today of the Palestinian "liberation movement."

A second characterization of this generation is that it includes most of the people who grew up in or came from Arab countries, about 55 percent of the Israeli population. Most of them know the bluff in Arab propaganda—either personally or from being told by their parents, or by a kind of instinct. The bluff is that Jews have always had a very good time in Moslem countries. Historically it is not true. Personally, most of the Israelis who come from Arab countries know that. This realization among Oriental Jews brings them—in their basic views on the Palestinian problem—into the Right. I'm not talking about their political or pragmatic solutions. I am saying only that among Oriental Jews in Israel, public opinion about the Palestinian question, and psychological attitudes towards the Palestinians, are quite strongly to the Right. Theirs is a generation with an overwhelming suspicion of any Palestinian state and the whole phenomenon of the Palestinian people.

The third characteristic is associated with those who have a stronger memory of the Holocaust. They take seriously, and they listen carefully to, anybody who says that he intends to destroy Jewish communities—whether called the Diaspora or the state of Israel. They have a strong feeling about the danger of self-delusion in this matter. They draw parallels, rightly or wrongly. Even simple people in Israel remember that those who represented the Palestinian cause in 1936 and 1939 were killing Jews, and that the same representatives collaborated with the Nazis, as did the Mufti of Jerusalem,* Haj Amin el-Hus-

---

*Dominant Palestinian political leader of mandate period, and religious head of the Muslim community.

seini. People know that, and they know now that those who represent the Palestinians today—the PLO—are ideologically continuing the same line. They're not talking about gas chambers, of course. But it doesn't matter. They are saying that they want to destroy a Jewish community. Some of you here would declare that many people in Israel who see things this way are wrong, but I think they're correct. This attitude characterizes the position of what you call the Right; it goes beyond the political or pragmatic questions. You can't avoid it. Maybe it is a kind of trauma which we should get rid of. Maybe we shouldn't. I don't know. This position is emotional. Why not? Certain things are legitimate even if—especially if—they are based on emotions. The burden of proof is on the other side to show that this is an illusion, to show that the associations made by these anti-Palestinian Israelis are wrong. They have to show that they are not like the Palestinians in 1936 and 1939, that it is not one continuous phenomenon.

We must very carefully distinguish between the two levels of our discussion. One is an historical or moral level—ideological, if you want to call it that. Is there a Palestinian nation with a right in Eretz Israel? Or isn't there? The other level is the pragmatic-political. Are we for or against a Palestinian state? Not because they deserve it, or have the right to it—but because this may be a kind of political solution for the conflict in the Middle East. The two levels should not be mixed up. A person may be on the Extreme Right—may be a Gush Emunim—on the first level, but on the Extreme Left on the second. There are people who say, "I don't think Palestinians have any right in Eretz Israel. The whole issue of Palestinian nationality is a bluff. But what can I do? I have certain American pressures. I can't go against public opinion. So I am giving up my right in Eretz Israel. I'll even agree to a Palestinian state." You will see later that this is not my

position; but it is possible for some people to have this view.

MEIR: Bitan has described, and quite rightly, the position of the man in the street. And he is probably right about the Oriental Jews. But he forgot to mention a quite different feeling—not exactly among the man in the street, but mostly among our youth—in the high schools, in universities, the people born after 1948. They also have a distinctive feeling. Bitan describes the feeling of the wrong done to Jews in the Arab countries, the Arabs killing the Jews, and he describes it very convincingly. But consider the youths generally of European or European-American background—it's a pity that they must be categorized this way, but let's describe the situation as it is. Among them there is an implicit or explicit feeling that a wrong was done to the Arabs. I see it even in the generation of my eldest son—and it's not just because he's my son.

Bitan also spoke of the Holocaust, saying that for many Israelis—obviously those of European origin, since I guess he wouldn't say the impact is the same for Oriental Jews because they are less aware of it—there is the memory of the Holocaust. He said that a logical conclusion follows from this memory. Beware of this naive attitude to the world. Maybe this is true for many people. For some people this is absolutely incorrect. Some, including myself, who are quite aware of the Holocaust and are Holocaust-conscious, have reached totally contrary conclusions.

For others in Israel there is also a memory of the thirties in Europe—not a personal memory, but a historical memory. It makes them sensitive to what is meant by extreme, mystical nationalism, and by mystical religious nationalism, which contributed to some movements that eventually led to the Holocaust. So for other

Israelis this type of movement is precisely what is repellent, and you should be aware that here there are currents which go very deep.

HANAN: I question whether you were right, Amir, to limit the spectrum to what exists within Zionist thinking in Israel. A segment of Israeli Jewish public opinion is frankly and sometimes vociferously non-Zionist or anti-Zionist. Also, your definition of the Extreme Right did not exhaust this philosophical territory.

The non-Zionists have a school of thought that says whatever happened in Israel in the last fifty or thirty years is basically our fault. We shouldn't have started this adventure of Jewish colonization in Palestine. Zionism is one big mistake. The country was someone else's. Sometimes you can detect such a feeling in what people say, without their saying it bluntly. They believe that we do not have peace, we have conflict in the Middle East, just because there is Zionism.

I think the Center, which is a much wider segment of opinion, maintains that it is the Arabs' fault. If they had been willing to accept us as a small entity, as a partitioned small state, either in the thirties, or after the 1947 resolution, then the Israelis would have been quite happy to remain where they were. There would have been no wars. Whatever happened since is the result of the Arabs' belligerence and total opposition to any Israeli existence. This is why you will find such a mixed appreciation of the situation, such mixed feelings among Jews and Israelis toward the Arabs. If the Arabs were not so belligerent and opposed to our existence, many people who are defined as Rightists would become much softer. The Rightists say: "There is no hope; the Arabs will never recognize us." Those who are in the Center, but more to the Left, will say: "Well, maybe one day

they will recognize us." Among right-wing people, sometimes, is the feeling: "Well, if they do recognize us and some day agree to take away their objection to Israel, then we might change our attitude." Then, farther to the Right are those who say: "All this is true maybe—but we don't care. Maybe we created the situation in the Middle East. But it's a clash, a historical clash. We are repeating Joshua's conquest of the country. We don't care. We have to conquer it. We are going to get it."

AMIR: Then 95 percent of Israeli society is in one category—your Center?

HANAN: Yes. You can make further subdivisions. But in order to understand what is going on in the Israeli mind, you first must see the three main groups. A small one on the Left, which denies any right on the Jewish part. The big bulk in the middle which has as its main problem—moral and political—the fact that the Arabs wouldn't agree to our existence. And then a fringe group on the Right which says we don't care about Arab resistance, or Arab objections, or Arab opposition to our state. We are going on.

This division is important because only through it can you understand the interplay among different views in Israel, the changes in the position of many Israelis, and sometimes in all parties. You will be able to understand the divisions within political parties; almost every one contains these nuances. "Schizophrenic" is a very important word to keep in mind if we want to have a clear understanding of Israeli public opinion about the Palestinians.

There is no one who tries to avoid the fact that there is a Palestinian problem. And the problem must be solved. The division of opinion starts when we try to define the problem. There are very few who would deny that there is "a Palestinian issue," but it becomes more difficult and complicated once you refer to "Palestinian entity," "Palestinian people," "Palestinian nation," and, of course, the "right of the Palestinians" to have political statehood.

Let us be very clear here. We are trying to find out our attitude towards political statehood for the Palestinians living in Israel, in Palestine, or outside. Amir confused two things. One is the current argument about issues that seem politically very urgent or concrete: territories; evacuation or no evacuation; the demographic problem and the fate of so many Arabs living within the Israeli Jewish political framework; recognizing or not recognizing the PLO. However, these are only the current appearances of a problem much older, much more profound, much more basic. The problem of territories didn't exist at all less than ten years ago—before the war of 1967. But the issue was exactly the same—whether we should let the Palestinian refugees come back to Israel of the Green Line, back to their homes. The issue started decades ago.

Furthermore, the problem of the Arab states around Israel is so deeply connected with the problem of the Palestinians that you must keep it in mind whenever you speak of Israeli public attitudes toward the Palestinians. The Palestinian problem wasn't created only gradually, just by Jewish colonization, and buying land, and driving the Palestinians away from the land. It was created by three or four wars waged upon Israel. The present situation of the Palestinians—being refugees, being away from their homes, being without a state— is an outcome of basically an Arab action. Before the Six Day War, the Arab attitude and demands toward Israel were aimed at Israel in its pre-1967 war borders. Israeli public opinion about Palestinians, and the suspicions of some of Israel's prominent political thinkers, include the fear that the Palestinian issue is just a means for Arab states to conquer and to dominate this very vital part of the Middle East.

MEIR: I'm glad we entered the subject through an ideological angle by this discussion of Zionism, because it's the heart of the matter. There are two extremes in Israeli views about this whole subject, and then there is the Center.

For the Center, the Palestinian problem exists, but as a technical question—a problem that has to be solved or not within a technical framework. The attitude toward it is pragmatic. For Golda Meir, there was a problem but it was a minor question. It could be solved, or it could be delayed.

For the two extremes, it's a fundamental ideological discussion about the essence of Zionism. This is the great dividing line. For the Center, it's a problem among others. For the Extreme Left and maybe the Left, and certainly for the Extreme Right and Right, the Palestinian problem is not only central to the conflict, it is central to a view of Zionism. That explains our basic internal confrontation. We are polarized today in Israel on this question because we are not only discussing the Palestinians, but also how we see Zionism.

The Israeli historian Yigal Ilam wrote some time ago about the change in views of Zionism. He says that for one group—let's say the Left and the Extreme Left—originally Zionism was to solve the problem of the Jews, not to solve the problem of Judaism. Solving the problem of the Jews meant to find a country where the Jews could live in peace—an answer to anti-Semitism. Now, however, there is a reversal of the trend in Zionism. Now we have a trend which did exist at the beginning but which is becoming stronger and stronger. According to this trend the problem is not to solve the Jewish situation in response to anti-Semitism, but to solve the problem of Judaism, to redeem Eretz Israel—eventually even to sacrifice Jews in order to do so. We certainly needn't go into its complex history here. But I will be very frank: isn't the redemption of Eretz Israel the major issue by now in Gush Emunim, and in others?

HANAN: It was so in Zionism from the beginning. That's your basic mistake.

MEIR: But these are two totally different attitudes to Zionism. If redeeming Eretz Israel is the purpose of Gush Emunim, then the Palestinian problem, from that viewpoint, is absolutely insoluble—for it cannot be solved totally outside the confines of Eretz Israel. The insolubility, then, turns on a matter of principle which is linked to a religious, Messianic view. As I see the Israeli spectrum, these are the basic questions, and the political issues are only a superstructure for the extremes of these two different views of Zionism.

NAHUM: But there's more to the development of the Zionist idea than what you describe. I would put it this way: Herzl failed.*

HANAN: No one failed. We failed.

NAHUM: I'll tell you why. The idea of Zionism, political Zionism, was to bring all the Jews to Israel. The idea was to bring about normalization for the Jews. This failed. Zionism went from maximum Zionism—bringing all the Jews to Palestine—to minimal Zionism—acknowledging that a big Diaspora will exist. Thus there will be a center for the Jews in Israel, but most of the Jews will live in the Diaspora. Ahad Ha'am, [the twentieth century Zionist philosopher], preached and hoped that the Jewish community in Israel would be of a very high spiritual quality. In that we failed. But he didn't err in his main idea that only a small minority of the Jewish people would be in Israel. Therefore the differentiation between Zionism and Judaism is much more complicated than represented by Ilam.

GAD: Amir's linear description is more or less the accepted model whether it uses the labels hawks and doves, Left or Right. But this way of describing the political map does a great injustice to many nuances because it fails to take account of the underlying reasoning that motivates people to adopt the various positions on this spectrum. I suggest, instead, another classification, which gets at these nuances by asking three sets of questions.

One is to ask how people answer the question of evacuation of territories. For or against? The question is answered on the basis of ideological reasons, strategic, and other reasons. Next, how do people evaluate the possibilities, the prospects, of reaching a peace agreement with the Arabs? How do they evaluate the Arab position? Are the Arabs ready to accept the existence of Israel or not? Third, there is a tactical point: With whom and how are those negotiations to be conducted? There are those who are ready to accept only a step-by-step process, those who are ready to accept only a comprehensive agreement—a final solution—and those who are ready to try to go both ways. Altogether, the possible combinations of basic approach and basic categories are over twenty.

We also ought to take into consideration the depth of conviction behind the positions adopted. And we should remember that public opinion in Israel usually tends to forget, not the question of which territories we can afford to evacuate, but the opposite question: Which territories can we afford to hold on to? Do we have support for holding certain territories? More specifically, how much American support do we have? It may be that we should hold a certain territory, but we can't do so because we have no ability to hold it.

NAHUM: I too believe that Amir's very important typology leaves out significant nuances because it mistakenly is based

*Theodore Herzl, 1860-1904, father of modern political Zionism.

only on the political prescriptions of each school of thought and ignores what lies underneath those prescriptions. The typology risks shallowness, and it gravitates to ideal types and abstractions. But my corrective would be different than Gad's.

One underlying element I would stress is: What are the assumptions about the other side? People often describe the Israeli side or the Arab side as if they are describing a boxing match while focusing on the movements of only one boxer. But the movements of one side, of course, are conditioned or influenced by those of the opponent. Therefore, for every school of thought, it is important to see its assumptions about the behavior, the threats, the actions, and the perspectives of the other side, and to see each school's evaluation of how the other side would react to given circumstances.

Another element of extreme importance is sometimes overlooked. In describing schools of thought or political trends, one has to take into consideration the way that they manage their contradictions. Every school enumerated here has some inconsistencies; none is completely free of internal contradictions. To give our picture a human and political depth, I think that these contradictions have to be spelled out—especially in such a complicated conflict as the Arab-Israeli one. It is not only a political conflict. It goes much deeper.

One school of thought was misrepresented—what was called the Tactical Left. Every school of thought has contradictions, but if any school controls these contradictions, it is this one. Because it is an ambivalent school of thought. What does it say? First, it says we recognize the Palestinians and the PLO.

HANAN: Please say "the Palestinian attitude."

NAHUM: No. I recognize the PLO be-cause I don't know of any other important group among the Palestinians. Second, it says we recognize the Palestinians' agony. Many times I ask myself how I would have behaved had I been a Palestinian. Let us have and show empathy for their anguish. This school does recognize the Palestinians' political aspirations. We cannot think ethnocentrically—as if we are alone. We have to take into consideration that they exist, and that they have the right to exist. We have our dreams. We have our national aspirations. They have theirs, which are legitimate. This school does take into consideration Arab attitudes. This school says, in other words, that Israeli approaches to Arab attitudes have become counterproductive, that Israelis should no longer persist in their tendency to fool themselves about what the Arabs want, and what is the Arab reality. Perhaps it comes from the history of the Jews. Historically Jews lived in a hostile environment. It caused them to try to ignore it. They survived by closing themselves off from their environment. But now, they cannot afford to ignore Arab attitudes.

Besides recognizing the Arab and Palestinian attitudes, this school recognizes the depth of their hostility. It is not hatred. It's not a question of emotions. It's a political idea, which they can justify and thus reinforce. They have a case, a relatively good one. Their ideology is cohesive. I wish Zionism would have been so cohesive, so rich in ideas as Arab nationalism. They have studied us; they know about our ideas. How many Jews know as much about Arab ideologies?

The Tactical Left, in order to escape its contradictions is tactical and strategic at the same time. It says: "We are ready to withdraw to the 1967 pre-war borders. We recognize the rights of the Palestinians. Once we withdraw, it's not up to us to say whether there will be a Palestinian state or not. They have to decide it. We must maintain a sympathetic indifference."

HANAN: You certainly have your contradictions.

NAHUM: I recognize the deep enmity of the Arabs. Because they have a case. It is much deeper than the German attitude was. The German attitude was pathological: the Arab enmity is not. Therefore, I can't close my eyes to the depth of their opposition, which is rational, not emotional.

The tactical school is ready to maintain the most lenient, the most dovish position. It's up to the Arabs, by their reaction, to determine whether it is a tactical step or a strategic one. If they are ready to make real peace, it is a strategic step. And a strategic step, would involve a need for change, for rethinking of Zionism. Israel is destined to stay a tiny, small state. We have to develop an ideology in which the quality of life is not dependent on the bigness of the state. If the Arabs are not ready to make peace, then this school's proposal to withdraw is a tactical step, enabling us to improve our position in world opinion.

OREN: What is your belief? How will the Arabs answer?

NAHUM: That is immaterial.

AMIR: You say, "if they are ready." Does this mean that in fact you see a possibility that they may accept your proposal?

NAHUM: One day, yes. I think that there is very grave danger to the existence of the state of Israel. I don't know any example in history of a state having to combat such odds. There has never been such an asymmetry between two sides. It's a grave danger to which I can't close my eyes. We have a qualitative advantage, but the qualitative advantage will be narrowed. It seems to me that history is with the big numbers. The Arabs are not subhuman, not inferior in their ability to adopt modern technology; they can begin to close the gap.

I think that it is an existential imperative for Israel to try to come to some kind of accommodation—peace. Because I'm afraid of the continuation of the conflict, I think Israel should be ready to pay very much for reaching an accommodation, an agreement.

Because of the asymmetry of the conflict, we must work to acquire the support of public opinion. Until now, our own policy has mistakenly allowed Israel to be isolated from public opinion and from the world. The Arabs have been impressed only partially by Israel's strength, because they always interpreted Israel's strength as transient. They have been very much impressed by world opinion. I'm sorry to say that the Arabs have made headway in public opinion and Israeli doves have helped to give legitimacy to the Arab position by describing it as more lenient than reality warrants and by describing the Arabs as willing to make peace with Israel. Unwittingly, the Israeli doves helped to give legitimacy to the Arab idea that the state of Israel has to be destroyed. The Palestinians would not have made so much headway in public opinion if their position had not been described by some Israelis as not so extreme, if it had not been said many times that the PLO showed signs of agreeing, at least acquiescing, to the existence of a Jewish state and coexistence.

PINHAS: But you also just said that you can understand very well the Palestinian case.

NAHUM: I understand it scientifically, which is quite different. I don't give legitimacy to it, and I don't advocate it. I do not describe Arab intentions as peaceful.

It is an existential imperative for us to take a moderate posture. Therefore, the Tactical Left is "tactical" in this respect: If the Arabs don't accept, then at least we have improved our position in the international arena, and I think this is very important. There is a danger that the Arabs will accept the tactic. This is a problem which I can't completely resolve, but we have to grapple with it. In any event, it seems to me that we are in a much better position if we argue our case in terms of the conditions of peace that satisfy us in exchange for withdrawal. We then have a better chance to make the conditions of peace the center of gravity in the debate. This is better than to debate questions like: Withdrawal or not withdrawal? Is there a PLO or is there no PLO? Who are the Palestinians?

The Arab position against Israel is basically hawkish to the extreme in its non-acceptance of Israel's legitimacy. This has deep reasons—historical, the nature of Islam and other factors. It doesn't seem to me that in order to counteract an Arab hawkish position, we have to assume an Israeli hawkish position. On the other hand, it seems to me that the big mistake of the doves in Israel has been that, in advocating a dovish policy for Israel, they have tended to describe the Arab position as containing dovish strains.

I do see a possibility of an erosion of the Arab position. It would be mistaken to discuss political situations in terms of eternity. The term eternity is for the theologians. Human groups change their position. The world changes. There is a great resilience in the Arab position. But between the negation and the acceptance of the state of Israel, it is very difficult to have intermediate stages. Therefore, the change has to be qualitative and that is what is difficult. But a possibility exists that the Arab position will change, and the main agent will be the Arabs finding themselves incongruent with world opinion.

PINHAS: But your views, Nahum, create a problem, for me at least. Within your case there are more contradictions, unresolved contradictions, than in any other school of thought I've heard described here.

First, if it is true—and I don't think it is—that Israel's entire situation today, vis-à-

vis the Arabs, is as you have described, then I could hardly think of any serious Arab leader who would be ready today to accept what you have to propose to him. Why would he be so stupid—given the total enmity and hostility that you say exists among the Arab countries and within the Palestinians—to accept your proposal just because of the potential pressures of public opinion in the future? I don't recall that past pressures of public opinion influenced Arab countries to make strategic changes in their positions. And you are suggesting today that the only hope of eventually changing the positions of the Arab countries—which is even worse, you say, than the Nazis—will be somehow through manipulating public opinion. What you said before in describing the currents within the Arab world was too serious to allow me to believe that you could really think they would change merely because of public relations manipulations.

Second, what troubles me even more is what you said about the Palestinians' case. I don't see much difference between understanding it from a scientific point of view, and providing justification for it. To make this distinction is very hard, especially from the point of view of the man in the street. For him, the scientific evaluation is no less harmful—for the very reasons you gave when criticizing the dovish position. You want to believe that a scientific evaluation says that the Palestinian believes he has got a case. And you want to believe that you can leave it on that scientific level. You want to believe that it doesn't create in your own people, and within the general public opinion around the world, an inevitable feeling that if this is so, then the Palestinians have a case—not only from their own point of view but from our point of view as well. The results—for public opinion and attitudes toward Israel—are the same.

PINHAS: Of all the issues between Israel and the Arab countries, the Palestinian problem is, strangely, the hardest for us to explain to the world, and the easiest for the Arabs to use against us. We are all very sensitive to the emotional, irrational element of the Israeli Right and Extreme Right, and how the whole world is intolerant of their arguments. At the same time, when you hear the arguments of the Palestinians, they are not less extreme than the arguments of the Right and Extreme Right in Israel. They are not less nationalistic, they are not less chauvinistic. But the outer world—and even many among us—tends to accept those arguments and their spirit as authentic expressions of the rising nationalism which we have to understand, accept, and somehow learn to live with. Remember that until now, the more extreme elements—or let's say not the more moderate elements—among the Palestinians have been accepted by the world. Arafat and his colleagues, for example, have been accepted with understanding. This shows that the Palestinian problem is a very good issue to be used against Israel, and it has been used widely by the Arabs, especially in the last two years.

There has, then, been a change since the last war in the centrality of the Palestinian problem, within Israel and within the whole world's attitude about the Middle East. I'm not sure that the Palestinian problem is the heart of the problem between Israel and the Arab countries, but it is one of the central problems.

As for whether Israeli public opinion changed towards the Palestinian problem after the 1973 war, we have to bear in mind that Israeli public opinion is not isolated from the trends around the world, and it was to a certain extent influenced by the international debate and the growing support for the Palestinians and the PLO. As a result, the debate within Israel has sharpened between and among different groups, and we have been hearing a greater number of extreme groups. But I still think that a majority, the overwhelming majority, is somewhere around the center.

Yet, we can be very easily misled by setting up categories such as Amir's. These and other categories do exist. I even tend to agree with Amir's spectrum as long as we are talking about the politicians or a certain elite which is sophisticated enough to develop various attitudes toward the Palestinians—for instance among the leaders of the parties, or the media, or the universities. But public opinion does not have all these shadings and sophisticated differences; nor does it have all the knowledge required for them. About public opinion at large, I tend to agree with Bitan's description of the general sentiment towards the Palestinians. This does not mean that the Israeli public is less ready to accept this solution or that solution. That readiness is conditional on many other things. But if we are judging general public opinion trends, most people do not accept the Palestinians and most have many memories very much influenced by the acts of Palestinian terrorists.

I agree with what has been said here about the younger generation, and about the Oriental Jews. The younger generation is troubled by the problem, and the sentiment of the Oriental Jews is as you described it, Bitan. But I want to caution everyone here not to draw from these observations any conclusions about the party divisions in Israel. For instance, Meir, you may ask on the one hand why the younger generation is so troubled, and on the other hand why the Likud is dominating all the universities, and why the percentage voting for the Likud in the last election within the army, which was then the reserves as well, was 42 percent, the highest in the history of the state? This happened because in the last elections the Palestinian problem was not dominant in deciding patterns of voting in Israel. Patterns of voting in Israel do not reflect voters' attitude toward the entire problem of our relations with the Arab countries; domestic factors play a very large and very important role.

DROR: I share Nahum's fears about the future balance of power. Not tomorrow or five years or seven years, but later on. I share his fear that gaps between us and the Arabs will be closed. And mainly I share his fear that the Palestinians themselves sense exactly what is going on in the balance of power; that for this reason they are so extremely against a real peace solution; and that therefore they are choosing the way which leads us only to war.

We used to say that there is a leadership crisis in Israel. I don't think it's a leadership crisis. It's more a confusion crisis. It's the first time since the establishment of the state that we have to find exact answers to a new challenge. I have to stress these apprehensions—I found them especially in the higher ranks of the defense community in Israel. Not everyone shares them in this community, but the assumptions are not so rosy for the future.

I don't want you to misunderstand me. It's not a change toward despair. The result could be that we shall find more readiness to compromise with the Palestinians if, of course, they will accept us, will accept the existence of Israel, will be ready to recognize our national sovereignty. But the result can be in just the other direction. Most of the Israeli public—the group in the middle—could jump to the Extreme Right in their viewpoints, and even in their readiness to use extreme methods. I don't think it was just by accident that the former defense minister, early in 1976, spoke in Paris about the possibility and the need

that Israel will have—possess—an atomic bomb. We never heard these things before—except in inside circles. And Dayan hasn't been the only one to speak about it since the Yom Kippur war.

Among soldiers and Israeli Defense Force higher rank officers, opinions do not conform to a party line or to the labels hawk or dove. Some military men are considered to be convinced hawks, and they object to any scheme of interim agreement. Yet they call themselves moderate on the Palestinian question. Among the armed forces, the Palestinian question is troubling—although not, of course, the top priority concern. The previous generation of armed forces' leadership, including the educators and commanders, ignored this question, left it dormant, and did not try to explain it to the youth. But what was perhaps clear to that generation is no longer obvious to our young people. So this young generation now finds a vacuum, which complicates their search for answers today. Moreover, the question marks of this generation don't relate only to the Palestinians, but also to the problem of Zionism as a national movement—this too is less crystal clear today than it was to the founding fathers.

In some major military schools, the Palestinian question tends to be one of the three main questions that a sample of students say are the most vital and interesting being discussed there. The discussion ranges across not only the rights of Palestinians, but the acts of terrorism by the Palestinian groups, the PLO official ideology, or our right to build settlements in the West Bank. There is no single direction in their answers. That it has been one of the crucial questions for this part of the young generation after the 1973 war was for many officers and army educators quite a surprise. They admit that they are called on to cope with these questions far more than in the past.

In the higher ranks and the high

command, the question takes on a different complexion. Many of them feel that the objectives of the war with the Palestinians are not clear for them personally and not clear for the army. The strategy is incomplete, or even faulty. Since the clash is between two national movements, and since one of them, the Palestinians, doesn't recognize the existence of the other, therefore it's a total war. So among officers in the high command, some argue that self-defense alone is not sufficient. They argue that sealing the borders, some sporadic reaction, delayed reactions, should not be accepted as sufficient. They argue that something more extensive is needed—comprehensive war in response to Palestinian extremism. This attitude leads, for example, to such tactics as the execution of the three Palestinian leaders in Beirut in April, 1973; or the suggestions to invade Lebanon during the civil war there, just to eliminate the Palestinian Liberation Army and the terror organizations.

But before as well as after the Yom Kippur war other officers have had another view. They say, for example, that we have a habit of telling the Arab countries that we will return territories for peace. But this is not Israel's official line with the Palestinians. For the Arab states, these officers say, there are interim agreements and talks about non-belligerency today. But not for the Palestinians. A senior officer, during a debate on the question, once reflected this view by saying, "What do you expect for the Palestinians to do today? To commit suicide? To drown themselves? Wouldn't it be more intelligent and better to offer them a political solution? And only if they refuse, fight them to the bitter end? This also would be correct as a tactical approach, as a way of arousing the Palestinians to argue between themselves."

Other officers suggest that we exploit an opportunity in any war in which Hussein would attack Israel in order to eliminate the Hashemite kingdom and allow the Palestinians to set up their sovereign territory there. Arik Sharon [a right-wing, politically active Israeli general], for example, is on public record with this opinion. Among the security community, the Palestinian question is not seen only in military terms, as a problem of controlling terrorist activities. The fact is that terror is not a serious military problem for Israel. Handling the problem does not pose special difficulties, whether the terrorist actions orginate from inside the country or from bases outside the country. After nine years of occupation in the territories, the million Arabs involved have not succeeded in creating any real underground. So the strictly defense aspects of the Palestinian problem are very limited.

My conclusion about the defense community is that the spectrum of opinion within it is no different than within the general public, though it's at a higher level of awareness because these men are involved daily much more in the question. Yet, there is much more pressure within this group for clear definitions and objectives in war and peace, for and against the Palestinians.

EITAN: The Israeli public realized after the 1973 war that the strategic balance of power had changed to our detriment. They became convinced that in the long run, we may not be able to hold on against the combined forces of the Arab world, because we have already reached the limits of our potential, whereas the Arabs are now only beginning to mobilize their human and financial power and their command of energy supplies.

This change was a deep shock to many, and it produced two groups in Israel. One group I will call the Tactical Right. The main line of thinking is that only by having atomic power, atomic bombs, do we have a chance to deter the Arabs. This group believes we are financially limited in going on with the arms race. And there is a limit beyond which even the United States wouldn't like to carry this burden. The Arabs will be in a position to build such huge armies that only by having atomic bombs can we deter them. Those who believe in the possibility of atomic deterrence are the optimistic wing of this new group. I don't say this happily, but I think really we are now reaching a position in which we would be fighting for the right, unlike Jews in the Second World War, to die with honor. That is to say, if worse comes to worst, the whole Middle East will this time go to the grave together with us. So this realization produces those who believe in the atomic deterrent capability, as well as those who are desperate and think that in the last resort this will be the path of general suicide.

The second group has two wings. One consists of the most extreme and totally despairing people, who vote with their feet and leave Israel. I think it's a factor among the 24,000 to 25,000 emigrants in 1974 and almost the same number in 1975. I don't know, I can't judge how many, but it seems to me that among emigrants from Israel in 1974 and 1975 there are people who left because of this realization that there is no point—we can't go on, we'll lose—not maybe the next war—but the war after the next. It's the end, and the end will be tragic. So let us go in time.

HANAN: Do you actually think this is the sole, or the main reason, for the emigration?

EITAN: No, I say there are some emigrants who left for this reason.

HANAN: You use numbers that are in themselves exaggerated.

EITAN: Why? They are certainly the official numbers.

HANAN: They aren't. You give the impression that 49,000 people left Israel be-

cause of this sole reason.

EITAN: No, this is your conclusion. I didn't say it. I said that among those who left Israel in 1974 and 1975—and their aggregate number is about 50,000—among them are people who left Israel because of despair over the possibility of the next war.

The other wing of this second group reached the conclusion, according to my judgment—I admit I don't have good tools for measuring public opinion, but from a very few people I have heard this conclusion—that Zionism may be morally good, morally valid, but we have no strength anymore to carry it on. When this experiment began, we couldn't assess the strong reactions we might engender in the other side. We were too late. If Zionism had been started in the beginning of the nineteenth century, we would have been much more successful. But since it began at almost the same time as the Arabs also began their national aspirations, we have reached a point in which the combined forces of the Arab world are strong enough to prevent us from going on. Let us try a new approach, this subgroup says. There is a hope, there is a possibility that a non-Zionist Israel would be more acceptable to the Arab world—to the Palestinians, but not only to the Palestinians—than a Zionist Israel.

BITAN: What do you mean? Without the Law of Return?

EITAN: Yes, Israel without the Law of Return. These two symbols—the Law of Return and the Law of Nationality of Israel—have consolidated the privileged position of Jews in Israeli law.* In order to

---

*The Law of Return, adopted in 1950, grants every Jew the automatic right to settle permanently in Israel; the Law of Nationality, adopted in 1952, grants automatic citizenship to any Jew who settles there.

try to convince themselves or others that their approach might be more successful than the Zionist attempt, this group quotes two facts. They point out that twice in recent months—once from the Egyptian foreign minister, and once from Dayan—there was confirmation that Egypt's conditions for peace include this notion of the de-Zionization of Israel. Fahmy's famous condition for a Middle East settlement was that Israel should stop immigration. And Dayan said in a TV interview that, unofficially and through intermediaries, in 1971, we asked Egypt, "What do you want for peace?" Egypt's reply contained several conditions, one of which was that Israel should be a non-Zionist state, that is, without the Law of Return.

BITAN: But who in Israel thinks like that? Give me one name.

EITAN: These were my views even before 1973. I dare to say, I hear this from people that I didn't hear it from before. There is a slight change. I know I speak of tiny changes, but since the source of this change is not ideological, but a despair of the possibility of carrying out Zionism in its original vision, it might grow stronger.

Among this defeatist group—if you want to call them that—the much more important segment, I'm afraid, is those who leave Israel, the emigrants. The emigrants are more important than those who remain and delude themselves into believing that a non-Zionist Israel would be more acceptable to the Arabs than a Zionist Israel. Much more important, of course, is the emergence of this Tactical Right, who—out of desperation—think that our main hope is atomic deterrence.

EITAN: I don't agree with Amir's classification because it includes only the Zionist spectrum of Israeli public opinion. Whether we want it or not, there are almost a half million Israeli Arabs. Certainly they cannot be included in the Zionist spectrum. But still they are Israelis, and what is going on among them is no doubt one of the most important results of the 1973 war, as far as public opinion is concerned: the stiffening, the consolidation of the Palestinian Arab feelings of the Israeli Arabs. Those who feel that way express themselves now. Whereas those who up to 1973 expressed pro-Israeli views or identified with Israel don't dare speak now as they once did.

AMIR: Do you regard them as Palestinians?

EITAN: I regard them as Israeli citizens of Arab origin. According to my beliefs and values, that is the way I would like them to be. But objectively, of course, they are part of the Palestinian Arab people.

AMIR: Then they do not belong in this part of our discussion because we are discussing the attitude of Israelis to Palestinian Arabs.

EITAN: But they are Israelis.

HANAN: Formally Israelis.

EITAN: Why? Not just formally.

HANAN: When you say Israelis, in the general connotation, you mean Israeli Jews.

EITAN: It's not only formally, because their behavior influences the behavior of the state. They vote. By voting they shape the political behavior of Israel. And by their growing indentification as Palestinian Arabs, they engender a reaction among the Israeli Jews—I do not mean only a reaction against them. Israeli-Arab behavior is one of the considerations the Israeli Jews take into account when they shape their attitude toward the general Palestinian problem. We shall come later in the discussion to the question of how the emergence of a Palestinian state in the West Bank would influence the Israeli Arabs. For now, let me say only that the direction of the changes in public opinion among Israeli Arabs since 1967—certainly after 1973—was towards Arab nationalism as the Palestinian Arabs present it.

And it seems to me, in answer to Pinhas, that the Palestinian Arabs succeeded to some extent—but not totally—in their propaganda because they have used this good gimmick of a secular democratic state. It is compatible with liberal notions of nationality. Because of the structure of Israel, we cannot present a countervailing picture—a picture that Israel also wants to be an open, secular, democratic state, for Israel by its nature is not secular and not open.

PINHAS: I'm afraid that here you are putting into an objective evaluation some of your personal views about the kind of Israel that you want.

EITAN: Maybe. Maybe. But don't mistake me—I don't believe for one single moment that the Palestinians want to establish a secular democratic state. What I am saying about our difficulty in presenting a countervailing view to this idea comes out of my experience in speaking to some people outside Israel, who told me what they believe is the Israeli alternative. They said to me that the Israeli reply to the Palestinian program was Golda Meir's attitude that every morning when she gets up and hears that more Arab children have been born, she becomes sad. And they also recalled to me the notorious quotation of Golda's that every Jew in a mixed marriage is for her someone who should be included in the six million Jews who were exterminated in the Holocaust. I think this is an example of what, to some extent, contributed to the Palestinian success in telling many people in the world, "We want to build an open society without barriers of race and religion; the Israelis are building a closed, racial, segregationist society."

But now the Palestinian success is not so complete, because after six, seven years, very few people really believe them about a democratic secular state. And it's not only because of Lebanon. People began to look at what they were writing, and they questioned the Palestinian leaders. They didn't get satisfactory answers to their questions, and they saw that the Palestinians don't want to build an open, democratic state, but an Arab state in Palestine.

EITAN: I do not see the purpose of speaking about the Palestinian agony, nor do I understand what Nahum really means when he speaks about it. I don't doubt for one moment that there were many, many personal agonies during the 1948 war. On both sides. But I don't see the point in acknowledging the Palestinian agony, as if it were one aggregate national agony. To me this seems an exaggerated notion. Immediately there is a comparison: the Jewish agony compared with the Palestinian agony. I think there is no basis for comparison. The Palestinians, when they were expelled—and many Palestinian Arabs were expelled in 1948—they could go places in which they lived among their brethren, among fellow Palestinians, not fellow Arabs in Morocco, but fellow Palestinians. I think we play into the hands of Palestinian propaganda when we speak about the Palestinian national agony. I agree that many, many personal problems should be solved, and—even more—that they shouldn't have been created. But I don't see the symmetry which was implied in your position.

NAHUM: I didn't say "symmetry."

EITAN: Yes, but you have to understand what you said: You acknowledge the Palestinian agony; then someone else says there is a Jewish agony. Both agonies are presented as equal or symmetrical and it plays into the hands of the Palestinian propaganda.

On the other hand, I also cannot accept Bitan's use of the past history of atrocities in Palestine as a justification for his characterization of the Arabs in this conflict. It's two-sided. You cite 1921; they cite Deir Yessin.* You cite 1936 to 1939; the Arabs cite many, many other places. When we are presented with such accusations by Arabs—that we were murderers, and so on—we have no alternative but to give our side. But I don't think that it serves any useful purpose to try to show that the Arabs—the Palestinian Arabs—have been butchers from the very beginning. There were atrocities committed by them, no doubt—in 1921 and 1929. In 1936 to 1939, most of the Arab atrocities were committed against Arabs, not against Jews. Maybe it's a question of definitions, but in 1936 to 1939, the Palestinian Arabs were engaging in guerrilla warfare, which is accepted by many people who believe in the right of self-determination and nationalism. I personally believe there is no right to kill other human beings, even in the name of nationalism. But if one does accept such a right, if one acknowledges the right to wage a popular war of liberation, and if one acclaims things done by other nationalities—then what the Palestinian guerrillas did in 1936 and 1939 is the same. Of course, each side should talk about the atrocities committed by his side. We should condemn our and their atrocities. But to present the Arabs as butchers is not true factually, and it doesn't serve any useful purpose.

BITAN: My purpose was not to recite Arab atrocities, and to say, "Look how the Arabs are." I tried to make an essential point about what it is that you find when you try to define the general attitude of the Palestinians toward the Jews in Palestine. I'm not talking about how many Jews they killed. I am talking about their attitude of not wanting to accept us here—physically. And that's not the same on both sides. Yes, you can have atrocities here and atrocities there. But the essential point is that there is a continuity in their basic position towards our being here.

EITAN: Of course, in the political sense. Yes.

BITAN: Not only political—but by saying that they have to kill as many Jews as are living here. I cited it not to show that they are butchers, but to illustrate their attitude toward the situation here. So there is no other way: Here I have to return to the past because I have only the past. What do I have? I don't have the future. Thus, many people in Israel don't see any essential change between the killing of Jews in 1929 and the PLO today.

ZVI: Until 1948 we had these two nations—the Palestinian Arab and the Jewish—within the same territorial framework, Western Palestine. And in the face of this geographic reality during the mandate period, the bulk of the Jewish population was willing to recognize the need for a division of this territory—to recognize the right of partition. After 1948, however, circumstances changed, and influenced many of the trends in Israeli public opinion we have been discussing here. One change has been demographic. A partition that might have been possible before 1948 has now become only a theoretical solution because about half of the Palestinian nation is outside this former mandate territory of Western Palestine. A second

*An Arab village near Jerusalem where in 1948 about 250 Arab civilians were killed by members of two right-wing Jewish underground units during an attack on the village.

change since the mandate period is that the problem of the Palestinians cannot be viewed in isolation—it cannot be divorced from the conflict between Israel and the Arab states. A third and more recent change is the emerging asymmetry, especially since the October war, in the balance of power. Israel has exhausted its military and economic potential, while the Arabs have been strengthening theirs— and time is on their side.

What is important for the Israeli public is that the October war did not bring any radical change in Arab attitudes about the existence of Israel, despite some peoples' expectations that those attitudes would be softened after the war. But most of the Israeli public believes—and I think they are right—that the war, if anything, has hardened and radicalized Arab attitudes toward Israel.

DROR: But something that you do not mention also happened after 1948 to change our approach to the Palestinian question. We have to remember that most of the Israeli public was, at first, indifferent about the Palestinian question because hundreds of thousands of immigrants came to Israel between 1948 and 1967, and for them the Palestinian question was just an abstract question. Their indifference was evident in the almost complete absence of the subject from educational curricula and even from press articles.

By comparison, the period after the Six Day War opened a new era for many people in Israel. After nineteen years, the two nations were linked again directly, and not this time only in war. There was a beginning of a new trend. Among many Israelis there was a feeling that daily contact at the human level would result in some understanding and political cooperation. There was talk, for example, of an easy solution to the refugee problem in the territories. Or it was said that our own Palestinians—the Israeli Arabs—would serve as a bridge to peace, as a model of successful cooperation for the Arabs of the territories. All of us remember that the early curiosity led to a great deal of travel between Israel and the territories.

We have lost some hope since 1967. Our high expectations have given way to disappointment. I don't want to speak about absolute failure, but many circles in the Israeli public feel that the chances are clearly diminished. We now agree that the Israeli Arabs were influenced, instead of influential.

The rendezvous we anticipated in 1967 continues, but it is almost one way, into Israel, through the commuting of thousands of Palestinian workers from the territories. I'm sorry to say it, but apart from the Israeli population settlements in the Jordan Valley and the Upper Hebron, Israeli civilians do not move around on their home ground—in the territories. And it's not because of the terror. Terror has not driven the Israeli civilians out of the territories; it was not strong enough or serious enough for that. The rendezvous has failed. Of course you can say that, since nine years in the life of a nation is really a drop in the ocean, the rendezvous has not really failed, it just wasn't put to use.

Other questions are bothering the Israeli public, some not yet mentioned here. One is the moral problem of dominion over others, over a large minority that doesn't want us. It's a fact. It bothers us. Another is the social-economic problem: thousands of Arabs from the territories doing the manual work in place of Israelis and in vital branches of industry. It, too, is a problem we cannot deny.

URI: Among segments of the Israeli society there is this feeling—without expressing it—that there is a "white man's burden" attitude towards the Palestinians. It's found in the Left, in the Right, in the Extreme Left, in the Extreme Right. People think that they know what the Palestinians should have. People think that they know whether or how the Palestinians should get a country or a homeland. They impose what they think on the Palestinians. There is a general tendency in Israel, especially among the working classes—what we call the silent majority—to ignore what's happening in the Palestinian community, our neighbors. It's true that the Israelis are no longer visiting the territories. I agree, Dror—it's not that terrorism is such a great problem. It's something more basic. I find many times when I bring Israelis to the territories—that for them it's a newer world than visiting Oxford Street in London. The problem, in my opinion, is that Israelis want to escape the Palestinian problem rather than know about it and deal with it.

Palestinians in the West Bank and Gaza or East Jerusalem often show more understanding of our political life in Israel than we do of theirs. Many Israelis—including those in the Knesset and in the universities—know much less, by comparison, about what's happening within the Palestinian community.

I also think, Amir, that you should add the non-Zionist elements such as the New Communist List (Rakah) [a political party whose principal source of support comes from Israel's Arab citizens] to your spectrum, on the Extreme Left. The 500,000 Israeli Arabs really are not Israelis. But there are also Israeli Jews among the New Communist List. To my great sorrow they are the only channels connecting us to the Palestinians, either in the occupied territory or in Israel. Look at the Palestinian community in Israel now, in the West Bank and in the Gaza Strip. Those people who regard a return to the boundaries of the 1947 partition plan as the right thing to do are considered to be moderate elements among the Palestinian community in Israel, and also abroad.

OREN: The question is whether Israel can survive in spite of Arab hostility. Nahum says he is worried about the continuation of the conflict. All of us are worried about it. The problem is: What is our answer? Ben-Gurion used to say that the fulfillment of the Zionist idea must not be dependent on an agreement with the Arabs. He was right, obviously. But probably ever since the late fifties or sixties, certainly a few years ago, the situation has changed. I want to put it very sharply. Today, possibilities are only two: either to reach an agreement or to be demolished. I don't think that wanting to reach an agreement means that we can reach one. Nobody can promise such things. It's a political gamble. But we have to try, because the alternative is a disaster.

YAIR: There is a Jewish saying: "Happy is the man who lives in fear." This is one saying that I am reluctant to accept. I join those who think that fear is a bad adviser. The evidence I see from experts leaves very little to the imagination about what are the real intentions of the Arabs—Palestinians and the Arab countries—and how deep these intentions go and how seriously one should take them. What I am going to say might be a simplification, but nevertheless true: the Arabs and the Palestinians are not going to rest until the state of Israel is abolished. In my view, this is the major fact. All the rest is beside the point. What Nahum said here about the depth of Arab opposition is only an intellectual and scientific corroboration of what is the gut feeling of the majority of Israelis.

If this feeling has been somewhat eroded since the Yom Kippur war, it is because the intellectual community—and I'm not blaming anyone, not accusing anyone—the intellectual community, the politicians, and the media have been debating the subject much more than before. Their main achievement has been to confuse a large part of the population, which either is not equipped or is not ready to examine all the subtleties of the subject. I think this argument about the Palestinian question, which has been going on for the third year now so intensively, has shattered some of the basic beliefs which people in Israel had.

This came about mainly because after 1973 the weakness of the Israeli leadership became more pronounced. Somehow the people felt that their leaders had lost their sense of purpose and direction, that they were groping in the darkness. People liked much more the simplicity—maybe even the fundamental way—in which Golda Meir expressed her attitude toward these problems. I reject the interpretation we've heard here of quotations attributed to her, which were taken out of context. She had a *weltanshauung* which, although it was a simplified one, the Israeli people could identify with.

The Israeli writer, Amos Oz, who undoubtedly belongs to what was defined here as the Extreme Left, said once in an interview that you can erase eternal enmity. This, of course, is a paradox. How can you erase something that is eternal? But I assume that many Israelis would like to believe that this is true. Yet the horrifying element in Nahum's analysis is his assertion that hatred is rational, that it has its "good" reasons, and that it is deep-rooted. I agree with him completely. And I think we can rectify this in only one way—to give up our sovereignty, to give up Zionism, to give up the state of Israel. What he said about public relations is one thing I can't accept. We can point, for example, to Arafat's UN appearance. He said terrible things before the whole world—things which have only one meaning: the obliteration of Israel. He's not so afraid of what the world might think. On the contrary, he believes that he can take the world with him.

Again, all the rest is almost beside the point. This means we all have only two options: either submission or, as I think, we should try to find our own way in this very dangerous world.

HANAN: In referring to whether the Jews are now visiting the territories more or less often, you should take into consideration the development of the Emunim group, and the tremendous sympathy they have had throughout the Israeli public and society. You can regard Gush Emunim as a sign of change in Israeli attitudes, and it is a change toward a greater and more profound self-conviction among Zionists. It might seem from our discussion that the changes in Israeli public opinion have been mostly toward the Left—which I think is not true.

AMIR: The spectrum of opinion I described in my opening remarks is based on my belief that the Arab-Israeli conflict is basically a conflict between two nationalist movements. I regard as relevant to our discussion those political forces on two sides which represent the two respective nationalist movements. Therefore, I thought that only the Zionist camp is really relevant and I omitted all groups which do not reflect the Israeli nationalist movement. In this sense, I fully accept the concepts of Neguib Azoury who wrote in his *Le Réveille de la Nation Arabe,* in 1904, that there are two forces in the Middle East—Arab nationalism and Zionism—and it's the clash between these two movements that is going to decide its future.

Some participants have suggested that we add other groups to our spectrum, such as "the desperate" or those who consider reliance on nuclear rather than conventional weapons. Of course these undercurrents are quite important and may be even more significant in the future. But if we discuss the Israeli public at the present time in terms of tangible political forces and schools of thought, it is very difficult to identify today a well-defined party or group or even a personality that has made a definite commitment to such a conception of the Arab-Israeli conflict. Moreover, questions concerning nuclear weapons do not have a direct bearing on public attitudes toward the Palestinians. So at the present moment, to include a nuclear school of thought within the spectrum, or to include any group reflecting desperation, is premature.

Various rightist schools of thought, it was explained here, are motivated by the genuine fear that Israelis have with regard to the Arabs' intentions of extermination, and it was pointed out that these fears are colored by the Jewish experiences. Of course, that is a very important dimension of the problem. We should never lose sight of the threat of extermination, and we should never underrate the determination of the Israeli community to prevent it.

But fears and anxieties are not the monopoly of the rightist wing in the Israeli camp. It is not that the Right has a "realistically pessimistic" view of Israel's position and prospects in the Middle East, while the Left has overoptimistic and unrealistic expectations about the feasibility of a peace settlement with the Arabs. I think this is a false representation of the differences between Right and Left. The Left is also motivated, to a large extent, by fears, although they are sometimes of a different nature. Leftists fear that the kind of rigidity sometimes demonstrated by the Right would seriously constrain the Israeli government and that the Israeli leadership might lose its flexibility and its ability to maneuver in circumstances of extreme complexity and danger. In a situation in which the Israeli government must take rapid decisions, make compromises, maneuver, suggest alternatives, produce policies which will be acceptable to Israel's allies—particularly the United States—Leftists fear that the government might be constrained to such an extent that it would be unable to prevent a disastrous outcome. The Right—being so anxious to defend the existence of the Israeli community—thus

might actually precipitate a process leading to the ruin of that community.

Israeli Leftists also fear that the self-centered rightist orientation would produce an esoteric Israeli society which is not conversant with the rest of the world and would bring about the isolation of Israel. Therefore, the rightist attitude may turn out to be a self-fulfilling prophecy—by speaking about Israel's isolation they might cause it to materialize—with detrimental consequences to the future of Israel.

Leftists are not necessarily, as they are sometimes assumed to be, overoptimistic about the ability to terminate the historic conflict between Israelis and Arabs. Leftists—if I may generalize about the leftist category—sometimes feel that precisely because it is impossible to terminate the conflict one must search for alternatives to total reconciliation—for interim agreements, for various arrangements designed to reduce the level of the conflict, to reduce the frequency of violent confrontations between Israelis and Arabs. In the long run the number of such confrontations may turn out to be the crucial question for the future of Israel.

I want to recall what Yair said following his suggestion that we learn about the Arabs' desire to destroy Israel from experts—who, indeed, do not differ on the basic interpretation of Arab attitudes and intentions. Then he added, "all the rest is beside the point." I suggest that all the rest is not beside the point. Precisely the opposite: all the rest is the crux of the matter. Once we have established the Arab intentions toward Israel, then the question arises: what do you do under such circumstances? Do you indulge in self-pity and the feeling of being isolated from the rest of the world, and in sentiments of irrational dependence on—I don't know—the eternal destiny of this nation? Do you indulge in despair or in hopes linked to the possible use of nuclear weapons? Or do you continue the search for any possible arrangements which can be worked out on the basis of the differences between the various Arab countries? Because, with all their common animosity toward the state of Israel, Arab states *are* motivated by different interests. In the Arab world there are different attitudes toward various practical questions regarding the conflict, and this allows a space of maneuvering for Israeli diplomacy. The tendency in the Israeli political public is to disregard Arab differences and to speak about *the* Arabs, which is a grave mistake. Therefore, I repeat, all the rest is the crux of the matter. This is the watershed between Left and Right, as I understand it.

The position I call the Tactical Left, has many merits. But not the merit you attributed to it, Nahum. Like Pinhas, I feel that the greatest weakness of that position is that there are more contradictions in it than in any of the other positions.

Either you assume that there is a reasonable chance of an agreement with the Arabs—in which case I do not see any difference between this opinion and that of the various left groups: You see a chance of settlement, you advocate it, and you take the necessary steps in order to reach it. Or, on the other hand, you assume that the depth of Arab hostility to Israel—the Arabs in general and the Palestinians in particular—prevents any progress towards a settlement. In this case, I cannot see how to describe this position as anything other than tactical. You are inviting the Arabs to do something that you know they will not do simply in order to benefit from the propaganda for Israel. I certainly do not see anything wrong in a tactical position. We need many good tactical positions. But in this forum let's call a spade a spade.

GAD: I believe that the key sentence that describes best the opinion since 1967 of about 60 percent of the Israeli population is: "Let's keep as many territories as we can and let's return only what we must." There is a deep wish for peace among this majority, and until 1973 there was a deep belief in the decisions of the Israeli leadership about what we must return.

Since 1973 the feeling has grown that we cannot keep too much, and we will probably have to return much more than we anticipated before. That's the general consensus of the people—whether they want it or whether they do not want it. A majority believes that we'll probably have to give much more because we are weaker than we expected, and the powers aligned against us are stronger than we expected. A big part of the public believes that this is a calamity for Israel, strategically and even morally. This prepares the ground for the readiness of larger segments of the population to follow a desperado policy.

On the other hand, a larger section of the population shows a degree of disbelief in the Israeli leadership. Now the leadership has a more difficult time proving to the people that it is going to hold on to whatever territories it can and return only what it must. This erosion of belief in the leadership means that the leadership has to make much stronger efforts to convince people that it conforms to the basic wish of holding onto the territories. There is thus an inhibition on the leadership. It cannot lead. It has to conform. It cannot initiate policies. It cannot initiate policies even along lines advised by the Tactical Left. It cannot follow the advice of someone like Yariv because it is always engaged in proving to the public that it's going to hold on to as many territories as possible.

According to certain Israeli public opinion polls in 1975, there is a polarization of views. More and more people now are ready to trade territories for peace, while more and more people are convinced that the Arab intentions are not peaceful. The basic reaction of the population is "Let's be tough with them because they are tough with us." But in my opinion, 60 percent of the population is swayable to one or the other side, according to the recommendations of the leadership.

PINHAS: Hearing you say, Gad, that greater numbers of Israelis are convinced about Arab intentions makes it clear, to me at least, that more and more we all here agree on some basic facts. The mainstream of thinking within the Arab world shows deep hostility and enmity toward the existence of Israel. I didn't hear anyone here denying these basic things. On the contrary, everyone insisted on emphasizing his agreement with this basic evaluation of the feelings within the Arab world towards Israel.

The differences among us lie in the political conclusions we draw, and some of the tactics that we propose. What disturbed me most, especially in Nahum's presentation, is that some of us here try to do the impossible: to accept these evaluations of Arab feelings and still propose or speak about a framework of some potential final agreement. This is self-contradictory—not logically perhaps—but at least under the circumstances we face. Amir is very conscious of this in that he does not want to commit himself to something more than some kind of practical arrangements—not peace or reconciliation with the existence of Israel. He too remains only on the tactical level, in the same way as the Tactical Left that he criticizes. He is not talking any more about any strategic aim or purpose.

I do share, basically, the feeling that perhaps a full, final solution is impossible. We have to think in terms of something more limited. The main question is: what tactical route is left for us? How much can a state like Israel allow itself the luxury of tactics since we are as weak as we are? Many on the Right and the Extreme Right

believe that it is impossible for Israel to engage in a process of negotiating practical steps because we might not be able to control the outcome of such a process. Even given all our resources, influence and ability, the Tactical Left's approach is one that perhaps only stronger and better-positioned countries could allow themselves to follow under these circumstances.

ZVI: It also bothers me personally—this contradiction between the way we represent the Arab attitudes as very stubborn or inflexible or hostile, and the way we try to face the situation.

Among most Israelis, there's a common agreement that the initial cause of the conflict is the clash between two national movements for the same piece of land—the Jewish Zionist and the Arab Palestinian. Most of us would say that the Arabs don't have the same right or the same deep-rooted feelings for their right, and that it is not as strong as the Jewish right. But even those of us who believe this would agree that there is a Palestinian claim here. In my own home, my daughter speaks about the right of the Palestinians.

I see a very sharp asymmetry in the attitudes of the Israelis and the Arabs, including the Palestinian Arabs. Most of the Israeli public—even, I would say, the Right—would recognize in one way or another the Palestinian entity—in principle. I'm not speaking now about any particular political solution, but about the principle of a Palestinian entity. But among the Arabs such attitudes do not exist at all. I'm talking particularly about the political elite, and the political community, whose attitude is to deny the right of the Jews to self-determination as a nation-state, for reasons that are essential in Arab political thinking.

But still I think that we ourselves have to be more flexible and to seize all opportunities for coexistence—although I don't believe the Arabs want peace. Yet, I have this little doubt about whether the Arab position is permanent, doubt about saying it would never change. Perhaps it might change.

YAIR: When did it change last?

ZVI: But things might be different under new circumstances such as a nuclear deterrent. Let them have it too.

NAHUM: You want them to have a nuclear deterrent?

ZVI: Yes, I do. The Arab position might change. The alternative would be worse for everybody. From the Israeli public's point of view, if things remain as they are now, I think there will be a great shift to the Right, to the Extreme Right.

NAHUM: Those who speak about going nuclear and, at the same time, acquiring American support are embroiling themselves in a contradiction in terms.

MEIR: Obviously.

EITAN: Is it not possible to go nuclear without the United States' knowledge?

DROR: The answer is yes.

MEIR: I am puzzled by this whole discussion today. Many of us assumed after 1973 that there was some change in the Arab positions. At what moment did this whole group come to the conclusion that this assumption was false? The question is central. I know that some of you never believed in the change. But many here did. In December, 1973, and January-February, 1974, there was a feeling that there were some changes here and there: Egypt was moving; eventually among the Syrians there were different voices; and even among the Palestinians there were some moderate voices. I know that some Israelis never changed their minds on this, but at some moment after the 1973 war Israeli public opinion—or part of it, or part

of the elite—had the right or wrong impression that there was a change in the Arab position. Therefore Israeli public opinion started to change its own position—toward the Egyptians and the Syrians—on the possibility of a settlement. But I get the impression from our discussion that actually—suddenly—all Israeli public opinion, except some fringes, is convinced that there is nothing to be done. Therefore, there is no possibility of settlement, and there is no solution to the Palestinian problem. There must have been a shift somewhere, in 1974 or 1975. When did this sudden reversal take place in Israeli opinion?

PINHAS: I think you misread me. I don't think there was any dramatic change. I get the impression that people, some of you here, do not express a belief in the chance for a final solution. As an alternative, you have been really trying to suggest to us a process of practical arrangements which would enable Israel to exist with lower pressures and to see what would happen in the future. Now I don't think this reflects a dramatic change within public opinion.

EITAN: I think that on this question there has been a change in public opinion, and it is directly connected to the behavior of the Israeli leadership after the war. In order to save their political control of Israel, the Labour Alignment and the Labour Party deliberately lied to the public in November, 1973, in saying that there were chances of peace, that there were forces that might bring peace through Geneva, and that Geneva might produce results because there had been change among the Arabs. And they won the December, 1973, Israeli elections because they succeeded in convincing a greater part of the public that the chances were real. The initial disengagement agreement with Egypt was presented as the first sign that this view was operational and was going to be fulfilled. But most Israelis didn't accept the second disengagement agreement with Egypt in the same way as they did the first. Very few believed the leadership's claim that it was really good. The public reaction was generally, "OK. We had no alternative. The United States forced it upon us." During the period of time separating these two agreements there emerged a deep crisis of trust. The leadership is not regarded anymore as trustworthy, as reliable, or as credible. And since they were the ones responsible for the image that something has really changed in the Arab world since 1973, their discreditation also brought challenge to this myth of change among the Arabs.

AMIR: I would answer you differently, Meir. When we discuss the problem on the level of principles, it is a matter of almost complete consensus in the Israeli public—it is certainly a consensus within the small community of Israeli experts on the Arab world—that no significant element in Arab society has accepted the legitimacy of the state of Israel; that no Arab element has adopted a view which completely abandons the hope that some day the state of Israel will disappear, or will transform itself and cease to be a Zionist Jewish state. This is the view, at the level of principle; but there is also the level of practical diplomacy.

Take a person like Mr. Rabin. In discussing the negotiations for the various interim agreements, he holds out the hope of some progress toward peace. But at the same time, he asserts consistently—and should get credit for it—that no Arab state and no Arab leader has really reconciled himself to the existence of the state of Israel. There is no contradiction between these two positions. There is no doubt that Arab society

feels that the creation of the state of Israel was an act of injustice. It would be almost impossible to expect the Arabs to see the problem in any other terms. Our claim to Eretz Israel—to which I as a Zionist fully adhere—is based on the unique historical experience of the Jewish people. Some societies in the West—especially those that have the same Biblical tradition or witnessed closely the predicament of the Jewish people in Europe—are ready to accept it. But most Afro-Asian peoples find it very peculiar. Certainly it is difficult for the Arabs to accept this claim, for they regard the establishment of the state of Israel as contrary to the "natural" course of history. Therefore, there is no Arab leader who adopts, as a matter of principle, the Israeli view about the right of Zionism to establish a Jewish state in this country. This is the area of consensus, and no change has taken place in this matter.

But beyond that, there have been various developments in the Arab world, before and after 1973, which might—I stress "might," for there is no certainty—constrain some Arab states in such a way that they would accept arrangements which in turn would reduce the level of the conflict. This offers a wide range of possibilities for a constructive Israeli diplomacy and for imaginative Israeli policymakers, as I have said. We might now have an opportunity for reaching a sort of *modus vivendi* with our neighbors which might at least reduce the risks of more wars for Israel. Given the terrible pressures operating now on this little state amidst a sea of animosity, this would be an achievement of the first order. No one knows if it can be achieved, but it should be tried. Here lies the controversy in Israel; and here, I believe, there is some fluidity in the situation.

Before Israel was established, we Zioni
never allowed anybody to formulate
aims for us. We were flexible on ta
points, never changing our basic aim
should we think that the Palestinia
different in this respect?

4

The Palestinians

Editors' Introduction

While reluctant to locate precisely a political center of gravity in Israeli public opinion, the participants are not so tentative about the distribution of political weight in the Palestinian Arab community. To discuss that community means for them to discuss primarily the Palestinian Liberation Organization (PLO), although they have contrasting reasons for attributing central importance to the PLO. Some make this attribution because they acknowledge, for practical purposes, the Arab world and the United Nations verdict that the PLO is the representative of the Palestinian people. Some do so because they conclude from observing developments in the West Bank, the Gaza Strip, and even among the Arab citizens of Israel, that the PLO enjoys an authentic monopoly—although not necessarily a complete one—on the symbols and the substance of Palestinian nationalism. Some do so because the PLO represents for them the confirmation of historical Palestinian hostility toward Zionism, which participants now find embodied in the official political programs and basic objectives of the PLO.

The group's assessment is not uniform either on the question of Israeli diplomatic strategy toward the PLO or on the question of whether the identification with the PLO among Palestinians under Israel's control could have been forestalled by Israeli encouragement after 1967 of rival or parallel Palestinian leadership in the West Bank and the Gaza Strip. Nor is the group of one mind about the depth or the durability of the PLO allegiance now evident among Palestinians in these two territories.

The Palestinian National Covenant*, formulated in the 1960s and accepted by all PLO-affiliated organizations, expresses for many of the participants, more than any other official document, the principles and goals animating Palestinian policies toward Israel. For many in the group the covenant *is* the PLO. To ask, as

*The full text of the covenant is reproduced in Appendix II.

y do, whether there has been any recent change in Palestinian objectives quires them to look at other, later political pronouncements. But the baseline from which the group evaluates possible change remains the covenant—even though participants diverge in their assessment of the covenant's political and diplomatic significance and in their interpretation of other evidence about possible transformation of Palestinian ambitions.

Historical memories also feed many participants' perceptions of the Palestinian Arabs and their present-day intentions. What matters for many in the group is not only what the PLO has decided or done in the 1960s and 1970s, but also the accumulated experience of the Israelis since 1948 and the Jews of Palestine before then. All the participants do not see this long history alike or read the same lessons from the half-century of violence and enmity. Nevertheless, participants who voice totally different political conclusions about the Palestinian-Israeli conflict do not deny that two national movements have collided in Palestine during the twentieth century—even if the participants do not all regard these rights as symmetrical or equal in priority.

The PLO and the Palestinian National Covenant were both born in 1964, as a result of Arab summit recommendations taken on Egypt's initiative. Yasser Arafat's organization, Fatah, was not then a member of the PLO. Fatah, which began to take shape as a movement during the late 1950s, received Syrian patronage during the next decade, and under guidance from Damascus, undertook in 1965-67 its first military activities within Israel, mostly by Fedayeen infiltrated from Jordan.

The aftermath of the Six Day War was a crucial period for the PLO. Before the war, intitial impulses toward a more assertive Palestinian movement were muted by chronic Arab world disunity that sidetracked Palestinian hopes of a decisive struggle aginst Israel as well as by inter-Arab manipulation of the Palestinian cause. With the shattering defeat of the Arab states in 1967, a Palestinian line more independent of Arab state tutelage seemed the only path, and Fatah led the way. Its reputation bolstered by a promise of Palestinian-centered struggle against Israel and its ranks enlarged by new members, Fatah tried just after the war to launch a conventional guerrilla campaign within the West Bank and the Gaza Strip. That effort failed, as did Fatah's first effort to gain control of the PLO in 1968. In 1969 Arafat was finally able to take over the organization, only to see the Fedayeen decimated by King Hussein in the 1970 Jordan civil war. Anti-Hussein feeling ran deep among the embittered Palestinians. They were now left only with Lebanon as a territorial base against Israel, because Syria maintained tight control of Fedayeen activities from Syrian territory. It was then that a strategy of international terrorism outside the Middle East was adopted by Palestinian groups.

Between the 1967 and 1973 wars, the Palestinian organizations went through a period of intricate factionalism, of ideological disputes, and of realignments with Arab-world protectors and supporters. Fatah played the leading role in the PLO after 1973. It remained the most ideologically pragmatic, the most tactically flexible within the constellation of Palestinian organizations, and the least dependent of them all on any Arab state. Fatah's main rival has been the Popular Front for the Liberation of Palestine (PFLP), the most single-mindedly ideological and Pan-Arab of the organizations, led by George Habash. Also highly ideological, but

taking a line different in certain essentials from the PFLP, is the Popula
cratic Front for the Liberation of Palestine (PDFLP), under the leadership ᴏ
Hawatmeh. The other leading organizations are the Syrian-sponsored Saiᴋ
headed by Zuheir Muhsan; the Popular Front-General Command, headed by
Ahmed Jibril and also Syrian-controlled; and the Arab Liberation Army, Palestinian Independents, and former residents of the West Bank.

The participants focus in this segment on the basic programmatic objectives of
the PLO, including the concept of a "democratic secular state" that was advanced
in the late 1960s. They also discuss two developments that took place after the
October War. The first is the split between the PLO establishment and the so-
called Rejection Front groups within the PLO, mainly Habash's PFLP. The split
was provoked by disagreement about whether the Palestinians should participate in international negotiations such as the Geneva Conference; whether they
should establish, if Israeli territorial withdrawals make it possible, a "national
authority" in the West Bank and the Gaza Strip. The "national authority"
question dominated the 1974 Palestinian National Council meeting in Cairo,
where it was favored by Fatah, Saika, and the PDFLP, and resisted by the PFLP
and the Popular Front-General Command. The second post-1973 development
discussed by the participants is the emergence since 1973 of voices within the
official PLO structure—such as the organization's London-based representative, Said Hammami—hinting at possible PLO acceptance of coexistence with
Israel, involving Palestinian acquisition of their own state on the West Bank and
the Gaza Strip.

A single question defines the group's main concern in this portion of their
dialogue: Has there been any change in Palestinian objectives and attitudes
toward Israel? Nahum, after listening to his colleagues' answers, made this observation: "Eitan... said there is no change in the Palestinian position—and then
went on and described some changes. The same happened with Zvi. It happens
with me too. And I ask myself, what does it mean?" His own answer, and the
answers of the others, come in response to Zvi's opening survey of developments that he regards as important in Palestinian thinking.

ZVI: There have been some changes in
the attitude of the Palestinians about the
Palestinian question and the future of
Israel. The most crystallized, weighty, and
representative views among the Palestinians are the views and basic positions of the
PLO. The PLO was recognized by the
international community as representing
the Palestinian people. In the inter-Arab
arena, the PLO was recognized at the
Rabat conference as the legitimate, sole
representative of the Palestinian nation. A
large part of the population in the West
Bank supports the PLO. Finally, the political standing of the PLO, as well as its
military might, doesn't give room to any

other Palestinian community to speak in a
different way—with one exception: the
Rejection Front. But I regard it as part of
the PLO.

Let me examine the changes in the position of the PLO since the war of 1973 on
two major issues: a secular democratic
state in the whole of Palestine and a Palestinian state next to Israel as a political
solution.

The National Covenant, as adopted in
1964 and amended in 1968 represents the
official, the most concentrated, and the
most cohesive attitude of the PLO. Four
points sum up the relevant clauses. One is
that Palestine, in the framework of the

The Palestine Resolution
e Seventh Arab Summit Conference,
Rabat, October 29, 1974

h Arab Summit Conference resolves the following:

To affirm the right of the Palestinian people to self-determination and to return to their homeland;

To affirm the right of the Palestinian people to establish an independent national authority under the command of the Palestine Liberation Organization, the sole legitimate representative of the Palestinian people in any Palestinian territory that is liberated...."

The full text of the Rabat Resolution appears in Appendix IV.

Palestinian National Covenant, 1968

ARTICLE 1:

Palestine is the homeland of the Arab Palestinian people; it is an indivisible part of the Arab homeland, and the Palestinian people are an integral part of the Arab nation.

ARTICLE 6:

The Jews who had normally resided in Palestine until the beginning of the Zionist invasion will be considered Palestinians.

ARTICLE 9:

Armed struggle is the only way to liberate Palestine. Thus it is the overall strategy, not merely a tactical phase....

ARTICLE 20:

... Judaism, being a religion, is not an independent nationality. Nor do Jews constitute a single nation with an identity of its own; they are citizens of the states to which they belong.

The full text of the covenant is reproduced in Appendix II.

British Mandate, is one integral unit which is undivided. All of it belongs to the Palestinian Arab nation, and the Palestinian Arab nation only has the right to this land. Second, Israel doesn't have a legitimate right to exist, even in the boundaries of the partition of 1947. It is a tool in the hand of Zionist imperialism and poses a threat, not only to Arabism, but also to humankind. Third, the great aim of the Arabs and the Palestinians is to liberate Palestine and to eliminate the "Zionist entity" through an armed struggle without compromise. Finally, the Jews are not a nation, but members of a religious community. They don't have the right of political or national self-determination. Those Jews who lived or settled in Palestine before the "Zionist invasion"—which is interpreted as 1917, [when Great Britain announced the Balfour Declaration promising a national home in Palestine for the Jews]—could be citizens of the Palestinian Arab state.

One important development in the attitude of the PLO is the idea of a democratic state. At least theoretically, this idea is intended to change the clause in the National Covenant which says that Jews who lived in Palestine before the "Zionist invasion" would be regarded as Palestinians. This idea has been expressed since 1971 in the various organs of the PLO but especially in speeches and interviews of the PLO leaders. And when these speeches were directed abroad, usually there was another dimension added—not only "democratic state," but "secular democratic state"—a formulation which doesn't appear, as far as I know, in the official resolutions of the PLO. In Arafat's famous speech at the United Nations in 1974, he said that he regarded all Jews living at present in Israel as part of this democratic secular state.*

I maintain that, according to the PLO, this state would be Arab, not bi-national. It would take the place of the state of Israel, instead of existing side by side with it. It wouldn't be secular, but Islamic. And it

Terrorist activities of '
Green Line agains'
don't encourag'
that they c'
state. Ar'
Israel'
Le'

wou...
that...

Ad...
dem...
lishe...
eral...
guara...
had ta...
tion. T...
the nu...
repatria...
and uni...
Jordan. ...
would be ......atus of a minority. One official clause says that only those who would like to live in peace would be allowed to remain. Other Palestinian publications say that the Jews who could remain would be those willing to give up their Zionist convictions, which are defined as working against peace. Also, there is a strong possibility that land would be taken from Jews and returned to their initial Arab owners, causing many Jews to leave. European Jews wouldn't like to live in this state and would go back to Europe. Oriental Jews, whom the Palestinians call "Arab Jews," would be invited to go back to their original countries.

The general feeling of the Israeli public is that in this so-called democratic state violent means would be used to reduce the number of Jews. Whether it's imaginary or not, whether true or not, the memory of 1921, 1929 and 1936-1939 is quite vivid. Many still remember the yells of Ahmad Shukiary to throw the Jews into the sea.

*"I proclaim before you that when we speak of our common hopes for the Palestine of tomorrow we include in our perspective all Jews now living in Palestine who choose to live with us there in peace and without discrimination."
—Yasser Arafat, Address to the United Nations General Assembly, November 13, 1974. The full text of Arafat's speech is in Appendix V.

...e PLO within the
...ivilians and children
...nany Israelis to believe
...u live peacefully in such a
...er trauma shared by many
...related to events in Lebanon.
...on has always been the image of a
...ti-communal, democratic state—if not
a secular one. Not long ago some PLO people said that this would be the model for a democratic Palestine. What is happening in Lebanon is again an indication that it wouldn't work. Moreover, the historical record of the Palestinian national movement and of the Arab national movement in establishing democratic and secular states is not very impressive. Also, Islamic influence on the PLO, and especially on Fatah, is well known. So for most Israelis this idea of a democratic, secular state is regarded as a gimmick—a propaganda gimmick—and not an ideological change.

There are, however, two exceptions I want to mention. One is found in the statement of the Palestinian Sabri Jiryis [now Head of the Israel department of the PLO Research Center in Beirut, and a former Arab citizen of Israel] who says that the idea or notion of the democratic state is void and empty, because it indicates a violent solution, which means the uprooting of 99 percent of the Jews living now in Israel. He urged changing the 6th article in the National Covenant. I also want to stress that the Popular Democratic Front of Naif Hawatmeh used to be the only genuine democratic and secular organization—in their terms—in the PLO. The Front initiated this notion of a Palestinian democratic state as an accepted principle of the PLO.

NAHUM: It's not a principle, it's a tactical slogan.

ZVI: Slogan in our view; that's right. The Jews in that state, according to the Front, should be granted the rights of a cultural minority. Hawatmeh has gone on record several times—especially in the European press—in favor of establishing a federated state in Palestine, Jewish-Arab or Arab-Jewish; something on the Czechoslovak-Yugoslav model. But unfortunately, after these declarations or interviews, he was harshly criticized by members of his organization, and many left him and went to another organization. So he had to step in line and withdraw his declarations. His later interviews are much more extreme, and in order to show that he was in line, he perpetrated the Maalot crime [a town in Galilee where twenty-six Israelis, mostly school children, were held as hostages by the Fedayeen and killed] in May, 1974.

The second change—so-called change—within the PLO concerns the national Palestinian state in the West Bank and the Gaza Strip. I want to stress that the basic attitudes of the PLO, as I've outlined them, were confirmed again and again in various national councils of the PLO—until the 1973 war. No compromise. All organizations within the PLO maintained a categorical objection to the establishment of a Palestinian ministate in part of Palestine.

PINHAS: Ministate within Judea and Samaria?

ZVI: Yes. But after the October war, some new views and nuances could be detected on the question of armed struggle versus a political solution. Usually the moderate trend was to advocate use of both political means and military measures in the struggle for Palestine. Also, a new moderate nuance was to establish a "national authority." From the beginning of 1975, they even spoke about a "state" in part of Palestine as a stage to the liberation of all Palestine. The official expression of this attitude—before the word "state" was mentioned—can be seen in the political program of the PLO in the 12th Session of the Palestinian National Council, June, 1974.

There have been many interviews and declarations by Palestinian leaders on the possibility of establishing a Palestinian state in Palestine side by side with Israel. I want to mention Said Hammami, the PLO spokesman in London. He said in March, 1975, at a symposium sponsored by the Council for the Advancement of Arab-British Understanding (CAABU) that he is for establishing a Palestinian state in the West Bank and the Gaza Strip and opening its border with Israel. In the course of mutual peaceful relations, he said, the Zionist nature of Israel will be eliminated as a result of the internal processes of its own inhabitants. Then, the two states will unite in one secular state.*

Ibrahim Souss, a PLO official assigned to UNESCO, has said that for them the durable and just peace is through the establishment of a "unified, democratic state," but to achieve this goal they have to pass through a "few stages and first must establish a Palestinian national authority."

NAHUM: Qaddoumi** said that Souss was not authorized to say that; and Souss later recanted.

ZVI: That's correct. Another expression of that idea comes from Sabri Jiryis, who has said he is for a Palestinian state in the West Bank and the Gaza Strip as a step towards the establishment of a state in all of Palestine. But he maintains that the idea of a democratic state is still premature, that it should be postponed until both the Arabs and Israelis would be ready to accept it. Both Ibrahim Souss and Said Hammami admit that an Israeli nation is in the process of formation. Sabri Jiryis even speaks about a Jewish nation, and he admits that the majority of Israelis stick to Zionist convictions. But he himself expects the disappearance of these convictions. He thinks that a small Israel would be less Zionist and cease to be a refuge for world Jews, that a small Israel would be more dependent on the Arab states and be forced to take back a large number of Palestinian refugees and to abolish the Law of Return. He adds that in the long range the PLO cannot achieve its final goal through political, economic

and demographic .
also would be used at ،
not the time.

One can regard these tre.
esting and new development ι.
prominent Palestinian scholar,
Hisham Sharabi,† in the lecture ι.
gave at the Institute for Strategic Stuc.
in September, 1974, said, "A pragmatic Palestinian position has evolved which calls for a separate and independent Palestinian state in this area as a basic condition for any political settlement. In this conception complex questions dealing with demilitarization, inspection, international guarantees, etc. will have to be settled, but without compromising the principle of Palestine sovereignty over Palestinian territory. As for the alternative to such a

*The Decision of the Palestinian National Council, Cairo, June 9, 1974, reads as follows concerning the Palestinian national authority: "The Liberation Organization will employ all means, and first and foremost armed struggle, to liberate Palestinian territory and to establish the independent combatant national authority for the people over every part of the Palestinian territory that is liberated. This will require further changes being effected in the balance of power in favour of our people and their struggle.

"The Liberation Organization will struggle against any proposal for Palestinian entity the price of which is recognition, peace, secure frontiers, renunciation of national rights and the deprival of our people of their right to return and their right to self-determination on the soil of their homeland."
The full text of this decision appears in Appendix VI.

**Farouk Qaddoumi is head of the PLO Political Department.

†Hisham Sharabi is editor of the *Journal of Palestine Studies*.

a probable outcome of any peace settlement is likely to ___ establishment of some kind of Palestinian State on the territory recovered from Israel, it seems to me that a very necessary and useful subject for discussion is whether we may then hope to pursue our unaltered, ultimate aim of a 'state in partnership' covering the whole area of Israel/Palestine by non-violent and evolutionary means rather than by a continuation of armed struggle."

"...consideration should be given to the maintenance of open frontiers between Israel and the Palestinian State and to permitting, even encouraging, a mutual interpenetration of commerce, industry and cultural activities."

"Once stability and peace are ensured the momentum [of Zionism] will be lost and the whole idea of political Zionism will lose much of its appeal both for Jews living in Israel and for their supporters outside."

"We hope that it will be possible before long to work out a form of co-existence which will enable the two peoples to live together within a reunited Palestine...."

The full text of Hammami's speech is reproduced in Appendix VII.

state, the idea of a Palestinian state confederated with Jordan seems unacceptable to a majority of the Palestinians. Equally unlikely would be the establishment of a Palestinian state divorced from the Palestinian resistance movement (the PLO) and the power and authority which it wields among the Palestinians. Confederation with Israel, another alternative, has no support whatsoever." He adds: "Among the moderate elements, however, there seems to be a growing willingness to reconsider the question of recognition. These elements hold that Israel cannot be destroyed by war and that refusal to achieve settlement now would inevitably lead to Israel's *de facto* absorption of the West Bank and the Gaza Strip, with the resultant obliteration of their Palestinian Arab character within a decade or so. Peace, on the other hand, may eventually bring about the de-Zionization of Israel, *i.e.*, the abandonment of expansionist policies and goals and of the idea of an exclusively Jewish state from which most Palestinians are automatically excluded on ethnic grounds.

"This possibility, the moderates contend, is not based on wishful thinking or merely on the hope that reason and goodwill one day will prevail. It rests on the certainty that economic necessity and some political sense in the face of an overwhelmingly powerful Arab world will force the Israelis in the direction of reconciliation, once their militance has been softened by a period of peace."

How can we evaluate these new trends? Leftist circles in Israel would say that this is a pragmatic, moderate tendency which is a break-through in Israeli-Palestinian relations. It will eventually lead to coexistence and peace in which the idea of a secular democratic state all over Palestine will be kind of a ritual, Messianic desire. The great majority of Israelis, however, regard this tendency not as pragmatic or moderate, but as tactics and propaganda not representing the real aims of the PLO.

Some people would argue that moderate statements by PLO spokesmen were voiced mostly abroad before European or American audiences. Some statements were denied or were denounced later. On the central issues, what was said was either not new or very vague. Not one of the PLO spokesmen would regard a Palestinian state in the West Bank and Gaza Strip as a final solution. Nobody. The final aim is still a democratic secular state throughout Palestine. No Palestinian spokesman was ready to accept a Zionist state of Israel— namely the right of self-determination of the Jewish people in Israel. And most Palestinians are not ready to recognize Israel, even if it agrees to the establishment of a Palestinian state in the West Bank and the Gaza Strip. Some might say that they recognize the state of Israel *de facto*—since it exists and they are fighting against it—but they would not recognize Israel's *right* to exist.

Palestinian spokesmen usually go out of their way not to stress, before a Western audience, that a Palestinian state is only a stage or a step toward a final solution. They usually avoid the issue, or they are noncommittal. But when pressed to answer, they say that the final stage is sort of a dream—the word that Arafat mentioned in his UN speech, something that the next generation can solve.

Some PLO leaders say that a Palestinian state along the 1947 boundaries could be a basis for a solution and for a settlement with Israel. Shafiq al-Hout, head of the PLO office in Beirut, Zuheir Muhsan, chief of the Saika, and others all say so. The Left in Israel claims that both the democratic secular state and the 1947 boundary proposals are bargaining positions from which the PLO is ready to retreat and eventually to come to terms along the 1967 boundaries. However, the main body of Israeli public opinion believes that the PLO has not changed its basic position.

What led the PLO to accept this notion of a political solution and a Palestinian state in part of Palestine? First, they wanted at all costs to prevent the return of this territory to Jordan, which would prevent the PLO from taking it. Second, the PLO has now developed a new policy, namely that the establishment of a state would strengthen the Palestinian position and their national identity, while weakening Israel. The argument for this policy is that the Palestinians badly need a territory to develop a political identity under the leadership of the PLO. When this identity is established, Israel would be weakened—militarily, politically, morally, and economically. It would stop attracting Jews from all over the world. It would be exposed more than ever to pressures from Arab states, the Palestinians, and the international community, including pressure to go back to the boundaries of 1947 and to take back the refugees. This pressure would come also from the Arabs living within Israel—especially in the Galilee, which was not part of Israel under the 1947 partition resolution. Finally, the PLO believes that if a Palestinian state is established in the West Bank and the Gaza Strip, it can turn into a kind of Middle Eastern North Vietnam, a base for guerrilla activities against Israel which might bring about its collapse from within. Or in case of an Arab-Israeli war the West Bank might serve as a springboard for an all-Arab offensive.

PLO acceptance of a West Bank-Gaza Strip state also is connected with the position of the Arab states, especially Egypt, Syria, and Saudi Arabia. The PLO knows very well that it alone can't achieve its full aims with a long-term military struggle; it also needs the assistance of the Arab states. On the ideological level, Arab states identify completely with the PLO aims regarding the rights of the Palestinians. However, the major Arab states, especially Egypt and Syria, despite the rivalry between them, are interested at this stage in a political solution which would lead to the return to the 1967 boundaries and the establishment of a Palestinian state in the West Bank and Gaza Strip as a first step. Thereafter, Syria would probably press for the 1947 boundaries, as would Saudi Arabia, Iraq, and Libya. Egypt and Jordan might be content with the 1967 borders. The PLO is well-aware of these Arab attitudes.

The standpoint of the superpowers also has influenced the PLO in its new policy toward a Palestinian state. Pressure on Israel to accept such a state would come from the USSR and from European countries. It also might come from the United States, which at present time wants to solve the Palestinian problem through a Palestinian state, but under the condition that the PLO recognizes Israel. The PLO has to take into account the US position because only Washington can press Israel to give back the territories. No less important, the PLO has to take into consideration the attitude of the Soviet Union, its great supporter. The Soviet Union favors a political solution that would include creation of a Palestinian state in part of Palestine.

It seems to me that the Soviet Union is inclined to see the process in two stages. In the first, the Palestinian state would be established in the West Bank and the Gaza Strip along the 1967 boundaries. The second state might be the boundaries envisaged in the UN resolution of 1947, which the Soviet Union recognized officially. I have some ground for believing that the Soviet leaders promised Yasser Arafat, on his various visits to the Soviet Union since the October war, that they would support this stand if the PLO were to agree to a political move. A joint communique published in Moscow at the beginning of November, 1975, after the visit of Yasser Arafat, could be interpreted as supporting the idea of a Palestinian state along the

1947 boundaries,* along with the repatria-
tion of refugees as called for by the UN
Resolution of December, 1948.** As you
know, the Soviets are against the elimination of the state of Israel, but they are for
the 1947 boundaries which perhaps
amounts to the same thing.

GAD: But there were two later statements—one by Gromyko and one by
Brezhnev—supporting the 1967 borders,
not the 1947.

ZVI: They were ambiguous about it. The
Soviet-PLO communique didn't mention—as was the case in other declarations—the right of all states to coexist in
the area, or the right of Israel to exist as a
state.

Another influence that the PLO has to
deal with—which contributes to a hardening of its position—is the Rejection Front. I
think that the Rejection Front, which still
sticks to the orthodox line of the PLO, represents a great bulk of Palestinians, especially in the refugee camps in Lebanon.
This makes it difficult for the PLO leadership to adopt more moderate attitudes
without splitting the organization. The
attitude of the Rejection Front stems from
ideology as well as other considerations.
They say that a Palestinian state in the
West Bank and the Gaza Strip would be a
disaster for the Palestinians because it
would be a ministate dependent on Jordan
and Israel and would serve as a reservoir
for manpower for Israeli industry. Such a
state would mean recognition of the state
of Israel and coexistence with it, and this
would lead to a weakening of the nationalist revolutionary drive among the Palestinians. In the Rejection Front's view, this
state in the West Bank would eventually
turn out to be a cemetery for the Palestinian nation. The Rejection Front is supported by Iraq and Libya, and it has much
sympathy among the Palestinian youth in
the occupied territories, and, I believe,
within the rank and file of the Fatah as

well. Sharabi maintains that the main bulk
of Palestinian public opinion sympathizes
with the Rejection Front and that many
politically conscious Palestinians think that
they can materialize their national rights
without giving up their principles—
without recognizing Israel—because they
believe that time is on their side.

Many Palestinians also draw much confidence from the UN resolutions favoring
the implementation of the rights of the
Palestinians and denouncing Zionism as
racist. They think that they can get back
the West Bank and the Gaza Strip through
political pressures from the international
community in return for a very vague and
noncommittal recognition of Israel in order
to satisfy the United States.

---

*"[the two sides] reaffirmed their con-
viction that a just and lasting settlement in the Middle East and on the
Palestine question cannot be achieved
without an Israeli withdrawal from all
occupied Arab territories and without
safeguarding the legitimate national
rights of the Palestinian Arab people,
including their rights to establish
their independent national state in
Palestine, in accordance with United
Nations resolutions."
—Moscow-PLO Joint Communique
November, 1975.
**"The General Assembly ... *Resolves*
that refugees wishing to return to
their homes and live at peace with
their neighbours should be permitted
to do so at the earliest practicable
date, and that compensation should
be paid for the property of those
choosing not to return and for loss of
or damage to property which, under
principles of international law or in
equity, should be made good by the
Governments or authorities responsible."

HANAN: Have there been any developments on the question of forming or not forming a Palestinian government-in-exile?

ZVI: The PLO thinks it would weaken their position in the international community.

NAHUM: Yes. They say a government has to have territory. Otherwise it has no roots. Furthermore, a government-in-exile would have to start operating, not as a fighting organization, but with all the paraphernalia of a government. And that is what they don't want. They have to maintain the climate of a struggling and fighting organization.

AMIR: I have a somewhat different explanation. The PLO at the present time is basically a federation of very diverse groups and organizations. Some are sponsored by Syria, others by Iraq or even Libya. Everybody ready to participate in the struggle is welcome. But if they try to convert that federation of terrorist organizations into a representative cabinet, it would be an entirely different matter. The question of who would be included in that cabinet would become a political stumbling block. Also, the question of representation of other elements of Palestinian society would be a very difficult one. The inevitable result would be a fierce struggle within the PLO, and this they want to avoid. The PLO has tried consistently to avoid internally controversial issues. At their National Council in 1974, where the issue was the possible participation in a Geneva peace conference, they wanted to avoid a showdown. Finally they reached a resolution to the effect that if participation in Geneva were to be proposed to them, they would convene again and adopt a resolution. It recalls some decisions of the Israeli government in the past: deciding not to decide. Forming a cabinet would be for the PLO a very crucial step making adoption of definite resolutions inevitable.

HANAN: You all know the story about Juha, the famous Arab folklore type—who is always outwitting his neighbors. Once Juha's neighbor came to ask for his donkey. Could he use it? Juha told him, "No, my son took it away to the marketplace." At that moment the donkey started to bray from his stable. So the neighbor asked him, "Why did you tell me he's not here?" Juha said, "Do you trust my donkey, or do you believe me?"

I trust the Arabs rather than the experts, in spite of the fact that if I try to sum up Zvi's speech, I think the answer is: "Developments within the Palestinian Arab Community? No."

ZVI: Question mark.

HANAN: Almost no. Nothing that is really discernible. What are the sources for what I am going to say? My sources are many years in Israel and more than eight years of very deep involvement in this matter—long talks, a lot of reading in the last eight months, meeting and becoming friendly with many Arabs.

ZVI: Some of your best friends...

HANAN: We have to define what is the "Palestinian Arab community" to start with. If we understand this terminology as parallel to, for instance, the "Israeli-Jewish community," we are mistaken. The word "community" for us has a completely different meaning—a truly democratic community, cohesive, national. It has a completely different meaning when it is applied to a Palestinian Arab community or, for that matter, to any Arab community in the Middle East. These statements might sound not very humanistic or progressive, but they are facts, bitter facts of life and history.

This Arab community is, to a far greater extent, divided into leaders and led; into those who have the day and are directing things and those who are passive, quiet, and very frequently an enslaved majority. This is largely a feudalist society with its entire structure based on things that in our community belong to the past. When we speak of "developments within the Palestinian Arab community," all we have to concentrate on is the leadership—those who have the say and those who are really influential.

I would title Zvi's remarks: "Changes in the Propaganda of a Group of Assassins." These are the changes in the practice and the propaganda of the PLO, all of whose power and influence stem from the fact that they committed acts of terror. They have no other source for their influence, their impact, or their acceptance in the international arena. One simple, straight, limited source—they killed people. They downed airplanes. They burned and bombed homes, cities, and schools. This is the only—the only—reason that they are being discussed, studied, taken into consideration, and the only reason they were given the position in Rabat of being the sole representatives of the Palestinian community. Even within that community their sole source of influence is fear and admiration of the fact that they are killers, because the killer is the hero in the Arab community. They have never been elected. On this, there has been no change or development within the Palestinian Arab community or within any Arab community, for that matter. War is a good thing in Arab thinking. War is something noble, is something that one mustn't shy away from. In the eyes of a democratic community and, of course, in the eyes of the Jewish-Israeli community, war is the epitome, the symbol, the concentration of evil. Not for the Arab. It is quite noble. It is justified. It is beautiful and positive to speak out for war.

We notice that there are more groups than before within the PLO, more divisions. With their gaining of strength and influence—almost dignity—in the eyes of the international family, why haven't they come together in one cohesive program? The fact is that they are not independent at all. They are less an expression of the Palestinian community and more an expression of diverse interests, funds, and influences in the Arab world and the entire international arena.

Now, what has actually taken place in the Palestinian Arab community? The only development is on a tactical level. They decided to try and take whatever can be taken—only because of their changed appraisal of what is happening to Israel. They think—they read the Israeli press—that Israel is starting to tremble. They believe that it received a terrible shock in the Yom Kippur war, and they feel that Israel is slowly crumbling, is ready to give in.

Before, they wouldn't budge from always stressing the very final goal, but now they are ready to concentrate on the near, first steps—and I agree that they also want to keep Jordan out of the picture. Before things start to move, when you feel that there is no opening at all, and when all that you say is theoretical, then you are inclined—and it is wise—always to put forward and to declare your maximum and most far-reaching aims. This is the period of self-education, or propaganda, or strengthening of your lines. It happened in Zionism too. It happened in socialism. It has happened in all revolutionary historical movements.

There is a pretense or an illusion of some kind of movement or development within the Palestinian, I mean the PLO, community. But this is not because they are now ready to get less. It is because they are convinced now that they are going to get it all.

EITAN: Hanan, I must say that your remarks are to some extent repugnant to me. Such a generalized description of the Arab world—I don't want to call names, but you said your description might not sound very humanistic or progressive. Your remarks are very, very far from "not being humanistic or progressive," if not to say much worse.

PINHAS: What do you think then of what the PLO says if this is what you say about Hanan's remarks?

EITAN: Almost the same. No, maybe PLO statements are worse. I don't know. Hanan sad "Arab community," but there are many Arab communities. The differences among them are profound. For example, a deep division between rulers and ruled certainly does not exist for Palestinian Arab society. This society was totally broken in 1948. There is no one line of continuity between the social and political structure of the Palestinian Arab community before and after 1948.

The leaders of the PLO, and also of the Palestinian Arab people, were from totally different social layers after 1948. They reached positions of leadership owing to their merits, not owing to their social status. The leaders of today are those who in the early fifties gave up personal life, personal career, their medical clinics, their jobs as engineers in Kuwait and in other places, and dedicated their life from then to now, with very strong devotion and resilience to cause they believe is right. By working day and night. By publishing newspapers. By educating their people. And since January, 1965, by fighting Israel. Because all this was regarded by their compatriots as good behavior, as the proper thing to do, they reached the positions of leadership. That's the reason. Not the fact that they succeeded in killing a thousand Jews rather than only a hundred Jews. Even before they started killing Jews their stars were rising. The fact that they successfully killed Jews and fought Israel, of course, strengthened and still strengthens their position of leadership. But they reached leadership because their political and military combat is praised by their compatriots. It has nothing to do with

the so-called national inclination of the Arabs to admire assassins.

It's true that they were not elected in a democratic way. But that would have been very difficult even to imagine, given how the Palestinian Arabs have been dispersed in various states, some of which strongly opposed any Palestinian activity internally. This situation is similar to all the movements that are called national liberation movements. I don't know of one— except the Zionist movement, which was working under the umbrella of the mandatory government and had statutory rights in Palestine—that behaved as a semi-independent state within a state.

HANAN: The Zionists held elections throughout the world.

EITAN: Anyone who follows what is going on inside the camps, inside the Palestinian community, understands clearly that their leaders enjoy and command the support of public opinion there.

BITAN: More than 95 percent of Israelis wouldn't need examples from Lebanon or anywhere else to convince themselves that the democratic state is another name for their own annihilation. Some people just see it as a joke. Some are frightened of it. But the idea is very vehemently rejected, and is extremely repugnant. I really don't understand—I really mean it—how the slogan of a democratic secular state can be considered in any sense a change. The real meaning is its disguised meaning—the elimination of the state of Israel. How can this be considered a change in any sense?

ZVI: It's a change in tactics.

BITAN: No. I don't see how it is a change in tactics. I have to ask a very naive and simpleminded question. If this is going to be a democratic state—and all the Jews living in Palestine now are going to remain here—not just those who came before 1917—how is this going to be democratic with three million Jews? Let us call things by their right name—it must mean the physical extermination of, let's say, about a million Jews living here. So I will have to be exterminated physically, because otherwise I am part of three million Jews who are going to vote in this democratic state. Therefore, I ask myself whether the democratic state wouldn't really be a final solution—the old term of "final solution"—of the Jewish problem. Like Mr. Qaddoumi said to *Newsweek:* "This Zionist ghetto of Israel must be destroyed."*

We are answered by the Israeli Left that the real change is the change of some PLO moderates, so-called moderates who accept two states. The rest is going to be a Messianic dream. It is just like—and this is something I hear always from the Israeli Left—just like the dream of the Extreme Right in Israel up to 1967, which had ambitions toward the other side of the Jordan River, and then relinquished them even though they considered Eretz Israel to be both sides of the Jordan River. This is a very unjust comparison. Because in the 1947 partition, the Jewish opposition came from a very, very small minority, the really ultra-Right, without any influence. Whereas the Palestinian dream about eliminating Israel is the explicit position of all Palestinian organizations.

MEIR: But you're misquoting the argument. The argument does not deal with the other side of the Jordan. What people on the Right say often is that within the borders we acquired after 1967—that there the dream will be realized.

BITAN: But even then, you must agree, that from 1947 to 1967 nothing was done politically or militarily to realize this dream.

And, finally, I don't see a change evident in the idea of accepting a small Palestinian state as a tactical step. Look at all of what is said for instance, by Sabri Jiryis and Said Hammami, who are considered moderates. Even they say in so many words that a small Palestinian state is a tactical step towards the elimination of the state of Israel. All of them say it. We haven't heard one voice giving up this idea. If every one of them says it, then how can I accept the interpretation of the Israeli Left, who tell me that they don't mean it? The Rejectionists don't deny that they and the moderates have the same goal. The difference is a tactical one: We have the same goal, they say, but we are afraid that your way will not achieve it.

MEIR: Certainly, Hanan, my vision of the Palestinians also is somewhat different than yours. I will not react now to what you said—except to say that there is more involved than just a description here of the Palestinians. There is an attitude which goes much deeper, an attitude that goes really to the essence of what we Israelis are, and what we want to be, and how we see the other side in this conflict.

But the main issue I wanted to put to everybody is this. The only dim hope is that something has been changing in the Palestinian position since 1973. We don't know. Most of you think there is no change. My question is, if there is no change, why does the Rejection Front attack so strenuously what they call the moderate element? You can say that this is a matter of international tactics, that it's a game organized beforehand. But it really doesn't look that way.

My feeling is that the Rejection Front is really fundamentally opposed to the line taken even by the, let's call it, the establishment. The Rejection Front is afraid that this line will lead to some kind of compromise. My feeling is that the Rejection Front

*Interview with Farouk Qaddoumi November 17, 1975.

is genuine in its rejection and genuine in its fear of what the so-called moderates are doing. That really is the crux of the matter; it means that something is happening in what we call the moderate camp.

EITAN: My answer to you is that, in the PLO's position since 1973, basically speaking, nothing has changed, although there have been some nuances by some people. I would even say that there are indications that some moderate expressions—especially of Naif Hawatmeh and his organization—have been muted during the four or five years since he first expressed them. When the Popular Front split in February, 1969, I think Naif Hawatmeh made the first real change in the accepted Arab and Palestinian attitude towards Israel and the Israeli people—in the issues concerning two states, which have been mentioned here: his acknowledgment that the Israeli Jews constitute a cultural community, not only a religious one, and his suggestion for a federative solution.

For an Arab to have acknowledged cultural autonomy for the Israeli Jews was really a breakthrough because of the accepted Arab notions of nationalism and national identity. They identify national identity with cultural identity. Arab nationalism is totally defined in terms of culture and language. I think—I am not sure—that when he was speaking about cultural autonomy for the Israeli Jews, he had in mind much more than pure cultural autonomy. As I understand the Arab usage of the term, cultural autonomy is really national autonomy.

On the federative solution what happened was that the Front published in *Le Monde*—afterwards it was propagated in Arabic—that Naif Hawatmeh visualized the possibility of solving the Israeli-Arab conflict, the Palestinian-Israeli conflict, by establishing a state something like the confederation of Yugoslavia or Czechoslovakia—integrated states based on multi-

national federations with various nations living together. I regarded it as an important development. But unfortunately, when his unorthodox views about Israel and Israeli nationality became clear, many of his supporters went back to George Habash. Hawatmeh's influence was diminished. He got taught a lesson and didn't repeat these unorthodox views. So if a change might have taken place, I think this could have been the source, but it was nipped in the bud.

Having said this, though, I still must agree with you, Zvi, that the introduction of the term "national authority" in the June, 1974, resolution is a change. I don't know whether it was a significant change or not. It was a compromise decision between those who totally rejected it—the Rejectionists—and those who supported it. Certainly, one could read in the Arabic press a more positive attitude towards the idea of a Palestinian state, a ministate, in the West Bank and the Gaza Strip. Now what did it mean?

Let us assume that Israel withdraws or is forced to withdraw, and they establish a national authority in the two territories. What is the practical difference between that authority and the government of a territory that is a state? The 1974 decision was a face-saving device, or a unity-saving device, to express a position in ambiguous terms in order to keep unity. It was made very clear that a ministate wouldn't be the end. The national authority would be only the basis to carry on the struggle until all of Palestine is redeemed. But, it is a change because they accepted, unlike before 1973, the possibility of advancing in stages.

And it is this possibility, Meir, that explains the attitude of the Rejection Front. The Front is opposed to the moderates because of the possibility that a "stages" approach might not work in the direction that those who initiated it expected. A stages approach might lead to a point—I'm not sure—in which the next stage wouldn't be liked so much. The Arabs might have to say: "When we began we had the vision of stages. We have succeeded partially and we have no power anymore. We are tired. We have been fatigued by the conflict. The Israelis are tougher than we had expected in the beginning." This is one of the reasons the Rejectionists didn't want even a mention of the Palestinian state and rejected in principle the stages approach.

The second reason is that the Rejectionists are ideologically motivated. This is important to understand. The Rejectionists are Pan-Arab, very strongly. The Popular Front is the daughter of the Arab Nationalist Movement, the most important Pan-Arab nationalist organization throughout the last ten, twenty, or thirty years. Certainly this is the orientation of the second small rejectionist organization, the Arab Liberation Front, supported by the Iraqi government. They don't want a Palestinian state. They want a Palestinian revolution as a spark for an Arab revolution. If the Palestinian revolution succeeds, it will be a combination of an Arab revolution and a unitary Arab state—not a Palestinian state. If this is their position, why should they establish a government-in-exile? A government-in-exile is directed toward a territory—a specific territory and a specific goal.

The position of the Rejection Front also is important because it reflects powerful currents of opinion within the Palestinian movement. The movement, as a relatively independent force, is now based mainly—even solely—on the Palestinians in the Lebanese refugee camps, where the Rejection Front is very, very strong. The refugees there are from Israel itself, from the Galilee; they would not be satisfied with the West Bank. I think these people are looking for a personal solution for themselves—returning to their proper homes, or at least their proper regions, which they left in 1948. A Palestinian state in the West Bank and the Gaza Strip is no

solution for them. Unlike some of my colleagues, I still believe that they are not that inspired by the notion of a Palestinian separate identity. They are either locally-oriented to the village in which they grew up or they identify with the Arabs—not solely, but these elements in their identification are still stronger than the Palestinian components. So a Palestinian state which recovers Palestinian dignity and self-identity in the West Bank for them is not sufficient. That's the reason why the opposition of the Rejection Front must be taken into consideration by the PLO, because they know very well that in the Lebanese camps the Rejectionists are a force and must be reckoned with.

AMIR: My belief is that there is only one way to learn something more tangible about possible changes in the PLO—by confronting the PLO with a positive option and by setting down specific conditions for negotiations with the PLO. This would either expose their real attitudes or perhaps lead to a showdown within their ranks from which, hopefully, a new attitude may emerge. Zvi has established that the PLO's formal attitudes, formal documents, and formal policies have not changed. And he showed that those new phenomena which can be perceived within the PLO can at best be described as something on which a question mark should be put. No really definite conclusions can be drawn from the Souss-Hammami syndrome, no definite policy can be formulated on the basis of these phenomena, and no new attitudes have yet crystallized within the PLO. I would add one other thing: the PLO's constituency is not the Palestinian society as such, but the Fedayeen organizations—and even though the PLO today is the only political body which appears as representative of the Palestinians—and apparently the great majority of Palestinians would assign this role to the PLO—it would be a mistake to identify completely the PLO with the Palestinian community.

_____

GAD: Most of you have approached this question of change by trying to appraise the enemy's intentions. But I think such an appraisal is based upon quite a lot of irrelevant information, which might be interesting itself but not always directly relevant to the process of arriving at policy recommendations. Also, the debate—which luckily enough was almost not mentioned here—about who has the national right or title to this country is a great debate in Israel and is in the back of everybody's mind, but it cannot make an important contribution to arriving at a policy recommendation. The discussion of national characteristics is also fruitless. Even the discussion of the true intentions of the Arabs, or the true goals they set for themselves, or the long-term ideological convictions which they hold—I won't say these are irrelevant, but too much debate about them is not as important to policy-making as appears to the eye.

Discussions of the intentions of the other side could be important if we look at the other side not as a single, monolithic entity, but as a summing up of many positions and many different factions. We've got to understand the forces that are working within the other side influencing its consensus, and the forces that could change that consensus. In addition we should not see the other side as having a static position. We should try to see its dynamics. How is the position that we might take going to influence the position of the other side? We should try to analyze the division of opinion on the other side, and to formulate a policy that will differentiate the positions on the other side, so that a majority there would support policies conducive to our policies and would be able to meet us, if not halfway, at least part of the way. Their position is not something

arrived at in a vacuum, unaffected by our positions. Looking at things this way, we have a premise for discussing the most suitable alternatives for Israeli policy.

Also important is a discussion not only of what the Palestinians want, but how they evaluate their prospects and abilities for achieving it. Recently—I won't say this is true for all the leadership of the PLO—it has become more apparent to bigger sections of the PLO that there is a futility in the armed struggle with Israel.

Sabri Jiryis said, for example, that a war of popular liberation—on a long-term basis, like the one in which the Palestinians are engaged now—harms the Palestinian struggle to a certain extent.

Jiryis, moreover, pointed out that he doesn't think that the question of recognizing Israel now is relevant because he is sure that Israel is not going to recognize the Palestinians. That is his main argument against recognizing Israel. This is, by the way, very reminiscent of arguments heard for many years inside the Labour Party: Why should we argue our position toward the Arab world or toward the Palestinians if a solution is not imminent? The similarity of arguments is striking. I mention this similarity or symmetry between certain Israeli and Palestinian positions, even though I understand that this is a very, very touchy subject. I know that Israelis hate to hear about the existence of such a symmetry. There is no symmetry in the situations; but there is a very striking similarity in stands and arguments, showing the parallel between our attitude and the Palestinians'.

Each side has a very deep conviction of its own justice and right. Each side has a very deep conviction that the other side has no right to exist. Each side is sure the other side is committing atrocities. Each side sees the atrocities of the other side and is very reluctant to see the atrocities commited on its own behalf. Each sees violence on his side as justified because they are acts of national liberation, while the acts of violence on the other side are condemned as contrary to human values.

There is a feeling on both sides—when I say "side," I mean official spokesmen—that the other side is not ready to acknowledge its national rights. Each side recognizes the *existence* of the other side; it doesn't recognize its *right* to exist. We know that the Palestinians will not recognize the Jewish state of Israel. The Palestinians have exactly the same feeling: Israel is not ready to recognize the Palestinian right to have its state in its own country. Our official position, adopted in the Knesset, is that Israel's right to al of the land of Eretz Israel is inalienable and cannot be taken away. The Palestinian Covenant says that Palestine is an Arab country and nobody else has rights on it.

BITAN: For some people, there is no symmetry.

GAD: I know. Also there is the Ben Gurion position in 1937, after the Peel report [the pro-partition findings of a special British commission charged in 1936 with defining a basis for resolving Arab-Jewish hostilities in Palestine].* Ben Gurion said: "I am ready to accept the partition only as a step towards establishment of all of the Jewish state in all Eretz Israel, and there is no step unless there are further steps after this."

The official resolution of the Zionist Congress in 1947 also adopted the United Nations partition program as a step toward fulfillment of Zionism's goal of establishing the homeland of Israel. So our own business of talking about steps is also very similar to the talk of steps inside the PLO now. We did not accept the partition because of rights, but as a pragmatic consideration, as an interim concession. But within the course of twenty years we got used to the idea that this is all there would be to the state of Israel. We gradually abandoned the idea that this would be just a step towards something else. Exactly the same dynamic may work in the Palestinian state

if it is ever established. National liberation movements accept compromises for practical reasons first and only later for ideological ones. They never admit to abandoning ideological goals right away. Even we did it only gradually. The Palestinians, after so many years of adhering to certain ideological goals, are definitely not going to abandon them overnight. The Palestinians are trying to gain time. They don't want to push any decisions. They think the time is not right to push because the Israelis are not ready. There are, I should add, important similarities and differences between Said Hammami and Ibrahim Souss. Hammami always has said the secular state is still the ideology, but it is impractical. Ibrahim Souss says something more. He says: This idea is impractical and because of that we should abandon it as ideology.

The creative way to try to influence the Palestinian attitude towards Israel would be to start a momentum, not just by using the stick but by using the carrot too. If you give the Palestinians the feeling only that you will react by force if they use force on you, and if you don't give them any hope that they can gain something by changing their basic attitudes towards coexistence, then they don't have any incentive to change their policy. There are certain sections in the Palestinian movement which present themselves as a majority, and they say they are ready to go step-by-step towards mutual recognition. The reason they are trying now to avoid a showdown with the Rejection Front is that they cannot bring any proof that their way would lead to any better results for the Palestinians than the road of the Rejection Front.

Of course, the Palestinians are not a single group that will spring suddenly into action if we promise them something nice. To evaluate how far we have to go to get

*A map of the proposed Peel Commission partition is reproduced in Appendix XI.

majority support for coexistence, we have to start a policy that will cause a differentiation between the extremists and the more moderate. We have to analyze the forces inside the Palestinian movement to see what kind of Israeli position presumably is going to bring about this break inside the Palestinian movement. Wise Israeli policy would be to show the Palestinians that a moderate policy pays and that an extremist policy does not pay.

PINHAS: Beyond the generalizations about the Palestinian society that were made by Hanan and which perhaps rightly provoked some emotional reactions, there is still something which has to be said. Some of you experts here should be more tolerant toward some of the things that a non-expert says. Naturally those things irritate you. Because of your knowledge and expertise and involvement in these matters, you are used to more refined and sophisticated distinctions. Yet such generalizations, to a very large extent, reflect a popular feeling of a large majority in Israel towards the Palestinians.

URI: How do you know the majority shares these feelings?

PINHAS: That's my opinion. What are those feelings? One should not overlook some characteristics—and I say "some"—within the different Arab communities, in different forms. I am always reminded of the famous speech by the defense minister of Syria. After the Yom Kippur war he decorated one of the heroes and described in Syria's parliament in very specific details why that soldier deserved the honor. It was because he killed twenty-eight soldiers, with an axe. The minister described how the soldier did this and how he then even ate part of the bodies. The minister said or insinuated that anyone who would do the same would be awarded the same highest

honor. It's an official document of the parliament. Why do I mention it? Because of the emotional impact that such a speech has on us.

We can bring many examples of these things. So, Gad, don't you come and tell me that there is symmetry, that there is no difference between us and them—because we did our things and they did their things. Of course, in the process of war, things happen even when you don't want it or when it's not a basic part of your approach. But I think what is obvious—beyond all else—is the difference in the ability of the two societies to be tolerant toward those things. I am talking in generalizations, intentionally so. This is a basic difference between our society and all Arab communities put together.

The earlier remarks here about different groups among the Palestinian organizations prompt me to say that I think we try too much to rely on those conflicts. Some of those disagreements have nothing to do with their approach towards Israel. None of these differences is strategic, and none shows a difference, ultimately, in their attitude towards Israel. Therefore, I would not like to build up a feeling that some hope perhaps lies within the moderate elements inside the Palestinian organizations.

Another question was raised by Hanon. I don't agree with his statement that the PLO really is not an authentic representative of the Palestinians because it was not elected in a proper democratic way. This whole question is irrelevant. It's sometimes good as a propaganda instrument when we want to show—and it is true— that they are not a democratic society. But the main question is whether it would make it easier for us if the PLO did really have a democratic mandate from the Palestinian society. For me it would be much easier if I could believe that they are not the representatives of their society. Because then I could try to deal with this society separately from the leadership. Unfortunately, I believe that, elected or not, basically they are accepted. They are popular. They reflect the general sentiment of the population in Judea, Samaria, and the Gaza Strip. This is the important factor.

I say this and even more. The "more" concerns the Arabs living within the state of Israel—I mean within the boundaries prior to the 1967 war—the Israeli Arabs. I don't call them Israeli any more. I am sorry—they are Israeli citizens, that is true—but they are Palestinians. And since they are Palestinians, I look at them as the same as the Palestinians who live in Judea and Samaria.

HANAN: You're playing into their hands.

PINHAS: No, I am not playing into their hands. I meet those Arabs in Israel. I talk to them, to students, to teachers, and I know what they think. The difference between them and the Arabs living in the territories is in the manner in which the Arabs of Israel allow themselves to say what they think. They have the tradition of twenty-eight years of living in a democracy, and they feel that they can be much more free in their expression.

URI: Even more radical.

PINHAS: Maybe. But we ought to face the facts, as hard as it is for us on this question. My conclusion is that perhaps no solution which differentiates in the future between the Arabs in the territories of Judea or Samaria or the Gaza Strip and the Palestinians who live in Israel's pre-1967 borders will hold for a long time. The distinction that existed because of special circumstances from 1948 to 1967 between the Arabs in the territories and the Arabs who live in Israel no longer exists.

EITAN: Why were those years different? Why could we then differentiate between our Arabs and King Hussein's Arabs in the West Bank? They are now, all of them, under our control and they have become more united. Faced with the implications for Israel of this greater unity, I say let's divide them again.

PINHAS: I know that my line of argument could very well be used in order to reach the conclusion that you are ready to reach. But it is not my intention. Why is it impossible now, but not impossible before 1967? Because of the developments that have taken place since 1967. Before then the Arabs who lived in Israel didn't speak the same way as they speak now.

GAD: All of this is true, and will also be true in ten years from now if we go on exactly as we are.

PINHAS: Our problem is to see what we can do, given the present feelings among the Palestinians who live in the state of Israel. Anyone who would support a return to the 1947 solution, the Partition Resolution, would find today's situation ideal. If there are such people in Israel, then they probably can justify their views by this analysis of the present feelings of Palestinians who live in Israel. But I think not only that a return to the 1947 borders is impossible, but also that even a return to the 1967 borders will eventually bring about the destruction of the state of Israel.

YAIR: Most participants here do not refute one basic premise: no peace is foreseeable, and no reconciliation is possible, at least according to the Arabs. What we are relying upon, however, is that there are Arabs who say that Israel is now strong, that the United States is still supporting her and is committed to her existence in one way or another, and therefore that there is no possibility of uprooting Israel in the very near future. In this straitjacket, some of us see enough room to maneuver.

That leaves me, and those who are convinced that the Arabs offer no hope for peaceful settlement, in an appearance of despair. We are supposedly advocating doomsday measures, shutting ourselves off from reality, and aggravating the situation—and by all this making our blackest dreams come true. I have tried hard to find anything to support the view that the Arabs regard the obliteration of Israel as a vision for the far off future. It is an uphill operation as far as I am concerned, and quite disappointing.

I must say that this whole phenomenon is characteristically Jewish. We indulge ourselves in hair-splitting exercises to find some redeeming traits, some faint expression of moderation on the part of the Arabs. We grasp some vague, usually misleading voices, as does a drowning man—at the same time trying, pathetically I think, not to hear the loud noise of the tom-tom all over the place. My impression, and I would be glad to be corrected, is that now more than before the Arabs see and think that the end of Israel is close at hand. My impression is that since 1973 they have become hardened, hardened much more than before. I see the Arabs, mainly the Palestinians, gaining the self-confidence they lacked before. They were impatient before because they couldn't see the fulfillment of their aspirations on the horizon.

Until 1973 Israel seemed to be flourishing. Since then Israel seems to be crumbling: diminishing American support, lack of European support, Third World currents against Israel, insurmountable financial difficulties, and deep social and political strife—all of which the Arabs are trying to exploit. On the other hand, there are all the signs of Arab might and its paraphernalia. And the world stands in awe because of it. Furthermore, after Vietnam, after the Kurds, after Angola, the Arabs don't think that American support should be regarded as permanent.

Even including some of the declarations of Hammami and Souss, I think an honest and realistic assessment will show that it is a fallacy—naive and wishful thinking, at best—to find some sign of moderation,

some chink in the armor of enmity. Now, very desperately seeking signals of moderation, we will go the length of finding support in the Rejectionist Front. Not finding one single redeeming hopeful sign in the PLO, we go to the devil and ask him to put his Kosher stamp on the PLO. It reminds me of Neville Chamberlain returning from one of his infamous trips to the Continent, telling the world that one can find common languages with Hitler, that one can satisfy Hitler's modest demands, and that his fire-eating speeches are only for internal consumption.

Should such conclusions lead us to despair, to the promotion of nuclear proliferation, to extreme measures like preemptive strike strategies, for example? I don't think so, and I hope to come to the alternatives later.

But at this point let me say one thing. I think that the Palestinian problem is not our central problem—if only because we Israelis cannot solve it. I thought it misguided in the years just after 1967 that some Israeli groups expected Israel to "raise moderate leadership" in the territories. Let us not delude ourselves again in the present circumstances. We cannot play one group of Palestinians off against another as a colonial power and derive some benefit. Some of you here have implied that we can, but I think we should be practical and limit ourselves to matters where our influence could be felt, where our resolve could have real and tangible results.

It is ridiculous to expect that Israel can solve the Palestinian problem, much less to try to suggest to the Palestinians what they should do. Before Israel was established as a state, we Zionists were assisted by many outside forces and factors, including the British Left, the French Right, the communist world, but we never allowed anybody to formulate our aims for us. We were ready to listen—not more than that. We were flexible on tactical points, never changing our basic aims. Why should we think that the Palestinians are different in this respect?

AMIR: I am struck by how deeply we differ, how different are the interpretations we have of the situation. Between the options of genuine peace based on the acceptance of Israel and that of endless struggle against Arab eternal enmity there is a wide range of possibilities—interim agreements, non-belligerency pacts, various types of political and strategic arrangements—which cannot be described as a "straitjacket." An exploration of these possibilities cannot be described as dealing with "hair-splitting" distinctions. I truly believe that the future survival of Israel may depend on the ability of its leadership to explore these possibilities and choose the best one for this country.

URI: June, 1976, marks the end of the ninth year of Israeli rule in the West Bank and the Gaza Strip. The population there was previously for many years involved in a military, political and emotional conflict with Israel and with Zionism and suddenly found itself subject to Israeli rule. To this population, too, we must look if we want to see whether Palestinian attitudes toward Israel have changed.

After nineteen years of Jordanian rule, the residents of the West Bank and East Jerusalem—the latter about 80,000 people, Arab inhabitants—were much more a part of Jordan than their brothers in the Gaza Strip. An early development was the Jericho Conference in December, 1948, which was initiated mainly by the Jordanian government with the assistance of West Bank personalities, and which called for union between the West Bank and Transjordan. Later, the residents of the West Bank became Jordanian citizens in every respect and received Jordanian passports. The refugees on the West Bank also had the status of Jordanian citizens in the

early fifties. However, the residents of the Gaza Strip, mostly refugees, did not receive Egyptian citizenship and were subjected for nineteen years to an Egyptian military government and military rule. They were not integrated into Egypt and did not undergo a process of Egyptianization.

The conditions of the refugees in the Gaza Strip hardly changed after 1948, while the condition of the refugees on the West Bank improved gradually. Even before 1948 there was emigration from the West Bank and from other places in Palestine to the East Bank. After 1949, this emigration intensified, encouraged by the Jordanian authorities in the name of unification of the two banks.

Over the next nineteen years there began a process of mutual understanding between the Palestinians and the Hashemite authorities. But there were a few islands of opposition on the West Bank to the regime, and some demonstrations and even attempted uprisings in the fifties and sixties.

Under Jordanian rule the economic development of the West Bank was intentionally neglected. Factories and investments were directed to the East Bank where they were granted very generous loans and concessions. The request of the population in East Jerusalem, made in 1950 and even later, that Jerusalem be recognized as the second capital was flatly refused. Most of the West Bank citizens, despite the attempts to integrate into the Hashemite establishment, felt that they were second class citizens. The Bedouin soldiers of the Jordanian Legion were frequently used against Palestinian demonstrators, and this served to increase the feelings of hostility towards the Hashemite regime.

In contrast to the Palestinians of the Gaza Strip, those on the West Bank who wanted to become a part of Jordan's ruling establishment were welcomed with open arms. King Hussein was not vindictive and received even well-known radicals into the establishment, once they moderated their views. There is no telling what would have occurred in the West Bank if the Six Day War had not broken out. But one can find some indications from what has occurred on the East Bank since 1967. The Palestinians in Jordan became more and more involved in Jordanian government and society. This was a continuation of the process that had begun much earlier, and it was not disrupted by the strengthening of the PLO, which received widespread recognition both among the Arab states and the international community. Nor was it disrupted by the armed conflicts between the Jordanian army and terrorist organizations in the early seventies.

The Israeli military victory in June of 1967 came as a great shock to the residents of the territories. For the first few weeks, there was complete calm in the territories and in East Jerusalem, but after about five weeks or more, the signal was given to begin what later came to be known as the attempted civil rebellion: women's demonstrations, pupils' strikes, commercial strikes, and petitions to international organizations. Supporters of both Jordan and of the PLO participated in these efforts, but without any advance coordination. The demonstrations as well as terrorist acts—originating both within and from outside the territories—were put down with an iron fist.

On the other hand, those who were not involved in rebellion were able to take part in the economic prosperity—the greatest that the region had ever known. Economic relationships began to develop almost immediately. There was a withdrawal of barriers between the modern economy in a relatively advanced stage of development, and a traditional economy, at a low stage of development which quickened the pace of economic growth and raised the standard of living in the territories. And the wages earned in Israel by the large influx of residents commuting every day from the territories to jobs in Israel were an important stimulus to growth. Israel, largely at the inspiration of the ex-minister of defense, Moshe Dayan, decided that the principle of free movement between the two banks—open bridges—should be preserved. In cooperation with Jordan, the Allenby and Damiya Bridges over the Jordan River were opened immediately after the war to civilian and commercial traffic. The great economic change did not lead to any serious social changes in the territories. This is a mostly conservative society in which the upper middle class is dominant.

Because the rapid and continuous economic growth of the territories is due to the close economic ties established with the Israeli economy, a political settlement which would not make it possible for the residents of the territories to maintain their economic ties with Israel would impose economic losses to both sides.

The political outlook of Moshe Dayan, which received the support of Prime Ministers Levi Eshkol and Golda Meir, was that the citizens of the West Bank are Jordanian citizens and Jordan is their government. Physically, and only physically, they happen to be in the West Bank. Moshe Dayan also encouraged the mayor of the Gaza Strip to grant Jordanian citizenship to thousands of Gaza residents—efforts that ceased because of the opposition of the PLO.

One feeling common to the vast majority of the residents of the territories and of East Jerusalem is the desire to see a rapid Israeli withdrawal. Beyond that, there are many disparate views. Up to the October, 1973, war, the Palestinians, both in the West Bank and in Gaza, seemed to have resigned themselves to the Israeli conquest, which many viewed as likely to continue for many more years. One can divide the nine years of Israeli rule, somewhat grossly, into three periods. The first was the period of resistance, which ended 1968-1969. The second is the period of reduced tensions that extended from the end of 1969 until October, 1973, marred somewhat by the terrorist activities in the Gaza Strip. The third period from the end of the Yom Kippur war up to the very present has been characterized by a tremendous turning point in local self-pride. The overall feeling was, and is, that as a result of the outcome of the Yom Kippur war, Israel must, sooner or later, withdraw from the territories or at least from most of them.

Who will receive the territories when Israel does withdraw? There are many differences of opinion and constant swings in sympathy for various views. In the Gaza Strip only a small stratum, property owners for the most part, view the Jordanian solution as desirable. By contrast, in the West Bank there are many more supporters of Jordan. During the entire nine-year period there was almost a constant struggle between the supporters of Jordan and the PLO. Even among supporters of the PLO, one finds a number of versions of the desired solution. The Rejection Front in the occupied territories tends to agree mostly on the democratic secular state solution. In the years 1967-69, one could also find those who supported the establishment of an independent Palestinian state on the West Bank without the participation of the PLO. But the supporters of this solution are few.

Another very important factor in the territories is the Communist Party, which in the West Bank has close ties with the Israeli New Communist List, Rakah, but which is also a subordinate branch of the Jordanian Communist Party. The Communist Party in the territories has close links with the PLO, and it consists of a few hundred activists—mostly white-collar, intellectuals, and students. Their underground newspaper, al-Watan, expresses—in comparison with other PLO elements—a rather moderate view, which recognizes Israel in the borders of 1947 and might even agree under some conditions to

recognize Israel in the 1967 borders. During and around Black September, 1970, the supporters of King Hussein did not dare to state their support openly. By contrast, since the Yom Kippur war, the status of the king has been consistently rising, particularly after the significant improvement of relationships between Jordan and Syria.

A small rival factor in the Gaza Strip, the pro-Egyptian people, still think the Gaza Strip should be back in the hands of the Egyptians. But most of the inhabitants of the Gaza Strip are followers of the PLO, either the Rejection Front or some other segment.

What role can the population of the territories and its leadership play in the pursuit of a solution to the problem? Can it really play the crucial role that some groups in Israel would attribute to it?

This is a population that generally unites against some step of the Israeli government or of some Arab government. For instance, the inhabitants of the West Bank, the Gaza Strip, East Jerusalem, and the Palestinians abroad regard East Jerusalem as a part of what they call their country; they do not recognize in any way the Israeli annexation of 1967. Public opinion in the West Bank and in the Gaza Strip also is consolidated against the Israeli settlements. But it is very difficult to unite public opinion behind a single, positive solution to the Israeli-Arab conflict or the Palestinian problem.

Some Israelis claim that in the early years of our rule in the territories we could have promoted new leadership as an alternative to the largely Jordanian-oriented older, conservative generation of local leaders and reached some kind of understanding with that leadership in respect to conflict. They claim that an alternative leadership would have had an interest in promoting negotiations and taking on an independent role in them. I believe this could not have happened. Israel did not come to a vacuum in 1967. There already was a leadership in the West Bank, and if we had tried to change it there would have been many hardships. We might even have inadvertently brought the most radical part of the population to rule—the opposite result from what we wanted.

In general, most of the territories' inhabitants are moderate compared to the Palestinians abroad. Living together with the Israelis over nine years shows even the most radical parts of the local PLO that they can live some way or another with us. Even people who were deported from the territories by the Israelis and were called dangerous PLO elements are considered among the Palestinian community abroad to be more moderate. The three major newspapers in East Jerusalem, which reflect the mainstream of opinion in the population (Al-Kuds, with its tendency to the Hashemite Kingdom; Al-Fajr, radical, very close to the Communist Party; and As-Shaab, with close ties with the PLO), are moderate in comparison to the publications of the PLO or even the Jordanian newspapers in Amman.

But in my opinion the opportunities to take advantage of this fact now are rather limited. Maybe we could have done something in the first months after 1967, but not now. We are dealing with a population that is in a trap. It is tied to the Arab states—Jordan in particular—and to the PLO. It cannot initiate, even if it wanted to, any independent measures or solutions. Only if a completely different set of circumstances were to arise, such as a sudden weakening of the Arab countries, could it be conceivable to bring about a change in the status and position of the residents of the territories.

AMIR: Maybe the population in the territories is, as you put it, in a trap. Nevertheless it would be a mistake for us to make a complete identification between the Palestinian community and the PLO—despite the PLO's apparent representative character today. Certain events during the years of Israel's rule over the territories showed how incomplete this identification was. For instance, the tens of thousands of Palestinians from the territories who have been working in Israel were at times under very strong pressure from the PLO to stay at home. However, the Palestinians in the territories voted on this practical issue with their feet, so to speak, against the PLO.

OREN: They don't want to starve.

AMIR: They don't have to starve. They didn't starve before there was Israeli employment. They want to benefit from the economic advantages that go with employment in Israel. They chose between the pragmatic considerations and the ideological-political pressures applied on them. It doesn't make them pro-Israeli and it doesn't make them anti-PLO—on the level of formal ideology. But when the practical question was presented, they opted against the line propagated by the PLO. The same is true of the local West Bank elections in 1972. The PLO was pressing strongly against them, and yet the elections were conducted, people voted and were elected in spite of the PLO and in defiance of its pressure.

I think it is quite obvious that the basic interest, say, of the elite in the administered territories does not coincide with that of the PLO. Many of them say candidly that they wouldn't like to see "the people with the Kalashnikovs" take over. Many remember bitterly the experience of 1936-39 when "the guerrilla organizations" of that time seized control of the same territories and terrorized the local population. Such statements evidently reflect their various self-interests but they also reflect genuine fears of what might happen if Arafat were allowed to gain control of the territories.

Now, even though I emphasize that there are questions on which the PLO and the West Bankers do not see eye to eye, I agree with those around this table who say that Israel cannot "produce a leadership" for another society. It is virtually inconceivable to imagine the Israelis selecting certain persons who might serve their purpose and making them "leaders of the Palestinians." This is completely self-deluding. I also agree that it is virtually impossible to imagine any separate deal, separate peace agreement, between these West Bank Palestinians and Israel.

But this does not rule out meaningful discussion of the political potentiality of this society. After all, Israel cannot conclude a separate peace with Jordan either, and, for that matter, she cannot conclude a separate peace even with Egypt. The Arab world should be seen as a combination of numerous factors. The question is whether it would serve a useful purpose to have—among the various Arab factors with which we must deal—also a local factor in the form of a representative leadership of the Palestinian society in the administered territories.

It is not too difficult to show that such leadership would represent a relatively more moderate attitude within the Arab camp. It has been shown here that the major trends among Palestinians in the territories are three: there are the pro-Hashemites, who are still quite strong—and Jordan has definitely been a moderate element in the Arab spectrum; there are the supporters of an independent Palestine entity without the PLO—and there is no question about their relative moderation; and there are the pro-PLO people in the West Bank—and today we heard from Uri that even they are more moderate than the PLO itself.

If these are the components which constitute that community, it seems to me that the addition of its leadership would affect, positively, on the whole, the chances of working out a settlement. I am not talking about a final peace solution but about a reduction in the level of the conflict with the remote hope that it may one day lead to

peace. This is a modest ambition, but I think it is the best that Israelis can hope for in the foreseeable future.

The next question obviously would be: To what extent are the Palestinians in the territories interested in producing such a leadership? At the present moment, the answer is that they are completely paralyzed politically. The PLO has been accepted as their only authoritative representative by the Rabat conference and by the United Nations. There's very little the Palestinians in the territories can and wish to do. But moods and political attitudes in the West Bank fluctuate according to changing circumstances. Therefore, it is not enough to examine just the present situation. We should instead examine their behavior over the last eight years, as an indication of their potentialities.

It was mentioned here that perhaps the period after the 1967 war offered an opportunity for the emergence of a moderate representation of the West Bank Arabs. At that time some leaders indicated their desire to talk to the Israeli government on behalf of the Palestinians. In June, 1967, Israeli officials were approached by a number of Palestinian politicians in the West Bank who suggested a meeting of about fifty Palestinian leaders to constitute an assembly, which would then request the government of Israel to recognize them as representatives of the Palestinians. Later there were other attempts by leaders in the West Bank to gain permission from the Israeli authorities to form a body, not in order—I stress this again—to negotiate a peace settlement with the Israeli government but in order to be allowed to play a constructive role in the search for some sort of settlement within the Israeli-Palestinian-Jordanian triangle. But all the efforts to establish wider regional forums in the West Bank (beyond the municipal level) met with Jordanian opposition and were prevented by the Israeli government.

In the following years, two periods in particular were significant. One was after Black September in 1970-71. Fedayeen prestige sank to a very low ebb. Shortly afterwards Nasser died and there was no longer a central authority in the Arab world. It was a period of potential fluidity. And at that time a number of requests were made by Palestinian leaders to be allowed to play a more meaningful political role.

The second period was in March, 1972, when King Husssein made his famous federation proposal, for the first time setting the ground for a meeting of the interests of the three components of the situation—the Palestinian, Jordanian, and Israeli.* His proposal might have been made for tactical reasons, but unfortunately it was rejected by the Israeli government and we shall never know for sure. However, a considerable number of Palestinian leaders in the West Bank did accept it, but of course nothing was done about it.

These opportunities to test the possibility of the emergence of a serious leadership in the West Bank could have prevented the present apparently exclusive position of the PLO. I remember a published interview with Dayan in which he was asked about lost opportunities in the West Bank. His answer was roughly this: If you are ready to withdraw to the former borders, then of course we lost opportunities, but I never considered for a moment giving up an inch of territory.

In referring to the potentiality of a West Bank leadership, I must stress I am not speaking of "quislings," but of genuine leaders who could represent reasonably the interests and the aspirations of their own political community. On this point, there was controversy among Israelis, including those who were more or less in the center of the political spectrum, many of whom tended to stress that the PLO was the only possible Palestinian representative—even at a time when this view was not accepted by Arab society itself.

There was a tendency to do two things which, I fear, resulted in a sort of intellectual paralysis and political immobility: First, to stress ideology at the expense of politics, to speak of the Palestinian National Covenant instead of speaking of realities in the West Bank and the opportunities those realities offered; second, to stress the PLO at the expense of Palestinian society itself. In some of the Israeli newspapers, whenever the term "Palestinians" was used it referred to the PLO, to the Fedayeen, disregarding completely the other elements in Palestinian society. What happened was another example of a self-fulfilling prophecy: Those Israelis who said that there was no Palestinian representation except the Fedayeen actually helped in

*1. The Hashemite Kingdom of Jordan shall become a United Arab Kingdom, and shall be thus named.
2. The United Arab Kingdom shall consist of two regions:
   A. The region of Palestine, and shall consist of the West Bank and any other Palestinian territories to be liberated and where the population opts to join it.
   B. The Region of Jordan, and shall consist of the East Bank.
3. Amman shall be the central capital of the Kingdom and at the same time shall be the capital of the Region of Jordan.
4. Jerusalem shall become the capital of the Region of Palestine.
5. The King shall be the Head of the State....

—King Hussein's Plan to Establish a United Arab Kingdom of Palestine and Jordan, March 15, 1972.

The full text can be found in Appendix VIII.

precipitating a process which removed all other alternatives—at least for the time being. Indeed, what happened after 1973 is that the PLO emerged, by a process of elimination, as the sole representive of the Palestinians.

───────────────

BITAN: I want to ask a few very short questions of Uri.

First: Do the Arabs in East Jerusalem believe that Israel is going to give up Jerusalem? If they believe that, what do you think are their plans about, let's say, Ramat Eshkol, [a post-1967 Israeli suburb near Jerusalem in former Jordanian territory] or the Jewish Quarter* [in the Old City of Jerusalem]? How do they envisage dealing with facts which have been established? Maybe they think Jerusalem is a lost cause—that we've annexed it. But if they don't, what do they think?

Second: What are the reactions of the Gaza Strip populations to projects such as the new housing for refugees?

Third: Do the Arabs in Judea and Samaria and the Gaza Strip believe that the Palestinian state under Fatah is going to be a democratic state? Do they want such a Palestinian state to be under Arafat or Fatah groups or the PLO?

Final question: Is it true that immediately after the Six Day War the municipality of Bethlehem asked to be annexed to unified Jerusalem?

URI: I think that most of the Arabs in East Jerusalem do believe that Israel would give up most of East Jerusalem. Some of them say there will have to be an agreement about the Wailing Wall, the Jewish Quarter, and maybe Ramat Eshkol and French Hill [another Israeli suburb in the formerly Jordanian environ of Jerusalem]. They also believe that there will be some kind of an agreement on Arab rule, Arab government—something like what was

before 1967—an Arab Jerusalem. That is what most of them believe.

PINHAS: This is what they have been thinking since the last war?

URI: This is what they thought all the time.

PINHAS: They thought even before the war that Israel eventually would give up the territories? Even Jerusalem?

URI: Jerusalem is the most important thing for them. Jerusalem is the heart of the matter for them. More important than the West Bank. This is the general reaction of 90 percent of them.

As for Israeli plans to rehabilitate the refugees, there were several attempts to resettle the refugees from the Gaza Strip in the nearby El-Arish area. Most of them did not want to move there—only a few hundred did. They know it's a political exercise by Israel. Most of the Gaza inhabitants believe the PLO is the sole solution. Except for a very thin layer of rich people—owners of a few factories—who are tied to Jordan, most of the people tend to agree with the PLO. In the West Bank, most of the people I know—the youngsters, for instance, in the Nablus area or the Hebron area—tend to join the Rejection Front.

BITAN: But among those who are moderate, those who are for a small Palestinian state in the Gaza Strip and the West Bank, do they want this Palestinian state to be governed by Arafat or the Fatah? Or do they say, no—we don't want the PLO?

URI: They give several answers. Some say the dominant factor would be the local leadership, not the PLO. The PLO will come, they say, and we will reject them. In the Gaza Strip they would say the PLO is the dominant factor. It depends. It varies.

*The location of the Jewish Quarter in the Old City is shown on a map of the holy places in Appendix XI.

The Palestinians 77

To answer your last question, yes, it is true that right after the Six Day War the municipality of Bethlehem asked to be annexed to a unified Jerusalem. They denied it afterwards. But it is true.

I would add a final point: There are, among the PLO people in the West Bank, those who think and will say openly that the 1967 borders might be a solution. By the way, there are many who think that way among the people who support Jordan. They say they can recognize today the 1967 borders, with minor modifications on both sides. There is one big addition: to let all the refugees have the right to return to their homeland. In the same breath, these people add, "We just have to say this." Because they believe that only 5,000-10,000 refugees, maximum, will come back.

PINHAS: Wait till we say it, then we'll see.

URI: That's what they say. But they stress that this is not the most important thing. They stress, these people of the PLO, that they are ready to accept the 1967 lines.

If we combine the moderate groups in the West Bank—not so much in the Gaza Strip—in the West Bank and East Jerusalem, we can find a group that could be one day a bridge of understanding with Arab countries and with Palestinians. There are the moderate pro-Jordanians, the people who want to have a Palestinian country without the PLO governing it. And there are the moderate PLO people who suggest the 1967 lines. The views of these groups will depend very much on how Jordan handles the situation in the future.

DROR: Among the developments which have taken place since 1973, there's the beginning of a change—a worrisome one—in the Israeli Arab community. We can sum it up in one sentence: their nationalism has increased since the Yom Kippur war. It has nothing to do with their high standard of living or with the fact that they are living in an open, democratic society. After nineteen years of relative quiet, when the Israeli Arabs played an apathetic role, or shall we say a dormant role, in Arab nationalism, we can now find a great many more Israeli Arabs who are enlisted in terrorism within Israel—a few hundred.

We also can see this nationalism in the results of the December, 1975, elections in Nazareth, which brought a communist Arab mayor to power. In my view, they reflect the tendency of the future, the tendency of Israeli Arabs to organize themselves in Arab parties instead of Jewish parties as they did previously. They are starting to look for a much more independent stand towards the Israeli establishment. This could be very important for the future balance of power within the Israeli parliament. It is not only for electoral purposes that the Israeli Arabs are showing a tendency to organize themselves on a national level; it is also to develop agreed positions on issues important to the Israeli Arab community.

Another sign is the readiness of young Israeli-Arabs, especially among the students in the Israeli universities, to recognize the PLO as their sole representative. Most of them admire the Fedayeen. I agree with Pinhas. They are much more extreme than we ever saw before, even though here and there we can hear voices of criticism of PLO terror activities. Nevertheless, we can sense that there is no political alternative today to the PLO, even among the Israeli-Palestinian youth. I am afraid we are only at the beginning of this path. The danger is that the extremists in the Arab community in Israel will carry the tune and lead the silent majority of the Arab population and the moderate elements. The unavoidable result will be tougher measures taken by the Israeli government against the entire Arab population. If we are talking about the possibility of a Palestinian state, we have to remember the Arab-Israeli community.

BITAN: Do you think, if there is a Palestinian state, that most or many of the Israeli Arabs would choose to become citizens of that state?

DROR: I don't know if "many" would. But I have no doubt that we shall face an irredentist tendency.

BITAN: No, I am asking if those Israeli Arabs would give up their Israeli citizenship and become citizens of that state?

DROR: It's not a question of Israeli citizenship. We have to face the fact that a Palestinian state in the West Bank raises the possibility that a great many Israeli Arabs will want to join this Palestinian state.

EITAN: Emigration with the land they live on.

HANAN: It is an immediate outcome of a Palestinian state.

OREN: To be Palestinian is a matter of political, pragmatic belief, not geography. And the tendency today in the West Bank, in Gaza, and in Israel is that the Arab population is becoming more and more Palestinian in terms of their political faith. That is what is important to me.

I am not sure that all these everyday connections and all these meetings between Israelis and the Arabs in the territories have made the Arabs there, especially in the West Bank, more moderate. On the contrary, I am sure that Israeli occupation made them much more radical and much more militant against Israel—more even than leadership elsewhere in the Arab world. The Palestinian issue in the Gaza Strip and in Lebanon, but not in the West Bank, was acute for twenty years, from 1948 to 1967. But after 1967 the Palestinians in the West Bank began to feel the

issue acutely, too. Until 1968 or 1969, most of the Palestinian leaders came from Gaza and Lebanon, not from the West Bank, not from East Jerusalem, and not from the Arabs in Israel. During the last five or six years, many people from the West Bank especially, from Jordan and from Israel, joined the organizations. For twenty years the West Bank had had an Arab regime. Maybe they were not satisfied with the regime, but it was an Arab regime, and it was Arab independence. They participated in all the institutions of the regime. But after 1967 this process of Jordanianization in the West Bank stopped; the West Bank became more and more Palestinian.

I think that the same process occurred in the Israeli-Arab population. But here the reason is much, much deeper. First of all, in Israel there is no possibility of absorption for any groups or individuals who are not of Jewish origin—there is in this sense no possibility for an Arab community to exist in Israel. The problem now is that you have nearly half a million Israeli Arabs. All of us remember that not many more than a half a million Israeli Jews were in the country and established the state of Israel by claiming self-determination for themselves.

PINHAS: Are you leading to a self-determination solution?

OREN: No. I am saying only that the Palestinian-oriented political tendencies among the total Arab population under Israeli authority are a severe problem; and it is most severe among those half million Arabs who are Israeli citizens.

AMIR: When you say that the political attitudes of the Palestinians in the West Bank are more radical than those of the leadership of other Arab countries, do you speak of the popular mood or do you include the leadership? Do you include such persons as Ja'abari, and Can'an, [the former mayors of Hebron and Nablus who were voted out of office in the March, 1976, West Bank municipal elections] and all the rest of the pro-Hashemites? Do you regard them as more radical than Assad, Arafat, Qadhafi, and Habash?

OREN: I think they are a slight minority.

AMIR: Leaders are always a minority.

OREN: But the tendency—I think 90 percent, even more—the tendency is toward the PLO, and to be Palestinian. And to be Palestinian means to be PLO. Yes, that's right. Social and economic development is transforming their political attitudes in a more radical direction, not a more conservative one. Of all the changes mentioned here, nowhere was there a change towards some kind of compromise or coexistence with Israel. A person like Ja'abari is an old-fashioned leader with conservative support. After a very short period he will disappear.

URI: Oren may have the impression that the West Bank is going radical. I do not tend to believe it. It might be so for a few days, a few weeks, a few months. But the flexibility within the territory is enormous. The leadership of the West Bank reflects the face of the population. The population wants and deserves a leadership that cannot organize itself, and cannot decide, and cannot come to one conclusion.

AMIR: I am afraid that both of you are projecting the present conditions backward over the past nine years, as well as forward into the future.

NAHUM: To come back to the question of change in the Arab position, it is clear that the Arabs are not monolithic, and we have seen, too, here in this gathering that we are not monolithic. Whenever we deal with social movements, we have to see what is the dominant view that is expressed. It would be a mistake to demand complete consistency from an individual or from a movement. Say, for example, that I've expressed myself one way on a question 98 times, and then I express myself differently twice. If someone were to take those two times because they suit him, and say, "That's his view," I believe that would be a big mistake. Therefore, if we see dissidence among the Palestinians we should take note of it but must keep it in its correct proportion. I would give much more importance, not to Hammami and to Souss, but to Qaddoumi. What Qaddoumi says carries much greater weight, and what he said to *Newsweek* was most extreme, bordering on genocide. He said the Jews in Israel have to accept the democratic state. If not, "they will surely die." And when he said "die," he didn't mean a natural death.

I rebel against the symmetries that were described today. I consider them condemnable morally. If you compare someone who killed a cat with a car to someone else who ran concentration camps—you can say both killed. But if you draw this comparison, you will arrive at a nihilistic moral view. I don't consider Israeli society impeccable. We have done things that we should not have done and that we should not be proud of. You cannot simply say that we are not impeccable and they are not impeccable, so therefore we are the same. Your comparisons of symmetries are wrong because you don't differentiate between the quality and quantity of the same acts. Even though Israeli society and the Zionists are not impeccable, on the whole our ideal of maintaining a high standard of morality is one of the things that we have to be proud of.

I also want to draw your attention to something that recurs, perhaps in what all of us have said, although not to the same extent. Eitan and I see eye-to-eye, I believe, on what is happening in the Arab world. He said there is no change in the Palestinian position—and then went on and described some changes. The same happened with Zvi. It happens with me too. And I ask myself, what does it mean?

I believe that there is deep ambivalence in us if we deny that there has been change. On the one hand, we describe the Arab position as it is, and it is very rabid, unpleasant. And still there is a tendency inside us to leave the door open for change and to describe the Arab position in much more moderate terms.

It happens to all of us—Amir, you said there is wide leeway for maneuvering. I believe that there is some leeway for maneuvering. But I think you are exaggerating. You yourself describe the position of the Arab mainstream. We deal in political phenomena, in international affairs, not in folklore. There is only some leeway for mañeuver.

AMIR: These are relative terms. I say "wide" compared to the sense of being at a dead end and to the feeling of helplessness which is so typical to some parts of Israeli society: there is nothing to do, "ein breira," no alternative. The scope is much wider than that.

NAHUM: You can find dissident views in Arab society. But it will be the gravest mistake to take dissident views and to describe them as if they are in the center of the society, as if they will influence political behavior.

EITAN: Presumably you don't believe that it would be a mistake to shape policies that might enlarge or strengthen the dissident views?

NAHUM: I understand that argument. Here, however, there is a limiting factor. Can you? I've seen the tendency in Israeli society: People are intoxicated with their own grandeur and tend to think that we can have this influence, that we can influence the growth of a moderate leadership.

NAHUM: We should remind ourselves that our assessment of the Arab position, and especially the PLO position, must also take in account the evolution of American attitudes toward the PLO. There is a problem in saying what *the* American attitude is. American society is so heterogeneous, and it is easy to overgeneralize about "the" American position. But we can see some distinct periods in the US approach to the Palestine problem. During the first period, covering the 1950s and 1960s, the United States was motivated primarily by humanitarian considerations: what to do with the refugees. The nationalism of the Palestinians was not salient in this period, neither on the Arab nor on the international level. Thus, there was no need to deal with the Palestinian problem except as a refugee question, and the United States gave hundreds of millions of dollars to the UN agency responsible for Arab refugees.

When the PLO came into being in 1964 the same attitude continued. The PLO started with very pronounced enmity towards the United States as a supporter of Israel. Its leadership did not spare abuse against the United States, and all its resolutions condemned the United States and supported the Soviet Union. PLO support for North Vietnam during the Vietnam War was clear. The PLO in those days brandished openly their "politicidal" objective: Israel has to go. They didn't hide it then behind any euphemistic slogans. The United States supported Jordan in September, 1970, when the PLO was crushed ruthlessly by Hussein. During this first period, then, these various factors produced estrangement between the United States and the Palestinians.

The situation changed. First, detente and the end of the Vietnam War moderated the old tendency to consider friends of our enemies as our enemies. "Guerrilla" in the

American public lost its negative image to the extent of taking on even a shade of positive appraisal. That Palestinians were ready to sacrifice their lives attested to the fact that they had a grievance. The cumulative effect of Palestinian terrorism, magnified by mass media, donned them with some heroic aura.

The second factor was Palestinian success in the United Nations. The United States voted very consistently from 1970 onwards against a long series of resolutions supporting the Palestinians and their right of self-determination. Despite this official US opposition, the American public could not fail to be impressed by the wide support in the world that the Palestinian problem and the PLO acquired over the years. The United States was, on this question, in an unpleasant state of isolation. The urge for conformity, it seems, does not operate only on the level of individuals, but operates too on the level of collectivities and nations.

Another factor was the October war of 1973. Though the role of the Palestinians was marginal in this war, they benefited from the rise of Arab importance—including oil—in international politics. Arabs and Palestinians were successful in public relations, especially the Palestinians. They had success in persuading people that they have a genuine grievance. People were impressed by that, and the grievance had not been known before that. Furthermore, the Palestinians were very successful tactically in posing as moderate, always stressing the positive side of their case—very often hiding the negative implications that it has for Israel. The PLO benefited too because the American media blamed Israel. Journalists were, and I think still are, sympathetic to Israel. But they blamed Israel for intransigence. This immediately caused, somehow, a tilt of the scales in favor of the PLO, although there is a great amount of American goodwill toward Israel.

Another factor is that there has been a very grave failure by the Israeli government in presenting its attitude on the Palestinian problem. It seems, for instance, that Golda Meir's miserable uttering that there were no Palestinians became part of modern culture, part of what an average man knows. Her intention was distorted—it will be a great injustice in history if Golda is to be remembered only for this saying.

None of these changes has altered the basic fact that, as far as general American public opinion is concerned, there is a great sympathy for Israel despite—and one has to say this—despite some erosion in recent years. We had a very good image in the United States; our image now has been tarnished in some respects. I don't think—and I will mention this only briefly here since we will return to it later in our discussion—it doesn't seem to me that there is a serious strategic American interest in Israel.

HANAN: You *don't* think so?

NAHUM: I don't. But there is a very important moral, ideological commitment which—and I want to stress this—is not weaker than a strategic interest.

In this changed situation, there is now the beginning of a debate in the United States on the problem of contact with the Palestinians. It didn't exist earlier, even though unofficial contacts were always maintained by the American embassy in Beirut.

Let me try to summarize the arguments from the American point of view. Those advocating the need for some recognition, or negotiations with the Palestinians, or at least talks of an exploratory nature, argue that the Palestinians are the core of the conflict. In Saunders' words, the Palestinian dimension is the "heart of the conflict." If the center of gravity of the PLO—which tends to be identified as the PLO establishment—can be persuaded to move toward a more accommodating position, toward a settlement, it will facilitate negotiations with the other Arabs. This argument says that the PLO holds the key. The Arab States cannot move without that. The PLO has some kind of *de facto* veto on the negotiations.

A second argument is that American-Palestinian contacts, irrespective of the results, will have a moderating effect on the PLO, and the PLO will not veer away from violence and terrorism unless it sees some advantage in a political approach. Ostracism—treating them as pariahs—will have only adverse results. There are, this argument says, moderates among the PLO whom such talks would strengthen. Americans are impressed by what some of the PLO people tell them in private, when they show much more forthcoming attitudes. Furthermore, Americans who spoke to the Palestinians are told that the PLO is the *de facto* representative of the Palestinians— this is the result of meetings between American officials, or American journalists, or American representatives with Palestinians.

Still another argument is that negotiations with the PLO do not necessarily mean recognition. Official recognition can be withheld as a means of pressure and persuasion. And there is no need to wait for PLO recognition of Israel. The situation is not symmetrical, with Israel's non-recognition of the PLO. The PLO cannot move first. PLO moderates express the view, according to this argument, that they would like to recognize Israel, but are afraid to endanger themselves. Only by the United States engaging in such talks with both sides can a formula be found for mutual acceptance, mutual recognition, mutual accommodation. The PLO cannot be expected to recognize Israel because by doing so the PLO would lose its main bargaining tool. Delay in such negotiations will encourage the extremists, who will prevail. The rift in the PLO may close, and

therefore there is need to start such negotiations, the earlier the better.

The final argument is that involving the PLO in the diplomatic process, in general negotiations, will force the PLO to formulate demands in a reasonable way, which of course is identified as moderate. Here there is a tendency to adopt a kind of agnostic attitude—we don't know what the PLO says, we have to bring them into a process to make them face the need to formulate their demands in a much more concrete form.

The countervailing American arguments are that open negotiations would be a blow to Israel, would weaken the moderates in Israel, may strengthen the extremists, and may make Israel desperate and desperately intransigent. Negotiations would constitute a precedent, suggesting that terrorism is the way to achieve results. There will be a harsh reaction of the US Jewish community. The United States is reluctant to displease Jordan in this matter. There is a false symmetry in the Israeli and the PLO reluctance to negotiate. The PLO wants to eliminate Israel, and Israel is therefore justified in its reluctance. So long as the PLO maintains such a position, there is no possibility of talks. Furthermore, the PLO has to give up terrorism.

Between these two sets of American arguments, which I intentionally polarized, there is give and take. Present policy is the result of compromise between them. I would define that policy as a sympathetic affirmative stance: to maintain secret, unofficial contacts with the PLO, contacts to get information and some exploratory talks—but without any real political commitment. This satisfies the Arab states that the Palestinian case is being taken into consideration. This serves to keep hopes alive within the PLO establishment that there will be some kind of recognition, which is a political weapon. This posture can be maintained without embarrassing any of the sides, without offending Israel as well. The

PLO is not left completely in the Soviet lap. And it all converges as part of the theory of the need to maintain momentum.

This posture gives express recognition to the importance of the Palestinian problem—a recognition that did not exist earlier. But there are reservations about whether the PLO is representative, even though it is acknowledged to be important. Official US statements say: We don't know about its representativeness. This is in Saunders's paper; the posture is not to offend Jordan, not the Palestinians, not the bourgeois circles among Palestinians.

There is recognition of "Palestinian interests"—and the word "interests" is used deliberately, not "rights." The semantic differentiation is that "rights" goes much further. The Palestinians define their rights as following by definition from their being Palestinians. Palestine—by definition—belongs to them as Palestinians, as the French are the owners of France and the English the lords of England. The United States also maintains an agnostic attitude towards these rights— that is, the Palestinians have to describe, or to spell out, what their rights are.

There is, therefore, an attempt to leave the door open by contending that the PLO has not yet made itself clear on its objective. It is a way of saying that if we describe the Palestinian demands as not clear, if we don't close the door, if we leave some kind of leeway for maneuvering, then it will have a moderating effect. It seems to me that this contention is half-believed and half-contrived. There is a continued and insistent demand that the PLO must recognize Israel as a condition for recognition or for contacts by the US government with the PLO; and there is also an attempt to explore the possibility that the PLO, instead of recognizing Israel as such, will declare acceptance of Resolution 242, and by that, in a vicarious way, will recognize Israel or escape from the recognition quandary.

PINHAS: I believe that the United States never desired the rise in the PLO's position. In a way, the policies of the United States reflected the objective developments in the rising position of the PLO in the Middle East and in the awareness of the big powers. I'm afraid that the Saunders paper is to a very large extent a very good and representative summary of the existing views. I myself heard, immediately after the Rabat Resolution, similar views in the State Department. The question is, of course, what are the Americans going to do as far as the PLO is concerned? I think that as long as Jordan will remain a reasonable option, the Americans will do almost everything possible to go in that direction, to support the king, and to force Israel into negotiations with him. They will try to avoid any PLO solution because of the difficulties it will create for almost all the parties concerned. Under almost all circumstances, the United States will prefer Hussein as a partner to any future agreement, rather than the PLO, with all its more radical views. I have no doubt, however, that if Jordan turns out not to be a realistic option, then the United States will adopt more seriously the PLO's position. Then they will have to impose on the PLO some more moderate expressions, perhaps acceptance of Resolutions 242 or 338 as a starting point for some further negotiations between Israel and the PLO—as Nahum just said. Then it will be possible for the United States to force the Israeli government to negotiate with the PLO. There is no illusion among the American policymakers today about the PLO—they accept the argument that the PLO is the sole representative of the Palestinians. I don't think Americans think there will be any future troubles within the Palestinian community which would somehow bring a different leadership onto the scene. But they are waiting. Maybe new developments among Jordan, Syria and the PLO will change the balance of power. While Americans will not do anything which would somehow lower the relative importance of Jordan, if its decline is brought about in a natural way within the Middle East, then the United States will adopt the PLO option, with all the accommodation necessary.

BITAN: Neitzsche once said about his doctrine: "I wish and pray with all my heart that I'm wrong." I'm still waiting for people to convince me that I'm wrong about this question of change in the Palestinian position. To say that we should not treat the Arab position as one unified position is a very good intellectual maxim, but as Nahum said, human beings always have different views. There is a certain unified position among the Arabs. Everybody here agrees about that. In this position, there is no change and there are no differences among the Palestinians. And to try to prove that there are Palestinians who want to stop, or are against, the armed struggle reminds me of the famous definition of metaphysics: somebody looking in a dark room for a black cat which isn't there.

I want also to say that there is no symmetry between the Palestinians and the Israelis. I wish, Gad, that there would have been symmetry. Because on the Israeli side there have been quite a lot of changes in position—in my opinion even too many changes, changes toward moderation. Here there is no symmetry on the other side.

You mentioned four points of symmetry. You said both sides are sure that they are right. On this there is no argument at all. It is neither here nor there. It doesn't say anything about the cases when both sides are sure that they are right but when in fact one is right and one is wrong. Then there is an argument.

You say that both sides don't recognize the rights of the other side. This is just not

true. Maybe I am one of those who doesn't recognize the national rights of the Palestinians to Eretz Israel, but it is not true to say that there is symmetry. Because on the Arab side, you cannot find things like the Israel-Palestinian Peace Committee, or a political party like Moked [a left-wing Socialist-Zionist Party with one Knesset member], you cannot find any doves at all.

Your third point was that both sides accepted a decision of partition because of tactical reasons. Therefore, because the Arabs are repeating here or there our words, they are only doing the same as the Zionists did. This is not true. I do not accept the argument that the Zionists accepted partition as a tactical step with the thought that when the time came they would take over the whole of Palestine.

This wasn't the Zionists' official policy. It is the official policy of the Palestinians now. That makes all the difference.

Your fourth point was that both sides don't recognize the atrocities of their own doing. I won't do a bookkeeping of atrocities, but I would like to bring a less absurd example than killing a cat. Intellectually, there was a difference between the bombing of Hamburg—or even of Dresden—and Auschwitz. I'm not talking morally, even. There is also a difference between bombing the Palestinian camps and Maalot.

There have been at least some people in Israel who have said that bombing the camps was wrong, even though it was the bombing of the enemy.

PINHAS: Even when we won't say it is wrong, we are not dancing in the streets and shouting "hallelujah."

MEIR: Yair's earlier remarks prompt me to say that history is not a science. To construct analogies is the most dangerous use of history, and I would say that the famous Munich analogies are one of the most dangerous uses of the recent European past. It really is irrelevant for our problem. It may look relevant, but it is totally different. Let's use less history and maybe more imagination.

The comments here about the Israeli Arabs may be completely right. But I remember a year or more ago Israeli television interviewing Israeli Arabs about what they would do if there were a Palestinian state. My impression was that the answers were quite different from what was said today. Some who were interested said that if there was a Palestinian state they would emigrate to the Palestinian state—not saying that they would take their land along—but they would leave. Some of them—and this was quite astonishing—said that the existence of such a state would help them to integrate into Israel, because then somehow they wouldn't feel the guilt they feel today.

MEIR: Now to the main point. Is there any sign of change among the Palestinians, or isn't there? I'm quite aware of the arguments against, but I want to point out again the logic of those who argue that maybe there is some kind of change. There are two arguments. First, there are Palestinians who are dissident voices—obviously they're dissident. Three or four years ago, there were no dissidents, no Hammami, no Souss.

I know that dissident voices are not an entirely new phenomenon in the long history of the Palestinian Arabs, and that they have existed since the twenties. But even so, there is something new in the last few years, in the post-1967 period. Now is this beginning of a trend or is it nothing? Maybe it's nothing. I come back to my argument about the Rejection Front. Herut abandoned the idea of two sides of the Jordan in the early fifties—that's exactly what the Rejection Front argues against the main PLO line. They say that if they start going in that step-by-step direc-tion, they will end up abandoning their final aims.

PINHAS: I must point out again that this is an attempt to build a symmetry which does not exist.

MEIR: There is no symmetry. I only put a question.

But never mind. Look. What is the rationale of my positon? Yair said it's a Jewish tendency to look for some fictitious good thing in a reality which is black as hell. The problem is the following: There is a conflict. Most of us here agree—I'm not sure all—that the Palestinian problem is the core of the conflict. If it is not solved, the conflict will go on. Many of us think that if this conflict goes on, it will be ruinous, maybe totally destructive, either for Israeli society—which maybe is the least of the evils—or even for the state of Israel in the long run.

If that is the situation—and not many will contradict me—the whole question is: Have you a 5 percent chance to see some way out of this kind of doomed situation? If there is a 5 percent possibility—I would say if there is a 3 percent possibility—maybe we should really use our whole imagination to see if there are cracks in the wall. If then you find that really there are none—well then you have to draw conclusions. You know there is nothing to be done. But as long as you are not convinced—really convinced—that there is not even a small possibility that there are really no dissidents who could be important, or that there are no trends which we should promote—as long as you are not convinced that there is really nothing to be done, you cannot dismiss the attitude that is behind my question. I'm more pessimistic than most of you here. But it's precisely because of that—not out of a kind of rosy stupidity—that I look at the dissidents and at their voices. In a framework of pessimism, one should really try to rely even on the least sign.

BITAN: But you have to prove that there are dissident views. And you didn't prove your supposition that the alternative is doom.

MEIR: We shall all speak later about alternatives. But for now, I shall only say that you should give credit to those of us here who are making another argument than yours, and you should be willing to accept the possibility that there is some goodwill and logic underlying this argument. You should not just dismiss it as a result of shallowness or stupidity or our inability to see reality. Because there is a view of reality that pushes us to our position.

HANAN: I have to respond to Eitan's references to Palestinian leadership that came to its position by merit. I beseech the historians among us to try hard to find another historical example when a leadership of a national insurrection had such a luxurious way of conducting their revolution. Never in history. Rich. Safe. They can have their headquarters anywhere. Open. This leadership is tied—everybody in it—is tied by strings to Arab states. There is absolutely no independence.

ZVI: But not everybody.

HANAN: Almost everybody. They would not function one day if they were not fed by Arab money. There are heaps and heaps of money. And there is no United Arab Appeal. It comes straight from the big bags. From oil.

I think all this talk about "chosen by merit" is one long, sentimental hogwash. There is so much corruption, and so much waste of money and waste of blood, and so much cynicism about the blood of their own people, and so much wasting of human life among them. So much, that I do not think that if the Arab Palestinians could express their feelings as human beings they would have tolerated this kind of leadership. Because of that, I think the only thing that gave this leadership their

very important step into the center of events today is because they have the revolver. They were the killers. We are now living now in a world where the killer is the one you are afraid of, the one you are giving in to. He is the leader.

As for the chances of making peace with the Arabs that were wasted after the 1967 war, here again some of us have made the mistake of talking about the Palestinian Arab problem as if it was cut off from the surrounding Middle East states. In June, July, and August of 1967 we were still contemplating our position vis-à-vis the Arab states. Now, however, when you speak of withdrawing and of giving back the Western Bank, it immediately has an association with solving the Palestinian problem. Thanks to their successful propaganda there now is a combination: Western Bank-Palestinian problem-PLO. That's the association. But in 1967 the idea was different. Withdrawal then would have meant giving the West Bank back to Jordan, the state that only yesterday you took it away from. The problem was whether you made peace with Jordan and with the other Arab states. We must be honest about our government, in spite of the fact that it is not terribly honest to us. Our government—from the very first moment in June, 1967—agreed and maintained and declared that the territories would be returned for peace.

Finally, I want to present a key problem to you. There are two completely contradictory characteristics of the Palestinian Arabs. One is that they collaborate with us. They live with us. They work, they sell, they buy. They are nice. I'm telling you frankly and honestly as a boy I lived among Arabs and I liked and loved them. Sometimes I wish the attitude of a municipal clerk or someone in Israel would be as beautiful, as nice and civilized as it is in the eastern side of Jerusalem. And a very big 99.9 percent of the Arabs of Palestine are collaborating with us.

While I know this is true, I also know that with even the slightest twist, the slightest change, they will become the murderers of the Jewish community. It will take no time. Very easily. None of them wants us, none of them is really ready for this kind of collaboration. We Israelis cannot even comprehend such a situation. If we were in their position, I'm sure that the Israeli resistance to Arab rule would be ten times greater, maybe a hundred times.

URI: There wouldn't have been a chance.

EITAN: You are too optimistic. You assume that there would have been Israelis under Arab rule.

HANAN: You know what I believe. The Jews of Israel will never be exterminated. Because even if they kill every single Jew in Israel, in a matter of a few years, we will start to immigrate to Israel again. And the entire story will start over again. There is no end to Jews in Israel.

ZVI: Hanan mentions the dichotomy between the friendliness of the Arabs to him and their real intentions. And he doesn't understand it. I also don't understand it. I try, and my conclusion is that the situation is not so simple, not black and white. It's very complicated.

In addition to possible nuances at the human level, there are some, perhaps, at the political level, which I tried to analyze. One was the idea of the democratic, secular state. This is a tactical maneuver.

But this is not true about another nuance which I mentioned: the positions of Hammami and Sabri Jiryis. Here there is something different, not just a tactical position. For Hammami and certainly for Jiryis it's a genuine conviction. Imagine what they think. They think there is no military solution to the conflict because of the Israeli deterrent, perhaps an atomic deterrent as well. The better way to settle things is to eliminate Israel through a peaceful way. Perhaps, I would say, like a kiss of death.

Imagine. We must put ourselves in their shoes. They look at Israel—three million Jews, more than half of the Oriental Jews. They are tired of twenty-eight years of wars; they've had it. You open the borders. The Oriental Jews will be influenced by the Arab culture. There will be economic ties with the Arab countries. The Jews in Israel will realize that they must integrate into the region in order to continue living. In this process, Israel will change. The European Jews would say, "We didn't come all this way to live in another Levantine country. We want to go back."

The closest example would be Lebanon's history—which has been cited by Arab intellectuals. Lebanon until 1920 was a kind of national home for the Maronites, developing a unique Maronite Christian nationalism based on the Phoenician heritage and religious ideas. Then the French came in 1920 and annexed some neighboring Muslim territories, and created Greater Lebanon. In Greater Lebanon, the Christians were outnumbered and lost their urge to continue to be different. They had to change the character of the state. The constitutional changes in 1943 were an important milestone in this process of making the state more Arab and more integrated with the Arab world.

Some would maintain that this position I described as Hammami's is even worse than the PLO official position. I don't know. I tend to think it's the same. But we should not just brush it aside and push it under the rug and say "it's tactics." Some are tactics, some are not tactics. I'm sure that Jiryis and even Hammami sincerely believe that this is the way to solve the problem. They call it a peaceful way.

And, as far as the stituation now developing in the Middle East is concerned, I think we should anticipate various other possibilities that might change the situation. One would be the rivalry between Syria and the PLO, with Syria taking over Lebanon and controlling the PLO. Or there could be an open rift within the PLO, with the Rejection Front strengthened by more PLO members rejecting Syrian domination. Or there could be a new Palestinian re-grouping based on the pro-Syrian PLO—Saika and others, including Palestinians from the West Bank and Jordan. The idea of a Syria-Jordan-Palestine federation is not new. Whether it's good for Israel to have around it a federated state under the fist of Syria is another question. Syria is able to curb the guerrillas. But it may be that the danger to Israel from Syria would afterwards be greater. Or perhaps it might be better for Israel that the PLO in Lebanon be pushed by the Syrians and crushed.

In the present situation, the main body of the PLO is still very extreme on the question of Israel, and rejects a political solution, even as a tactical step. The war of 1973 hasn't mitigated their position. On the contrary. Now they say the war has undermined the *status quo* which Israel tried to establish in the Middle East after 1967. Why cannot another war undermine even the earlier *status quo*—that of 1948? They believe time is on their side; Israel is weakening, and the Arabs are getting stronger; They believe that it's the beginning of the end of Israel, and they will be able to get the territories back, even without war. War is a later step.

We can even see occasional indications in the Arab world that the views of the main body of the PLO are not completely satisfactory—in terms of Arab interests vis-à-vis Israel. The Egyptian newspaper *Al Akbar*, for example, on the 4th of December, 1975, offered some advice to the PLO by saying that its position is not clear, and Israel can utilize this ambiguity and take advantage of it. I quote: "We didn't hear any official, clear voice on the part of the PLO saying that the PLO agrees to join the Geneva Conference, and that it accepts the principle of looking for a complete solution in the Middle East. Now we ask our-

selves, what will happen if you reject the last chance you have? What would be the outcome? Who would back you—the PLO—to destroy Israel eventually? If this is your official position, your official attitude, you make things easy for Israel. And this is a real tragedy. The struggle today is not about what will happen. But it is a race against time. What would be reached first? Either it would be a Palestinian state on part of the land, or a nuclear guarantee to Israel, which will make her keep the territories forever."

This Egyptian position can be called tactical—let's take what we can, and then we shall help the PLO to gain the rest. But basically the PLO so far hasn't changed, partly because of the Rejection Front fears that I mentioned before.

I want to turn briefly to what Gad said. True, the Palestinian front is not monolithic. But the common ground—the common denominator among them—is the idea that Israel is not legitimate. Here there has been no change whatsoever among the Arabs. I'm talking about the political leadership, not about the people in the street. They want peace. They don't want to kill and to be killed, to destroy and to be destroyed. Everybody wants to live in peace. But they don't have any influence.

You spoke about the symmetry between Israel and the Arabs. I can't accept it. There are no Moked and Mapam among the Arabs. There is nothing comparable to the fourteen points of the Israeli Labour Party among the Palestinians. The asymmetry is large. Within the Jewish community—both during the moderate sector has always been the dominant one. Maybe now it's changing. I'm not sure about it. But with the Palestinian Arabs, it has been the other way around—the extremists have had the upper hand.

EITAN: What do you mean when you say the Jewish leadership was moderate?

ZVI: I am referring to those Jewish leaders

who believed in the principle of partition, for example.

EITAN: I am quite doubtful whether the leadership was so moderate, at least in the Ahdut Ha'avoda component of Mapai [Ahdut Ha'avoda was the party of Ben Gurion, which had merged in 1930 with Hapoel Hatzair, the other leading Socialist-Zionist party, to form Mapai]. The internal discussions of partition show that not one of them accepted partition in principle in the late 1930s.

ZVI: But eventually they accepted it.

A Palestinian state would regard itself as the culmination of fifty or sixty years of struggle against Zionism in Palestine.

5

The Eastern Frontier

Editors' Introduction

The participants now move from the PLO to the triangular relationship among Israel, the Palestinians, and Jordan. In doing so, they are merely shifting their angle of vision, not the basic subject-matter. Most of them say that they regard the PLO today as the primary if not the sole representative of the Palestinians. They know that more than three-quarters of all Palestinians reside in the West Bank, the Gaza Strip, East Jerusalem, and the Hashemite kingdom of Jordan combined. They know that in the territories administered under Israeli military government since the Six Day War live more Palestinians under a single political authority than anywhere else in the world—the total, in 1976, according to Israeli military government sources, was 1,141,000 West Bank and Gaza Strip Palestinians. They know that these territories are the main political battleground between Israel and the Palestinians.

In sum, even if the participants regard the PLO program negatively and skeptically, they see no choice but to confront somehow the practical alternatives facing Israel concerning the future of these territories. Among what they regard as the available alternatives, some shape their preference because of their judgments about the PLO, some in spite of those judgments, and others because of considerations having mainly to do with Israel and Jordan. In the previous segment of the discussion, there was no unanimity among the group about the PLO, but there wasn't wide disparity in their views either. In this segment a much greater range of opinion emerges, both in basic appraisals and in conclusions.

The starting point for the dialogue, not surprisingly, is the so-called "Jordan Option"—the formula that since 1967 has dominated official Israeli thinking about peace on its eastern frontier. Details and interpretations of the formula have varied, but the underlying principle has remained constant: Israel would negotiate territorial concessions on the West Bank directly with Jordan in the context of a mutually acceptable peace agreement. King Hussein would regain land lost in 1967, and Palestinian self-expression, the Israel government now stresses, would be satisfied within the Jordanian political framework. Any such negotiations presumably would take place within the framework of what Israelis call their Oral Doctrine—unwritten understandings that add up to an official consensus about the broad contours of peace terms: Jerusalem would remain united and the capital of Israel, the Jordan River would be Israel's effective security border, and no third state would be tolerated between Israel and Jordan. Although the future of the Gaza Strip under the Jordan Option has not been spelled out publicly, the Oral Doctrine precludes its reversion to Arab control even with a peace agreement.

Behind the attachment to the Jordan Option lies a conviction that important mutual interests continue to be shared by Israel and Jordan, stretching back to Zionist-Arab ties at the beginning of this century. But current developments and their unpredictable future implications—developments within Israel as well as outside—have brought this option under increasing challenge. Both the conviction and the challenge figure prominently in the participants' evaluation.

So do certain historical milestones. One is 1922—when Hussein's grandfather, Abdullah, was approved by the British as ruler of Transjordan, which included the area east of the Jordan River that had been part of the original British Mandate for Palestine. That year, also, Transjordan was excluded from the application of the Balfour Declaration promising a national home for the Jewish people, and separately administered within the League of Nations mandatory regime. The West Bank came under Abdullah's control when his Arab Legion occupied the area in the 1948-49 Middle East war. His annexation of the territory in 1950, however, was never officially recognized by an Arab world unwilling to bless Hashemite acquisition of land allotted to the Arabs of Palestine in the UN Partition Resolution of 1947. Jordan's conservative and pro-Western orientation in the following years gained for it the support of Great Britain and then the United States, the enmity of revolutionary Arab countries, and a tacit working understanding with Israel that served their respective purposes. It was the closest Israel has ever come to *de facto* recognition from an Arab leader.

How far Israel would go to protect King Hussein in order to preserve this relationship was hinted at occasionally before 1967, when Israel let it be known that it took an extraordinary interest in seeing that Hashemite rule was maintained in Jordan. The king reciprocated by not allowing foreign troops on his soil before 1967 and by restraining Palestinian Fedayeen attacks on Israel from Jordanian territory. Israel took the relationship less for granted after the Six Day War, which Hussein joined at the last moment. The earlier Israeli hints became alarm bells in 1970. That year, Hussein's showdown with the Fedayeen during the Jordan civil war peaked in the "Black September" success by the king's army, and, to stem the Syrian invasion of Jordan on the Palestinians' behalf, Israel readied intervention plans to save Hussein. That the planned intervention never happened didn't matter. The episode confirmed—more visibly than ever before—that Israel still regarded Hussein's survival as vital. For most Israelis, Hussein's decision to stay essentially out of the October, 1973, war underlined the persistence of Israeli-Hashemite mutuality, however incomplete and fragile it has been. Moreover, Hussein's willingness to meet discreetly with Israeli leaders after 1967 to discuss peace terms, even though it produced no results, sustained some hope in Israel that an accommodation could be worked out.

In the West Bank and Gaza Strip during these years, the Israeli cabinet's "decision not to decide" their political future meant that there would be neither annexation nor withdrawal. Within this broad latitude, Israeli official policy was shaped by leading figures in the political and defense establishment. Former Defense Minister Moshe Dayan was highly influential. His ministry was responsible for the territories and his ideas had the most impact there on the course of daily life. There was a return to normalcy after the security situation was stabilized, first in the West Bank and somewhat later in the Gaza Strip. Local residents retained their Jordanian citizenship, and most Jordanian laws were allowed to remain in force. The bridges across the River Jordan were reopened—a step that was to become the centerpiece of Israeli occupation policy. Selective economic transactions could be thereby maintained between the East and West Banks, including the marketing of surplus agricultural production eastward and the maintenance of financial connections westward between King Hussein and his supporters, former civil servants, and local municipalities whose development continued along lines approved by both Israel and Jordan. Arabs under Israeli rule could visit, and be visited by, their families outside the territories; and they could travel, work, or study outside. This entailed substantial population traffic over the bridges at levels risky enough in security terms to be opposed by some Israeli military officials. And the "Green Line" 1967 borders were made more porous, enabling movement of goods and people in both directions, including eventually the daily commuting of tens of thousands of West Bank and Gaza Strip residents to jobs mainly in Israel's construction and agricultural sectors.

If Dayan most decisively shaped the contours of daily life in the territories, then Deputy Prime Minister Yigal Allon's concepts produced the geographic and demographic contours of the Israeli physical presence, especially in the West Bank. The formerly Jordanian sector of Jerusalem was annexed in the summer of 1967, and the city's municipal boundaries were extended by Israeli decision during the next several years.* Beyond these areas, the Allon Plan became informally the blueprint that substituted for the official cabinet decision never taken concerning the territories. First circulated in 1967, Allon's idea gave concrete expression to the Oral Doctrine that the Jordan River must be Israel's eastern security border. He proposed Israeli retention of a band of territory along the entire length of the Jordan Valley, plus certain strategic areas in the West Bank, and the establishment of paramilitary *nahal* settlements, or regular civilian settlements, within these areas, altogether totaling about a third of the territory. The bulk of the West Bank's populated areas Allon would reserve as potentially negotiable with Jordan.**

The realities on the West Bank today show the stamp of both Dayan and Allon. The integration of this territory, as well as the Gaza Strip, has proceeded quite far, especially in certain economic spheres. Ties between the local population and Jordan have not been broken, and the open bridges are accepted as a fact of life. Israel's military presence is normally kept in low profile throughout the territories, although most of the Israeli Defense Force training bases have been moved to the West Bank since 1967. During the period of Israeli rule, active underground resistance was minimal. To control the security situation, the military authorities used selective punishments that included destruction of houses, detention

*See Appendix XI for a map of Jerusalem boundary extension.
**See Appendix XI for a map of the Allon Plan.

measures, arrests, and deportation; but Israel has avoided application of the death penalty as a sanction.

The Israeli government, in deciding where to place officially authorized settlements in the West Bank, has generally followed the geography of the Allon Plan.* There are currently twenty-two settlements in the West Bank, thirteen of them flanking the Jordan River or located on the adjacent slopes. Although the Allon Plan is generally thought to be associated with the West Bank, Allon's own formulation to the government, which is excerpted in Appendix III, also refers to the Gaza Strip and North Sinai, where eleven settlements have been established.

But today's realities also show the stamp of two developments that architects of Israeli policy could not have foreseen clearly just after the Six Day War. First, the Oral Doctrine has been challenged increasingly severely from within Israel by religious and secular groups insisting that the Jordan River be not only Israel's security border but its sovereign border as well. For some holding this view, security arguments motivate the belief that Israel takes unacceptable risks by returning any part of the West Bank to Arab rule. For others, historical and religious arguments are decisive in the case for a Greater Israel extending to the Jordan River—the West Bank is biblical Judea and Samaria, the centers of ancient Jewish life. To underscore what is seen as an inalienable and overriding Jewish right to this land, and to preclude its return to Arab hands in any future peace negotiations, some Israelis have rallied to the efforts of Gush Emunim, an activist, highly nationalist, primarily youthful and religious movement committed to massive Israeli settlement of the territories. If necessary, Gush Emunim has shown itself determined to establish settlements illegally, without prior government authorization.

Second, Palestinian nationalist sentiment has asserted itself in the West Bank much more vigorously than might have been expected in 1967. The underlying opposition to continuation of the occupation has been strong since the beginning; demonstrations and protest strikes were initiated within months after Israeli rule was established in the West Bank and the Gaza Strip. And in the years that followed, the local elites and leaders debated what political path would most likely lead to termination of the occupation—a debate that took its cues less from developments within the territories themselves than from external developments affecting the fortunes of Jordan, the Arab world at-large, the Palestinian organizations, or Israel. Whether the preferred path was to press for an independent entity of some sort, to return to Jordan, to seek UN trusteeship, or whatever, the fact remained that the local population was little able to influence by itself the course of events.

That the local leadership has at times embraced or rejected one or another political outcome may well turn out in the long run to be less significant for the territories than the March, 1976, West Bank elections. Their outcome fundamentally changed the character of the local leadership by confirming trends already evident in earlier local elections in 1972. Most of the old guard of conservative, generally pro-Hashemite, and traditionalist leaders were replaced by younger, more nationalistic, and more vocal politicians whose generalized pro-PLO allegiance was clearly expressed during and after the election. The new

*See Appendix XI for a map of Israeli settlements in the West Bank.

leadership was brought to power on the crest of anti-Israel demonstrations in the West Bank that were unprecedented in their intensity and duration. They occurred, furthermore, at a time when the neighboring Arab community in Israel was also experiencing unprecedented political ferment. A communist Arab mayor was elected in Nazareth in December, 1975. Three months later an Israeli Arab protest against government land expropriation plans in the Galilee triggered riots and confrontations between Arabs and government security forces that were the worst in the history of the state.

These fluid local developments contrasted with the absence at the time of any active diplomacy bearing directly on the status of the Israeli-held territories. Jordan had begun in 1975 to edge toward Syria in the Arab realignments after the Cairo-Damascus split over the Sinai II Pact. From Israel's point of view, a closer Jordanian-Syrian relationship dampened enthusiasm for active exploration of the Jordan Option. And Jordan's own freedom of action to consider negotiations with Israel, even on the most favorable of terms, was still formally constrained by the 1974 Rabat Arab Summit decision to thrust the PLO into the primary responsibility for the West Bank and the Gaza Strip. Months before that summit decision, Israel and Jordan, despite some American intermediary services, failed to get even within negotiating range of each other about the West Bank. If West Bank negotiations had been promising, moreover, they would have raised for the Israeli government the prospect of national elections on the issue before any agreement could be implemented—a promise that the National Religious Party extracted from the Labour Party as a condition for joining the ruling Alignment Coalition. Most Israeli leaders, and many outside Israel, continue to believe that Jordan has not given up its hope to regain the West Bank if conditions permit. To do so, the king is assumed to be willing to offer West Bankers a degree of political autonomy. The arrangement might follow roughly the lines of his well-known March, 1972, Federation Proposal for the West and East Banks, which at the time evoked little enthusiasm.* It was rejected abruptly by the government of former Prime Minister Golda Meir. It was received coolly by those West Bankers who could not forgive the king for his harsh treatment of the Palestinian Fedayeen in the recent civil war. And it was severely criticized throughout the Arab world as an overture toward a separate peace with Israel at the expense of the Palestinians.

Although the participants' discussion preceded the West Bank municipal election and the outbreak of violence in Galilee, the deeper political trends among both the Israeli Arabs and those of the West Bank and the Gaza Strip are recurring threads in the dialogue. In one way or another, all participants make it clear that the West Bank and Gaza Strip future touches some of the most crucial issues in the Israeli-Palestinian relationship: the basic conflict over territorial rights, the implications of demographic trends implicit in the higher birthrates among the Palestinian population under Israel's control, the influence of Jewish religious and historical attachments to the contested land, and the strength both of Israeli security apprehensions and of Palestinian national identification.

That the participants weigh those considerations differently was one reason their views tended to cluster around four future alternatives, put forward by them as either inevitable or preferable. In no particular order they are: (1) the Jor-

*The full text appears in Appendix VIII.

dan option, (2) a PLO state on the East Bank, with Israeli retention of the West Bank and the Gaza Strip, (3) a third state composed of the West Bank, with or without the Gaza Strip, and (4) a PLO state on both the East and West Banks. In the discussion of these alternatives, several themes emerged as particularly important.

Jordan: How Moderate? How Enduring? For some of the participants, choices among future alternatives rest on conclusions about Hussein's rule and Israel's proper posture towards it. The conference heard restatements of Israeli conventional wisdom about Hussein's moderation, with participants arguing at length that strong self-interest still motivates King Hussein to preserve the main lines of Hashemite moderation. And the conference heard a wholesale reevaluation of this interpretation, prompted not only by Jordan's closer relations with Syria, but also by a retrospective rethinking of whether Israel has really benefited from her tacit entente with Jordan. The group does not agree about the degree of Jordanian moderation historically, or about its causes. Nor does the group agree about whether Jordan, in the long-run, would be able to maintain moderate policy directions even if it wanted to. For example, participants who imply their willingness to endorse a West Bank Palestinian state separate from Jordan, *as well as* participants who believe Israel must retain the West Bank, both base their conclusion on the premise that if the West Bank were to be returned to Jordan, Hussein could not hold on to it. Either the West Bankers would exert pressures to break the link, or Arab states would press Hussein to give it up to the Palestinians.

These perceptions of Jordan influenced the participants' judgments about past Israeli policies as well as future ones. According to one line of argument, for example, Israel was mistaken when it helped King Hussein during the Jordanian civil war. According to another, excessive reliance on Jordan's presumed moderation caused Israel to miss opportunities to give encouragement to more independent West Bank leaders. Challenges were raised to these arguments. And they were raised even more vigorously—in this portion of the dialogue and in the final statements—to the suggestion that Israel's future posture toward Jordan, as one participant put it, should be "to bless the fall of King Hussein."

A Third State—Why, and Why Not? Observers outside Israel frequently see an independent Palestinian state on the West Bank and possibly the Gaza Strip as an essential ingredient in any negotiated settlement. The participants displayed a range of reactions to this possibility—a range not necessarily the same as the one that characterizes outside debates. Arguments about whether a neighboring independent Palestinian state would threaten Israel's security by increasing the country's vulnerability to either guerrilla or conventional military actions, or whether such a state might in fact be less of a security problem for Israel than a larger state composed of both East and West Banks, are part of the Israeli calculus. These arguments are raised in the group. But other factors also intervene. Most striking, perhaps, is the question of how a Palestinian state would affect the Israeli Arabs, whose nationalism and identification with Palestinian aspirations, participants feel, have intensified since 1967 and particularly since 1973. Would a Palestinian state reduce their political anxieties and thereby make their integration into Israel easier? Or would it stimulate irredentist tendencies and magnify the predicament of the Arab minority in Israel? Is self-determination for the residents of the West Bank and the Gaza Strip tantamount to eventual self-determination for the Israeli Arabs? And is it, therefore, an invitation to reopen the question of Israel within its 1947 borders, since areas inhabited today by Arab citizens were outside the boundaries set for the Jewish state in the UN Partition Plan?

The Implications of Palestinian Identity. Resistance to a third state among the participants is not necessarily a product of negative judgments about the validity of a Palestinian identity or the PLO's status as its representative. Indeed, some of those who oppose a third state—and most in the group do—are prepared to see the PLO in power, either in the East Bank alone, or on both the East and West Banks. And some of those who prefer a Jordanian option do so not because they undervalue the force of Palestinian nationalism, but because they fear that its very strength and persistance endangers Israel precisely because of its authenticity, and that its aspirations cannot be reconciled or compromised with Zionism.

Here lies one of the group's most fundamental debates: Most participants do not challenge the contemporary reality of a Palestinian identity, most are treating it as a phenomenon with an essential political dimension, and most are inclined to satisfy it with some kind of territorial solution. But the nuances and opposing views in the group turn on differences: About the maturity of this identity. About its territorial focus. About Israel's ability to channel it in one or another direction. About its impact on the Israeli Arabs. About the degree of compatibility between the Hashemite and the Palestinian identities. And about the extent to which the Palestinian identity can be satisfied by one or the other of the four political alternatives discussed by the group. Not all participants who accept the reality of a Palestinian identity and even its intimate connections with the Israeli Arab community believe that it must be satisfied by either an independent state or a Jordanian solution.

The Triangle and a Zionist Israel. The Israel-Palestinian-Jordan triangle encloses familiar issues of Israeli foreign policy—whom to negotiate with, where to draw boundaries, how to ensure security. But much more than that is at stake. Revealingly, it is in the upcoming discussion of this triangle that participants first sketch the practical consequences of projections about future *aliyah*—Jewish immigration to Israel. For some participants this is one of the central factors in Israel's choice about whether to continue to rule over the Palestinians who came under Israel's control in the Six Day War. If the Jewish population of Israel within those extended boundaries will not grow sufficiently to preserve a Jewish majority, then the internal political and social consequences of Israeli rule over a larger Arab minority must be faced. The participants voice varied expectations about prospects for *aliyah,* and they reach differing conclusions about the moral and practical dilemmas of preserving an Israel that is both Jewish and democratic as the present demographic ratio changes. But in addressing these questions, which have bedeviled the internal debate in Israel about the future of the territories since 1967, they highlight one of the most critical ways the entire Palestinian question affects the core concerns of Israelis.

EITAN: I want to appraise Israel's interest in the triangular relationship among Israel, the Palestinians, and Jordan, and I want to do so not just on the basis of current and local developments. Rather, I want to set out for you five broader premises that, for me, define the situation facing Israel as far as this triangle is concerned. The first concerns how I define Israel's national interests. The second, my assumptions about the compatibility of Arab and Zionist ideologies. The third concerns my expectations about *aliyah* and future Jewish-Arab demographic balance in this area. The fourth concerns my conclusions, from the demographic situation, about the workability of annexation. And the fifth concerns the character of the Palestinian Arab identity.

First, Israel has, or should have, one interest—to insure its survival. I don't see a place for ideological factors, and I don't take them into consideration when I discuss this triangle—neither the Israeli ideological motivations nor the Palestinian Arab ones. What concerns me is to find the way that will enable Israel to go on, to survive, and to let her Palestinian Arab neighbors live in the way least objectionable to them.

I am fully aware that about 98 percent of Israeli Jews are Zionists. Israel will be for a long time a Jewish state. This means not only the state in which Jews are the majority, but a state that will be Jewish in its symbols, in its public appearance, and in its basic constitutional arrangements. The Law of Return is here to stay; the Law of Nationality will continue to be applied; and these two laws will continue to exemplify the preferential position of Jews in Israel according to the basic Zionist principles.

My next premise is that for a long time to come perhaps 100 percent of the Arabs and the Palestinian Arabs wherever they live will share the beliefs of Arab nationalism and accept the basic assumption that the Arabs are one people. They believe they share one language and culture. They believe they have a common history and territory. And they believe they will some day constitute one state in which there will be one nation. I think it is impossible to overcome the gap between these two ideological approaches—the Zionist and the Arab—within a single state.

I am also assuming, in a third premise, that there is no chance that the number of Jews in Israel will grow so much that the number of Palestinian Arabs will become negligible. There is no real chance to convince Western Jewry to emigrate to Israel in any meaningful numbers—the Western world of South and North America and the great Jewish communities of France and Britain. And the other reservoir of Jews, those in the Soviet Union, is less Zionist than Israelis are led to believe. The main sources of immigration were the newcomers to the Soviet Union—the Baltic Jews, and the traditional Jewish communities of Georgia and Central Asia. These sources are gradually drying out. Most of the Baltic Jews have already emigrated to Israel. The only remaining reservoir is the central Asian Jews. As far as I can judge, the Russian Jews—the Jews of Moscow, Leningrad, Kiev, and the Ukraine—are just not that enthusiastic to emigrate to Israel.

What is more important to the growth of community is natural increase, not foreign immigration. Immigration is capable of increasing numbers only for the generation when the immigration takes place. The rate of natural increase among the Russian Jews is even lower than the average of Israeli Jews, or even than what is now common among the Israeli Jews of European and American origin. This is extremely important because it will finalize the number of Jews in Israel.

The demographic history of Israel shows a decrease in the rate of natural growth since the beginning, because the Oriental Jews have drastically decreased their rate of growth whereas the Western Jews only slightly increased theirs. For the last seven years, the birth rate has been stable—1.7 percent. The parallel rate among Israeli Arabs, also stable for the last seven years, is 3.9 percent. It is, of course, less than the record reached from 1963 to 1965, which was an unparalleled record in the world—4.5 percent. The Israeli Arab rate exceeds that of their Palestinian Arab brethren beyond the Green Line, although among them there is now an increase owing to the better standard of living. It has grown from

2.6 to about 3 percent during our occupation.

Because this is the picture, my fourth premise is that I don't think Israel can annex or incorporate the occupied territories. Israeli Jews would not then be in a position to carry on their dream of having a Jewish state, which means the Zionist vision of bringing as many Jews as possible to Israel. I don't think that an Arab minority of 30 or 40 percent would agree to the Law of Return and the Law of Nationality, two basic laws that discriminate against them. Therefore, it is out of the question for Israel to incorporate these territories in a democratic way—meaning, conferring nationality and political rights on these Arabs.

My fifth premise is that the national identity of the Palestinian Arabs has not been fixed once and for all. The Palestinian Arabs are still going through a process of crystallizing and consolidating their sense of national identity. Historically they have fluctuated according to the situation. Once they were Pan-Arabs, or Pan-Syrians, desiring to be united with a greater Arab state. In other times, they preferred to rely on themselves and to behave as a distinct, self-oriented political community, struggling against Zionism according to their capabilities and led by their own leaders.

What was decisive for them was their assessment of their chances to fight Zionism. When confident that they might do it on their own, they preferred the local orientation. When they lost their self-confidence and were confronted with a big influx of Jewish immigrants in Palestine, or when they were sure that the world at-large supported Zionism, they tried to mobilize the support of the Arab world, and they preferred that their fight be carried out by the combined forces of the Arabs.

So far as I can judge, the Palestinian Arabs have not yet decided whether they are Palestinians or whether they want to be incorporated in a greater Arab state, immediately or in the future. There certainly is no doubt here about their ideological stand: the Palestinian Arabs are Pan-Arab. All their documents are deeply imbued with Pan-Arab expressions, symbols, visions, and terminology. Of course it's not new. The Palestinian Arabs during the mandatory period used to call themselves "Palestine Arabs," not "the Palestinians." The most important nomenclatural evidence—which no one would reject—concerns the definition of their nationalism. When the Palestinian Arabs describe their nationalism, they always say "Arab." You can never find "Palestinian." The very term "Palestinian nationalism" is totally a foreign, non-Arab invention. In this case, as well as in many others, political development and political history could national identity—more than the other way around. That's why I will argue in a moment that either a Jordanian or a Palestinian state is valid and that a Jordanian solution would not be detrimental to Palestinian national identity, as some people try to say.

We also have to remind ourselves that Palestinian Arab political or social developments in this century were not in one direction only. Before the mandatory period, when Palestine was part of the Ottoman Empire, all Palestinians were Muslim Arabs, loyal subjects of the sultan, and in close connection with the southern part of Syria, or Transjordan. When Abdullah was ruling Transjordan under the British Mandate, for all practical purposes the area of western Palestine and Transjordan was one as far as the Arabs were concerned. They could move freely from one part to another. It was one economic unit. Immigration was in both directions. Many educated Muslims who found difficulties finding jobs in Palestine found them in Transjordan. All of Abdullah's prime ministers up to 1948—except one—were of Palestinian origin. During the entire period, it was not so much a process of integration, as one of keeping the connection between the two communities.

On the other hand, political history and the political struggle developed in another direction. The Palestinians of the West Bank fought Zionism and crystallized their identity, leadership, and organizations, without any reference to Transjordan. They tried to mobilize the Transjordanians behind their cause but failed because Abdullah didn't let them. Pure and simple: he didn't let them. He did his best to make sure that his subjects would not be involved in the anti-Zionist struggle, and certainly not in the anti-British struggle afterwards. So, unlike the natural processes of immigration or movement from one bank to another in the economic and administrative fields, in the political arena development was one-sided: Palestinian-centered without ties to Transjordan.

After 1948, even in the political sphere, the situation changed. There was the annexation of the West Bank and the granting of nationality to Palestinians in 1950. And the amendment to the Jordanian nationality law in 1960 was a pure repetition of the Jewish Law of Return. According to this amendment, a Palestinian, if he retained his refugee status and didn't take another Arab nationality, was entitled to come to Jordan, to settle there, and to get Jordanian nationality. Or if he was living elsewhere he could apply. It's symbolically significant that Jordan wanted to present itself as a state to which the Palestinians could apply.

NAHUM: The problem is that many Palestinians didn't apply.

EITAN: Yes. But it has been basically a political problem for them, ever since 1948. The Palestinians only grudgingly—in the beginning very grudgingly—found a place in the Hashemite Kingdom. At the beginning the antagonism was strong, but in the sixties, it was less strong than in the fifties. The numbers of those who were involved in opposing the regime decreased

in Transjordan. Even in the army there was a process of integration. In 1967 about 30 to 35 percent of the army was Palestinian, and during the Jordan civil war of 1970 most of the Palestinians remained loyal to the regime.

This brings me to my conclusion: Palestinian identity is an open question. Therefore I think we can influence and shape it. We can, because, if we reach agreement with the Hashemite regime in Amman about the restoration of the West Bank to Jordan, the political future and the national identity of Palestinians will be deeply influenced. It seems to me that from our point of view, it would be much better if the government of the West Bank and Gaza Strip derived its legitimacy from a peace agreement rather than from the 1947 Partition Resolution, because any separate state would rest its legitimacy on that resolution and would try to return to at least those boundaries.

A Palestinian state would regard itself as the culmination of fifty or sixty years of struggle against Zionism in Palestine. The struggle would be the source of inspiration, would provide the national heroes and symbols to strengthen society and to establish a common ground for national movements and for the body politic. Those in this state would desire to carry on the struggle and to redeem the whole of Palestine, because their forefathers dreamed and died for that cause.

I have no doubt that a Palestinian state would deeply influence the Israeli Arabs. Up to 1967 they were docile because beyond the border there was a Jordanian state and Palestinians who lived there and got some benefit from living there were willing to become a part of it. What remained for the Israeli Arabs was only the memory of Abdullah's betrayal. A Palestinian state would therefore engender a process of irredentism among the Israeli Arabs and would make trouble—I have no doubt. I'm personally not so opposed to the possibility of a change even in the pre-1967 boundaries. For example, I would give some areas of Israeli-Arab concentration in the "Little Triangle"* back even if there were no irredentism there that pressured us to do so. If there is an agreement which includes demilitarization of the West Bank and real safeguards assuring that the West Bank wouldn't serve for bases against Israel, I think it would be beneficial to Israel that the boundary wouldn't be east of Tira and Taybeh, but west of these two villages that together have a fairly large Israeli Arab population in the Little Triangle. Israel cannot absorb a large Arab minority, and to decrease the number of Arabs is a first priority for Israel as a Zionist state.

PINHAS: You are talking about the whole Little Triangle?

EITAN: Yes, that's right. I didn't mention the Galilee. Because there exists a much more important interest. The Galilee supplies all of Israel's water. Since we need the water from the Lake of Tiberias, we must live with the Arab minority in Galilee. Otherwise, I would say that the Galilee, for me, is in the same position as the Little Triangle.

PINHAS: If we could find alternative sources for water from Galilee, what then?

EITAN: Then the significance of Galilee, for me, reverts to what I said about the Little Triangle.

DROR: Do you know that one source of Lake Tiberias is in the Golan Heights?

EITAN: Yes, and when the Golan Heights is returned to Syria, I think it is highly important that the source of the Jordan River that is in the Golan Heights would remain under Israeli control.

If we were to find under the Dome of the Rock the greatest well of oil in the world, then I would support the incorporation of the Old City into Israel, as well.

PINHAS: A very important condition.

HANAN: What he wants to say is to hell with all ideologies. To hell with thinking and poetry and sentiment. To hell with all this and with history. We have facts. He wants things that can be measured.

EITAN: My last point is that a Jordanian state would be much better for us and not bad for them. The Jordanian state doesn't look for its legitimacy in the Partition Resolution of 1947. The regime has tried to convince its population for the last two generations that this state is the culmination of the great "Arab Revolt" of World War I [during which some of the Arabs under Ottoman rule cooperated with the Allies against the Turks.] This Hashemite regime for generations has maintained quite friendly relations with Jewish, and afterwards Israeli, authorities, and the Hashemite regime tried to prevent the Palestinians from harassing Israel. We didn't always understand this. For example, the infamous retaliatory action in the West Bank village, Samu, in November, 1966, was an extremely stupid thing for us to have done.

I think the Jordan solution would work. It should be the way to a compromise arrangement. But I must make one thing clear: this solution must include the Arab part of Jerusalem. Without Jerusalem there is no chance whatsoever that an Arab leader would agree. There must be a compromise in Jerusalem. We have to find a solution by which Jerusalem is shared by these two states. Otherwise everything that I said up to now is not valid, for there is no way to circumvent the problem of Jerusalem. The Israeli public should make up their minds. If there is a possibility for an arrangement with Jordan, and the only stumbling block is Jerusalem, then the population should decide whether they prefer to prolong the present state of affairs or to have an arrangement with Jordan.

There is a trend in the Jordanian regime, in the Hashemite establishment, to give up the West Bank, to say let it go, we are now

*See frontispiece.

prosperous without it. Crown Prince Hassan—the king's brother and the heir apparent—holds this view and he is supported by some other people. But the king still counts more. And he wants the West Bank back. As far as I can understand Hassan's exact views, he wants the West Bank—but on his terms. He says, let the Palestinians establish a West Bank state, such a state could not exist, and after three or four years of failure at government and killing each other and economic isolation, the Palestinians would crawl on their knees from Jerusalem to Amman. Then we shall get the West Bank back on our conditions.

But the prevalent view in Jordan is still Hussein's. He wants the West Bank back if he can get all of it with an overall solution for Jerusalem. I think, of course, the Jordan solution should be part of advances on other fronts as well. If Egypt gets back territory by one process or another, then chances are higher that it would not reject the Jordan solution. Egypt is, after all, mainly interested in the Sinai. But I don't belittle its interest in the general Arab world. And I admit that it is not certain that Hussein would dare to undertake this agreement against very strong opposition of the whole Arab world.

I think the Palestinians would swallow the Jordan solution—certainly if it is put in the form of the March, 1972, Federation Proposal. I was sure then, as I am sure now, that most of the population in the West Bank, including the pro-Palestinian, the Palestinian-oriented people, don't regard the federation as so horrible. It's better than the continuation of Israeli occupation. If federation were the only way to end the occupation, they would certainly take it. No one can be 100 percent sure. But I am sure that the best thing for Israel is to attempt such an agreement. And I think it is still possible.

BITAN: Do you think that Jordan is ready to have a peace agreement under these conditions? If you don't, you are playing chess with yourself.

EITAN: Yes, I think so.

DROR: In talking about Israeli interests in the Israeli-Jordanian-Palestinian triangle, I would define Israel's main interest as the preservation of her existence, peace, and security. Israel's interest is to select an alternative that promises a solution to the conflict, or at least its dilution to the extent that dangers to Israel's survival and security are considerably minimized. Anything else is secondary and subservient to that.

The desire to assure this interest is in fact the cause of Israel's opting for the Jordan rib of the triangle. The Palestinian side rejects compromise on partition and recognition of the existence of an Israeli national movement. Our assumption has been that the Hussein-Jordan factor is more moderate, less dangerous to Israel, and pro-West. And this assumption convinced Israel that it should favor and support Jordan. Both Abdullah and Hussein in practice recognized *de facto*. Israel responded by unofficially recognizing Jordan's annexation of the West Bank in 1950, and by protecting Jordan's flank at a later stage during the 1970 Syrian invasion.

American interest in the survival of Hussein's Jordan has made Israel's choice that much easier. There were periods when Israel gave tacit approval to the supply of American weapons to Jordan; the *quid pro quo*, of course, was weapons for the Israeli army. The US administration insured, in the sixties, that tanks supplied to Jordan would not be transferred to the West Bank.

Hussein's moderation continued until the waiting period preceding the Six Day War. Afterward, not only did Radio Amman provoke the Egyptians into closing the Sharm el-Sheik Strait and expelling the UN forces, but American-made Patton tanks crossed the Jordan River, and Egyptian commandos were transferred to that front. Hussein joined the war against Israel, even though he had been warned by us; and even though he would obviously lose. From that moment on, Hussein's moderation was a thing of the past.

I find similarities today—observing Hussein with the Syrians. In hindsight, and with the benefit of a second thought, it may well be that over-dependence on Hussein's moderation and our consideration for American interests in Hussein's survival caused Israel to lose opportunities, or at least tactical advantages. The feeling of obligation to support Hussein was certainly our motive in not thinking about more serious contact with the Palestinians. This prevented us from seeking in late 1967 and the beginning of 1968 an alternative to Hussein, and again, in late 1970, after the Jordanian civil war, when proposals for self-government of the West Bank—now rejected by the West Bank Palestinians—might have been accepted. Had such a plan been adopted then, it would have been possible to create an alternative to the PLO and to the Palestinian extremists. But we also have to admit that Israel did not offer Hussein any real solution for final peace.

The strategic importance of Israel's eastern frontier was very great up to 1967. This is the frontier that many suggest today as the withdrawal line in the framework either of a Jordanian-Palestine solution or of an independent Palestinian state. True, the army to the east of the Jordan River is not the biggest or strongest Arab force. But most of Israel's vital centers lie in close proximity to this frontier; the big centers of population—Tel Aviv, Jerusalem; the centers of industry, or energy, the transport junctions, and civil and military airports. It is therefore important that Israel should have an eastern neighbor who represents a minimal threat and whose hostility should not impel him to cooperate or enter a coalition with Israel's other enemies.

The theoretical answer given to this argument is that in an age of sophisticated weaponry, when missiles play a considerable role, terrain and what happens close to the frontier and across it are unimportant. This viewpoint contends that there is little point in obstinacy about pushing Jordanian artillery back from Qalqilyah and East Jerusalem, when missiles from across the Jordan River can easily hit the same targets. This presentation of the problem is wrong. Missiles, like artillery, do have a destructive capability. They can kill, cause damage, and disrupt reserve mobilization. But if the eastern neighbor also has a capacity to penetrate quickly with armor into Israel's vital centers, then the destructive capability of missiles is augmented— by a capacity for victory and extermination. This fact underlies our security problem in the east. And most of the Israeli Defense Force commanders, even the most moderate doves among them, are afraid to leave Israel in such a vulnerable situation. Most Israelis share this fear.

When we take into account the present size of the Middle Eastern armies and the power of modern weapons systems, then it is very doubtful whether an offensive against Israel's 1967 eastern borders could be contained, particularly if accompanied by a simultaneous offensive from other frontiers. Moreover, it is doubtful whether Israel can base her future strategy for the eastern frontier on the concept of a pre-emptive strike. No matter who the neighbor to the east is, Israel will be better off without this strategy and free of the fears that would accompany withdrawal to the 1967 line. In other words, it is precisely the modern weapon systems, including missiles, that accord importance to certain terrain, as in the case of the West Bank vis-à-vis Israel.

My conclusion is that Israel's vital interest lies in denying and fighting against the possibility that the terrain to the immediate east be occupied by anyone who operates on the principles of the Palestinian Covenant—more precisely, on those clauses which speak of the elimination of Israel. Unfortunately, there is at present no political alternative to the PLO. If there are Palestinians who think differently, they are neither heard nor seen. Yesterday, and the day before, I heard no names except Souss and Hammami, Hammami and Souss.

Yet we must assume, as a hypothesis, that there will be a change in the Palestinian attitude, that a constructive element will be found, that their inclination for genocide will decline, and that the PLO will change its image—in which case the PLO won't be the PLO. Under such an assumption, there are various proposals as to how Israel should preserve her interests. One of them is to lean on the Palestinian rib of the triangle. In other words, to accept a Palestinian state in Judea and Samaria without or with the Gaza Strip. There are military men who argue that from a security viewpoint this would be a good solution—better a small Palestinian state than a large Jordanian-Palestinian entity to the east.

However, the fear is that a small Palestinian state would be unable to solve the refugee problem of those who now live in Lebanon and Syria. We also have to keep in mind that a Palestinian state would mean not only a direct and real danger to Israel but also, no doubt, the destruction of an American ally, the Hashemite kingdom of Jordan. Furthermore, it would severely endanger the Arab country which American interests lean upon most today—Saudi Arabia. More than that, pushing the PLO towards Geneva would mean the indirect recognition of PLO willingness to destroy Israel and the cultivation of a Soviet-supported organization. Would it be good for American global interests and interests in the Middle East to reward terror and extremist factors among the Palestinians? The extreme approach of the PLO is proven by their refusal to accept the challenge of the Saunders paper to recognize Israel in return for US recognition of the PLO—even though American recognition is so important to the PLO. The Palestinians would continue to be a destructive element as they have been in Jordan and recently in Lebanon. A Palestinian state would renew the conflict from a different baseline. On the other hand, there is also the fear that a Palestinian state might integrate into a greater Syria. Damascus aspires to such a historic program and puts considerable energy into its achievement. Israel cannot ignore this possibility, which would present a new threat. The triangle would become a rectangle: Israel, Syria-Jordan and the Palestinians. Such a rectangle would bring new elements into the conflict and invite guaranteed intervention of a Soviet Union hostile to Israel.

HANAN: Eitan said that without a compromise for Jerusalem there is no possibility whatsoever for any kind of agreement with either the Jordanians or any other Arab entity. Now he didn't ask himself, or at least he didn't tell us why it is so. Why is Jerusalem that important to the Arabs? I think the answer is ideological on their side. In other words, he is ready to recognize and respect an ideological factor on the Arab side; but he is more than a cynic when it comes to ideological factors on the Jewish or Zionist side.

EITAN: I'm for a compromise—I don't want to give up all Jerusalem.

HANAN: I don't now speak of how much, but of the principle of this, which is something that nothing in the world could change. Why, on our side, don't you even want to take into consideration these trifling, imponderable things that are called ideas and ideologies? Ideology is the most important thing. Anyone who wants to assess the situation in the Middle East without taking ideologies into account won't ever see the true picture.

Israel's topmost interest is not to secure

its survival. Israel's topmost interest is to carry on with materializing the Zionists' great vision. We, of course, have to secure our survival, but I do not think that it is so questionable as might have appeared from some of the words uttered around this table. Israel still is the strongest state in the Middle East. Israel can still repeat its victories twice and thrice and four times in the future. Israel can take care of itself.

What has happened to Israel is more on the ideological level. Successive governments have concentrated too much on securing their own standing, while losing the main aims of going on with materializing the Zionist vision. The entire gloomy picture drawn for us by Eitan about the end of it all—for all practical purposes about the end of Zionism, because the end of *aliyah* is the end of Zionism—this picture has no legs, as we say in Hebrew, no feet, no basis in reality. There is one simple fact: since the Six Day War the Jewish majority has been growing.

EITAN: Only up to 1973.

HANAN: *Aliyah,* immigration to Israel, is the soul of Zionism, is the main purpose, the topmost interest. No Israeli leader of any importance will agree to discount it, will fail to take into account continuation of *aliyah* as a realistic, viable factor in the future. In the Jewish communities of the world, the sources are not tapped, not exhausted. There can be a constant wave of *aliyah,* of a very substantial number, and it will keep the Jewish population in Eretz Israel growing for many years to come.

With the present Arab regimes, I do not believe that we will get any kind of peace, either with or without a Palestinian state in the West Bank. The interests of Arab countries bordering Israel have their own dynamism and will carry on with their enmity to Israel's existence even after what we call the Palestinian problem is solved. The same goes for Jordan. It is not true that Jordan ever was less hostile to the state of Israel. It was only weaker. Neither was

Lebanon ever less hostile. Lebanon was weaker. She simply didn't dare. The reason the Jordanian authorities stopped the terrorists from shooting across the border into Israel before or after the Six Day War was because of our retaliation.

We have to keep this in mind when we speak of letting the Palestinians have a certain area in the West Bank or not letting them, trusting them or not trusting them, believing that they will be better, or not believing it. They will not be better. As in any other case, a gain for them—a territorial gain or a political gain for them—gives them a greater initiative, a greater encouragement to be more aggressive toward Israel. I think all our history is one long proof of this assumption.

You didn't mention an adjective that has been applicable to Jordan since the days of its birth—it's an artificial state. The problem of the artificiality of states in the Middle East is very important. The map of the Middle East is just a photocopy of the colonialist map of the region. Not one single Middle Eastern country was created by a historical process of national statehood.

ZVI: Egypt—that was the only one.

HANAN: I'm not so sure. Look, in my opinion, Egypt is in Africa and it should stay there and not the Middle East. This is why I think Suez should be the border between Israel and Egypt.

PINHAS: It's not any more, by the way.

HANAN: It should be. We'll return there in the next war. We'll be there again.

In terms of this artificiality, the most distinctive is Jordan. Because of that, I offer my suggestion: to agree to help Jordan—east of the Jordan River—to become the national home of the Palestinians.

In other words, Israel's position toward the Jordanian-Palestinian-Israeli triangle should be to make the triangle into a parallel. To take the three elements and make out of them only two. This is roughly agreed upon by many Israelis. I think there is only a very small minority of Israelis that would agree to a third state, as we say, "between the desert and the sea," in what was the British Mandate originally. The question is, what should the dividing line be between these two elements? My opinion is that the only viable dividing line is the River Jordan. Even here, many, many Israelis—more than the majority, including the Center and the Tactical Left—believe that at least the security border between the two should be the river. Even Yigal Allon thinks this. If we say that the Palestinians should get Jordan, and say this emphatically, if we work for this, this is an achievable goal. This is something which is obtainable and historically feasible. And maybe one day we will see it.

The crux of the matter is that the conflict in the Middle East is the father of the Palestinian problem, and not the son of it. It all stems from the war of the Arab countries and states between themselves, and, of course, against Israel.

EITAN: Who triggered the war? Who triggered it? The Palestinian Arabs.

HANAN: I think the Palestinian problem was created by the Arabs' refusal to accept the state of Israel.

EITAN: Not the state. Zionism. In 1920—take the beginning.

HANAN: Even then.

EITAN: In 1920?

HANAN: Yes.

EITAN: It's simply not true. Factual truth is factual truth.

BITAN: I am confused. Up to now, everybody here was crying to heaven that to say "the Palestinians" means the PLO. Now I hear from Eitan that a Jordanian solution to the Palestinian problem is the best solu-

tion. You sound convincing. I hope you are right in your assumption. Nevertheless, I think we have a serious problem because you can't get away from the dilemma.

What do the Palestinians say? All of them are very much against Hussein, against Jordan—"reactionary" Jordan. From all I have heard here from my friends, most of the Palestinians want a Palestinian state and not a Jordanian state, whether they will get it freely or whether they will take it over by force. What are we going to have if we accept the Jordanian solution? We are going to have all the bad aspects of a Palestinian state without any of its good aspects.

Hussein may be murdered. Why don't you take seriously the Palestinians who are powerful, militant agents of the PLO? They all say in so many words: It's not just finishing off Israel; we first have to finish off King Hussein and have a Palestinian state. Israel then would have to deal with a big Palestinian state comprising Jordan and the West Bank, and all of Jerusalem and whatever. And all benefits we might have from the Jordanian solution would be gone, and we would not have anything.

What do you think about the proposal, made by certain people in Israel, that it is in the Israeli interest—that it is in the Israeli interest that the PLO should take over Jordan? But, as these people say, it should happen in a controlled way. Israel made a most severe mistake in September, 1970. We should have supported the PLO; we shouldn't have supported Jordan.

The point is that a PLO victory over Hussein—without a Palestinian state—would give the Palestinians a big state east of the river which they would have to manage themselves, which would give them their own troubles. Then the whole idea of having a state in the West Bank would be a secondary interest for the Palestinians.

MEIR: You are deciding for them.

BITAN: No, I am not deciding, I am suggesting a possibility.

URI: But not letting them decide for themselves?

BITAN: No. They are deciding; they would be the ones to take over.

I say that it may be in Israel's interest for the East Bank of Jordan to be a Palestinian state. That means that the Jordanian-Hussein-Hashemite regime should be overthrown. I don't know. It's a possibility. If that doesn't happen, there is the danger that the PLO might take over the West Bank from Hussein—or maybe Hussein would give it to them after getting it back from us.

AMIR: The historical perspective looms very large in our discussion today. It should be welcomed.

Even among deterministic historians many would admit that there are periods, there are circumstances, when there is great flexibility, great latitude for a variety of options. When social and political orders are amorphous, when different belief systems and different institutions are competing with each other—then many things may happen. In the Middle East, particularly in the Fertile Crescent, the years after the disintegration of the Ottoman Empire was such a period. In the Fertile Crescent, the two dominant powers, Britain and France, were able to mold, create, invent states and nations almost at will.

We cannot, however, extrapolate from that situation that this game can be played *ad infinitum*. In periods of transition identities may change according to circumstances, but after a certain time the situation solidifies. In the Middle East this took place after World War II. It turned out that the Arabic-speaking population of this area tended to identify itself as Arab. It also turned out that this identity by itself was

not enough. For every individual Arab, this identity had to be supplemented with attachment to a local nation-state.

These facts cannot be changed in the foreseeable future. Arabs are Arabs, but they also have local nationalities without which their self-image and identity would be lacking. In the case of the Syrians, it is Syria. In the case of the Iraqis, it is Iraq. In the case of the Palestinians, it is Palestine. To me this is one of the given facts which must be considered—not manipulated or ignored.

Therefore, Israeli political thinking must accept two premises. First, there is a Palestinian identity which must be recognized and satisfied, at least to a reasonable degree. Second, there is a Jordanian-Hashemite factor which is different in nature and in whose viability and relative moderation there is a clear Israeli interest.

If my analysis so far is correct, I do not see how we can make suggestions like "tell the Palestinians that the East Bank is their homeland." This kind of manipulation really exceeds the boundaries of possible options. We might as well tell the Palestinians that "Kuwait is their homeland," or that "Somalia is their homeland." The fact is that as far as national sentiments and symbols are concerned, the national identity of the Palestinian Arabs focuses on that territory called Palestine, and not on the East Bank. Directing the Palestinians exclusively onto the East Bank is actually a contradiction in terms. Look at the focus of the Palestinian identity. Look at their symbols. Read their poems, their stories, their histories. They all concentrate on the Palestine west of the Jordan.

I am willing to accept the paradoxical formulation that it is Zionism which created the Palestinian identity. Historically it is true; now it cannot be undone. Israel should get credit not only for crystallizing the Palestinian identity, but actually for stimulating their political and social development—unintentionally, of course. This we did, but we cannot turn the clock back.

However, two crucial questions remain open. The first emerges primarily from Dror's presentation on the security dimension—which for Israel is definitely more important than the ideological one: To what extent can the West Bank be demilitarized effectively, with inspection arrangements, with some sort of a barrier along the Jordan Valley (not necessarily an annexation in political terms) which would reasonably insure that no attack such as that described by Dror would threaten the existence of the state of Israel? And, second: To what extent will the Hashemite factor remain a stable and moderate factor which the Israelis can safely include in their plans for the future?

Referring to the second question, it is true that in the past the Hashemite element functioned on many occasions as a moderating force in the framework of the Arab-Israeli arena. However, the main problem is not what happened in the past, but what the situation is in Jordan today and what might happen in the future. Recent developments bringing Jordan and Syria closer together are quite alarming. We should ask ourselves whether a new situation is not emerging which would make it necessary for the Israelis who include the Hashemite factor in their planning to reconsider their position. But I do not think that the Jordanians have already passed the point of no return. This has not yet happened.

MEIR: I am astonished that nobody has asked Eitan to clarify his basic non-ideological assumption. It is extremely fascinating—although he says quite correctly that 99 percent of the Israelis and 100 percent of the Arabs are ideologically motivated. I must remind you of a story you may know—a German-Jewish story told in the thirties. Kohn from Breslau meets Levy from Berlin: "Levy," he says, "you are

here because of Hitler?" And Levy answers: "No, because of the weather." If there is no ideology or anything like that—you know, why be there except for the weather—it has no great logic. Without ideology, the whole thing is a little problematic.

HANAN: Meaningless.

MEIR: Eitan based his argument on the Jordanian solution, on a sociological explanation—historical-sociological. Even more important than the sociology, I think, are nationalism and its symbols. Sociological proof is not proof in an argument about nationalism. It's not whether the majority of the population moves to this or that area, but whether an area becomes the center of its national consciousness.

Now the political point: I must say I agree with Bitan. For once we really agree. The main argument against the Jordanian political solution is that nobody can guarantee that it will last. You say that Hussein will be murdered. A more probable scenario is a second Rabat scenario: He will get the West Bank back, and then pressure from the Arab states, or whatever else, will in one way or another make him hand it over to the Palestinians. Then you would have all the negative results, and you would not have any of the positive.

Dror convinced me of most of the things he said. But he said one thing too quickly, and maybe not convincingly. He said the creation of a Palestinian state would harm American interests in Jordan and Saudi Arabia. It may well be true. But the Americans are not yet in favor of a Palestinian state. There is still a lot of hesitation. But assume the United States moves in that direction. They must have asked themselves the question that you asked about Jordan and Saudi Arabia. They must have arrived at some answers. One wouldn't think that you are the first who thought of that.

DROR: I'm sure that they are very aware

of the danger. They haven't decided that a Palestinian state on the West Bank is the solution. On the contrary. But at the same time, after reading the Saunders paper, we have to be on the alert.

MEIR: Your other point about the strategic situation on our eastern frontier worries the Left as much as it worries the Right. But I find a flaw in it. Can the security border be on the Jordan River? First of all, politically such a military border is unacceptable to the Arabs. But let's assume that it will be imposed on them. From purely military logic, there is something which I do not understand. Dror quite convincingly said that it's not the missiles. It's missiles plus armored advance across a West Bank that is not demilitarized. But what distances are we talking about? Let's say that Jordan, for some reason, gets back into the conflict or into a situation of tension. Forget Tel Aviv for a moment. Speak of Jerusalem. The distances are so small that this is no basic strategic argument. It's a matter of nuances. To move armor from the Jordan River 60 kilometers to Jerusalem is not such an insuperable technological feat.

YAIR: The difference is that from the Green Line border, if they have the new weapons or new masses of armor, one or two days means a complete defeat.

OREN: I share much of Bitan's attitude, only with the opposite result. In this Israel-Palestine-Jordan triangle emerges a very special phenomenon: an implicit or a reluctant agreement between the state of Israel and the Hashemite kingdom of Jordan. This phenomenon has been evident since the early 1930s, and has lasted for almost fifty years. The Jewish state of Israel and the Hashemite kingdom of Jordan share the same enemy—the Palestinian National Movement. There is no possibility of bringing about a Palestinian political structure, however small it might be, without tearing land and population from both Jordan and

Israel. This very basic element played a major role in the calculation of both sides in the past. And it is also the basic common denominator between King Hussein and Israeli leaders today.

From a social and economic point of view, for the Palestinians living in the two banks, the Jordan River is not a border. The two banks have gradually become one unit that cannot be separated. The Palestinians' identity is a constant threat to the Hashemite regime. That is why I believe the Palestinian state can be built only at the expense of Jordan, and not side by side with it; and only in Nablus and Amman together. It is like a balance of the scales: if Jordan has the upper hand, the PLO must go down, and vice versa. The contrast between the two is sharp. The Hashemite kingdom is based on rather conservative elements and principles, while the PLO is based on rather modern and radical elements.

King Hussein has today the ability to threaten the population of the West Bank and, I think, the Palestinians in general. He can cut them off immediately from the East Bank once he closes the bridges. For the residents of the West Bank and East Jerusalem, this means a separation of families and business—losing the only channel to the Arab world. The Arabs of the West Bank are faced with two bad alternatives. One is to agree with the PLO to a Palestinian state in the future, having the risk of such separation, or to accept a rather hated regime that would assure the unity of the two banks.

PINHAS: I was extremely depressed this morning to hear Eitan's extreme non-ideological conception, perhaps more than by anything else that was said until now. There was, however, discontinuity between his non-ideological conception and his later analysis, which resulted in an artificial solution. With all the detailed background he presented about the Palestinians, he simply couldn't adopt the Palestinian solution. But he created a dilemma by trying to go back to the Jordanian solution.

I think that the Jordanian solution not only is not feasible, but perhaps is not good from the point of view of Israel's interests. Going back to 1970, I agree with those who think that perhaps Israel committed the greatest mistake after 1967 when we protected the Hashemite kingdom and cooperated with America. Israel was tempted by the Americans to serve their interests, mainly by doing something which in the long run, I think, damaged some of our best interests. Israel's interests in common with the Hashemites—before the independence war, and for nearly two decades after, were seen correctly by Israel. Our policy was right and justifiable. But not in 1970— and I must admit that then I didn't share this view. Later, after analyzing developments I came to the conclusion that perhaps we made a great mistake in not letting the Palestinians take over in the East Bank. We protected mainly American interests, and not necessarily Israeli interests.

EITAN: But even this is not wrong, you know. From time to time the United States also protects Israeli interests. So it's a *quid pro quo.*

PINHAS: I don't object to the principle. I just say that I am not sure whether then it was in the long-range interest of Israel to prevent a certain development, which could perhaps have planted the Palestinians later in the East Bank of the Jordan and perhaps also could have made them feel they had realized some of their aspirations, which could lessen their determination to get a part of Eretz Israel. Perhaps it could have imposed on the Palestinians some of the things they are trying to avoid—some kind of moderation that could have resulted from new responsibility for that territory.

Under no circumstances could we today come back to the Jordanian option just because we all share the knowledge that the Palestinian option, within the limited territory of Judea and Samaria, or even more than that, is detrimental to the very existence of the state of Israel. It goes back to the security problems that might be created by the presence of the Palestinians, or even the Jordanian army, within the territories of Judea and Samaria.

Without negating Oren's argument that from a social and economic point of view, the two banks of Jordan have been inseparable in the past, I don't think this necessarily implies that from a military point of view they might not be separated as they are now. The model that Dayan was trying to create in the last nine years was exactly that. On the one hand, the two banks were separated, from the military point of view, and the Israeli army was placed on the Jordan. But socially and mainly economically, they have been connected by the open bridges.

GAD: I think Hussein is very popular in Israel. He also satisfied a certain need for recognition-hungry Israelis by agreeing to meet with Israeli leaders and having those meetings publicized, more or less. He was tough on Palestinian terrorists. I think if he would run for election in Israel, he could get himself a very sure place in the Knesset.

OREN: In the Likud—only in the Likud.

GAD: I'm not so sure. Every party would like to have him. Anyway, I think the Jordan Option was feasible right after the 1967 war. Jordan could have made peace, a separate peace, with Israel if Israel would have been ready at that time to give back almost all of the territories with the minor border changes suggested by Hussein. And it might have been feasible to reach a satisfactory solution to the problem of Jerusalem, which was suggested at that time even by Dayan. He said something about a Jordanian flag inside the old city, and there was an idea of mixed jeeps policing the area. If it could have been acted upon fast, it would have been feasible.

It was desirable at that time from the point of view of the interest of Israel. It would have stopped the irredentist tendencies among the Israeli Arabs at the outset. In those years we waited for a telephone call from the Arabs. We thought that at a later date we might get better territorial results, but we forgot to think of the other implications of prolonging this agony for everybody else.

HANAN: You only have to prove that he was ready to sign a separate peace. This is unprovable.

GAD: Yes, he was.

EITAN: He was ready for everything.

GAD: His main claim was that he could prove to the Arab world that he could get back the territories, that he could actually deliver.

The feasibility of such a claim is doubtful now. Even its desirability is very doubtful. I agree with the security-motivated notion. Until recently, I favored the Jordanian option. But now I think that an agreement establishing the Jordanians on the West Bank can be, from a security point of view, more dangerous to Israel than a third state. A third state in the West Bank and Gaza—with a very precarious link between the two sections—which is dependent upon Israel for its lifeline, whose borders to the Arab world on the east can be sealed at any moment by Hussein himself, is a much smaller risk for Israel than a Hussein-dominated West Bank, open to direct contact with the rest of the Arab world.

DROR: Even a PLO-dominated Palestinian state?

GAD: I think that a PLO-dominated third state is impossible without a basic change in the PLO, without mutual recognition. It is not at all feasible or concrete now to suggest this, with the PLO's 6th Article of the Palestinian Charter. This is the gist of the matter—war only will continue if the PLO does not change its basic policy. But with a change in basic PLO policy, I think, from a security point of view, a third state is even more desirable than the Jordanian option at present. The alternative of keeping the territories one way or another—with full annexation, with semi-annexation, or even without annexation—is even less desirable.

This discussion about the relevance of ideology reminds me of the famous simplistic, insoluble problem—of the rhinoceros that can break everything that meets a stone that nothing can break. There is no solution, of course, to such a situation—except a compromise. When two ideologies conflict, the only solution is for each side to stick to its own ideology, while they compromise on the practical level.

YAIR: Your third state would be a buffer state. But since you favor forming this Palestinian state in the West Bank, what is your answer to what Eitan has said about the viability of such a state?

GAD: I did not say that I am for a Palestinian state on the West Bank.

ZVI: Welcome.

GAD: I agree that if the Palestinians choose to have a state of their own, it's not up to us to tell them whether their state is viable. Whether it is viable or not is a problem for the Palestinians. An argument about viability might be their reason for not establishing a state like that; but it shouldn't be an argument on our part.

There is no contradiction between this and what I said earlier. I was talking about something the Palestinians might choose, and I happened to mention that from a security point of view there are certain advantages to an independent Palestinian state compared to a Jordanian solution. This does not mean that we can enforce either one. We can only try to get the best solution for ensuring our security. But we are not going to have a *Pax Hebraica* here. It is impossible for us to tell everyone to behave according to the needs of our security. If we could do that, we would be a world power; and even a world power is not able to arrange every situation in which it is involved according to what is best for security.

ZVI: A Palestinian state in the West Bank and the Gaza Strip would be a grave danger to the state of Israel. What Eitan said about 1947 is true. There couldn't be a compromise between these two national movements west of the River Jordan. The main focus of a Palestinian state should be east of the River Jordan. The solution to the Palestinian question should not be seen in the context of what I would call Western Palestine, but in historical Palestine—the original British Mandate for Palestine before 1922, on both sides of the river. I wouldn't label it a Palestinian state or a Jordanian state. Maybe it could be called a Jordanian-Palestinian solution, but that's up to them to decide. There are, of course, differences between Jordanian identity and Palestinian identity. But there is much in common now. If we look at Jordan, in many respects it is a Palestinian state. The majority of the population is Palestinian—55 percent. The educational system is staffed mainly by Palestinians. The machinery of government and the cabinets have been greatly marked by the Palestinian presence. Since the West Bank and the Gaza Strip are also Palestinian, they should have political and cultural links to Transjordan, but Transjordan should be maintained as the focus of this state. The West Bank must be demilitarized and placed for a period under Israeli military control.

If the West Bank goes back to Jordan or to the Palestinians, it goes back to Arab hands. This territory is next to the underbelly of Israel—and it is sensitive for that reason. My concern stems from security—strategic considerations, not historical or religious ones. Jordan used to be moderate and flexible; now Jordan is establishing a dangerous coalition with Syria. A West Bank returned to Jordan might become an aggressive Arab springboard against Israel. Alternatively, Jordan will be forced to hand it back to the Palestinians. And even if moderate Palestinian elements were to dominate the West Bank, members of the Hawatmeh, or Jibril, or Habash groups might still sit along the Israeli border with SAM-7 or Strella missiles and hit any airplane which takes off—to give only one example. Therefore Israel's military border should be drawn along the Jordan River with Israeli military supervision—west of the river not merely because of Israel's fear of massive attack from the West Bank against Israel, but also because of our need to assure daily security, current security. We can prevent the massive attack if we dominate the routes from Transjordan to the West side of the Jordan River, and in case of war we can prevent hardware from entering the West Bank. I am worried about more massacres such as in Maalot if the West Bank and the Gaza Strip were to fall into Arab hands. We'll have then much more bloodshed, and this is why Israelis, as we all know, are very sensitive to such a prospect. It would undermine the fabric of life in Israel. Even an atomic deterrent couldn't prevent this kind of guerrilla war from making life in Israel unbearable. People will leave the country, and there will be complete chaos.

Finally, I must stress that Transjordan is regarded by some Palestinians as part of their homeland.

OREN: They say that the way to liberate Tel Aviv is through Amman.

ZVI: They have said that a Palestinian state in the West Bank would be landlocked under the pressure of both Israel and Jordan. It couldn't survive; therefore the best thing is first to take over Transjordan, and then to turn it into a base against Israel. I believe that we can influence things. So let us perhaps influence them in the direction I have suggested.

The Arabs wouldn't accept what I propose. But this is the most that we can do to try and solve the problem and not endanger our security.

BITAN: You play chess with yourself.

HANAN: It's better than Russian Roulette.

YAIR: Let me come straight to the main point. I believe that Israel should bless the fall of King Hussein and the termination of the rule of the illustrious Hashemite kingdom of Jordan. Moreover, I think that Israel should, and can, be instrumental in such a development. Many of the speakers here today supported the idea of the Palestinization of the East Bank. Pinhas even thought that Israel took the wrong approach in 1970 by assisting, in a way, King Hussein to hold to his crown. I don't share this view. If the fall of Hussein were to take place in the future, somewhere before 1980, in my humble opinion, that would be an opportune time, a good time. If it were possible to arrange the timing, to fix it at the most appropriate hour, then it should happen when pressures on Israel—all kinds of pressures—insisting on the solution of the so-called Palestinian problem reach their peak. I, for one, think that the next four years might be the hardest in this respect. Gad pointed out humorously, but correctly I think, that Hussein could easily be elected to the Israeli parliament. I agree. And as an almost-member of the Israeli parliament, he should be told by us, paraphrasing the famous words of Cromwell to the Long Parliament, "You sat here too long for the good of our country. In the name of God, go!"

We should get rid of the Hashemite syndrome. We have a romantic, sentimental, and even paternalistic approach—which inflicts even the most unsentimental of us here. While I deride the paternalistic approach some of us tend to take toward King Hussein or the PLO, I am not saying that we should refrain from making our influence felt where it can be done. Again, we cannot play God and decide for others, on the basis of what is best for us. But if we are convinced—and I am—that Hussein, or any of the Hashemites ruling Jordan are damaging Israeli vital interests, we should try to contribute our share to his downfall. I am not blind to the dangers lurking alongside of this trail, but I don't think that the envisioned dangers of the alternatives are easier to bear, and they may be harder. And calling a spade a spade, I have in mind in particular the dangers of a third state, a PLO state, forced upon us by friend and foe. Maybe it's a brutal way of putting it, but we are engaged, like it or not, in a brutal game. So let us be shorn of all the sentimental feathers.

The first question that arises, of course, is "how?" I don't think we should elaborate on this point, but let me say a few sentences. Hussein's rule is the oldest in the Middle East, no doubt about it. But this doesn't make the position of his throne less precarious. He maneuvered beautifully in the past, but let us not forget that during most of the period we played along with him. We can rise from this chess table and take the queen with us.

Secondly, it is common knowledge that as much as the inhabitants in the West Bank benefit from the open bridges, Hussein benefits from them too. Disconnection will cut his influence at least by half, I think. I am not advocating. I am just saying that there is such a possibility. Here, as in all other questions, the main problem posed to us is the American problem. But it is not an insurmountable one.

The famous Hashemite moderation and levelheaded policies were not a result of ideology or of purity of character. Their behavior, at best, was opportunistic. And I put it to you that this kind of moderation can very likely be repeated or inherited by the Palestinians. In a telegraphic way: They will have to mind their own store for the first time, and responsibility is the mother of moderation. Some here say that the Palestinians on the West Bank would become an irredentist force. Well, there is always the other side of the coin. Allow me to use here an unpleasant word, but not in its literal sense: they would also be hostages. And the Palestinians in the East Bank with all their disregard for human life will have to consider every move, as Hussein is doing now. Hussein's moderation of the past derived as much from the geopolitical situation as from genealogical considerations. In short, by contributing to the process of institutionalizing the PLO in the form of a state, we might dampen its enthusiasm for fighting.

I don't know if we will thereby solve completely the Palestinian problem. Probably not. But we will be able to release much of the political pressure on ourselves.

It has been said here that the task of the Palestinians is to be a buffer state between us and the Jordanians. The main attribute of this third state, according to Gad, is its weakness. It's like adopting a week-old baby in the hope that it will not grow up. I hope the Palestinians accept this offer in that spirit.

EITAN: Let me speak to a few points that have come up in answer to what I said. First, for Jordan, I think, it is quite clear that up to 1948 Abdullah was moderate in his approach; he didn't support the Palestinian Arabs. He publicly accepted the Peel partition. He accepted the 1947 partition. His Arab Legion took part in the 1948 war according to this concept of the UN Partition Plan—in order to take what the plan said should become the Arab Palestine state next to Israel.

BITAN: He took Jerusalem.

EITAN: He never tried to cross the partition boundaries. Jerusalem, according to

the plan, was designated as an internationalized area.

BITAN: For months Jerusalem was under seige—he tried to take over Jerusalem.

EITAN: Read every historical book in the world.

BITAN: I don't have to read the books; I heard the guns.

EITAN: No. The Jordanians in 1948 didn't try to cross the partition line.

After 1948 the relations with Jordan also were moderate. So too with Lebanon. Because the Maronites—with their anti-Arab nationalism and ideology, with their fight for a separate national identity—regarded us as their only allies. In 1946 they even signed an official pact with the Jewish Agency.

As for Jordan, in the 1967 war, the first Jordanian action was not an immediate advance of the armored corps from the Jordan Valley, but some shooting on Jerusalem and elsewhere. There was no moving of Jordanian forces until we took the initiative. I think this was our greatest historical mistake.

I don't believe that Hussein today really intends to make a unified military front with Syria—for different and important reasons. It's a matter of interests. In the past too, he was motivated by self-interest—for example, the Hashemites had an interest in not supporting Palestinian-Arab nationalism because it was also directed against them. The same holds true now concerning Syria. Jordan is now going through its most prosperous period. I don't think that his Pan-Arab conviction and his great love for the Syrian state after the whole past history of their relationship is going to make Hussein risk all these developments. He is playing the same cards as usual: to be a good guy with Syria, with the Americans, and—I don't know—with Arab history, as well as with the Israelis. He tries to play all the cards he can.

On the Jerusalem question I did not ignore the fact that there are ideological drives on both sides. That is why I said there should be a compromise in Jerusalem, and not Arab sovereignty there. And I take into consideration the feelings that many Israelis, though I don't say most Israelis, have about free access to the Wailing Wall.

HANAN: Western Wall.

EITAN: Historically, this was the name which was used in English—"Wailing Wall." "Western Wall" is the translation from the Hebrew name. So when I speak English, I use the English term. That's my way. Even though I say "Eretz Israel" in Hebrew, in English I say "Palestine." I think that names shouldn't be loaded with ideological connotations.

In Jerusalem, it seems logical to me that the Jews should have their holy places and an area inhabited by Jews; the Arabs also live there and have their holy places. It's not only that one should take into consideration two conflicting ideologies that must be compromised. I also take into consideration that 75,000 Arabs in East Jerusalem don't want to be under Israeli control. For me this is important. It's difficult and complicated to rule them. These people are the elite of the West Bank, and it would be very strange for the West Bankers to be cut off from their leaders. If I can find a solution in which my vital interests are not jeopardized and which allows the Arabs to live according to their wishes, then that is my approach. And this includes Jerusalem. I don't see any difference between Jerusalem and other parts of Israel-Palestine, except for my personal love for the city.

Another of you said that the Palestinian issue is now not the central factor. I am surprised. I don't agree. It is self-evident that the Palestinian Arabs were those who began to fight against Zionism. They were alone in it up to the late 1930s. To our sorrow, they succeeded in Pan-Arabizing the conflict. They succeeded in bringing into the orbit of the Palestine conflict the Arab countries—and to some extent even non-Arab Muslims.

I agree that there is an American interest in the continuation of the existence of Jordan. It was an ally. There may be old sentiments. But I don't think only these are important. The United States wants to avoid a pro-Soviet or anti-Western state on the borders of oil-rich Saudi Arabia. A revolutionary state next to Saudi Arabia would not serve the United States interest in keeping the oil under a pro-Western regime. Despite the Saunders paper, I am not convinced that there would be an American stake in a Palestinian mini-state in the Gaza Strip and the West Bank. Such a state, if not part of a broader Jordanian-Palestinian agreement, would be located between two not very friendly states—to say the least. What would those responsible for its existence do? It seems to me self-evident that the first thing they would like to arrange is a Soviet guarantee and support. So why would the United States back such a possibility, when the Soviets would be involved in guaranteeing it and when Israel would be provoked? Such a state no doubt would be a haven for those who are against Israel. Maybe it is even true that the ruling people would be more moderate. But George Habash and even more extreme people would come. They wouldn't try so hard to prevent violations of the borders, and Israel would be provoked to retaliate. Such a state wouldn't exist more than two or three weeks. Israel would be forced to occupy it again. The whole story would begin again. And if such a state had a Soviet guarantee, then it would trigger real international trouble. The best interests of the United States are served by a process of stabilization. I don't see how a third state under these conditions could be compatible with the interest.

My last point concerns the comment about Arab states and the Palestinian Arabs sharing a similar historical process.

There is a difference between what happened with the process among the Palestinian Arabs and the other Arab states. The Second World War definitely was the dividing point; for us as Jews, certainly—for me it's the dividing of everything in the world, up to the Holocaust, and from there onwards. The Second World War was not the critical point in the process of shaping national identity for all Arabs. And for the Palestinians—certainly not. What changed in 1945? Nothing. Up to 1948 they were part of the British Mandate. Afterwards, the war of 1948 broke out. Nothing crystallized then. Some of the Palestinians were incorporated into Jordan. Others became refugees, and those refugees didn't cherish the Palestinian identity then. They were followers of Pan-Arabism. George Habash's organization—I think the most important organization—didn't fight only for the redemption of Palestine. It was part of a general conception of the Arab revolution—that Arab unity would be the goal of the Arab struggle, a part of which would be the redemption of Palestine. Look at the Palestine Arabs inside the West Bank up to 1967. Those who were stubborn—the die-hards who fought Hussein to the end—they didn't fight under the banner of Palestinian orientation. They fought under the banner of Pan-Arabism. All the Palestinian opposition, all of the opposition in Jordan against the Hashemites up to 1967 was by Pan-Arab organizations, under Pan-Arab slogans. There was no pro-Palestinian voice except for one voice in the early fifities—the voice of the Palestine Communist Party, only afterwards transformed into the Jordanian Communist Party. It is true that among the Pan-Arabs outside, in the late fifties and early sixties, there was a change to more pro-Palestinian orientation. It grew and gained momentum.

The Palestinian identity among the Palestinian Arabs, however, is much less strong than, say, the Lebanese identity for the Christian Maronite Lebanese. The same is true for the Egyptians. For them too, there are two forms of identification—Egyptian and Pan-Arab. You cannot say with the same conviction that these two forms exist with the Palestinians. The Palestinian component of identity is much weaker. The people of Gaza, Nablus and Jericho and Hebron identify themselves very clearly as Hebronites, Nablusites—and as Arabs. The Palestinian identity is much weaker than the two others.

BITAN: What can you say about the very likely possibility that if we return the West Bank to Hussein, the Palestinians are going to overthrow him and then you won't have the benefit of a moderate Hussein?

EITAN: First, look at historical developments, at the lessons from the 1970 civil war between the revolutionary Palestinians and conservative Hashemites. Also, I don't believe for a moment that the West Bank is going to rise against the king.

BITAN: But here in this room our experts told us that most of the Palestinians want a Palestinian state.

EITAN: So there are disputes among the experts. Experts are not messengers of God. I think there is a strong—I cannot measure it—a strong pro-Jordanian, pro-Hashemite, pro-unity stream in the West Bank. The possibility of a widespread uprising against the Hashemite regime—it may happen one day, I don't know, but I don't think so.

YAIR: You don't agree that most of the inhabitants of the West Bank are pro-PLO?

BITAN: And the Gaza Strip?

EITAN: I will tell you the truth: I don't know.

NAHUM: They are. The question is, what are they ready to do? There is some kind of verbal loyalty.

We also have another historical case: not only September, 1970, but also 1966 in Nablus, when Hussein suppressed them—

after Samu.

EITAN: They prefer to be oppressed by an Arab ruler, not by a Jewish defense minister.

YAIR: If they are only giving lip service to the PLO and they are not going to rise up against the Hashemites, why do you think they are going to rise up against Israel?

NAHUM: It is a false analogy to compare Israeli rule over Arabs and an Arab rule over Arabs. We are not efficient enough in these matters. We should seek a way—perhaps it's too ironical to say—like the way Hussein used in suppressing them when he had problems.

ZVI: Not efficient. Ruthless.

NAHUM: That is efficiency.

MEIR: We are not putting the question in the best way. The problem is not whether the population on the West Bank leans this way or that way. The Palestinian issue—or the fact that there is a Palestinian nationality—has become the central problem for the Arab consciousness in a sense. The question is not whether the people on the West Bank will rise up against Jordan. They won't probably; Hussein's police or army could manage. It is the pressure of the Arab states on Hussein which will compel him to give it back. A new Rabat—that is the real flaw in the Jordanian position.

AMIR: A few years ago I went to Turkey and visited the formerly-Syrian Iskenderun area, which is one of the few parts of the Middle East which is populated by Arabs and yet open to Israelis. I went from one Arab village to another and talked with the people. My repeated question was: "Who are you, what is your national identity?" The unanimous answer was "We are Turks. Arabs? Who are Arabs? The Syrians perhaps, on the other side of the border." I couldn't find a single Arab in half a dozen Arabic-speaking villages. What does it prove? Merely that people would say almost anything under political pressure, and that it would be a great mistake to confuse this with genuine identities.

I must say I am really surprised by some of the things that have been said here about the Palestinians identity. I fear that our living in Bellagio has somewhat detached us from reality. Some of us have just established that there is hardly any Palestinian identity at all. It now remains to establish that there are hardly any Arabs in the West Bank and then by Shabbat the whole problem will be solved.

Israel cannot take United States support for granted.... There is the danger that America will tire—seeing our aid requests and the conflict as endless.

6

Israel and America: Impressions

Editors' Introduction

The relationship between Israel and the United States is an obvioulsy unavoidable topic in any Israeli portrayal of the future. During the course of the meeting, most of the participants shared impressions of this relationship—some of its foundations, problems, and prospects. These, in turn, shaped the individual perspectives that were articulated in the closing segments of the dialogue. Therefore, as background for the final statements and cross-examination, we provide a selection from the participants' overall impressions of America's role in the Middle East and its meaning for Israel. Nahum's comment earlier in the discussion—that he does not believe that there is a serious strategic American interest in Israel—was the provocative take-off point for many of the comments that follow.

BITAN: The history of American policy regarding Zionism and Israel shows that in not such a remote past, the United States, and especially the State Department, was extremely hostile to Israel. I have just read Truman's autobiography, and we all know what troubles he had from the State Department about the problem of Zionism. The hostility of the State Department in those times makes the Saunders document something really sweet for Israel by comparison. I must say, though,

that if the statement we heard earlier is correct—that there is no American strategic interest in Israel—then our situation is very bad.

MEIR: You are discovering America.

BITAN: It is bad—if it is correct, and I do not think it is—because in our century we have seen quite well what happens when there's no strategic interest in the fate or destiny of a people—if there's only a moral issue or humane issue. We have seen how much this is worth. When it comes to sending an American army, even to save Israel from extermination, if only the moral issue is present, then we can't dream of any help. If the gamble of the Left in Israel—on Hammami—is going to fail, and if there is going to be a need for American soldiers, then I'm afraid that past experience shows us that those soldiers will not be sent.

There's no way to avoid a conflict between Israel and the United States in the next few years. A moment is coming when there will be a conflict because of our being pressured to make concessions—about the Golan Heights, about Judea and Samaria, and about Jerusalem—under conditions that 90 percent of the Israeli public will not agree to and which no government in Israel could accept. Isn't it preferable to have difficulties with American policy now, rather than after we have made concessions which will make our position in this conflict much more difficult? I think that the answer is yes, that this is the lesser of the two evils.

I ask a hypothetical question: What would have happened, for instance, if Israel had gone on with its refusal of March, 1975, about the Sinai agreement? What if we hadn't surrendered to pressure? Even more: What would have been the American reaction if we had annexed the West Bank? I'm not so sure that the answer is that we would have been finished. There are two possibilities. One is that the Americans would have abandoned Israel by consistently stopping the support of arms and money to a point where Israel would have been in danger. If this is the answer, then we might as well sign a blank check for anything which America decides to dictate to Israel. Or—and I think this is the answer—there is another possibility. It is like a poker game. We have to play our cards the right way. Golda Meir did it, for instance in 1971, in answer to the proposal by the Jarring Mission. She said, "No, we can't accept it." The American government was unhappy with Israel; and therefore the Phantoms which had been promised didn't arrive for about four or five months. But in the end, they did arrive, even though Israel had said "no." So either we can't say "no"—and we have lost our independence. Or we haven't.

———

MEIR: Three forces are molding US policy: the strategic question, political factors, and some emotional considerations. I would slightly qualify the statement that there are no US strategic interests as far as Israel is concerned—although all in all, I would agree. In the past, the United States considered that it had some strategic interests in Israel. In 1970, the fact that Israel was a threat to Syrian forces in the Jordanian war clearly changed the situation—at least in the Syrian-Jordanian-Palestinian triangle. The United States was able to use Israel to put pressure on some parts of the Mideast. There was, therefore, a strategic interest. It is, in my view, diminishing. I would now define it as an indirect interest. Through Israel the United States still has some leverage on the Arab countries. But the more the United States enters the Arab world, the less is the weight of the Israeli strategic factor.

Now the political factor. A lot has been said—maybe not here, but certainly in general—about the importance of the Jewish lobby in the United States, about the importance of Israel's position on the Hill, and now about the erosion of this importance. My feeling, from what I know of the US scene, is that the importance of the Jewish lobby—let's call it the Jewish lobby for discussion's sake, everybody understands the intricacies of it—is still very crucial. On the surface there is no clear erosion of the Israeli lobby on the Hill. Israel seems to be able to mobilize its whole potential, politically and in moments of crisis. But potentially, below the surface, there is erosion. I would call it latent erosion. Senators and representatives, some of them at least, are developing a grudge against Israel, and it will come out at an opportune moment for them. It is linked with the increase of the strength of the Arab lobby.

The third, the emotional factor, concerns public opinion. There is a general pro-Israeli attitude in the United States. It is something quite basic—this sympathy for Israel. Bitan said that if the United States has only a moral interest, and if there is no strategic factor, then it's really bad for Israel. This is a misunderstanding of the American scene. You cannot judge it according to European standards. What Bitan said would be true for France, England or other European countries—for any other country for that matter. But there is an idealistic streak in America which is very basic in American history and American politics. That's America. That's the United States. In the case of Israel, it's linked with deep religious motivation, this fundamental, Protestant, Bible influence or sympathy. You meet it at every step. It's a very strong factor, and you cannot dismiss it. But again, this is something which has to be qualified.

The Arab and mostly the Palestinian case is becoming more known, people are more aware of it, because of propaganda, because of the case itself. And then—and for me this is the essential point—Israel is becoming a nuisance. The financial aspect of the nuisance is perhaps the most important, because the American public is getting somewhat annoyed about these huge sums. Nothing is black and white. There are no clear strategic interests. Israel has strong political leverage, but it is being undermined.

These are the forces molding policy. How far will those forces be detrimental or positive for vital Israeli interests? Here is the crux of the matter: Do the Americans—the administration, the Hill, and the public— see the Israeli interests in the same way as Israel sees them?

There was an American policy—and a clear one—concerning the Middle East in the early seventies. That was the Rogers Plan.* It was never cancelled, only put in deep freeze. But then in 1973, because of our own faults maybe, the plan came back—if not officially, at least unofficially. Today the framework for American policy is a modified Rogers Plan. The ultimate aim would be a settlement based on an Israeli retreat, not necessarily to the 1967 borders, but close to them. Today perhaps the case for a Jordanian option is not as clear as it was in the original Rogers Plan. The outcome now may be Jordanian or Palestinian. Certainly, on the point of guarantees and help for Israel, the conviction is stronger today than it was in the original Rogers Plan: everybody understands that Israel cannot go back to anything like the 1967 borders without security and guarantees.

My feeling is that at some stage, this plan will be brought to the American public by the administration and will be shown as the reasonable solution—from the American point of view. Then the question will be: If this is shown as the reasonable solution by a president and a secretary of state, will not then the Hill—because of latent erosion in Israel's influence there—and the public— because it is fed up—say, "Well, actually, it's quite reasonable. It makes sense." So the problem is—when?

In America there is still an attachment to the Jordanian solution, which is seen apparently as the main solution of the Jordan-Palestinian problem, as it was in the Rogers Plan. Indeed there are a lot of contacts with the Palestinians, and there is the Saunders document. But in the US-Israel understandings attached to the 1975 Sinai II Pact, the United States promised not to back the PLO. And that promise has been restated. So one has the impression that Jordan is still the main card in this American game, although there is a growing awareness of the Palestinians.

*The main elements of the Rogers Plan are found in Appendix IX.

The Israeli public, however, and perhaps even the Israeli government, seems to feel that the Americans have already switched over to the Palestinian solution—even though the United States is still playing the Jordanian game. This misperception on our part could become self-fulfilling if Israel opposes the Jordanian solution, for such opposition obviously will result in making a Palestinian solution more probable. As I see it, the situation today is that Rabin himself has been convinced, more or less, to go ahead and try for some kind of Jordanian solution. But let's assume that for some reason he cannot get it approved in Israel—and I guess he won't be able to—because of the opposition from the Likud, Gush Emunim, even from within the Labour Party, and because of the need for elections before relinquishing Judea and Samaria. This means that the solution actually favored by the United States will be wrecked because of our own internal politics. The result will be that we will face a much worse situation—the Palestinian option—because pressure for a settlement will increase after the American presidential elections and because the Palestinian case will come more and more to the fore.

What are the possibilities of US pressure? Even after the American elections, I think that extreme changes in US policy are highly improbable. However, if the US administration succeeds in convincing the public that there is a reasonable framework for a solution—including probably the Palestinians, if in the meantime nothing has happened on the Jordanian front—then we shall be, I think, in total isolation. All the latent opposition to Israel will then come to the surface. Then, there are two possibilities: Either we shall give in—and I can imagine that some members of the Israeli government will be quite happy at this dramatic pressure, because it will allow them to get through policies which otherwise would be blocked at home. Or there will be, obviously, a drastic opposi-

tion and a frontal confrontation with the country on which we totally depend.

HANAN: And 1977 will be an Israeli election year, remember.

MEIR: Yes, and I believe that forces opposing a settlement along these lines probably will win in Israel.

I will just add one thing about such a frontal confrontation. Some time ago I asked a leading American academic, "What can a small country do when it totally depends on a big power like the United States, yet doesn't agree with the policies imposed by the big power?" His answer was that this dependence also creates difficulties for the United States. If the United States were not the sole protector of Israel, and if Israel were not totally dependent, it would be easier for the Americans to maneuver. But as it is, the United States feels that if it makes a harmful move, Israel is finished because nobody else is there to help. This is the difficulty for the United States.

EITAN: I don't see any deep division between moral interests and strategic interests as far as American interests are concerned. It's very difficult, if not impossible, to differentiate between the two. What is clear to me, however, is that the Americans—the American public, the American policymakers—behave as human beings. We Israelis don't like to be preached to by foreigners about what is good for our survival. I carry the responsibility. I would like to decide for myself. I have no doubt that the American public and American policymakers are the same. They don't like to hear Israel, which depends for its very existence on the United States, preaching to them about what is good not only for American policy in the Middle East, but for its global policies as well. It is acceptable to maintain a dialogue with the Israeli public, to hear our views, our national aspirations—but certainly not to hear a sermon.

Whether there is an American strategic interest in Israel or not is something for the Americans to decide—not for us. But if it is true that the United States is interested in stabilizing this region, one thing is quite clear, and I think it has been hinted here: that an Israel composed of desperadoes is not good for the process of stabilization. All of us, including the most extreme doves, agree on one assumption. If we are defeated in a new war with the Arabs, we will be exterminated. And in order to prevent such a thing from happening, we are ready to do everything. All of us agree. All of us. I think I presented myself in very clear terms, with my non-nationalistic approach. And I share this attitude. Here there is a total unanimity in Israel. And the American public should know that an Israel composed of desperadoes would do everything in order to prevent a new extermination, a new Holocaust. If the United States wants stabilization in the Middle East, the last thing it should do is to push us into a corner and bring us to the conclusion that it's the end, and that we must do the most horrible things in order to prevent what is to us a repetition of the Second World War situation. I think it is in American interest to avoid having such a mood become widespread and prevailing in Israel.

ZVI: Israel's choices are not so simple, partly because Israel is not a free agent. We have to know our limitations, as well as our red lines. Israel is dependent up to its neck on the United States; and the United States doesn't see eye to eye with Israeli interests. My reading is that the US government has an interest in peace and stability in the Middle East, but being a superpower it also has an interest in penetrating, influencing, and establishing its presence in the Arab countries. And the United States wants to contain and, if possible, push out the USSR from the Middle East. The United States is trying to penetrate the Arab world by investments, selling arms, developing markets—and by supporting the interests of the Arabs, all of which is quite legitimate. This could mean giving territories back to the Arabs which belong to them—to Egypt, Syria, Jordan. And it could mean materializing the "legitimate interests of the Palestinians." This phrase, which Americans used a number of years ago, might imply the establishment of a Palestinian state in the West Bank and the Gaza Strip, linked to Jordan. But the United States might support even a PLO state. As a superpower, it tries to keep all options open. Yet America requires that any solution should be in the framework of an overall Arab-Israeli settlement and that it should be accepted by all the major Arab countries, Egypt, Syria, Saudi Arabia. The Americans are trying to achieve a coexistence settlement in the Middle East between the Arabs and the Israelis, under a kind of *Pax-Americana,* a coexistence guaranteed by the American umbrella. If it works, this could be a good solution for the Middle East problem, even though it would bring only coexistence and not peace.

But the picture is not so rosy. In this triangle, with America on the top and Israel and the Arabs on both sides, there is a very clear asymmetry. It's obvious that the American interest in the Arab world is much greater than its interest in Israel. I don't agree with the line of argument heard in Israel that the Arab regimes are not stable and America therefore shouldn't rely on them. It's not the case. Saudi Arabia, after King Faisal was assassinated, did not collapse as many thought it would. Syria is now a very stable state after its long and notorious instability. Egypt too.

Another asymmetry concerns Israel's dependency on the United States. Perhaps Israel should be blamed, because it has not been willing to work harder in order to lessen this dependence. But our dependence is a fact. As time goes on and the arms race accelerates, this dependence will be greater and greater. By contrast, the Arabs are not dependent on the United States, certainly not to the same extent as Israel. This is so even for the pro-West Arabs. Arab pressure can be applied on the United States. The Cairo-Riyadh axis plays the American card as long as it suits Arab interests. American leverage on the Arabs is not as great as it is on Israel. So the risk is that once the Arabs get back their territories, they will feel free to change their pro-West policies. We have to remember that there's kind of a megalomania among some Arab states—Syria, for sure, but also Egypt—this feeling of being a new superpower. One shouldn't overestimate their potential; nor, more importantly, should one undervalue the Arabs' tendency, illustrated in history, to give reality to their pride and sense of collective destiny. Despite their quarrels, ultimately there is understanding and cooperation—or "unity of action," as the Arabs call it—on the major issues of Arab nationalism.

Because American interests are not identical with what the Israelis see as their interests, the United States will not protect or guarantee the Israeli occupation territories held since 1967. These are not our territories, and we have to give them back. But I would expect America, having some leverage on Arab countries, to use its influence and to use the territories in order to set in motion the process towards peace or a settlement. Unfortunately, this hasn't been the case in the recent past. In the Sinai II agreement with Egypt, for example, Israel gave back territories and got very little in return.

America might be eager to penetrate the Arab world, and this is legitimate. But this eagerness must not endanger the vital interests of Israel, or the existence of Israel. We can swallow the Sinai interim agreement; perhaps even an agreement on

the Golan Heights. But if it comes to an independent Palestinian state, the very existence of Israel will be endangered. This case must be clearly stated and put forward in America.

PINHAS: No one will deny that the relationship between Israel and America is tense, and full of Israeli suspicions. Naturally, under those circumstances some voices in Israel express their frustration by saying that America is selling out Israel. I don't share this opinion, when it is phrased in these specific terms. This is exaggerated. Yet, we have to ask ourselves what we can expect from America.

What is, and what will be, the profile of American foreign policy in the future? Israelis are not in a position to decide for America what its foreign policy should be. But one can't ask the Israelis not to pay important attention to recent developments—for instance, in Angola or in some other parts of the world. One can't escape sober conclusions about what we can expect from the United States. One can't ask Israelis not to question how American foreign policy might influence the Mideastern scene.

No matter what will be the specific shape of any future agreement between Israel and any Arab countries, the model will be very simple: Israeli withdrawals, very vague undertakings from the Arabs, and American commitments given to Israel as a substitute for its withdrawals. In the future, the deterrent element in any agreement will not be so much Arab commitments or a changed Arab attitude towards Israel, but rather, Israel's military power, and the kind of commitment that America will give to us. What is the value of American commitments? To what extent could we rest all future hopes for the very existence of the state of Israel on America's commitments, or any other outside power's commitments?

While we have reason to have legitimate doubts about the value of these commitments, I think we should not exaggerate our readiness to accept the notion, which exists here and there, that Israel has no strategic importance to the United States. The moral element in American public opinion is vitally important in shaping American policy, but I would not like to rest all my hopes only on the moral commitment to Israel. America has not only an indirect interest in using Israel as leverage against the Arab countries, but also an interest in Israel as a power in itself. The new developments in the Mediterranean, with Spain and Portugal and Italy, the instability of Greece and Turkey—all are developments whose implications the Americans do not ignore. I think these implications underline the importance of the status of Israel for the long-range global interests of the United States. This interest is not as important from a strategic point of view as perhaps some Israelis would like to believe. Of course, we would like to believe that without Israel, America can't exist. But, nor would I go to the other extreme and say that America has no strategic interest in Israel under any foreseeable circumstances. I don't share this view, and I don't think that the mainstream of American foreign policy shares this view. However, I'm not sure that it serves Israel's interest very well if we try to emphasize this specific argument more than the Americans do themselves.

No doubt there are strong and perhaps decisive voices among American foreign-policymakers who think that America should shift positions and develop new relationships with Arab countries. One should not overlook, however, the maneuverability that Israel has in influencing such a shift. Israel could influence developments within the Middle East in a way that could shatter some of the hopes that America has about rebuilding relations with the Arab countries.

Changed American-Arab relations could create a whole new situation for Israel. The question is: What will be the shape of these renewed relationships between the Arab countries and the United States? Will they necessarily mean that America will gather influence and power within the Arab countries mainly by selling territories from which Israel has to retreat? Or will America's shift be accompanied by appropriate pressures on Arabs to pay some price and to contribute something more substantial to future agreements with Israel?

Until now, the model has been the first one—we deliver the goods, the Americans increase their influence on the Arab countries, and the Arab countries get the goods. But the goods that we get from Arab countries and from America are not good enough to rely on for the future.

This brings me to the problem of a possible future confrontation between Israel and America. I think when we use words, we have to be very careful and very cautious. I wouldn't like to use the word "confrontation." I see it this way. If America is not going to change its basic policies, if it is going to carry on with this recent model, then I think Israel will have to put the question to American public opinion and to the Congress. Instead of trying to maneuver within the limited official community, we will have to try to bring this question into the open. We will have to force a serious reassessment of American policies. I too am aware of new winds within the Congress. It's true that the power of the Jewish lobby within the United States, with all its importance, is not unlimited. Yet I think that if it is clear to public opinion and to the Congress, not that Israel objects to withdrawals or retreats from territories, but that what is asked of us is not going to lead to any serious accommodation by the Arab countries, and that Israel will have to rest its own existence on vague and insecure

American commitments, then I'm not sure that the outcome will be as unfavorable for Israel as Meir fears.

DROR: One of the main American interests today in the Middle East is similar to our interests—to solve the Israel-Arab conflict, but in a way that shall provide Israel's peace and security. The differences between us arise because some, or most, American policymakers do not define Israel's security as we do, and do not see eye to eye on how to achieve it. The debate between Israel and Washington concentrates on the question of what should be the width of the security margin which Israel has to maintain to assure its peace and security. Washington says the smallest margin, plus international guarantees, and United Nations guarantees. We answer on the basis of our experience since the Holocaust—five wars, our readings of Arab intentions, our observation of how the Arabs behave toward each other, including the way they disrespect agreements among themselves. Based on all this, we want and need a wider and larger security margin—especially because of our national Jewish responsibility after what happened during the Holocaust. In this debate the Americans have pushed us to the corner several times and have made mistakes. One example was the pressure on Israel to withdraw in 1956 from Sinai without a peace settlement and with ridiculous guarantees. The result was the war of 1967. The problem has not been the one stated here, that we are telling the Americans what is good for them. It is that they are saying what is good for us in this debate about the security margin.

GAD: Because we need strong allies to help us, I consider all the talk about being able to exist without the support of the United States as empty talk. Invoking memories of 1948 is ridiculous, because in 1948, without the help of the United States, we got the armaments needed to win that war from another major world power, the Soviet Union. We don't have the option of relying on ourselves. We cannot get along without the United States; we cannot afford a major conflict with the United States.

I agree with those who said that the basic American interest in the Middle East is not the Palestinians, but a settlement of the conflict. American interest in the Palestinian question arose inasmuch as the Palestinians have some nuisance value, by being able to disrupt any agreement that can be reached. As long as they possess this ability, they have to be reckoned with. As long as this ability becomes stronger with time—which it has until now—there is a growing tendency on the part of the American public to take the Palestinian question into consideration.

Basic American motives at work in the Middle East are a combination of idealism and national interests. This is healthy. Idealism without national interests is not going to last long, while interests without a certain measure of idealism can become very ruthless. But I see two other contradictory features of American Middle East interests. On the one hand America wants to arrive at a settlement—I don't say a solution of the conflict, but a settlement. A settlement is enough for them. They are realistic enough not to strive for a lasting peace or anything else in the realm of abstract ideas. They strive to find a settlement, and to lower the profile of the conflict in order to preserve their interests. On the other hand, they want to try to prolong as much as possible the period during which a settlement is reached, because the very process of reaching a settlement enables the United States to serve its own interests by expanding and deepening its hold in this area. Such prolongation, I might add, poses some difficulties for the United States. The more the stalemate continues, the more the feeling grows among Arabs that they are dependent on the Americans to get back the territories. This we saw very well between 1967 and 1973. But the more the American influence expands for this reason, the greater the motivations for the Soviet Union to spoil such a solution, and the stronger its ability to undermine such a solution. The danger of a war then becomes more imminent. In case of a war, America has to take sides. To support Israel again works against the basic interest of America when there is a real showdown. And America would not support Israel at great length if it is contrary to its own interests. We find ourselves in a "regrettable" situation in which American interests are defined by the proper American authorities, and not by us. Our preaching and moralizing to the Americans is not going to help anything; it will only antagonize those who are responsible for making policy.

Israel, because of its dependency on the United States, is forced to adjust its basic goals so that they will not contradict fundamentally basic American interests. It is as ridiculous for us to claim that America's interests are Israel's interests, as it is to claim that what is good for Israel is good for America.

With its basic interest of prolonging the process of finding a solution, America found itself in complete agreement for years with basic Israeli policy, as interpreted by Golda's government and then by Rabin's. But now, when the American interest is for some momentum, it's not possible for the basic Israeli policy to be for stalemate without eventually contradicting America's basic interests.

By formulating unobtainable or unrealistic goals, we are not pushing the American goals nearer to ours; we are risking that one day we will find ourselves completely alienated. But there are obtainable goals. One is to make sure that there is no American commitment to the self-determination of the Palestinians without—and emphasis on the "without"—a simultaneous recognition by the Palestinians of the state of Israel and its self-determination. There must be reciprocity. If Israel tries to avoid this thorny problem of recognizing the Palestinians, we are simply releasing the other side from its need to recognize us, and we are releasing the Americans from insisting on this reciprocity. Another obtainable goal is to get the Americans to be mediators—I'm not afraid to use this word—between Israel and the Arab world and between Israel and the Palestinians. But we are losing the opportunity of a friendly and, to a certain extent, idealistically motivated involvement of Americans as mediators between them and us.

HANAN: It is true that America has always been a reserved and cool friend of Israel's, to put it mildly. Remember, America hasn't yet recognized Jerusalem as the capital of Israel. After the defeat of America in Vietnam, what we perceive in American policy in the Middle East is only a part of the famous detente, which is based on the philosophy of buying peaceful conditions from anti-American elements in the world by sacrificing interests here and there—friends, allies—and by appeasement. "Withdrawal" has been a cornerstone of American foreign policy for the last four or five years. It might sound paradoxical, but the very fact that America, at this same time, is our sole massive supporter and supplier of arms is a very good sign that there is a basic, very deep strategic, political and geopolitical American interest in the existence of Israel.

While detente is the overall situation that led to America's becoming more and more estranged from Israel, another contributing factor has been the internal crisis in the United States of the last two decades—the Negro problem, and then the Vietnam conflict as an internal social problem in America. These produced what amounts to a guilt complex, not only in America, but in the entire Western world. It is a guilt complex towards the have-nots—in the world and inside America. Once the Palestinians are identified with the have-nots, with the poor, with the underdogs, there is an inclination to be more sympathetic towards their cause or towards their demands. And there is a great strengthening of what are called Leftist sentiments, ideologies, and slogans in the American intellectual and academic communities. This is another reason why the Palestinians cause becomes more and more important in the American political mind.

Furthermore, there is a decline in the importance of considerations and associations that derive from the Second World War. Its villains are not villains any more. Germany and Japan have become part and parcel of the international community. The victims of the Second World War do not receive as strong a sympathy among the human community as they used to. The Jewish-Israeli-Zionist claim, based on the suffering and inflictions of the Second World War, is not as powerful as it used to be. In fact, a whole series of new so-called victims is now on the human agenda; they replace those of the Second World War.

The famous domino effect of Southeastern Asia went much, much farther than many people were afraid it would. It reached Africa. It may reach Latin America. It is now coming our way, and so is the same betrayal of allies that characterized American policy in the last decade, like the betrayal of Formosa and the betrayal of South Vietnam. There are inclinations to abandon the understanding and the sympathy that were once felt for the suffering Jew.

At the same time, there are forces working in the opposite direction. The disappointments and the awakening of American public opinion could be seen over the Angola affair. There is a growing awareness by American policymakers that what is happening now is the rape of Western civilization. Soviet Russian policy and Chinese policy are more and more concentrating on helping and encouraging the movements that are driving out American and Western influence. In Africa people are now speaking about the last stage of wiping away all white colonization, all white states, all the white population.

I believe that American policy understands the great importance of Israel as a bulwark, as a frontal position in the worldwide clash that might be ahead. American policymakers do not overlook the tremendous growth of the Russian naval force or the overwhelming strength of continental Russian capabilities vis-à-vis the declining power of the NATO states. It is in the American interest that the Sixth Fleet continue to be operative and effective. And so long as the United States is in the Mediterranean Sea, so long as they are in the Indian Ocean, a frontal post like Israel is an interest, is a strategic interest. This interest requires that Israel is indeed a fighting unit, that Israel is indeed ready to suffer difficulties and to mobilize all its resources.

American policy has until now been affected by certain circles in Israel that are saying that the Palestinians are the right side, that Israel is the wrongdoer. Indeed, the Israeli government, by accepting so easily and without qualms the Security Council 242 decision only a very short time after the Six Day War, showed that it does not take itself very seriously. Before even trying any other approach, it gave in to a resolution that was almost 100 percent anti-Israeli. Israel agreed that the resolution would be adopted without mentioning her name. Thus Israel becomes a non-state, non-human. This victorious state accepted a resolution based on the assumption that her name is profane, or that she is a pariah.

Therefore it is to a very great extent Israel's fault that American policy is not as sympathetic or as visibly pro-Israeli as it should be. But because there is a deep, very concrete American interest in the existence of a strong Israel, as the global crisis approaches the importance of Israel in America's eyes is going to grow. This means that we have the option—and we should utilize it—of struggling with American policy, negotiating with America, of demanding from it a give-and-take policy.

I say one simple thing: If the United States were totally or even largely against us, then, indeed, it would be a very, very tough situation for Israel. Because America is in a position to tell us to go to hell. But this is not the case, as I have said. We have to allow ourselves to bargain with America. The question is, how one bargains with America.

A nation like Israel can show stubbornness because of our moral might and our ability to clench our teeth a little longer. It is beyond rationalism. It becomes a matter of what kind of human beings we are. And I think that Israel, in its proudest periods, showed signs of being of much sterner stuff. I'm sure that Israel with leadership and determination, can fight inside America. America being a great democracy, Israel can fight for her cause, fight for her policy, recruit the Jewish community and its leadership in America. We can influence the American administration and the Congress through the leadership in America that is more inclined toward our philosophy.

YAIR: Ours is a conflict whose dangers cannot be exaggerated, but whose solution is beyond the horizon, if visible at all. We should be neither starry-eyed, seeing the shadow of dissent within the Palestinians as a mountain of hope, nor possessed of a *götterdämmerung* feeling, especially when talking about the United States. I daresay that the American attitude toward the conflict is our central problem. We have heard here several historical interpretations of the past relations between the United States and Israel. They were interesting and important. But I'm not sure that we can draw from them significant conclusions for the present and future.

All of us are probably worried about some of the trends and currents in the world today. But to show everything in cataclysmic proportions, looks to me totally out of place. Israel and Israelis should refrain from trying to preach to the United States about what is the best policy for her and where her real interests lie. Let us be generous and allow the United States, at long last, to define her own interests.

Furthermore, I feel completely uncomfortable trying to be a strategic asset for another country, friendly as it might be. Sometimes as a result of such reasoning we can be caught in an encounter with unpleasant answers. It's counterproductive. To be someone else's tool should not be, I think, our *raison d'être* even though the purpose might be noble. We have a just case. Luckily, this is still the prevalent notion in the United States. Our task should be to strengthen this notion in every way conceivable. And our energies should be directed to stop the process of erosion. This great nation—democratic, liberal, generous, the mainstay of the free world—will support Israel, I believe, as long as we remain just. And we can prove that we are just, in spite of difficulties.

So if staying alive, if to remain in existence, is not a just case, then there is no just case at all. I regard American recognition of the PLO as a very grave matter for Israel.

We should make a great effort to convince the United States that that is so, before it becomes irrevocable. And I think that the trend toward this recognition, in some way or other, is still reversible. During our discussions here, I think it was proved beyond doubt how important and serious what the PLO says is. In the light of this, I regard America's continuing support of Israel and the simultaneous recognition of the PLO as incompatible, as mutually exclusive.

The political fences between the United States and Israel should be mended in regard to the Palestinian question. We should not abhor, in principle, the idea of a US-Palestinian dialogue at some later phase. But we have to be able to convince the United States of several basic and vital moves that should come before that. First of all, there must be a broad and truthful discussion between the United States and Israel about the practical solution of the Palestinian problem. I would take the stance of the Tactical Left and think about the unthinkable. For, as I've said, in our search for true and complete peace, we should be able to show our readiness for great concessions, even sacrifices. But— and this is a crucial "but"—only after being assured that there is no erosion, no step-by-step tactics, no attrition of the Israeli will.

It might greatly help Israel in deciding her own mind if it got clear and unambiguous answers to at least the following basic questions: 1. How would the United States regard a PLO state on the eastern bank, as this is part of the declared and repeated aim of the PLO? 2. Would a PLO state absorb all the refugees from all Arab countries within its borders, and would the refugee problem then be considered as eliminated? As everybody agrees that refugees are the root of the situation in the Middle East, settling them has to be dealt with in the first place. 3. Would the United States be able to make the PLO agree to repeal all the clauses in the Palestinian Covenant which refer to a continuation of the conflict and continued demands against Israel? 4. What commitments and guarantees would the United States be ready to make in return, and what would their future validity be?

I see the American question as crucial to Israel, more than any other one, and I think these questions are completely legitimate, and deserve answers.

NAHUM: Israel cannot take US support for granted. The United States has many grave internal problems demanding solutions. These problems contribute to a greater isolationism—not isolationism in the classical meaning, but opposition to being forced into entanglements externally, to being the policeman of the world. All this affects the preparedness to support Israel and to support Israel in concrete terms. Israel can expect financial help. But I don't believe that Israel can expect this financial help to go on at the same level for long. There is the danger that America will tire—seeing our aid requests and the conflict as endless. The Israeli public does not correctly appreciate what two billion dollars means in the United States.

There is an imperative need for Israel to coordinate policy with the United States. This does not mean that we always have to be good boys. But on the whole we should see our limitations and our dependence on the United States. There is leeway for persuasion and negotiation on a wide front between us. We have one large identity of interest: We both want to finalize this conflict. One can find this identity of interest formulated in the Brookings report, which I see as favorable to Israel. It insists—and I must stress this—that Israel's concessions will be dependent not only on arrangements, but on a change of heart on the Arab side. So it seems to me that Israel could improve its position by assuming a more moderate stance, even tactically—and for me this doesn't mean only as a cover. At the same time we must be more successful in explaining our limitations. We are not without limits in the concessions we can offer. Within the United States there is a tendency to explain that Israel's limitations exist either because of lack of national consensus or because the government is weak. There is a mistaken theory that a strong government could offer more concessions, and this is believed by some people because we don't explain the objective limitations to what we can do.

Let me also say that many Israelis are more like American patriots than the Americans themselves. I consider myself a big admirer of the United States—not only for emotional reasons, but because of its general outlook on the future of the world. Yet I do take exception to Hanan's attitude. There is something of a megalomanic streak in it—in this notion that we are going to persuade the Americans. It works both ways: the Americans, by the same token, have the right to persuade us. That Israelis consider themselves American patriots is very nice. But it too has its dangers.

The assertion that Israel is a major strategic asset for the United States recurs in Israeli arguments. I think it is very counterproductive for our relations with the United States. One gets the impression that Israelis pretend that they have a "civilizing mission" towards the United States, a mission to teach the United States what its strategic interests are. Let me remind you that many Americans would say that Israel is a strategic liability, and not a strategic asset. They would say that had Israel not existed, for example, the US ability to get bases or support in the Arab world would have been completely different.

When I said earlier that Israel was not a strategic asset to the United States, it uncovered much sensitivity here. Why?

Because such an assertion takes away an important cornerstone from the position of the Extreme Right, which derives from this argument the conclusion that Israel has leverage over the United States and that Israel can force the United States to acquiesce in the Israeli occupation—or at least to adjust itself more or less to an extreme Israeli policy.

On what does the Right base this conclusion? True, sometimes Americans come to Israel and, being guests, they express themselves courteously. They say, "Yes, you are very important to us. You are an asset." But one has to take it with more than a grain of salt. The United States is a very heterogeneous country. There are many views in the United States. Who represents the US interest? On questions of strategy, it is the people who think in strategic terms, people in the Defense Department, in the military and elsewhere who think about and develop American strategy. These people don't consider Israel a strategic asset. Strategic thinking in the United States is mostly focused on nuclear war. In a nuclear war, we don't count—at all. The United States is reducing its military presence in Europe, and they lost some of their bases in the Mediterranean. But they are not interested in Israel giving them the services they used to get in Turkey, Greece and perhaps in Italy.

HANAN: Why then do they put Israel on the top of the foreign aid list? Why are they such a massive supporter of this unimportant, lousy Israel?

NAHUM: Because there is a national interest. Not a strategic interest. The difference is that the national interest stems from general political considerations; strategic interest has to do with the conduct of war, or the prevention of it. This national interest is more on the ideological level, on the moral level, and—as we said here earlier—it is not weaker than a strategic interest. Yet many Israelis consider it pejorative to their self-image if they are not important strategically. If we are important morally, in my view that is very important.

BITAN: But we have seen how little that means to Jews. We had a terrible experience, a terrible experience.

NAHUM: It was terrible. But look at history with some kind of relativity, and see things in that light, even if the facts are unpleasant. Let me say also that a US moral commitment makes an important demand on Israel: Israel must be such a state in its internal quality of life that the United States will consider it worthwhile to support it and to make large sacrifices. If we want US support to go on, we must be worthy of it internally.

A danger in emphasizing that Israel is a strategic asset is that it is a small step toward taking sides in the internal debate about detente in the United States. Thus, some circles in the United States may get the impression that Israel thrives on the cold war. It is extremely counterproductive for us. We should not align ourselves in the United States with the more hawkish elements. Because by that, we immediately estrange another sector of the American community. We have to try to put our case above the hustle and bustle of the internal politics of the United States. It is possible. We should preferably present Israel as a gem in modern civilization, and we should strive to become one.

HANAN: Speaking of megalomania.

NAHUM: No. Israel has something unique to contribute, and Israel is a very special case. By stressing this I believe we can get much wider American consensus in support of Israel. This tendency of ours to think that only strategic assets are important in history is an unrealistic pretension to realpolitik and realism. The motivation of people and nations is mixed. What endears the United States to me is that its

motivation transcends strategic considerations and rests on moral and ideological considerations as well.

URI: What about the Jewish leadership in the United States? Might they show a more independent stand toward Israel than they did in the past, when they were much more united?

NAHUM: I can speak only in very impressionistic terms. It seems to me that there is weakness in the Jewish leadership in the United States, and that it is part of the general phenomenon of the decline of leadership. Furthermore, many among the leadership represent more the old generation than the new generation. There is a new generation coming. Before 1973 they tended to accept the authority of the leaders of Israel without question. Now their attitude is much more skeptical. They tended to accept Golda as an authority, and she impressed them, much more than they accept Rabin. This ties up with another problem—the rethinking of Zionism. It seems to me that in this rethinking, there should be some trend toward a decentralization of the Jewish people. Despite the fact that Israel is the center for the Jewish people and an open haven for any Jews who are persecuted, I don't think that for long we can dictate to the leaders of the Jews. I say with very deep sorrow that the intellectual standard of the Jewish community in the United States is higher than the intellectual standard of the Jews in Israel.

BITAN: It's very easy there.

NAHUM: Let me say it in very, very bitter terms. When the cornerstone of the Hebrew university was laid in 1925, there was great hope that the institution would be a center of Jewish genius and a radiating source. Unfortunately it did not come true. Influence is related to the intellectual standard.

As for whether the American Jewish leadership can go further to show an independent stand, from time to time they criticize Israeli policy, sometimes quite strongly. I think they are quite responsible. They know their limitations, and they are also caught, as we are, in dilemmas.

AMIR: When you speak about the erosion of the credibility of the Israeli leadership—is it because Rabin replaced Golda Meir or because the American Jewish community realized where the Golda Meir policies led the country?

NAHUM: When Golda appeared she made a terrific impact. Now, they criticize. There is less readiness to accept everything that came from Israel—as before.

DROR: She spoke fundamentals about our just case.

HANAN: Yes. And by the way, there are, among the American Jewish leadership, people who are more hawkish even than Golda. So don't give the impression that all of them are critical.

NAHUM: Among the Jews in the United States, among the older generation, there are people who are much more hawkish than the Israelis.

AMIR: And there are people who are much more liberal.

NAHUM: But the center of gravity among the old generation is hawkish. Furthermore, they are intolerant of criticism of Israel. We Israelis can rise to self-criticism. But when they hear something said against Israel, it irritates them very much. Yet when I meet the American Jews I am always filled with admiration, and that too makes me very convinced of the greatness of the Jewish people, and of Israel's part in the greatness of the Jewish people.

YAIR: You said that you are saying bitter words about the university vision not being fulfilled until now. Do you despair of its being fulfilled in the future?

NAHUM: I believe that the Arab-Israeli conflict should be used as a major motivation for excellence—to persuade people who are in a difficult situation that they have to exert themselves in all walks of life. Others might argue that a conflict, as a negative thing, cannot be mobilized as leverage for excellence. But I think that the difficult situation in which we find ourselves—war—can serve as some kind of a purgative, to cleanse Israel of many unpleasant things. Especially things that grew after 1967—the smugness that we had. And it can serve to drive us, in order to exist, to improve our quality.

I don't know if we here represent all the nuances of Israeli public opinion, but I guess most of them.

7

Point and Counterpoint

"I suggest that we be radical."

BITAN: The long conflict between the Jews and the Arabs over Eretz Israel continues to produce strain and tension in everyday life—I myself don't remember from the age of six one peaceful year—and the recurring wars have influenced some Israelis into accepting the moral evaluation of the other side. In Jewish history, this is not a new phenomenon but today it even perverts the historical perspective by denying the link between modern Zionism and the continuous, deep historical ties of the Jewish people to this land. The assertion is that the conflict, on the moral ground, is between two peoples who have an equal national right on the same homeland—as if there is symmetry between the relation of the Jewish people to Eretz Israel, which is a story three thousand years old, and a Palestinian nationality, which is maybe fifty years old.

There is a moral problem concerning the Palestinians. But it is purely humanistic: how to realize the return of the Jewish people to their homeland without doing personal injustice to the Arabs living in Palestine. It is true that the Arabs have been living in Palestine and have a right to go on living there, but I deny that there was a Palestinian nation in Palestine according to

any definition of nationality. On the other hand, Eretz Israel was an integral part of Jewish nationality.

We have heard it argued here that historical rights are not relevant, because in front of our eyes the Palestinian nation now is being created. On the pragmatic level this is decisive. But on the moral level the issue of historical rights is decisive because it establishes the overwhelming justification of the Jewish claim on Palestine and breaks the false symmetry.

It is impossible to discuss any political question without a broader historical outlook. And this is especially true in relation to the Jewish people whose consciousness of the historical dimension is essential and central—more than for any other people. Anybody who talks about Zionism as a solution just for the problem of the Jewish people in modern times, but not as a continuation of Jewish nationality that always had Eretz Israel in its center—whoever talks like that talks about Zionism without Zion.

The Palestinian national problem should not be resolved at the expense of the Jewish homeland, which includes Judea and Samaria. I will argue my position from pragmatic viewpoints—without using historical or religious justifications. But to label such justifications neo-Messianic, in an abusive sense, and to consider a movement like Gush Emunim a terrible nationalistic danger that will ruin Israel means the denial of the basis of Zionism. It means taking from Israel and Zionism its moving spirit, its inner strength. Without ideology—or mysticism, not, of course, in a derogatory sense—there would not have been an Israel. Israel can't go on without our believing in these dreams. They are something more pragmatically important than American money or even arms supplies. We have no chance if we believe only in cold calculations, numbers, and statistics.

I still haven't heard any convincing answer to the banal question: Why do we have the right to live in Lydda, Lod, Ramle, Ashdod, and Acre, and not in Jericho and Hebron? Remember, these places in which we live were not even included in the legitimate Jewish state in the partition of 1947. This is just not an ideological or moral question, but a political one. How is a Palestinian state in Shechem, Hebron, or Gaza going to solve the problem of Palestinians who came from Jaffa and Haifa? When they sit in their own state in the West Bank, they will just feel that their final goal is nearer. They will have greater temptation and a greater initiative to realize that goal. An acceptance of the basic standpoint of the PLO will mean a legitimization of the elimination of Israel—first ideologically and then practically.

Our experience shows that any concessions have hardened the other side. The Israeli government talks tough, but when has a state ever given up so much to an enemy in return for so little, as in the September, 1975, Sinai agreement? And the Israeli government uses the slogan "territories for peace," but the truth is that we have merely sold territories—our only cards for peace—for American dollars. The Tactical Left argues that we have to get the

support of world public opinion. Yet, how is it that the more we give in, the less we are supported? So maybe a real hardening on our side will bring, in the long run, other results.

The first step has to be a large settlement effort in the West Bank, with or without annexation at this stage. This position looks like madness, or craziness, according to the description some of you here gave of Israel's situation today. But it is not as crazy as it looks. Maybe the rest of you here are not so remote from a crazy position. Even those who are willing to give back the West Bank to Jordan or to the PLO are insisting that certain conditions be fulfilled. Now let's admit that there is no sign that the Arabs, and especially the Palestinians represented by the PLO, will agree to the conditions of even the most dovish of the doves in Israel.

We are sitting here and talking very soberly—and sometimes so cynically that I am a little ashamed to use certain expressions and concepts which once we were proud of. When was something achieved in history without transcending sober and merely pragmatic thinking—without any grain of what may be called "craziness?" In Jewish history, and in general history, the rationalists in many cases have been the non-rationalists, not to say the fools; the crazy ones have been the rationalists. I suggest that we be radical, and part of the power of my position is that it is radical. Some here have said that they are ready to pay a lot for the termination of the conflict. So am I. For peace I am willing to give up all the territories, and give up my historical right to them. But I am not ready to endanger the lives of my children and the existence of my country for nonsense such as the formulas suggested and explained with hair-splitting distinctions by certain dovish Israeli ministers.

Moreover, Israeli doves tell us that we shouldn't decide for the Palestinians. But the doves do exactly that—more than anyone else. It's fantastic. They are really playing games with themselves. They know what the Arabs want and what they say—and in our century we should believe that such things as these can happen. The doves want the Jordan River as a security border. From the Center to the Left, they want the Jordan River as a security border. They want the demilitarization of the West Bank. They are not going to agree to the intrusion of Soviet advisers. The doves say Gush Emunim is irrational and non-realistic. Who is now being unrealistic or irrational? Who really thinks that the Arabs are ready to agree to these conditions that would secure our existence? Or that they are not going to go to war the moment they think they can win? You really need a mystical experience to see in the words of Hammami a vision of the acceptance of Israel.

We are told that the gap between us and the Arabs is closing and that we are going to be doomed without an agreement—an agreement or death. What is the logic here? For an agreement you need two sides. If there are no moderates, we are doomed. We don't want to be doomed, ergo, there are moderates. What a non-sequitur! The true premise is that there are no moderates on the other side when it comes to basic essentials. Nobody here has refuted it. Furthermore, if we are lost without an agreement, then the Arabs, too, know it. Why should the Arabs make an agreement at all? Why should they give up anything if they can sit and wait peacefully until the bitter end—our bitter end—as long as we do not do anything in the meanwhile that makes the situation worse for them in Judea and Samaria?

Instead of following the advice of the doves, instead of waiting for a miracle like PLO recognition of Israel, maybe we should depend on other, maybe less fantastic, miracles. For instance, there may be larger changes in the world. New energy sources would be one. The Western world may get fed up one day, not with Israel, but

with Arab blackmail and Palestinian terror. There may come a time, maybe not too far off, when public opinion will come back to us and will not ask us to be good children and give back the territories.

Hopes like these are more rational and less ridiculous than gambling our future on Hammami's vague hints. We should put our hope in the resources of the Jewish people in Israel and in the Diaspora. Those resources are not exhausted. Against the pessimism we have heard here, there are many thousands who are optimists—who may be considered a little "crazy," but they are optimists. They are ready to accept this challenge. I have no doubt that if my position had been followed in 1967, there would have been a great *aliyah* of young people from the Western countries, and I hope that we haven't lost this opportunity entirely. Great vision and daring plans can actualize the spirit of a people—forgive me for the dirty words—the spirit of a people. And the spirit of a people can do things which seem quite impossible.

In 1967 we should have put clearly to the Arabs the alternatives—giving back all the territories for full peace, or their annexation. It wasn't done because the Right was against the first alternative, and the Left against the second. I was for the first alternative. I can prove it. I signed a petition.

EITAN: Really?

BITAN: Yes. But the first alternative was taken from us by the Arabs. Only the second one remains. Everything in between is the worst of two worlds. Annexation right away or not right away—that depends partly on tactical considerations.

Practically my position means, first of all, the establishment, in any way it is going to be fulfilled, of a Palestinian state in the east of Jordan. We have heard all the arguments for a small Palestinian state—that it would not attack Israel because it would have its own troubles and its own government, that it would have its own prestige and would be afraid to lose what it had. But I don't see why these arguments don't apply equally to a much bigger Palestinian state in the East Bank of Jordan. I don't know if the annexation of Judea and Samaria would have caused or will cause terrorism in these areas, worse than it is now. Nobody knows. Maybe the opposite will be true—on the conditions that the Arabs are going to take us seriously on this matter.

The Palestinians living in Judea and Samaria and the Gaza Strip who wished to stay in Israel would get, they would have to get, full citizenship. There can't be any argument against this from anyone who still wants an Israel in the 1967 borders, from anyone ready to rule over the Palestinians against their will in Nazareth or in Galilee. And most Israelis are ready to rule 75,000 Palestinians in Jerusalem. We took a risk by annexing territories with a great majority of Arabs in 1948, when we established Israel with 600,000 Jews, and when we annexed Nazareth. We now should take this risk in annexing Nablus. Of course there is a difference in numbers. But we don't have any choice but to take this risk again. Comparing the strength of Israel in 1948, and today, I am not sure that the chances today are worse than they were then.

This position depends wholly on faith in the resources of the Jewish people. If we have no reason to believe in these resources, then I admit that we are doomed anyhow. Then no agreement will help us, because we will remain three million against one hundred million. Some say, and we have heard it here, that there is no chance of a Jewish majority in Eretz Israel. Well, strange things happen in Jewish history. Whoever would have said ten years ago that after a few years there would be in Israel more than one hundred thousand Jews from Russia? The pessimists don't know either what's going to happen tomorrow in Russia, in South America, in

South Africa, and even in the United States itself. I do not mean just bad things, but certain ideological, cultural developments.

Of course, it will be a long time before peace is established. But national movements of liberation often take a long time. And Zionism is a movement of liberation for the Jewish people. The Jewish people have showed until now very strong vitality and very great perseverance. Maybe it will show it during this long time, up to the moment of peace.

The weakness in my position is very deep, very crucial. It is not what you may think—not that this position means war. I think there is going to be war anyway, unless there is a total collapse of the Israeli side—giving in just to bring the last war in twenty years or fifty years, instead of in three or four years. The majority of Israelis are going to come to a point where they will not be able to accept the conditions of the Arabs. Then we are going to have war anyway. So this is not the point. I don't think that if we now annexed the territories, we would have a war.

The weak point in this position is that there's no agreement on it in Israel. This is a position which can succeed. It would have succeeded even as a tactical position. We would have had real peace now, without the territories, but peace, if this position had been adopted in 1967. It could have succeeded on one condition: that we would have been fully determined to carry it out. To succeed now would involve a very tough lowering of the standard of living to give us a minimal freedom from dependence on the United States. If I may say so, I think it would be a blessing to Israel if we didn't have to get money from the United States under the circumstances I am talking about.

This position has no chance now. We are a democracy. There is no agreement on it, and it can not be carried out half-heartedly. This was the whole difference between France and England in 1940. The current Israeli government acts in the opposite direction from what I suggest, leading us to a war in the worst conditions. Everything being done now is eroding national morale to the lowest level. But if we do not win this war—and I can't even imagine the tens of thousands of casualties which Yuval Ne'eman mentioned in his article*—then it's the end. But if we win, then maybe we will learn, at last, from experience and do the next time what we should do now.

NAHUM: Could you spell out the conditions that you consider "peace"—the conditions under which you are ready to give up the territories?

BITAN: The conditions are a risk, but one I am willing to take. The first step is direct negotiation. The Arabs must be willing to sit down and talk about getting back their territories for peace. Then, a peace agreement which is going to be called a peace agreement—I insist upon that.

ZVI: Recognition? Is that what you mean?

BITAN: I mean a peace treaty. It would be called peace, and it would be negotiated directly. Every war came out of peace, I know. But I am willing to take an historical risk.

HANAN: What about Jerusalem?

BITAN: Jerusalem is included. I'm willing, if there's real peace. I am willing. There's no point in not including Jerusalem. I'm willing to give up half of Jerusalem because human life for me is vital.

AMIR: What is your concept of a compromise? Is it necessarily between right and wrong? Or do you allow for the possibility of a compromise between two rights, in which each side gives up something of what he believes is his? If it is the latter, then why is giving up Jericho or Hebron in any way a renunciation of your right to Tel Aviv?

BITAN: I think there are cases where a compromise is not only pragmatic, but also between two rights. But in this case we don't have two rights—speaking purely from the moral point of view. I mean national rights. The Palestinian nationality is an artifical creation which doesn't have a national right on this land. I can't accept any other conclusion. The only problem I can see here is a pragmatic one—and not an ideological one.

MEIR: I'm almost of the same opinion as you—you'd be astonished—because of your concept of peace. Do you think that most of Gush Emunim—not some, but most—would be ready, for real peace, to give back the territories, including East Jerusalem?

BITAN: It's an important question. The answer is "no."

HANAN: Does peace include, in your mind, the right of the Jews to settle in all of the land of Israel, in all of Eretz Israel?

BITAN: Under the same conditions that Frenchmen are allowed to settle in Belgium—there has to be someting like that, yes.

PINHAS: Under the sovereignty of another state?

BITAN: Of course.

HANAN: Would you take the PLO leadership as it is today, minus some of their principles, as a party to such a peace?

*A former president of Tel Aviv University and ex-advisor to the defense minister, Ne'eman wrote a much-publicized article—after resigning from the ministry because of his opposition to the Sinai II agreement—in which he projected losses of 50,000 to 100,000 if Israel had to fight a war from the 1967 boundaries. His article is reprinted in *The Jerusalem Post* of February 11, 1976.

BITAN: No doubt. I have nothing against talking with murderers—if they want to talk about peace with me. I am not for the slogan "we will not talk to murderers."

"It's not so much the physical existence of Israel that worries me, but the whole sense of our enterprise."

MEIR: Bitan started with some moral postulates. Allow me also to refer to the moral dimension of this problem.

First, the rights of Zionism. Certainly there is a historical link to Eretz Israel; Bitan and I agree on that. It doesn't mean, necessarily, that this long historical link leads, or has led, to any practical implementation. The link was there the moment Zionism started, but for eighteen hundred years it didn't really lead to practical settlement in Eretz Israel, as you know, except for some short-lived Messianic movements.

For me, Zionism is the expression of the right to rebel—the fundamental right of an individual or a group, tortured or exploited beyond a certain point. Everyone has this right. This was our right. This is the argument that can be understood by everybody, because it is a general argument, not a particular one. Historically, Eretz Israel has had a special meaning for us; I know that very well. But our immediate right stems from what we had to suffer in Europe during modern times. Rebellion against suffering is an inalienable right. But you have to ask yourself: doesn't my fundamental right hurt the rights of other people? This, in a sense, is the basic moral dilemma of Zionism. Our right of rebellion, which led us to Eretz Israel because of historical links with this country, clashed with the rights of other people living in Eretz Israel. There is an answer to our dilemma, and it is evident to any person with any sense of morality: You have to admit your right, and establish it, but you have to limit it as much as possible—the criterion being your own existence obviously—in order to lessen the injustice to other people. If you have to do something out of sheer necessity which entails injustice for somebody else, then the moral corollary is that you must limit that injustice as much as you can. This explains both our right and, in a sense, our duty toward the people who lived in Eretz Israel—the Palestinians.

And there is even more to it. How do we see Zionism in the context of Judaism? In my view, the Palestinian question really makes no sense if we do not speak on that level. I see in Zionism a continuity. Zionism is a continuation of something that I call Judaism. I know, as does everybody here, that in Judaism there were always two opposite tendencies. One is particularistic, with a closed system of values. The other has always tended toward universalism. Throughout Jewish history there has been a seesaw. Never mind whether the prophets were on this side or that. For me the prophets were on both sides. But I take the universalistic side.

For me Zionism makes sense if it links up with the universalistic tradition. It doesn't make any sense if it brings us to a total closure, to a renewed particularism, a new chauvinism. It makes sense only if it is a new stage in the development of Judaism as a spiritual process. This brings me back to the Palestinians, the people we have wronged. They have a moral right that we must admit according to our own principles—the principles which give meaning to what we are doing in Eretz Israel, within the context of the Jewish ethical tradition, our tradition of universal justice.

Let me now turn to political trends and options. We agree here that this conflict may go on for a long time. As long as the conflict goes on, the gap in power between the Arabs and ourselves is narrowing and not widening. We have some advantage over them, but we may be losing this advantage.

For reasons that all of us know, we are more and more isolated on the international scene—the Third World, the Arab world obviously, Europe, the Communist world. And there may be an erosion in the American position too. We may find ourselves rather alone if the present trend continues.

And then there is a manifest deterioration of the situation in Israel itself. I won't go into the details, but each person sitting here knows that the situation in Israel is deteriorating right now.

We have to accept that if we don't succeed in solving the Palestinian problem, there will be no solution to the conflict. This means that all the trends which I have just mentioned will maintain themselves—the gap will close more and more, we shall be more isolated, there may be a change in the US position, and our internal situation may continue to deteriorate.

What is the implication in my mind? It is not, as some of you may have understood, that there will be some catastrophe—some crumbling of the state. This could happen, but I don't believe so. What worries me is something more subtle. It is that the trends will produce a growing despair among the people living in Israel, a growing feeling of loneliness, abandonment, *ein breira*, in the worst sense of the term. Because of continued deterioration of social and economic life, and also because of the hopeless kind of situation outside, there will be the growth of a narrow, militant, destructive nationalism which will make a tragic irony of our whole Zionist enterprise. Instead of reaching a new stage in Jewish life, in which we open somehow the ghetto to get to normalcy with a new spiritual dimension, we shall suddenly find ourselves closed in by enemies and getting back into what is, in my mind, our worst

tradition: the closed, obstinate, and actually sometimes suicidal kind of attitude—"all the world is against us." And the worst that is in us could come to the surface. There is an attitude like that. It's not Masada. Morally, it's much worse than that. That is what really worries me.

What are the options? The whole idea which I tried to convey—I will call it the 5 percent policy—is this: If there is a 5 percent chance, that is, a very minimal chance, to escape this type of evolution, then we have to put all our cards on that 5 percent until we are convinced that it won't work. My feeling is that we have never tried, up until this very moment. We have always said, "It won't work, so why should we try?"

I totally agree with Bitan that we should have made a determined and total attempt in 1967. We didn't. I say let's do it now. For total peace I—like him—am willing to give back all the territories, so he and I actually agree on the level of principle, although perhaps not on the tactics and approach. We may fail in such a total attempt now. But we may have a 5 percent chance, and we should try. I have one proviso, and I want my position to be absolutely clear. We must draw, before we start, a very clear red line: the line beyond which we will not go because otherwise we would totally jeopardize our security. We are dealing with an extremely dangerous situation, and everybody here knows it. So we are not going one inch beyond the red line, but within that line we should make a total attempt.

Concerning the Palestinian question, what does a total attempt mean? It means to adopt the Yariv formula: If the Palestinians, who are the core of the conflict, are ready to discuss with us, to recognize the state of Israel—which means obviously canceling the clauses of their covenant excluding the sovereignty of Israel, and so on—then we are ready to discuss with them, to divide the country, and to have a Palestinian state. This implies, on our part, a refusal of annexation; it implies the 1967 borders plus a few strategic changes.

Let us assume that they say "yes." Why assume this when there is so much evidence that they will say "no"? Because there are some new trends among them—as we detect from the arguments against these trends by the Rejection Front. So let's see if the trends can develop into something. Moreover, our unilateral declaration may start something in the Palestinian camp. Maybe those like Souss and Hammami and other people we never heard about—will suddenly come forward in London, Paris, Beirut or wherever, and say, "OK, finally Rabin has really said something; so we are ready to talk." There is little chance for that, I know. But at least let us be absolutely sure of that before we close all the doors, before we take the very, very risky road of no settlement at all.

If they say "yes," how can we know that there is not a "Tactical Left" on the Palestinian side, that we will not get back to the 1967 borders only to have the whole story start again? The only way is to follow two very simple principles: to be very clear at the outset about what our final aims are, and to ask for a very clear definition of what their final aims are. This means having, at the intitial stage, a precise declaration of intentions. We have never asked the Arabs—I mean at the negotiating table—what exactly they mean by peace. We have never gone into details. And we have never said what we are ready to give for ultimate peace. We always equivocated about it. Then you have to discuss implementation step-by-step, going slowly from the first position to the final position, over the years. You can do this with the Palestinians as well as with the Egyptians, although you cannot do it on a territorial basis because you obviously cannot divide Judea and Samaria into small slices. But you can do it functionally. You can first give the areas local autonomy under UN supervision or whatever. You can keep police or other forces. You can keep some strongholds, and then leave them after a few

years. You can establish economic links. You can see over two, three, four, five years whether the process is towards normalization, or whether they renew hostile propaganda activities, sabotage, and so forth. The moment you see that the process is the reversal of what you want, you stop it. All the stages are negotiable before you start implementation, and the implementation has to be a rather lengthy, step-by-step process.

If they say "no," we have to fall back on the Jordanian position—although I don't believe in its logic, for the same reason as was pointed out here. We will give back to Jordan whatever we give back. Then, for internal or external reasons, the Jordanians will turn it over to the Palestinians, you will have exactly the same dangers that you had with the worst Palestinian situation, without any kind of negotiations.

The truth is that if they say "no," our options are very poor. The "best" then remains the Jordanian solution. If that doesn't work, then we have the *status quo*, but without annexation. Here it is not only the moral principle, but the demographic argument which is really very strong. You say, Bitan, that a miracle might happen, that suddenly developments may occur in America. But either you are calling for anti-Semitism in the Western world, or you really expect demographic changes that probably won't come about; and then, if they do not, you will have a binational state in Israel before you can say Jack Robinson. The danger of annexation with equal rights for the Arabs (because without equal rights for them it's like Rhodesia or South Africa, and then where is Zionism?) is much greater than the danger of keeping the *status quo* without annexation.

What do I believe will happen? I don't believe the option I suggest will be chosen. Not that I don't wish it. I really wish that we could go in this direction. I don't believe that the Israeli government will do it. Why? Because the 5 percent policy, as I call it, would need a government ready to fight a very strong group of opponents in Israel. I do not believe that any conceivable government—speaking realistically now—is ready to take such a step after our leadership has been so extreme in pointing to the grave dangers of a third-state solution. Yariv had to swallow his formula. Allon says half-hearted words but really doesn't go beyond that. The prime minister and others have been so strongly opposed to anything going in that direction, they have made such an effort to show the danger of a third state, and most of the public is so convinced about it, that when I look at it coolly I really don't believe that anybody will dare to take that step. But let's assume that some government dares. If so, there will have to be elections. The trouble is that, whatever way you look at it, elections will bring a 50-50 division of the country, or a 45-55 division. With such a division you cannot implement such a radical solution. You cannot start any negotiations with Palestinians against 45 percent opposition. This is simply impossible. It's a matter of practical politics. You would have civil strife, if not civil war in Israel.

What do I believe about the Jordanian solution? I don't believe it will succeed either. Not because the Jordanians will not be willing to enter into an agreement. But because when we come to the problem of Jerusalem we shall face exactly the same thing I said just before about the Palestinians. On Jerusalem we shall not be able, I think, to compromise because of the state of public opinion, and the position of the government. And I don't think the Jordanians would be ready for any peace without getting back their part of Jerusalem.

So there are actually two possible courses. The one I hope for—and we have heard this line argued here—is that somehow by unilateral declarations and moving here and moving there we'll manage to lower the level of conflict. Maybe this can happen. I believe this is perhaps the only thing we can now count on as reasonable.

You understand that I wish for much more. The worst scenario is that we shall enter more and more into the siege situation with all the implications I mentioned. And then it's not so much the physical existence of Israel that worries me, but the whole sense of our enterprise.

When I am in a more optimistic mood I think that, after all, in this situation there is something which is not totally negative. And I would put it this way. The one argument against Zionism—on a level which we did not discuss here—has been that it has stifled something in the Jewish situation which flourished in the Diaspora in the 19th and 20th centuries and which was the real grandeur of Judaism. It was a kind of disquiet, which brought forth a special sensitivity. It cost us a lot in terms of suffering. But certainly it gave a unique aspect to some of our achievements in the Western Diaspora. We find ourselves with a paradox, a real paradox. Zionism has tried to normalize Jewish life. It is not succeeding. My guess is that it will not succeed because of what I foresee. So we shall face a new anomalous situation. Instead of the individual anomaly of the Jew in the Diaspora, we shall face a collective anomaly. I sometimes think that this collective anomaly may recreate some of the "Diaspora characteristics" that we were losing through the process of normalization when the Zionist enterprise started. And then I would use, in my optimistic mood, the following formula: Try to seek normalization as if there were no anomaly, but try to live within the anomalous situation as if the normalization were impossible. That is the optimistic mood.

In my pessimistic mood, an image often plagues me; it was used by a Jewish philosopher in the 1930s. He spoke of the angel of history. He said that the angel of history is an angel who goes backwards into the future. He looks toward the past, and he is pushed by a big wind backwards into the future. And I'm afraid sometimes in my pessimistic mood that in Israel, if we

Dialogue Fragments

"The Palestinian national problem should not be resolved at the expense of the Jewish homeland, which includes Judea and Samaria."

"The first step . . . has to be a large settlement effort in the West Bank, with or without annexation at this stage."

" . . . my position means . . . the establishment, in any way it is going to be fulfilled, of a Palestinian state in the east of Jordan."

—*Bitan*

"For me Zionism makes sense only if it links up with the universalistic tradition. It doesn't make any sense if it brings us to a total closure, to a renewed particularism, a new chauvinism."

" . . . the Palestinians, the people we have wronged . . . have a moral right that we must admit according to our own principles—the principles which give meaning to what we are doing in Eretz Israel, within the context of the Jewish ethical tradition, our tradition of universal justice."

" . . . if we don't succeed in solving the Palestinian problem, there will be no solution to the conflict."

—*Meir*

"They are terrorists, it is true. But I accept the approach that sees the PLO mainly as a political body."

"Any possibility might be dangerous for us. The most dangerous is annexation or continuation of the present situation."

" . . . settling in the West Bank is complicating the problem to an unnecessary extent—especially when settlement is only symbolic, as it is now, when only a very few Jews are residing within the West Bank. All these settlements are an obstacle to any chance of understanding that could be reached either now or in the future."

—*Uri*

cannot take the really courageous decisions, we shall be like the angel of history—with our faces turned toward the past, but with the wind really pushing us backwards into the future, without our knowing or seeing where we are going.

NAHUM: What is your red line? And what if the Palestinians say that their purpose is a democratic state?

MEIR: If they say a democratic state, it's "no." Obviously. I really cannot give you my red line. We have to sit down, and to decide once and for all, taking various scenarios, obviously, into account. For a period of ten, fifteen, or twenty years, and according to new weapons developments and so on, what are the minimum territorial necessities for our existence? I don't know today if Sharm el-Sheikh is essential. I really don't know. And I think nobody really ever thought it through to the end. I don't know if Qalqilya is really essential. Some here said the Jordan River must be the security border. I am not ready to believe this. However, it has become a kind of accepted idea in Israel. Has anybody really thought it through? Aren't we saying things in a very general way? On a red line you fight and die. That's what I want to say. In order to fight and die you have to be absolutely sure that you are not fighting and dying beyond the red line. The concept of the red line is important. Not being a specialist, I cannot tell you exactly what is the necessary red line. It's more concept than content. Content is up to the military people and specialists.

NAHUM: Does that mean you assume, as a possibility, that Sharm el-Sheikh is within the red line?

MEIR: I assume it, but I would like specialists to tell me that it is really so.

HANAN: My first question is about the price. I assume that what you mean is that we will demand a declaration of peace, an intention for peace.

MEIR: Absolutely.

HANAN: We know from what has taken place that there is a reduction in the price we are demanding.

MEIR: Peace. Not non-belligerency. Otherwise it's a completely different answer.

HANAN: OK. This is why you become even more like Bitan. My second question: you drew a gloomy and dark picture of what is going to happen to us if we do not gamble on this 5 percent chance. Right?

MEIR: You understand that my point is more the internal developments than the physical.

HANAN: Yes. You say we are slowly developing toward our doomsday. Now, after all, 5 percent is a little less than 95 percent. So there is a very great chance that the gamble will fail, and we will return to this same gloomy perspective.

MEIR: Yes. But with one difference.

ZVI: Public opinion.

MEIR: No. I really thought this was quite clear. It makes all the difference in the world if you know that you have absolutely no choice in something. Let me be more concrete. Take the kids now in their last year of high school and their first year in the army. Among them I see this deterioration of principles. It is coming out of sheer confusion and despair—not knowing where they are going, what they are doing. But the moment you know you have really done everything, the process which I fear—which may happen anyhow—may be reversed. If my son asks me: "Did we really do everything to try to make peace with the Arabs?" Or, when he goes to the army, if he says: "I have to stand in Jenin and hit some of the school children over the head there—did we do everything to avoid this?" If I tell him, we really did everything we could for peace, but they didn't want it, then he will know that he has to hit them over the head, that it is necessary. It will not cause the moral disintegration—I hope—that we see now. Because then there will be no choice. But if he knows that we didn't do everything to avoid it—because Israel likes to equivocate or because of party politics—then the process may be one of doubt, despair, and cynicism. So the 5 percent is more than arithmetic.

ZVI: You presented an argument for the Yariv formula. But people outside the government have discussed it with some Palestinians, and still the most moderate of them say, "a democratic secular state."

MEIR: I am aware of this. But Yariv is not Rabin. It makes a great difference if the prime minister says: "This is, now, the government of Israel's position"—this means something more than a junior minister saying something.

ZVI: Before 1967 we didn't have the West Bank and the Gaza Strip; we nevertheless had Arab hostility and Palestinian intentions as expressed in 1964 in the Palestinian Covenant. What has changed? Why now would they be more ready?

MEIR: We know the question—it is the usual question—and we know the answer. History changes. It is 1976. So let's now try it in 1976. If the answer is going to be "no," we will find out.

BITAN: If the Arabs will not accept the Yariv formula—and we know that they actually will not—then why not Israeli set-

tlement in the West Bank—without annexation?

MEIR: I don't want it.

BITAN: Why not?

MEIR: I won't even discuss that. Some people want it, so they will have to fight for it within the democratic process in Israel. I'm against it.

BITAN: But why are you?

MEIR: I will tell you. Because as a kind of stupid, actually basically optimistic Jew, I think that maybe in the future the situation might improve. And I know that every settlement creates one more impossibility. Settlement for me is not an important thing. For you it's vital. I can settle in the Negev if I want to settle. Do you understand me?

BITAN: No. That's a demagogic answer.

MEIR: The question is demagogic.

NAHUM: Why don't you describe yourself as Tactical Left?

MEIR: I would describe myself on the Left, not on the Tactical Left. Because the Tactical Left does not believe in the 5 percent. It believes there is no chance at all. I say 5 percent. But the Tactical Left is convinced there is nothing.

NAHUM: Then the difference is the 5 percent?

MEIR: Yes, but, you know, that is the whole difference.

"Ultimately, we have to divide this country."

URI: The Palestinian problem, in my opinion, is the most important issue within the Arab-Israeli conflict. The present official policy of Israel towards this problem is very clear: the only desirable solution for Israel is the Jordanian solution; Israel will nego-

tiate only with Jordan about the future of the West Bank and maybe even the Gaza Strip; Israel disregards officially the PLO as a political body of the Palestinians; the PLO is a terrorist organization and is dealt with only as such. The proposals heard in

Israel—that we state our readiness to negotiate with any Palestinian faction that is ready to recognize Israel—are not accepted by the government. In trying to be the common denominator for almost every important political faction in Israel, my government, to my great sorrow, did not initiate any steps to solve this problem, even within the boundaries of Israel.

An important issue is the Israeli settlements in the territories, and in particular the West Bank. One should be honest about the future. I do not see any chances in the foreseeable future to start solving the Palestinian problem or the Arab-Israeli conflict. I am very skeptical. But in my opinion, settling in the West Bank is complicating the problem to an unnecessary extent—especially when settlement is only symbolic, as it is now when only a very few Jews are residing in the West Bank. All these settlements are an obstacle to any chance of understanding that could be reached either now or in the future.

We, the Zionist Jews who came to Israel after a long exile, have the same right to be in Nablus as to be in Tel Aviv—or to be in Gaza as we are in Ashdod. But we do not have to stretch this right to its maximum length. And if, by not stretching it, we can help to start solving the Palestinian issue, it is better to do so. In short, I think that keeping the West Bank and Gaza as a bargaining card is much better than establishing symbolic settlements that are used like a red cloth in front of a bull.

We cannot decide for the Palestinians what is good for them. We can only state what is good for us. Annexing the territories, either gradually or quickly, will no doubt cause more war, more bloodshed, without finding any proper solution to this problem. The in-between way of the present Israeli government would also, in my opinion, lead us to the same result. It would not please anybody, and would serve only a domestic need. We have to leave to the Palestinians themselves the opportunity to decide what is their favored solution. The initiative taken by the minister of defense, Shimon Peres, to form in some way or another a self-governing body for the territories' inhabitants—which was refused almost totally by most of the people to whom he addressed it—was but an illusion.

Some among us think that the Jordanian solution is favorable. King Hussein is a stable and quite moderate element in the Middle East, most of his subordinates are Palestinians, and they are participating in the governing process without creating a serious opposition to the ruler. On the other hand, the PLO is recognized by the world and accepted among Palestinians in the territories, Lebanon and elsewhere. There could be a situation in which the PLO might take over Jordan with the assistance or help of some Arab countries. How would we negotiate with them then— after we preferred King Hussein to them? They are terrorists, it is true. But I accept the approach that sees the PLO mainly as a political body.

I would adopt the Yariv suggestion, and would be ready to come to terms with any Palestinian faction that is ready to recognize Israel—without totally shutting off the Jordanian alternative. For the short term, the Hashemite solution is my preference. This is because in the short run the PLO is really very extreme. We see that only a few of the PLO—Souss and others outside, and also some people in the territories—are really calling for a 1967 border solution.

For the long term, I think there should be a Palestinian entity—be it led by the PLO, or a combined PLO-territories leadership, or whatever. But it should be, I feel, a national Palestinian entity that would have support from a reasonable majority of the Palestinians in the Arab countries, and in the territories. However, I believe that an independent Palestinian country in the West Bank, Gaza Strip, and even some parts of East Jerusalem, without an outlet to the sea, and without ties to the East Bank, could not survive for a long time.

Any possibility might be dangerous for us. The most dangerous is annexation or continuation of the present situation. Ultimately, we have to divide this country. And we have to let the Palestinians fulfill their rights either within a Hashemite country as a confederation or otherwise, or in a Palestinian country, PLO or otherwise. I think the preferable solution might be a PLO country in the East and West Banks, with Amman or East Jerusalem as a capital. The Hashemites have proved themselves masters in the art of survival, but they cannot last forever. The solution must be on both East and West Banks, because it is one country. I say in all honesty, however, that in the near future I do not see a good chance for either solution.

BITAN: What are the security conditions which you would demand from Jordan or from the Palestinian state?

URI: I am for a 1967 border solution, and I think that we should demilitarize the West Bank. I mean demilitarization of the West Bank with King Hussein or with the Palestinian solution.

BITAN: Do you think they would agree?

URI: Not now. But we have to leave a door open for the future.

PINHAS: Do you think that they would agree in the future? Can you believe that, in any foreseeable future, any of the masters of the territories—either King Hussein or the Palestinians—would let you tell them whether or not they would ever be able to put munitions or military forces into the territories? Second, would it ever be possible for any of us, under any circumstances, to detect whether they violated these rules? Third, would it be a *casus belli* for you? Would you state beforehand that if they did it, that would be a good reason for you immediately to invade the territories and take over again?

URI: I admit that this is my weakest point. But, yes, after the demilitarization of the West Bank, if they violated it, I would regard it as *casus belli*.

"We have to choose the lesser evil, and it is the Jordanian option."

EITAN: Unlike Bitan I believe that in Palestine, in Eretz Israel, two national movements clash, one Jewish-Zionist, the second Arab or Palestinian-Arab. Both of them have their right, even though it is very hard to measure the amount of right. I'm sure that during Jewish history there was a connection with Palestine—through the Messianic link. But from an objective point of view you see that Palestine has been an overwhelmingly Muslim area—all through its history from the Arab occupation, including the Crusader period. There were very few Jews—almost none from the 15th to the 18th centuries. Only with the renewal of the Jewish community in Jerusalem at the beginning of the 19th century did the number of Jews really begin to increase. There have been Jews ever since the 16th century in Safed, I know, but very few. The connection was mainly spiritual and Messianic. On the other hand, most of the Jews living outside hoped Messianically to return one day. But many gradually assimilated—willingly assimilated—certainly in the 19th century. This has been the main trend in Jewish history: the process of gradual assimilation. While all other trends had moral, religious, and ideological significance, the practical reality is that more Jews have assimilated than have preserved their Jewish identity.

BITAN: That's not true.

EITAN: It's true—at times under pressure, no doubt. On the other hand, there was in Palestine a continuation of a Muslim, Arabic-speaking community. In the 20th century all Arabs reached the initial stage of regaining a distinct national identity—whether it's Palestinian or Pan-Arab, it doesn't matter. No, it doesn't matter. They are going through a process of national crystallization. They have been living continuously in territory which they rightfully regard as their own. They are encouraged by what is going on all over the world, where populations no doubt less developed in this respect have gained independence according to the same principle—without searching too far for historical connections with a specific territory. Everyone can see it in the new African states.

There are two national movements that exist by right in Eretz Israel or Palestine. And there is no chance that a demographic change will drastically alter the face of Palestine to make the Arab side negligible. Even more, I certainly don't share the expectations that something terrible might happen to Diaspora Jews in order that the Zionist dream will materialize.

BITAN: I didn't say that. I said cultural and ideological developments in US Jewry. For South America, however, I do think that terrible things could happen.

EITAN: OK. My expectation is that Jews won't suffer anti-Semitic persecution. They will live peacefully wherever they live. And they will decide whether they want to assimilate or keep their Jewish identity, in peace as accepted citizens in liberal societies. That's my vision. Whereas what you really expect is something else, at least for the South American Jews. I apologize, but I must say it—you share the basic assumptions of the anti-Semites. That's what drove me away from Zionism. Because Zionism is based on the assumption that there would always be anti-Semitism, that anti-Semitism is immanent in human nature, and that one sort of people must always hate another sort of people.

DROR: Only that assumption?

EITAN: That was the main thing—the non-humanistic basic premise of Zionism. So I don't think that there will be a demographic revolution in Palestine. I don't expect terrible things to happen again in order to bring more Jews to Palestine.

BITAN: Expecting it doesn't mean I wish it to be.

EITAN: No. Certainly you don't wish it. But, more than that, my conclusion is not only that we shouldn't expect or foresee it. We have to do whatever we can in order that it wouldn't happen again—by lessening the force of mutual national hostilities. From this basic assumption, I draw my concrete conclusions.

Also, you cannot draw a parallel between now and what we did in 1948. In 1948, it was clear that the Jewish community in Palestine would immediately grow very fast. There were, first of all, at least 300,000 displaced people in camps in Germany, Austria and other places in Europe, most of whom were waiting to emigrate—not all of them, mind you, but most of them. The majority fulfilled their aspirations to come to Israel, to Palestine. So the 600,000 Jews already there in 1948 were not really the starting point; rather it was about a million. That's why there was no demographic problem in the annexation of the Western Galilee, which had not been allotted to us in the partition. And why there was no problem in accepting the Little Triangle according to the armistice agreement with the Hashemite kingdom. It was a completely different situation that cannot be repeated today. If we annex today—and this is an important factor for me—we shall inevitably have a situation like Rhodesia or South Africa—maybe in a less rigid form. The ugly facets of apartheid will not be repeated by us. The human separation—you know, "only for Arabs, only for Jews"—I have no doubt that we will not reach this stage. But politically speaking, it will happen. It is very similar to what is going on in Rhodesia. The Ian Smith regime also didn't copy the ugly facets of South African apartheid. The Blacks are only denied political rights. They don't go to Parliament, except some of the tribal chiefs who get appointed. Anyway, for us it would be political apartheid. But I still wouldn't like to live in such a state, where there would be a 60 percent majority with full political rights in a marvelous democracy, while the 40-45 percent would be denied political rights.

BITAN: Nobody said they would.

EITAN: If tomorrow the territories were annexed, it would happen. Don't tell me otherwise. I know the trick: We would say that we wouldn't enforce nationality on them; we instead would wait until they came and applied for it. But the result would be that they wouldn't apply for nationality from us, because doing so would require from them an implicit recognition of the annexation. We would be satisfied. We would have annexed the territories without conferring on the Palestinians the right of nationality. That would be it. Everyone would say—"Of course, we wouldn't force Israeli nationality on them. If they want to, they can come to us, if not, they don't have to." Yet everyone would know they wouldn't come—as they didn't come in Jerusalem.

How to get out? It seems to me that the most practical way is to declare that we are ready to give everything back for peace and to negotiate about the West Bank with the Hashemites. I want to stress one argument against a separate Palestinian state in the West Bank and Gaza: the ideological component of it. This separate state would be a Zionist state—they would do the same as we do. They would establish a mechanism to keep the Palestinian identity of the refugees and other Palestinians all over the world, to get money, to encourage them to emigrate, and to have solidarity.

PINHAS: The comparison is appalling.

EITAN: The notion of Palestinian Zionism was invented by them. And this similarity, I think, is the best recipe for a prolongation of the conflict. The Jordanian state, on the other hand, wouldn't like this idea, for it is incompatible with Jordanian views about their state and how it should develop. Therefore a Jordanian state would reduce tension. And the chances for prolongation of the conflict would be much less, even diminishing in the future.

What is my red line? I don't share Meir's approach. He made his life easier by giving this job to military experts. Every expert will have one, maybe two, views. The politicians and the public—we shall have to decide according to the learned views of the experts. The experts wouldn't decide such an important question for us. It seems to me that the *sine qua non* is not full demilitarization. Israel should demand that there will be a Jordanian army in the West Bank in order to prevent those bandits from coming back to kill us. Only the tanks and long-range guns jeopardize our security. I admit it would be inconceivable if they had armor in big numbers in Qalqilya. But with infantry the Jordanians cannot do anything except to safeguard our security by sitting there as they did up until 1967, but then we idiotically didn't understand it. So my red line is demilitarization of heavy tanks and artillery, as happened up until 1967.

If the United States would underwrite such an agreement, it would have more credibility in my eyes. I know it's dangerous. I don't want to delude myself, or delude the public—everything that we should do is dangerous. But I am 100 percent convinced that going on with the *status quo* is also dangerous. We have to choose the lesser evil, and it is the Jordanian option.

I don't think—although I wish it could happen—that there can be a direct agreement with the Palestinians. Why? We should demand not only a change of words, but a change of heart. How can we measure it? For example, we might ask them to abolish some of these infamous articles of the National Covenant. But there is no doubt in my mind that if they agree one day, they would ask us to pay in the same currency: to abolish the Law of Return and the Law of Nationality. If both sides are ready, I am ready. I am ready. But I know very well that I am in the tiniest minority in Israel in this respect. And I haven't yet seen Palestinians who are ready, except for Sabri Jiryis. He was the only one who asked to abolish the 6th Article. But it's not enough. For me the 1st Article is much worse—if the Palestinians adhere to the Pan-Arab vision that Palestine is part of the Arab world and the Palestinian people are part of the greater Arab nation, the whole problem of Palestine is totally different. The whole notion of living together in Palestine in a democratic state is a lie. They don't mean it. But I think that if it were possible, if there were many people, both Jews and Arabs, who were not so ideologically motivated—as I am not—this would be my first choice. We give up the Law of Nationality and the Law of Return. They give up the 1st and 6th clauses. Then we shall try to shape a compromise solution. It may be cantonized Palestine, federated Palestine, or bicultural Palestine. I would take every one of these three possibilities. I mentioned them only in order to be coherent in terms of my basic approach. I know very well that only maybe two hours before the second coming of Jesus will any such solution take place, because most of the Jews and most of the Arabs don't want it.

Even not going to that extreme, a process of de-ideologization of the conflict is necessary. Let us be less Zionist, and let the Arabs be less Pan-Arab, less Arab nationalist, and more Palestinian-oriented. This is really important. Because if we are really Zionists to the end, and the Palestinians are Pan-Arabs to the end, then there is no chance whatsoever of compromise.

MEIR: The question I put to you is about Jerusalem. Do you believe any Israeli government in the foreseeable future would be either ready or able to give back East Jerusalem, and do you believe that Hussein would sign a peace treaty without getting it back?

EITAN: No, to both questions. If it came to the critical moment, there will be those Israelis who would be courageous enough to explain to the public that this is the best we can get. If the public in a properly democratic way decided that East Jerusalem was more important than the possibility of reaching an agreement with Jordan—well, that would be it. Now, I don't think there is a chance that the government would be ready to give back East Jerusalem.

AMIR: You advocate a Jordanian solution. This means, of course, a Jordanian state—including the East and West Banks—in which the Palestinians would become the predominant majority, the very same Palestinians who would have been completely ignored in the negotiating process. Why can't you visualize the probability that the situation in this Jordanian state would eventually explode and those Palestinians would take over? Then they would owe nothing to the state of Israel because they would never have been part of the peace agreement or the settlement.

EITAN: I cannot give a 100 percent guarantee. It seems to me that what happened after 1967 is what would happen later, as it is now happening in Jordan. The process of integration into the Jordanian orbit would make the Palestinians less Palestinian-motivated. The greatest tragedy of the 1967 war was that this process was stopped. Palestinians were very hostile to Jordan in the fifties. They were much less hostile to the regime in the sixties. It seems to me that in being governed by the Hashemites for many years to come, they would gradually integrate. The outcome would be that, even if the king and the dynasty are overthrown, the Palestinians would adopt the practical policies that Jordan had followed previously. Time would play a role in the process of their moderation inside the Jordanian orbit. But I cannot say that I am sure. I am not.

HANAN: In your Jordanian recipe, do you mean that we would negotiate with the existing Jordanian authorities?

EITAN: No doubt.

HANAN: With or without the collaboration of the Palestinian leadership?

EITAN: It can't be without. We don't determine who the king will send to Geneva. The last Jordanian delegation was combined, Jordanian-Palestinian.

HANAN: But in the future—including probably the PLO?

EITAN: If the king decides to send the PLO, then it will include the PLO.

HANAN: If the PLO is left out, will they agree to such a settlement?

EITAN: They won't.

HANAN: So they will go on with whatever they are doing against us.

EITAN: I have no doubt that if we reach agreement—with whomever it be—there will be enough extremists to go on. If we reach agreement with Arafat, Habash will do the job. If with Habash, then there will be an Ahmad Jibril. I take into consideration that this is the picture we face. I have no other answers.

HANAN: You painted so beautifully—I must say almost heart-touchingly—the Zionism of the Palestinians. What makes you hope that this kind of strong and vital nationalism will somehow all of a sudden cease to operate because we get some settlement with King Hussein?

EITAN: Since the Palestinian movement is a Palestinian Arab movement, there is a strong Arab component in it. There is a possibility that in Jordan, a nearby Arab state with almost the same objective ingredients of ethnic identity, they will settle themselves quite easily. I base my judgment on what is already happening. The Palestinians in Jordan, if they are encouraged or helped by the government, are quite easily absorbed. An agreement with Jordan, according to which the West Bank is returned to Jordan, will solve a great part of the Palestinian problem. It won't solve, I agree, the problem of those in the camps in Lebanon by one stroke. That will have to be solved differently.

URI: How?

EITAN: The Gaza Strip should be part of this Palestinian-Jordanian state, and I think that then the problem would be partly solved—not fully. We have to face the possibility that, in a not alarming proportion, the Palestinian problem would be with us for many years to come. That is the most optimistic vision that I can have.

DROR: Can you tell us what you mean by giving up the Law of Return? You are giving up the basis of Zionism. But in practical terms, what does it mean? Let us say that tomorrow Jews are persecuted in

South America or in South Africa or somewhere else. Does it mean that you will not allow them to enter Israel? And if they can enter, who will be allowed to come? Will the Arabs decide this?

YAIR: Also, in what way do you think the Law of Return would be harmful to the Palestinians if there were two separate countries? Could we ask for a limitation on immigration to the Palestinian country too?

EITAN: From the Arab point of view the Law of Return has become the symbol of Zionism and of the inherent expansionist nature of Zionism. Now, of course, symbols are not necessarily logical. But they are believed. I have no doubt that that is the basic belief of the Arabs. It is repeated everywhere when they write about the Jewish state, Israel, and Zionism. In their view, the Law of Return is the symbol of our need to expand, because if millions of Jews came, then our boundaries would be too tight or narrow for them, and Israel would be necessarily expansionist.

I won't run away from Dror's question. I admit it is the weakest point in my presentation, but still I must confront it. Zionism, or the Zionists, tried to change the nature of the Jewish existence. They presented a vision. Zionism was always a minority movement among the Jews—even in the heyday of Zionism, in the heartland of Zionism, in pre-1939 Poland. It seems to me—and this is an outcome of my evaluation—that the Zionist movement has already passed its peak. It can't do it any more. I must draw a logical conclusion, even though I admit that I don't do it gladly. We Israelis, we Zionists, we tried to bring as many Jews to Israel as possible. Most of the Jews made the choice for themselves. They could have come to Palestine, to Israel, from 1948 up to 1976. They decided not to come. From the establishment of the state up to 1976, the South American Jews, the North American Jews, the West European Jews all were able to decide for themselves whether they wanted to come. They had the experience of the Second World War to influence them in deciding what to do. Everything has now been offered to them. They have decided. They decide every day. They don't want to come. So I now say very frankly: If the future of the Israeli community or the Israeli nation or the Israeli state—to which I belong very willingly—is threatened by a prolongation of the Zionist dream, I don't want to risk three million Jews in order to give a free option to twelve million Jews who are now living where they choose to live, in order that they could one day come to their place of refuge if something happens to them.

YAIR: Why are you more privileged than the other Jews?

EITAN: I'm not more privileged.

DROR: In some ways, what you are saying is a renewal of the White Paper of 1939.*

EITAN: You can bring very extreme examples which will make my position even weaker. I know it. But still I think that the situation is that most of world Jewry doesn't want to emigrate to Israel. We try our best. We send messengers, and we do everything we can in order to convince them—and we fail. So if it is possible to reach agreement even at this price, I am ready to pay it.

YAIR: You want to freeze the situation?

EITAN: Yes, that's right. To freeze the situation.

*The White Paper, issued by Great Britain in the aftermath of the Arab Revolt of 1936-1939, reversed the Peel recommendation by proposing a unified independent Palestine within ten years with restricted immigration and land-purchase rights for the Jewish minority.

PINHAS: And we will always remain at three million, or three and a half million, or four million—forever? Surrounded by one hundred and fifty million Arabs?

EITAN: If I should be a member of a small nation, what's so wrong with that?

DROR: You didn't answer the question: Who will decide who could come?

EITAN: We, the Israeli government.

HANAN: The tragedy that you do not realize is that your proposal would mean the annihilation of Israel.

BITAN: It's the *raison d'être* of it all.

ZVI: In your Jordanian solution, can you foresee a situation in which there would be an agreement between the Jordanians and the PLO—out of their free will or under Syrian pressure—to let the PLO operate from the West Bank, from Jordanian territory, as was the case in the fifties. What then?

EITAN: I accept your point. It is a possibility. But Jordan doesn't want to be a satellite of Syria. Up to now I have not been convinced that Jordan, except for verbal concessions, has done anything to change its position or policy; they are playing games. I don't think it is a serious possibility that the PLO will come into the West Bank with Jordanian permission after the territory has been given back to Jordan. If that happens, and if the PLO begins operating again from there against us, it will change everything. We shall react—maybe not immediately—and it will regenerate the whole process of retaliation.

"My suggestion is to work for an overall settlement."

ZVI: I see the conflict, at least in its initial stages, as one between two national movements struggling for the same territory. One movement is the Jewish-Zionist, having a right in Palestine based on a long history, and on strong Jewish longing for Zion. Palestine or Eretz Israel has been part and parcel of Jewish history. There is no alternative for Jewish cultural and national life, no other solution for the Jewish problem, except in Eretz Israel. The rival movement is the Palestinian Arab national movement, which is fairly new and which was formed under artificial circumstances. Never in Islamic-Arab history was Palestine a territorial, political administrative unit of its own. When it was a political entity, it was Jewish or Crusader.

The Palestinian Arab identity is not crystallized yet. Quite a great number of Palestinians, especially among the masses, nourish the Islamic identity. Some have a Pan-Arab loyalty which is stronger. Both of these identities are stronger than the Palestinian one. Some regard themselves as belonging to South Syria. Some identify with Jordan. Some have the local identification—with Nablus or Hebron, for example. Several of these loyalties we can see also in the PLO: five out of its six component organizations are affiliated with Arab states or have Pan-Arab orientations.

Nevertheless, there exists a Palestinian identity—despite its weaknesses, despite its shortcomings. The same could be said about the Syrian identity, the Iraqi identity, the Lebanese identity—all are superficial and weak, but they exist. And the Palestinian national identity is not weaker than the Iraqi—maybe it's even stronger. Nor for that matter is it weaker than the Syrian or the Jordanian. It is a political fact which we can't overlook. The Palestinian Arab nation is struggling for self-determination, as other Arab nations have done. And it is the only Arab nation which hasn't achieved self-determination.

Theoretically, we can settle the conflict

Dialogue Fragments

"Let us be less Zionist, and let the Arabs be less Pan-Arab, less Arab nationalist, and more Palestinian-oriented. This is really important. Because if we are really Zionists to the end, and the Palestinians are Pan-Arab to the end, then there is no chance whatsoever of compromise."

" ... we might ask them to abolish some of these infamous articles of the National Covenant. But there is no doubt in my mind that if they agree one day, they would ask us to pay in the same currency: to abolish the Law of Return and the Law of Nationality."

"If we annex today—and this is an important factor for me—we shall inevitably have a situation of Rhodesia or South Africa— maybe in a less rigid form."

—Eitan

"And the Palestinian national identity is not weaker than the Iraqi— maybe it's even stronger. Nor for that matter is it weaker than the Syrian or the Jordanian. It is a political fact which we can't overlook."

"We have to recognize, in principle, the right of the Palestinians to self-determination in what I would consider 75 percent of total Palestine on both sides of the Jordan—West Bank, East Bank, and the Gaza Strip."

" ... we can't solve the Palestinian problem without solving the Arab-Israeli conflict, and vice versa—it's a vicious circle."

—Zvi

between the two national movements by mutual recognition, by partition and by compromise.

Most Israelis recognize the Palestinian right. Most, if not all, Israelis want peace. I can't say the same for sure about Arabs. The Arabs have never recognized the right of the Jews on part of their homeland, Eretz Israel. We and the Palestinians could perhaps have solved the problem if we had been tackling it between ourselves. But the Palestinians are not by themselves; they are part of the Arab nation. The Palestinian-Jewish conflict over Palestine has turned out to be an Arab-Israeli conflict, and the Arab countries are deeply involved and committed. Palestine is the litmus test of Arab nationalism. One Egyptian scholar writing recently in *Al-Ahram* said that from the national point of view, Palestine is in the heart of every Arab, and from the geographic standpoint, Palestine is the heart of the Arab homeland. Giving it up would mean that the Arab people are then not a nation, for a nation would never agree to cut off one of its limbs. In my view, it follows then that we can't solve the Palestinian problem without solving the Arab-Israeli conflict, and vice versa—it's a vicious circle.

But there seems to be no solution because of the Arab position. I must emphasize the denial of Israel's legitimacy on the part of the Arabs. Some Arabs recognize the fact of our existence; none recognizes our right to exist. This applies to the Palestinians, and to all Arab nations. Palestinians feel more strongly about it because for many of them it is also a personal issue—they want to go back to their places. It's not only an ideological goal.

The Arabs don't recognize Jewish nationalism and self-determination. According to them, Jews—like Christians—are not a nation, but a religious community without a right to a national life in Palestine, which they regard as Arab land. This intolerant attitude of militant Pan-Arabism is that the Middle East must be Arab-Islamic, and that there is no room for non-Arab, non-Islamic political entities. There must be a uniformity, not pluralism among Middle East communities. The Jews pose a great threat to this ideology. Moreover, the Jews also are regarded by the Arabs as part of the imperialistic West which humiliated and frustrated the Arabs for several generations through military, political, economic, and cultural domination. The imperialistic West has retreated from the region, but Israel is still there to remind the Arabs of their humiliation; and Israel has done this convincingly by defeating the Arab states in four wars.

The 1973 war, it is argued, enabled the Arab states to recover their wounded pride as a consequence of their initial military success and their eventual political and psychological victory. Now, the argument runs, they have gained confidence and are ready to make peace. In some Arab countries, especially Egypt, there are people who would like to coexist and live in peace, but unfortunately they are not influential. The mainstream of Arab political thinking since the October War has advocated a continuation of the conflict—to change tactics, but not the strategic aim. Many Arabs are now overconfident. They claim that time is on their side. They possess the great potential of the Arab world, 140 million Arabs against 3 million Jews, oil money, and also international support. The UN Resolution against Zionism laid the moral basis for legitimation of the war against Israel, and the Arabs take courage from this.

If my analysis is correct—I hope it's not, but if it is true—the logical conclusion for Israel would be that of Gush Emunim: to retain maximum territory, especially Judea and Samaria, to annex, to settle. But this is not my position because things are not that simple. Despite what I have said, there is a discrepancy between Arab ideology and the leaders' readiness or ability to fulfill it.

To what extent is a country like Egypt or Syria willing to go in order to materialize its ideology? What is the price in human lives and resources that each country is willing to pay? Also, I can't foresee the future. There may develop in the Arab world new classes who have vested interests in socio-economic growth and in a change of policy. There are some signs in this direction, at least in Egypt. On all sides, we are dealing with human lives, and we therefore have to exhaust all possibilities to avoid a disaster.

My suggestion, therefore, is to work for an overall settlement which would take into account the Palestinians, but without a third independent state between Israel and Jordan. This settlement should be based on UN Resolutions 242 and 338. In principle Israel would agree to return all territories conquered in 1967 and to grant recognition of the right of the Palestinians to self-determination in the area which was pre-1967 Jordan plus the Gaza Strip—all this on condition of reciprocal Arab recognition of the right of Israel to exist and the Jewish people to self-determination in Eretz Israel in the pre-1967 borders.

Why do we need this program for an overall settlement? First to foster and encourage moderate streams in the Arab world, if they exist. And even more important, to offer to the Arabs, both moderate and extremist, an alternative to total war. What we have heard here about desperadoes is perhaps one hint of how important it is to find such an alternative, for total war could be disasterous for all Middle East countries.

Second, to convince the United States—the administration, the Congress, public opinion—of Israel's readiness for peace, and the readiness to take a great risk for peace. This we must do in order to secure the continuance of American support. I think the American public and the Congress would understand that a country like Israel wants peace and has a right to it.

Third, we owe it to ourselves. I don't need to prove to myself that Israel wants peace, but I know that some people in Israel—perhaps in the Left, perhaps the young generations—are doubtful. We have to prove to our people that we have made the maximum efforts toward the Arabs, trying to achieve a settlement while undertaking very heavy risks. If our efforts are not accepted by the Arabs, we don't have any choice.

The beginning of such *via dolorosa* would be a declaration of intentions of both sides. We should state what we are willing to give; and the Arabs should recognize Israel's self-determination and sovereignty. Then, we have to go gradually towards a settlement, stage-by-stage, taking first Egypt, then Syria, and then, only in the last stage, the Palestinian issue. At the outset we have to recognize, in principle, the right of the Palestinians to self-determination in what I would consider 75 percent of total Palestine on both sides of the Jordan—West Bank , East Bank, and the Gaza Strip.

The weakness of my proposal is that the Arabs are not going to accept it. But I still maintain that we have to put it forward, and I trust that the United States will be willing to support it.

EITAN: We should beware of slogans, and especially the holiest of all slogans—the right of self-determination. Out of political and practical considerations we might reach a conclusion that we should give back the West Bank and the Gaza Strip to the Palestinians or to the PLO. But such a step shouldn't be presented as the implementation of the right of self-determination of the Palestinian people. Otherwise I can't explain to myself why this right doesn't belong also to the Palestinian Arabs living in the Galilee, in Nazareth, and in the Little Triangle. They are Palestinian Arabs. And if the Palestinian people have the right to self-determination, naturally and logically they too should share the same right.

Moreover, nowhere in the world has this slogan been implemented. Boundaries have not been delineated according to self-determination, even though the accepted mythology is that it is the basis of modern nationhood and modern international relations.

ZVI: But I mentioned also that the Arabs must recognize the sovereignty of Israel in the 1967 boundaries, which includes the Israeli Arabs. This is a limitation on their self-determination.

AMIR: Up to a certain point I found myself in agreement with you. But then you declared, in a very unequivocal way, that the Arabs will not accept what you are proposing. You don't seem to qualify it in any way. You are not saying "not in the foreseeable future," or "the prospects of their accepting it are limited." You say categorically, "they are not going to accept it." If so, why should we take the trouble of working out the stages and the elements of an overall settlement?

ZVI: I am sure that at present the Arabs would not accept it, but it would throw the ball into their court. I am doing it mainly for the international community, not for the Arabs—and especially for the United States and for ourselves. If there are mod-

erate elements in the Arab world, they might be encouraged by such a proposition.

AMIR: Then say so.

ZVI: I said so, although I am not very optimistic about the outcome because the forces for peace in the Arab world are much weaker—insignificant as a counterweight to the forces for war.

Now, if the Arabs reject such a settlement, I would still be against annexation of the West Bank and the Gaza Strip because I'm afraid of the demographic problem. I might, though, suggest taking some steps to deliver the Arabs a message—for example, by annexing Judea, but not Samaria. Why? Because Judea has a much lower Arab population—70,000.

NAHUM: Deferring the Palestinian problem, as you do, to the last stage, cannot be accepted by an Arab state. Will Egypt agree at the outset with you on some final settlement without the Palestinians?

ZVI: I didn't say they would. I said in the first stage there must be an overall agreement on all issues, including the Palestinians. We would be ready to recognize their right to self-determination as part of an overall plan to be implemented in stages.

"We will have to live with their rejection."

PINHAS: The broader premises which influence and even decide my final position stem, first, from my Zionist outlook with its three main ingredients: the Jewish people, the land of Israel, and the state of Israel. The foremost idea of Zionism was to save the Jewish people and guarantee them a secure physical framework for their existence. This could not be achieved except by creating a sovereign country ruled and directed primarily by Jews. Naturally,

such a state could not be created except in the land linked inseparably to the history of this nation for more than 3,000 years, where for the first time the Jewish people conducted their own sovereign life. The undoubted rights of the Jewish people over the entire land of Eretz Israel is an integral part of our historical heritage. No other people's rights equal or transcend ours. A sovereign Jewish state is indispensible to Jewish existence—even if it is obvious that all Jews never will be physically part of this state. Israel ought to live and conduct herself in view of its moral commitment to those Jews who are not yet part of it. Certainly I approve of the Law of Return.

One can't overlook our special history and its traumas. Although it is often a subject for satire and irony, we in Israel have to bear in mind the persecution, massacres, pogroms, and exterminations which resulted in the mass killing of Jews. Our history is full of tragedies which started basically with prejudices. One has to completely ignore reality to believe that the impact of years of anti-Semitic indoctrination and anti-Jewish propaganda has totally disappeared. This is the context for what I feel is perhaps the most crucial characteristic of the Middle East conflict. Although there have been many confrontations between two or more national movements over the same land, our conflict is perhaps the only one in recent history where a whole nation is not only in danger of losing its own freedom but is also under the threat of potential extermination. My perspective on our traumas crucially determines the amount of risk I am ready to take upon ourselves.

Had I taken part in this forum eight or ten years ago I might have expressed completely different views on the scope of the Palestinian problem. Yet, as much as I would like to escape it, I feel we can't escape admitting that recently the problem once known as "the refugee problem" has passed a substantial transformation and is now an issue on a national level. I do accept the fact that a process has started which can very well result in the creation of a new people within the broad sense of this word—the Palestinian people. We ought to deal with the question within this framework. While saying this—and believe me it wasn't simple for me to arrive at this conclusion—I want to state firmly and unequivocally: the conflict in the Middle East is not between two national movements that have equal rights to the same national territory. Rather it is between a nation whose right for its own state and land had been shaped and recognized hundreds of years before there were any Palestinians, and another nation in the process of being made.

As was so convincingly shown here, the basic objective of this new nation in creation is the abolishment of Israel—and subsequently the annihilation of its citizens. Without diminishing the importance of the conflict with the Palestinians, I believe that the whole conflict in the Middle East did not originate with the Palestinians and its solution does not depend solely on some agreement with them. Yet I do believe, at the same time, that without some progress on the Palestinian issue, no progress towards final true peace is possible because of the commitment of the whole Arab world to the Palestinians.

I must admit that had I been asked immediately after the war of 1967, I would have answered quickly that for full, final peace I was ready to withdraw to the 1967 boundaries—excluding Jerusalem. I don't say this anymore. Times have changed, and so have circumstances and options.

Given our security needs and the depth of the enmity and hatred toward Israel among the Arab countries generally, and among the Palestinians specifically, we ought not to withdraw from Judea, Samaria, and the Gaza Strip. Under no circumstances in the future will I be ready to maintain the boundaries of 1967, and thus bring upon ourselves effects which might acutely endanger our very existence. Our state can't exist within those boundaries. That we did so for nineteen years does not prove anything. Things have completely changed. I therefore don't really see any difference between the Jordan and the Palestinian options. Both are impossible as far as evacuation from Judea and Samaria are concerned.

At the same time, I believe that some

consideration must be given as to how to channel the Palestinians' nationalist aspirations to Transjordan, which is to a very large extent a Palestinian state.

I have listened to the discouraging assessments here about the Palestinians who have been citizens of Israel ever since the 1948 war, and I know the situation of the people in the territories occupied since 1967. I believe that all of these Palestinians have to be given three options: (a) to remain citizens of the Palestinian state which will be established in Transjordan and inhabitants of their old homes under Israeli control, or (b) to be full citizens and inhabitants of their new state, or (c) to retain their position as Israeli citizens. Whoever is afraid of the consequences of living together with 1.5 million Arabs, either from the moral or from the practical point of view, will have to explain why living with only half a million—as we already do, with our Arab citizens— will change the perspective on this problem. Of course, it is far from being an ideal state of affairs. Yet we have no other choice.

I don't believe in half-solutions and arrangements which include demilitarization, which is a thing of the past. No Arab country will seriously consider demilitarization on its soil. And even if accepted, it would not hold for long. Experience shows that, however much you declare otherwise beforehand, no one is prepared to start a war when demilitarization is violated, and it can be violated gradually, in a way that will make war impossible.

All this week I hoped that some more optimistic assessment would shatter my convictions. None was given. On the contrary, some of you trapped yourselves with the naive thought that, given all these facts, we still have to offer either the Palestinians or Jordan all the territory for even a 5 percent chance for peace. I object to this road, which will inevitably lead us to total evacuation with zero peace. The last two interim agreements are the model for what

would happen.

I call upon you here who would challenge this to explain how Israel would be able to control the process of negotiations. One day we would face the inevitable collapse of the whole structure. It is presumptuous to believe that Israel will be able to get from the Arabs and America the political considerations which will match the concessions that it is ready to make. Even now all the hints suggest the opposite. The nature of any such process is that the more you penetrate it, the less you are capable of objecting to its damaging outcomes. If the 5 percent chance does not materialize, we will not be able to stop the process. Within the framework of any limited agreement in the future, the relative importance of the American commitment to Israel will be greater than before, and I assume that relying on such commitments in the future is a risky business. There is another risk too. Perhaps having America too deeply committed to Israel may even be a prescription for troubles for Israel within the United States itself and the administration and Congress.

We ought to admit that all of us here, without any exception, have given up the hope for peace—true, simple peace as any one of us understands the term. We ought to admit that peace is not at hand under any foreseeable circumstances—including circumstances of serious and far-reaching concessions by Israel. The differences among us lie in the extent of our readiness to take serious risks upon ourselves, given on the one hand the shattered hope for peace, and on the other hand the depth of the Arab enmity toward us.

Perhaps our collective conclusion is shocking. But shocking as it is, I am much more afraid of those who offer us substitutions where the danger is obvious and concrete and the chance is 5 percent or even less.

As for settlements in Judea and Samaria, those of us who depend upon some future hope for miraculous peace, detached from any existing reality, will naturally oppose settlements. Since I do not share this baseless vision of the future, I support Israeli settlements in Judea and Samaria. I think that we don't have to wait anymore. I sympathize with Gush Emunim in this matter. But with all due respect to them, settling is not a private business. It ought to be a governmental initiative and not a Gush Emunim one, since it is a matter of national necessity.

I share the fears of those who are afraid of the continued *status quo* in the territories. Had they been able to offer us an alternative worthy of our expectations, I would have grasped it, and would have been ready to pay the price. Since all they can offer is one-sided retreats, I prefer to take the risks involved in remaining where we are now.

I can't ignore the weaknesses and risks of my position. My position might lead one day to a renewed military confrontation. Israel might find itself one day isolated and deprived of some basic needs for our future confrontation with the Arabs. Life in Israel with 1.5 million Arabs might be very difficult. I am aware of these risks. But I believe that the process of pushing us away from the territories will not avoid war, but will only bring it on us when we are weaker and less prepared for it. America, not to mention the Arab countries, will not approve of my position. Yet, if we cannot get something from them which is close to peace when we have all the cards in our hands, who will ever give us that precious thing when we have nothing to give in return, because everything has been given away for nothing?

I would not look forward with great desire to isolation, and I don't think that isolation is inevitable. The Arab countries must realize, and so too must America, that the stake is peace and only peace. America has to remember also that its own move into the Middle East is based on the assumption that the Arab countries must be appeased in order to avoid the damage that war can bring to American interests. Israel must be appeased as well if America does not want to turn her into a nuisance factor.

Finally, a lot has been said here about the ordeal Israel must face in the near future. In contrast to the fears of some of my colleagues, I think what we face is not beyond our national capabilities. I agree that we need to pull ourselves together and to express our full potential strength and qualities. Much has to be changed in our internal affairs. For the long-run, being a negligible minority as we are in the Middle East, we will never be able to exist if our unique qualities and abilities do not manifest themselves clearly, if they do not again become characteristics of our society as they were in the past.

MEIR: You have stated your position very clearly, and you have hinted that the United States would have some doubts about it. Could you explain how you will settle officially and massively in the territories, and forego the assistance of the US government—when you know that our country cannot live one more year without the yearly injection of two and a half billion dollars and cannot wage a war without American assistance? There is a total discrepancy here.

PINHAS: I object to your basic assumption. It is true that Israel cannot exist at its present standard of living without the yearly injection of two and a half billion in American dollars. However, with different circumstances inside Israel, we could manage. I see the difficulties, but we ought to realize that Israel is living in an emergency situation.

The confrontation, the dispute, with the United States is merely a question of time. I am afraid that what you offer is that one day we will find ourselves without almost all the territories, in total dependence on the United States. Because the more we

Dialogue Fragments

" . . . we ought not to withdraw from Judea, Samaria, and the Gaza Strip. Under no circumstances in the future will I be ready to maintain the boundaries of 1967."

"We will have to deal not with four Arab members of the Knesset, as now, but with twelve, fifteen, or twenty Arab members. We simply ought to come out of our ghetto mentality. With this number of Arab members in the Knesset, it's not the end of the world."

" . . . I support Israeli settlements in Judea and Samaria. . . . It ought to be a governmental initiative and not a Gush Emunim one. . . ."

—*Pinhas*

"No other nation in the world is confronted with neighbors whose express wish is to annihilate it."

"Eastern Jordan must be the homeland and the state of whichever Palestinians want to live there. Territory now in the hands of Israel will remain there."

"We have to tell the full truth to ourselves, and to the Arabs, to the world: the land of Israel, Palestine, is the land of the Jewish people."

—*Hanan*

"It's not true that the conflict is about the lands conquered in the Six Day War. . . ."

" . . . an evenhanded Western approach is bound to shift the balance to the Arabs."

"I am for declaring outright that, for a limited period, we are ready to exchange the territories—all of them—for a real, full, complete, and lasting peace. But not for a semblance of it.

—*Yair*

have to retreat, the more we will have to rely on American support, money, and commitments. Then, we will realize that we ought to confront the United States, but we will never be able to do it. Yet, we don't have to bow and to panic suddenly at the thought of having disputes with the United States. Our history is full of them. It will not be easy. I know that this is the most difficult ordeal that Israel will have to face. The more we postpone it artificially, the more we enter a situation from which it will be difficult for us to escape.

This is, in a way, a weakness in my position. It would be much easier for me to come here and declare that I expect the support of the United States. I don't mislead myself. Nevertheless I don't think that in another year or two we will get from the United States the amount of money needed for the kind of agreement that you support, Meir. Therefore, bad consequences will follow whether we have an agreement or whether we don't. In either case we will have to prepare ourselves for a different kind of life within the country.

ZVI: You claim that some of us are willing to give the territories back to Jordan or the Palestinians for a 5 percent chance. I think you misunderstood us. I want your reaction to the following quotation from the Brookings report, which I would like to endorse: "In peaceful relations, Arab parties undertake not only to end such hostile actions against Israel as armed incursions, blockages, boycotts, and propaganda attacks, but also to give evidence of progress toward development of normal international, and regional political relations." And "Withdrawal to agreed boundaries and the establishment of peaceful relations carried out in stages over a period of years, each stage being undertaken only when the agreed provisions of the previous stage have been faithfully implemented."*

BITAN: That's not an Arab document.

ZVI: But doesn't it provide you with the

necessary checks and balances after each stage? If it doesn't work, we stop the process. Would you sign such a document?

PINHAS: I say it very clearly: the nature of this process is that you can't control it. We have the model of the last two interim agreements, which show this very clearly.

ZVI: But the stages would be part of an overall settlement.

PINHAS: Yes, I know. But the problem with all these proposals is that once you present your readiness to withdraw, then immediately the whole framework, which is not yet a signed agreement, is debated, negotiated, and cut into pieces in the negotiating process. Taking into consideration the weaknesses of the entire Israeli position and our difficulties in persuading the United States and the Arab countries, I can clearly see that this would be the outcome of the process.

ZVI: You also mentioned that demilitarization is unacceptable. What about an Israeli military presence in the West Bank without annexation?

PINHAS: You didn't hear the word "annexation" in my remarks. I think that annexation — formal annexation — is something which will come in due time. What I am talking about is creating facts through settling in the territories. Of course, an Israeli military presence is part of it.

We will have to find practical arrangements for the inhabitants of the territories, which brings me to something you all overlooked: the problem of the Israeli Arabs. None of you has mentioned this yet in your final statement. After talking here so much about the difficulties, the burdens, the potential dangers among the Israeli Arabs—suddenly they disappear.

*Report of a study group. *Toward Peace in the Middle East*, (Washington, D.C.: The Brookings Institution, 1975).

Only Eitan hinted at it. I want your reaction to my conviction that there is no substantial difference from the moral or practical point of view between one and a half million Arabs and a half million Arabs.

ZVI: The half million are Israeli Arabs.

PINHAS: Yes, but what does it mean—"Israeli Arabs"? For me, the number in itself does not change our entire national and moral perspective on this problem. I don't want the one and a half million to become part of the Jewish state because of practical difficulties. I offer them the three options; I give them the choice to decide themselves.

NAHUM: It seems to me that your position is the most consistent we have heard until now. The irony is that here lies its weakness. It seems to me that you don't see the conflict as an eternal one. You have hopes that one day the conflict will end. None of us want to indulge ourselves in a vision of eternal conflict. But I ask: Why do you think that the Arabs in the future will agree to a much larger Israel? Why do you think they will prefer this to a smaller Israel, according to what has been called here the gambit of the Tactical Left?

PINHAS: I put the question in the opposite direction. All of you have said that they are not going to accept even the smallest Israel that you propose. Why then should I take all the risks inherent in such a position without any hope? At least I have no illusions. And I know that America, not to mention the Arab countries, will not accept my position. But at least I will retain under my control some of the ingredients which enable me to keep face and to fight for our interests.

We will have to live with their rejection. I rest my only hope on a very, very slow reconciliation. It will happen mainly because, I think, some of the Palestinian problem will be quieted down if we are able to help them channel their national aspirations into Transjordan and to settle themselves there. And it will happen if we are able to find practical accommodations for the population within the territories. I am even ready to make very generous proposals to the Palestinians—for instance, some status for Jerusalem as their capital city.

EITAN: Our dependence on the United States is not only economic and financial, but also military—in terms of arms. Let us assume that we reach economic self-sufficiency, that our exports cover our imports, together with private donations we get from American Jewry.

MEIR: A Messianic dream.

EITAN: But let us assume. Then, we still would need a foreign supply of weapons because even with the greatest development in our technology we couldn't match Soviet technology. You cannot go to the free market in the world and buy arms needed for waging modern war.

PINHAS: It's simply untrue. It depends on what weapons we are talking about. We can't buy Phantoms. But some of the best Israeli experts think that we ought not to spend all this money on buying Phantoms in America, and that we would be better off investing it in Israeli arms industries. We are in the process of doing so.

EITAN: I am skeptical. It's not only armaments, but all the other sophisticated things—lasers, and so on, for which we cannot reach such self-sufficiency in the foreseeable future.

On another point, you were inconsistent. You didn't say "annexation," and you said you had not implied that the territories should be annexed formally. But you said that the Palestinian Arab people under Israeli control should be given three choices: Jordanian citizenship and going there, Jordanian citizenship and staying here, and Israeli citizenship. That amounts to annexation. Let us assume they got Israeli citizenship. They will be Israeli citizens under Israeli legal jurisdiction. So it's annexation. Then we would one day be confronted with the problem of a big minority. During the past twenty-five years, we have reached the point where these Israeli Arabs cannot be maneuvered easily any more—but still they are only 13 percent of the population. When they are 35-40 percent, then they will constitute a political force of their own, and they will have the balance of power in parliament. I can't run away from the historical precedent of the Irish Nationalist Party which used its power in the British Parliament to extort home-rule, which led afterwards to independence. Unless we cease to be a democracy, there is no doubt that the Palestinian Arabs would behave in the same way.

Today our political system is such that the Israeli Arabs are not discriminated against—they are separated. The situation in Israel resembles what existed in the Hapsburg Empire: the Staadtsburg are the Jews. The state is ours. We defend it. We fight for it. And we enjoy full rights and liberties. The Israeli Arabs don't fight for it. We don't requre them to do it, they don't want to do it. Since they are exempted from military service, no one can expect them to get certain jobs or positions. No doubt both sides share the same attitudes toward this situation. It is a separation on which both Zionism and Arab nationalism agree.

PINHAS: About the total reliance on the United States: Look gentlemen, if this is the case, if Israel really is so totally dependent that we are unable to move independently on any issues, then we have to close the doors, give the keys to the president of the United States, and appoint a secretary of state as our prime minister.

We don't have to panic. We do rely and depend on the United States. We do need their support, their money, their airplanes, their munitions—everything. There will be some problems. It will be very difficult. I am not trying to reflect a very optimistic and euphoric mood here. Yet I think that we are exaggerating. The US pressures will not be total, comprehensive, unyielding, and immediate. We will just have to live with ups and downs in these pressures. There will be an open debate in the United States. I am not certain of the outcome. I have some fears about the Congress position, about the entire Eastern establishment position, and about the academics' position. Yet if our position is presented properly, the American public and the American Congress will give support to it. And we will have to fight for it.

You are wrong, Eitan, from the legal point of view, in your comment about the law and annexation. It is possible for us to grant Israeli citizenship to those who want it in the territories, without at the same time applying Israeli law completely.

And on the demographic question, the main problem is that Israel will eventually have many more citizens who will not be Jews. This is not a question of a one-day process. It will take a lot of time. I don't think, in the end, that all of these Arabs will become Israeli citizens. Many of them will prefer to remain citizens of the Palestinian state which will be established on the other side of the Jordan, while remaining inhabitants of the territories controlled by Israel. We will have to deal not with four Arab members of the Knesset, as now, but with twelve, fifteen, or twenty Arab members. This is something that we can live with. We simply ought to come out of our ghetto mentality. With this number of Arab members in the Knesset, it's not the end of the world.

"The only possibility is for us and the Arabs to reach an agreement on establishing a Palestinian state on both the East and West Banks of the Jordan River."

OREN: My brief remarks will concentrate on what I see as the dominant trend in Arab Palestinian society. Judging by the developments of the past, recent and remote, it seems to me that there is no way to escape certain facts that make up this trend. Arab Palestinian society is in the process of rapid transformation from a traditional into a modern society. One and a half million Palestinians under Israeli authority are developing from a rural, isolated society into an urban one—with all its implications. Primitive agriculture, crafts and commerce, and the whole traditional way of life have changed, and many of the Arab villages in Eretz Israel today are urban suburbs. Penetration of modern technology, the spread of education, and many other factors are ruining the old family system, and the whole traditional social structure is crumbling. In the place of the older generations of conservative leaders, a new, modern leadership is emerging—a leadership that is completely transforming the nature of Palestinian nationality. It has been said here several times that Palestinian nationality has not crystallized yet. I do not doubt this. But it seems to me obvious that the modernization process is going hand-in-hand with nationalist ideology and the PLO leadership. The trend of modernization makes the young less dependent on the family; it means the emancipation of women and the dominance of city culture; it chalenges local loyalties to Nablus or Hebron, for example; and it even undermines some religious loyalties.

The Palestinians are looking for new symbols of national loyalty. And the PLO is the only one supplying them. The Hashemite kingdom of Jordan symbolizes today for the Palestinians—a new generation on the two banks of the Jordan River—all the anachronistic norms which are bound to disappear. Everybody is fascinated by King Hussein's maneuvers and his capability to keep a stable regime for so long. Only recently Jordan has enjoyed a flourishing economic and industrial development—but in time it will put an end to the present regime. Hussein, as an absolute monarch, derives his power from obsolete local political and religious figures, and the whole process of modernization will wipe them out. The modern, new Palestinian identity being created before our eyes is unfortunately hostile to Israel. But it is also a result of social protest against the principles of the former generation's social system.

The state of Israel, and before that the Yishuv, [the pre-state Jewish community of Palestine] succeeded in the past in holding off the traditional Palestinian nationalism of Haj Amin el Husseini and others. The Jews in Eretz Israel utilized all the weaknesses of that nationalism: Bedouin society, poverty, illiteracy, corruption, faulty organization. The new Palestinian nationalism, mainly now PLO, preserves the same principles of hostility towards Israel, but bases them on a modern, urban, and educated society.

The Arabs in Eretz Israel are going to identify mainly with the modern symbols of the PLO. Moreover, the chances are that this identification is going to be revolutionary and radical—becoming more and more similar to some neighboring Arab countries, maybe Syria, and other parts of the Third World. That is why I think that the sole alternative before Israel is to form its policy in relation to that new nationalism which has found its expression in the PLO. The only possibility, I believe, is for both us and the Arabs to reach an agreement on establishing a Palestinian state on both the East and West Banks of the Jordan River, roughly on the 1967 borders. The single way for Israel to remain in existence as a Jewish state is to try to reduce the level of hostility and enmity around and within her, and to lower the Arab motivation for fighting. This can be achieved by a readiness to make real concessions, and at the same time by fixing it in the Arab mind that the destruction of Israel will bring disaster on the Palestinians.

What is most dangerous is that the Palestinians do not have a political outlet. This is what has made their position so tough. A young Arab growing up today in Nablus, Nazareth or East Jerusalem has almost no choice but to be a supporter of PLO terrorism. The continuation of current Israeli policy will result in making the comparatively safe borders of Lebanon and Jordan dangerous like the Golan and the Suez borders in October of 1973. The continuation of Israeli rule over one and a half million Arabs, in my opinion, is as risky as an unsafe border. More than 70,000 workers from the territories are working daily in Israel. Add to this number an equivalent number of workers from among the Israeli Arabs. They are the hard laborers of Israel. As a result we, the Jews, become a nation that is governing the Arabs in every aspect—politically as well as economically and socially. I cannot point to the political tactics that should be used by Israel. But a future solution must be, in my opinion, a state with a vast Jewish majority, side by side with an Arab Palestinian state on both sides of the River Jordan. What I want to emphasize is that the continuation of the present situation is as risky as giving up some territories.

PINHAS Some? But you want to give up all of them.

OREN: It's a matter of process. I am not in a position to give up any of my historical or national rights in the territories, and even not in East Jordan. That's because these rights are possessed by Jewish tradition, by the Jewish people. I take this argument from the Palestinian Arabs. I have often heard them say that they can't give up their rights in Jaffa. But I think that the quantitative problem of the number of Arabs within the borders of Israel has changed into a qualitative problem. Because you can give some rights, some individual rights, to a minority which is 7 percent or even 10 or 12 percent. But quite a different problem arises if it is 25, 30, or 35 percent.

URI: You mentioned before that we might threaten the Palestinians with a disaster. Do you think that this threat will deter the Arab countries from trying to annihilate the Jews in Israel?

OREN: I completely agree with the description we've heard here about desperadoes. And I think that we might have to stress this.

PINHAS: Your mention of the lack of some political outlet for Arabs from Nablus, as well as those from Nazareth implies that you and I actually agree that Arabs from these two sides of the so-called Green Line are almost in the same category as the Arab in Nablus. And you say that the political outlets that they have today in Israel are insufficient, and therefore the only outlet is either a Palestinian state, or the terrorists' activities. If the outlet you propose is a Palestinian state, do you imply that such a state will include the Arab from Nazareth, which means an all-embracing Palestinian state including Galilee? If not, do you think that the existence of a Palestinian state in Judea and Samaria will give the Arab in Nazareth the political outlet he does not have today?

OREN: I think that the most important thing is to have a vast Jewish majority in the state of Israel. So I am ready to give up, for example, Umm el-Fahm in the Little Triangle; but at the same time I am prepared to annex a few kilometers of territory, for example, near the Egyptian border.

PINHAS: No, that doesn't answer my question. The great bulk of Arabs in Israel are not in the Little Triangle, but in the Galilee. This is a very important point for me, so I want to make it clear. Morally, you are ready not to give a political outlet to the Arab from Nazareth in terms of his being able to be part of a Palestinian state. To him you say, "You are a Palestinian, an Arab, but you ought to remain in the Israeli state,

and you will never, within your own city, also be able to be part of a Palestinian state. If you would like to be a part of such a state, you have to leave." Don't you see any moral difference between saying this to an Arab from Nazareth and saying it to an Arab from Nablus?

OREN: If there were a small Arab minority in Israel, there would be a great difference for me.

PINHAS: From our point of view, yes. But what about from the moral point of view of the Arab?

EITAN: There's no moral solution to the problem.

"Three partitions have taken place in Palestine. We now have to have the fourth partition—in a final peace solution."

DROR: I too regard our conflict with the Palestinians as historically a clash between two national movements—although I want to stress that the Arabs who have enjoyed self-determination in immense areas since World War I have been hostile, not only to our right of self-determination, but also to the rights of millions of non-Arabs. Since 1921 seven waves of riots and wars have taken place in the Middle East. And during this period, a Palestinian people was created. In fact, we played an important role in encouraging this process. There is a Palestinian people and a Palestinian problem which we cannot deny. I don't want—and I have to state this—to exercise dominion over them. The struggle between the two people or national movements is on the territory of Palestine, and from the beginning, it was clear that a Jewish state and an Arab state should emerge within the territory of Palestine. Three partitions have taken place in Palestine: the first in 1922, the second in 1947-49, and the third in

1967. We now have to have the fourth partition—in a final peace solution.

In 1948, the Palestinian Arabs could have created their own state in the portion alloted to them under the UN Partition Plan. The Arab states, not the Jews, destroyed the proposed Arab Palestinian state as they sought to grab territory for themselves. The Arab countries were excellent partners in putting the baby to sleep. If the struggle is about the partition of Palestine, the problem is how to do it. Keeping in mind the instability of Arab society and its tendency to disrespect agreements, we have to reach this partition with those who tend to moderation—and not with those who are bearing the Palestinian Covenant. It brings me, therefore, to the Jordan-Palestinian solution. I would like to solve the Palestinian problem within the new partition, which would come out of a peace agreement between Israel and a single Jordanian-Palestinian delegation in Geneva. But we have to be

Dialogue Fragments

"The Palestinians are looking for new symbols of national loyalty. And the PLO is the only one supplying them."

"The Hashemite kingdom of Jordan symbolizes today for the Palestinians—a new generation on the two banks of the Jordan River— all the anachronistic norms which are bound to disappear."

"The continuation of Israeli rule over one and a half million Arabs, in my opinion, is as risky as an unsafe border."

—*Oren*

"Keeping in mind the instability of Arab society and its tendency to disrespect agreements, we have to reach this partition with those who tend to moderation—and not with those who are bearing the Palestinian Covenant."

" . . . we have to be courageous enough to talk even with the PLO and to look for their real and final goals. . . ."

"We have to worry about the balance of power—especially when we talk about the 1980s. There is a political meaning to this: we have to do our best to reach a political solution as soon as possible."

—*Dror*

" . . . Israel must do whatever is in its ability to lower the profile of the conflict, and to try to behave in such a way that would reduce, not the belligerency, but at least the grievances and animosity and the readiness of the other side to wage war."

"Winning another war might even cause a faster deterioration of the situation, and it might bring an imposed solution faster than we have expected until now."

"I don't believe the words 'full peace.' There's no such thing. It will be enough, as far as I am concerned, for us to have peace like any two countries."

—*Gad*

courageous enough to talk even with the PLO and to look for their real and final goals—even though we must not negotiate with them until they give up their proclaimed objectives, as described in detail in the Palestinian Covenant.

I am ready to give up territories for real security and peace. The line of the future partition has to be in the West Bank, with the agreement of both sides, and with the approval of the Egyptians and the United States. I think that the Gaza Strip should be a part of the Jordanian-Palestinian state; in exchange for this, Jordan would give Israel some of the northern part of the Jordan Valley for security reasons. I do not mean all of the area proposed in the Allon Plan; I mean only the part up to the Damiya bridge. Furthermore, the Gaza Strip has to be separated by a buffer zone from Egypt.

The weakness of my proposal—although it's quite moderate, in my view—is that the Arabs will hesitate to accept it. One factor I take into account is the problem of demilitarization. No country in the world will accept a complete demilitarization. This is one reason why I am against a Palestinian state. An army is security, and an army is a national essential. A demilitarized West Bank, a Palestinian state, would be a country without an army. But a federation between the West Bank and Jordan could include demilitarization. The implications would not be the same because demilitarization would apply only for one part of this country, the West Bank.

We will have to insist on demilitarization of all the West Bank; not only armor, but also missiles, including ground-to-air missiles must be kept out. Missiles stationed in the West Bank would be within range of Israeli military and civil airports. We will have to insist on demilitarization even of artillery. Furthermore, we will have to demand an early-warning radar station in the West Bank, at least for ten years. The Jordan River will be a security boundary, but without any Israeli units on the Jordan, and without an Arab army on the 1967 borders. Because of the short distances between the Jordan River and the Green Line, this may look like a small nuance—as was argued here. But what I am suggesting is no doubt much better than keeping armor near Tel Aviv on the 1967 borders. The river will serve our intelligence as a line for an early warning, and any crossing of it in violation of the agreement on demilitarization will serve as a *casus belli*.

The possibility of Israel's adopting an open nuclear deterrent concept has been mentioned here and was offered by Professor Tucker in his article in the November, 1975, issue of *Commentary*. I personally am against nuclearizing the Middle East. But we have to admit that we are approaching a new era of nuclearization of the Middle East. It doesn't depend only on us. The Arabs have already decided to reach this goal, whether or not Israel has an atomic option. An atomic concept cannot solve all our security problems. It is useless, for example, against terror. I doubt even that we can reach a nuclear balance of terror in the Middle East, not only because we are facing leaders like Qadhafi, but mainly because a great power can neutralize us by threatening us with greater atomic capacity. An atomic concept is good only as an open or tacit deterrent against a general attack by the Arab armies, or as a second strike— but it can't be used against targets close to us.

In mentioning the atomic option, I have to stress that I reject what is called the Masada complex. I agree that we have to be ready to do anything—anything, I say—for our survival. But not in a Masada way. Maybe, to the outermost, we could compare it to the act of Samson.

We have to worry about the balance of power—especially when we talk about the 1980s. There is a political meaning to this: we have to do our best to reach a political solution as soon as possible. Although the balance of power in the future is not so favorable for us, it doesn't mean that there is no political solution. We are not going to lose another war. With a good strategy, high morale, determined and high quality leadership, we can defend ourselves even in the far future, and inflict on our enemies heavy losses and destruction.

Maybe Israel is confused about the alternatives she is facing. But we are in complete agreement—even non-Zionists, as we saw here—on one issue: the issue of our survival. We know that there is a danger of more wars in the Middle East. Israel doesn't want them, and this is the reason for her fears. But we are far from a mood of despair. I must add that I completely oppose the suggestion voiced here, that Israel be prepared to give up the Law of Return; this would mean cutting the lifeline of Israel. I am sure that the Israeli public is ready to give great concessions for real peace. Yet, at the same time, there is a danger that this readiness will change if the Arabs do not answer our claim for peace. If there is no alternative, Israel will take a sharp turn toward an extreme line.

BITAN: What do you suggest Israel should do if the United States objects to such a line?

DROR: I am opposed to the step-by-step approach. Israel should hold on to the territories until the Arabs agree to make peace, and Israel could hold on to them even if the United States is against this tactic. But it would be best for Israel to try to convince the United States to support its position. I don't believe there will be unlimited pressure from the United States if Israel is firm.

AMIR: Does Israel have any evidence that the Arab states are doing any more than developing an option for nuclear weapons? That they are actually acquiring an operational nuclear capability?

DROR: The line between developing an option and developing a capability is a thin one. There is considerable evidence of activity in the Arab world concerning the development of nuclear reactors—scientific study, publications and exchange of information.

AMIR: But is there any hard evidence?

DROR: Beyond such indications as I mentioned, the answer is no.

"It should be an ultimatum: no peace agreement without the Palestinians."

GAD: We should distinguish between assumptions or assessments of the situation and our policy recommendations. I don't find too much point in arguing the basic assumptions. I think it is much more important to try to see whether we can arrive at certain mutually-agreed solutions or policy recommendations—on which, surprisingly, people can often agree no matter what their basic analyses.

And in developing policy recommendations we should remember one thing said here—that it's not necessarily an answer to a hawkish stand on the other side if we adopt a hawkish stand on our side. Maybe just the opposite is correct. It has to be analyzed on its merits. In this respect, the special stress on the real intentions of the Arabs is not as important as it seems. What we have to discuss is our basic situation, our capabilities and options; and we have to judge them according to how they contribute to our existence, well-being and security.

We also ought to set aside arguments about the basic problem of national rights of both sides. Readiness to compromise on certain rights does not mean that you say that these rights don't exist; it just means that you don't possess enough power to achieve those rights. And if you don't possess enough power to achieve them by force, then there's no sense in discussing those rights. It's just too much talk about nothing. I don't think we should even argue about whether we do have rights, or whether our right has existed longer than the Palestinians' or whether it's 50 years or 2000 years. The point is whether we can enforce certain solutions that will achieve our rights. I think most of us agree that we can't. So the various solutions for the territories and their Arab population shouldn't be discussed in terms of whether they are immoral or moral, but only on the basis of whether they are practical or impractical. And I believe that a majority of us will agree that we don't possess now the power necessary to impose a solution that involves occupying all the territories, or forcing the Arabs there to emigrate, or other ideas along these lines.

Most of the people here agree that the balance of power in the Middle East is not shifting to our side. There are different assessments on how fast it's turning against us, but I think we should, if we are honest, admit this fact.

It's true that a certain amount of danger from the outside serves to weld national unity and to bring out some inner strength, as it has in the past for Israelis. But too much external danger has an eroding influence in the long term on our ability not only to hold on but to develop a society that could keep its quality-edge on the surrounding countries. Somebody mentioned before that if we are ready to lower our standard of living, then maybe we will be less dependent on America. This might have been true in the past. Our balance-of-trade deficit is going to be four and a half billion dollars this year, and it will grow. This is about half the national income. Suppose you cut the standard of living by half—which is almost impossible because a majority of the consumption is public consumption. Only if you cut it by half will you be able to cover the balance-of-trade deficit. Then we will become a society which will look more-or-less like any one of the small developing countries, and we will not have this necessary quality-edge.

Nonetheless, given the deteriorating balance of power, we here agree that Israel needs deterrent power for its existence. Whether the Arabs do actually want to kill us or whether they don't is immaterial now. We need enough military power to deter any power combination in the Middle East from over-running Israel. As for nuclear armaments, it seems clear to me that we will never depend on a first-strike capacity, only on a second-strike capacity in case our very existence is being threatened. We won't be able to use it as a threat of our own, as a threat of escalation in regular conventional war. Yet if we have an atomic balance of terror, it will be even more difficult for us to use our past strategy of threatening escalation into a major war in which we can have the edge. So I don't think that nuclear deterrence will solve our problem.

What also won't solve our problem is another war. We can win another war. We can win maybe two other wars, but it won't change the basic facts of the conflict. Winning another war might even cause a faster deterioration of the situation, and it might bring an imposed solution faster than we have expected until now.

My basic assumption is that Israel must do whatever is in its ability to lower the profile of the conflict, and to try to behave in such a way that would reduce, not the belligerency, but at least the grievances and animosity and the readiness of the other side to wage war. I'm going to suggest an outline for a national security policy for Israel. It is what, in terms of practical policy, I think can become the national policy of Israel with the agreement of the majority of the population.

Everybody here will agree that we cannot base our national security policy on an assumption that the Arabs are ready for peace. Anyone who bases his policy on such an assumption, or such a prognosis, is a fool. We need a national policy that possesses enough teeth, enough deterrent power so that in case we find out that the Arabs are not ready for peace, we still will be able to survive.

I also think it would be foolish to base a policy on the assumption that *aliyah* is going to continue. We all want *aliyah* to continue. We hope it will grow. But a national policy based on that hope would be sheer folly—even suicidal—in the event that *aliyah* did not continue.

Finally, I think it is impossible to base a national policy on the assumption or the prognosis that we will not get agreement from the Arabs. They might surprise us and agree. We must have a policy that is valid whether or not the Arabs agree to it. My reservation about the suggestion that Israel annex the territories on the assumption that the Arabs won't apply for Israeli citizenship is that this assumption might be right for five years, ten, maybe fifteen years. Lebanon had this assumption when it was established as "Grand Liban" in the 1920s. The assumption that their situation would remain stable turned out to be false. Lebanon's troubles emerged as its large Arab Muslim minority eventually became a majority over the Christians.

The basic premise of a desirable national security policy must be that it will deter the other side from war, that it will set a penalty for war, that it will not close the option for peace, and that it will promise rewards for peace. This national security policy should also be such that it secures international support and the support of the United States.

To meet these tests, our policy has to completely remove, as a problem between us and the Arabs, the question of the territories. This does not mean giving back the territories outright. It means removing our claim to the territories, making it crystal clear that we don't intend to use the fact of the occupation in order to realize our national rights to those territories. I believe that's the only way to make sure that the international community has on its agenda the problem of peace and not the problem of Israel's demand for territories. The reward for peace would be return of the territories. The penalty for non-agreement would be the stopping of any momentum towards peace with the Arabs and the prospect of continued war. The penalty could not be annexation, as suggested here. That would penalize us by getting us more entangled with the territories and by risking the danger of turning Israel into a future Lebanon. So neither annexation nor continued Israeli settlement is the proper penalty.

In this light we have to see our approach to the Palestinian problem. Since the major problem of the Palestinians is their ability to disrupt any peace agreements, I think that bringing the Palestinians, and even the PLO, into the negotiations should be Israel's major interest. Israel should demand that the Palestinians be represented in any peace agreement. It should be an ultimatum: no peace agreement without the Palestinians. Those Palestinians that the Arab world recognizes as representative must sign the agreement. In our blindness we have demanded that Geneva be convened without the Palestinians. If this happens, we will go through the agonizing process of coming to some agreement, only to discover that the Palestinians won't accept it, and that the Arab world therefore will not be able to abide by it.

Israel should and can be the first one to make a reciprocal, conditional announcement of recognition of the Palestinians, in a statement such as: "We will recognize the Palestinians if and when they recognize us." This should be the cornerstone of the Israeli position right now vis-à-vis the Palestinians.

HANAN: The PLO or Palestinians?

GAD: The Palestinians. It's not up to us to decide who represents the Palestinians. Any agency of the Palestinians that the Arab world recognizes and that itself recognizes us, will benefit from this reciprocal statement.

I see two major weaknesses in my position. The first one is not that the Arabs are not ready to accept it. The trouble is that the Israelis are not ready to accept it. I think this new Israeli readiness to discuss non-belligerency rather than peace stems from the fact that we are not ready, mainly because of internal politics, to say openly we are prepared to give all the territories for peace. And as long as we are offering only part of the deal, then we are ready to be satisfied with only part of the price. The only way to be able to demand the whole price is to offer the whole deal. We are now in a position of discussing territories and not peace, something that enables the Arabs to avoid giving an answer about the basic problem of peace and the Palestinians. Moreover, we are being forced, because the Americans need the momentum, into these step-by-step agreements. I agree that this will lead to giving back all the territories without achieving any peace, to a reopening of the question of the 1949-67 borders, and eventually to another war. Our government sounds like that lady who wanted to cut off her puppy's tail, but she was a little too good-hearted and merciful so she didn't cut it all off at once. But she cut one piece off every day, so the dog wouldn't suffer too much. Our government cuts a little piece of the territories off every half a year or year when the pressures mount and hopes that it will hurt less. I am sure of one thing: it's going to hurt more.

The second weakness of my position is

this counter-argument: If it's true that we are going to go back to the 1949-67 borders without peace, why should the Arabs—if they know that—be ready for peace? The only way to test this argument, of course, is to adopt my policy. I don't believe the words "full peace." There's no such thing. It will be enough, as far as I am concerned, for us to have peace like any two countries. War begins from peace and peace begins from a situation of war.

Negotiations can occur when both sides to a conflict feel themselves equally strong or equally weak. I'm afraid that the whole Middle East is going to be led into a position of equal weakness after a couple of other wars, and then maybe from a position of equal weakness perhaps we'll find ourselves willing to propose such a policy. I think, rather, that now is the time—in our strength—to adopt it.

BITAN: If we declare at once that we give up our claim to the territories, what will be the penalty left to us if they refuse it?

GAD: The answer is that only by making such a declaration will we be in a position to hold on to the territories with the support of America and a part of the international community. With a declaration, we have a reasonable stand as far as America is concerned, a stand that they can bargain on. The penalty will be a continuation of the situation. For Israel to hold on to the territories as cards to be traded for peace is a strong penalty for the Arab world now. A declaration can put Israel in a position to resist a piece-by-piece process pushed by the Americans that will deprive us of the territories in a very few years, without peace. And with nothing to trade for peace, we'll surely have another war.

BITAN: If the United States wants, as you said, momentum, and if momentum now means step-by-step, since you are against step-by-step, how are you going to avoid the conflict with America which you say we can't afford?

GAD: If we adopt my policy there could be momentum without American pressure. Unless we offer a clear alternative to the step-by-step policy, we will have to submit to it. We can't just object to it and say, "I don't like it." A concrete alternative is the declaration I suggest. It can produce momentum too.

BITAN: Are you willing to be less vague about the question of what "peace" would mean?

GAD: Yes. I don't think anything can be gained by trying to make an absolutely clear definition of what peace is. There is an understanding of what it means. Peace is open borders. And if peace means the right for Israelis to settle on the West Bank, then—as Said Hammami pointed out rightly—it also means the right of the Palestinians to settle inside their own land, so long as both sides accept the laws of the country where they're staying. You don't arrive at peace in one day. It will probably demand many safeguards and many delay mechanisms. We would have to negotiate, for example, certain positions to be occupied by our army for a certain number of years, which would only be evacuated after the process of peace takes shape. It's a process that begins with an agreement and ends with the type of relations that exist between Switzerland and the rest of Europe.

ZVI: Can you be more specific about the place of the Palestinians in this process of peace? A Palestinian state—where and when?

GAD: I agree with those who believe we cannot patronize the Palestinians and decide for them how they are going to express their feeling of national identity. If they choose to do it in the framework of one state with Jordan, I think we should welcome it, as long as we can have all the necessary safeguards for our security. If they choose to have a separate state, I think it should be left entirely up to them, within a process of making peace. We should make clear that we will not interfere with their realization of national identity as long as our basic interests are safeguarded, and as long as they recognize our existence as an independent state within viable borders.

DROR: In expecting some sort of a mutual recognition—Israel and the Palestinians— are you ready to accept a PLO delegation in the Geneva talks?

GAD: I said that it is in our interest to demand that a delegation of Palestinians participate.

DROR: Even before mutual recognition?

GAD: We should demand it, providing they recognize the existence of the state of Israel. You remember what happened with the Egyptians. We also put a demand like that to them. Then Sadat was pressed to announce that the mere fact that he sits in Geneva with Israel means that he recognizes the existence of Israel.

HANAN: Would you accept such recognition from the Palestinians?

GAD: I don't believe there is room for any agreement with any Palestinian faction that is not going to be based upon mutual recognition. I do think that there is some room for discussion—even with people who don't recognize you. You discuss the terms of recognition. Recognition too is a process. For that process we need two things: a conditional declaration that we would be ready to grant recognition if there is reciprocity, and the process of negotiation itself. I believe that the negotiations should be part of the process.

"Jews: 100 percent caution. Do not trust the Arabs."

HANAN: These have been great days for the science of zoology. We have seen the emergence of an entirely new species—the hoves or the dawks. Part hawk, part dove. Too many of us got cold feet around this table and executed a retreat, which they are so afraid to do in Israel. The doves became a little hawkish; the hawks, a little dovish. What is common to all of us is that we know that this is a terribly serious business. This is actually a dialogue with the United States of America. We are speaking to America here. So I must start with one small remark. In spite of our great dependence, friendship and admiration for the United States of America, I deplore the extreme statements here that amount to something very near to submission to America, very near a call that Israel really toe the line with any American whim or wish. Because of the respect we hold for this great democracy, we have to leave much greater leeway for struggle, fight, and sometimes maybe even crisis with this friend of ours.

There is a feeling which I think is quite common to all of us, a lesson of our symposium. It says, "Jews: 100 percent caution." Be careful. Caution. I would put it even more bluntly, and maybe you all won't share it with me: Do not trust the Arabs. This is what I keep telling myself all the time. Attach all the names in the world to me, I will hold to that. I do not trust Arabs as they are today—with their regimes, with their rulers, with their societies, with their lack of democracy. Their only aim now is to get rid of us. No central idea in Arab policy today is stronger and more concentrated than this aim.

For a moment we must forget our wonderful atmosphere. In twenty-four hours we'll be on our way home. There are the famous homing pigeons, homing doves, and even the hawks are homing. We are on our way home, and let us be now home. And let us ask ourselves, "What is going to happen in the near future?" There is one simple answer to it. What you call the conflict—I call it the war—is going on. It is not going to be discontinued. I don't see when, not in the near future—precisely because of this almost perfect asymmetry between Israel and its foes in the Arab world and among the Palestinians themselves. A huge asymmetry gives them all the advantages of carrying on with the war. The first Arab is still to be born who will say to himself and to his brethren, "This war is bad for me." There is a state of war and we have to prepare ourselves for it. We and America—the two of us. And for that, determination and strength—moral and spiritual—is terribly important. This is why so much of the philosophy of the doves in Israel is, I believe, detrimental to the national tasks before us. Because they, to a very great extent, erode the very tissue of our national body and soul.

I suggest that we not make too much of a division between our conflict with the Palestinians and our conflict with Arab states. The source of the conflict between Israel and the Palestinians is Pan-Arabism and the Arab nations. But for them, this conflict would have never existed. So the challenges and difficulties that will confront us for a very long time will face us on a broad and complicated front; it is on the borders; it is inside our homes; it is in our streets; it's in the world arena; it is on all levels. We have to keep telling our friends the Americans not to forget—we have to survive this war day by day and hour by hour.

I think that I express the feelings of

many Israelis, and at least a number of policymakers in Israel, if I suggest that we refrain completely from speaking or even making any calculations about nuclear armaments for Israel. It will be a terrible mistake. Israel can only lose from it. I think that Israel is strong enough—if it will use its political and military power wisely—without using this terrible and self-defeating weapon.

My prescription for Israeli policy today towards the Palestinians and towards all our Arab foes is to start with a very radical change. We must stop all the maneuvers and contacts now being conducted or prepared, and say, "The hell with all this—we are being cheated." During the policy fed to us throughout the last three or four years, we have been cheated. Let us now go to square one, which means direct negotiations. This was long the declared policy of the state of Israel. Let us go back to it. Direct negotiations would have all the benefits that all of us here want, without the bad smell of bazaar bargaining. The civilized family of nations will understand and sympathize with such a standpoint because it has a very basic human approach in it. It is based on our demand to be recognized as human beings. It is based on the demand that we be regarded as good to be spoken to, to be met, to be shaken hands with. It implies, too, something new: recognition for recognition, peace for peace. At some stage this demand for direct negotiations will meet with understanding on the side of the Arabs—I don't know when, but I'm sure that it will some day. Only if we change completely our attitude and think about peace as something that is exchangeable only for peace, and recognition exchangeable only for recognition—only then we might one day, not very soon, one day, get the same thing from the other side.

Has the weakness of the Arabs come to an end? For decades, actually since the conquest of Ottoman Palestine by the British,

the fact that Arabs were weak internationally helped us a lot, enabling us to build, in spite of them, what we built in Israel. There are many people who think that the weakness of the Arab world came to an end somewhere around October, 1973. I think it has not come to an end. The Arab world as a whole is still essentially weak. Of course, there are some very important elements that make it stronger temporarily—massive support of the Communists and the Third World, and the growing dependence of the Western world on oil, and so on. The fundamental weakness of the Arab world is the poverty of the masses, the lack of solid social and national structures, submissive dependence on the Communists and the Third World, and the monolithic or dictatorial character of Arab regimes. In view of those weaknesses, it is not necessarily Israel's fate from now on to be on the decline, with our power diminishing.

I will conclude by saying that I have a vision for Israel's future. I believe that in a way this symposium was actually about Zionism. It was about whether we believe or not any more in Zionism, and about how hard we are ready to fight or how much we are ready to sacrifice for Zionism. We have to go back to the basic beliefs of Zionism. Most important, Zionism has only begun. What our fathers and forefathers demanded of themselves and their generation—the belief in *aliyah*, the fight for *aliyah*, settlement, advancing step-by-step—we have to demand from ourselves. We have to tell the full truth to ourselves, and to the Arabs, to the world: the land of Israel, Palestine, is the land of the Jewish people.

The solution of all problems emanating from the conflict must be on a Middle Eastern scale. All the states of the region were the producers of the problem; they now should contribute to the solution. Palestinian refugees should be settled throughout the Middle East. Eastern Jordan must be the homeland and the state of whichever Palestinians want to live there. Territory now in the hands of Israel will remain there.

What is the weakness of my presentation? There is something very weak—it is we: WE. It is the Jewish people. Because what I am presenting to you is a challenge, to a very great degree a war cry, for ourselves. The Arabs won't make peace with us. In such a situation, we have to decide whether we are afraid, whether we are tired. If we are not ready, then we must face the gloomiest of gloomy predictions. Unless we dare, we will see no future.

MEIR: Let's imagine a totally hypothetical situation. Tomorrow, or the day after, you have a real guarantee that the Arabs want peace, and that somebody can assure you that it is real peace. But there is a condition. For that real peace, you have to give back part of Eretz Israel, that is, the West Bank. Would you, for real peace, within your vision and your concept of Zionism—and I mean a real peace which would assure the future of the state of Israel—be ready to give up the West Bank? If not, how do you imagine that the Americans can bargain with the Arab world, if they have nothing to offer the Arabs?

HANAN: My answer is no.

MEIR: I expected it.

HANAN: The reason is that I do not believe, I do not believe, in an offer based just on withdrawal from all the territories. Because I will answer the Arabs, "I want your peace more than anything—well, almost more than anything. Zionism is more important to me. But why is it that with peace you want these territories back? Look, I am planning to have fifteen million Jews in this country in a matter of thirty or forty years. I'm working for this. Without this, my life is meaningless. Can you understand? My country is small. There is no oil, no nothing—almost no

water. And there are problems—let us solve them together." For instance, I will agree that the Arabs who live in Eretz Israel will have the most developed self-expression and self-determination. Not political and not military. Not statehood. The state will be the state of Israel. But we will do everything to please those who live with us.

More than that. Let us cooperate. Let us, for instance, take Sinai and make it into a place where all sorts of scientific, sociological, economic experiments are undertaken by the nearby nations.

And about Jerusalem. Once there is peace, once you do not demand political rule over Jerusalem, I'll give you everything you want. You will be able to build more mosques, if you want. You will be able to put up all the flags you want. If you want to declare King Hussein as king of all Palestine, you can do so, provided that the president of Israel will be the president of all Palestine, including the East Bank.

MEIR: I ask again: you say America is bargaining with the Arabs and should drive a hard bargain. Yet you don't want to give anything back. What are you giving the Americans as a card? What will they give the Arabs?

HANAN: The bargaining will be about the arrangements in the entire Middle East—development plans and investments in the Middle East, things like that.

AMIR: You said, very wisely, that you do not trust the Arabs. Do you trust the Russians?

HANAN: No.

AMIR: Do you trust the Americans? If they give you guarantees, would you trust them?

HANAN: Much more than the Russians.

AMIR: But you basically do not trust them?

HANAN: Not before I examine everything. Not blindfolded.

AMIR: Then why—in a similar way—don't you visualize the possibility of examining arrangements with Arabs? The hidden assumption of your statement is that international relations are based on trust—but the Arabs are somehow an exception. When you say we shouldn't trust the Arabs, it implies that we could trust others, while Arabs must be treated differently. It has always been my assump-

tion that international relations are not based on trust—but on systems of checks and balances, and they always necessitate the acceptance of a certain degree of risk.

HANAN: But not in this case—for one simple reason. No other nation in the world is confronted with neighbors whose express wish is to annihilate it. All other conflicts in the world are about territories, relative strength, and resources. Our situation is completely unique.

"I am ready to pay very much for peace. I don't see another more lenient and more dovish gambit."

NAHUM: I call my position "existential Zionism." Its essence is that it gives real value to the existence of the state of Israel. Its nationalism is Zionism.

I begin by stressing that the phrase "Tactical Left" is a misnomer. For the adjective "tactical" was meant pejoratively—as if it is a frivolous, even hypocritical, deceptive attempt at public relations. In fact, its merit is that it combines tactics and strategy more or less in a coherent whole. Any position which is only strategic, or is only tactical, is deficient. Even though the Tactical Left is not devoid of danger, its detractors among us will find to their astonishment that they are converging on it. As long as any position on the Left insists on a conditional withdrawal—that is, predicated on Arab acceptance of the state of Israel—it gravitates towards what has been called the Tactical Left. And any position on the Right giving importance to the problem of political plausibility in the eyes of world public opinion will also find itself roaming towards it.

According to my position, Israel should declare readiness to withdraw to the pre-1967 borders. I go further than Meir whose definition of his red line is that if Sharm el-

Sheikh is needed for the defense of Israel it should be retained. By that logic, if Irbid in East Jordan is needed for the defense of Israel, it too should be included. The logic is obviously not plausible.

My position recognizes the Palestinians' grievance. I agree that the use of the word Palestinian "agony" goes too far. But I also believe that evincing empathy towards Arab suffering partially disarms foes and pleases friends. In any case, my position maintains that Palestinian grievances and their demand for self-determination should be met outside Israel's borders once Israel withdraws. Israel should adopt an open-ended, sympathetic indifference to the nature of the solution—whether this state is Jordanian or Palestinian. This posture would return the Palestinian problem to its natural habitat—inter-Arab politics.

I do not believe in the possibility of a ministate on the West Bank, to which the Palestinians themselves refer in derogatory terms. I think that it is an impossibility because of geopolitical considerations. It would be landlocked and would need an outlet. If the outlet was through Israel, we would have leverage over them, for instance by our ability to block passage to Gaza. If it was through Jordan, then such a state would be subservient to Jordan. The Palestinians cannot Palestinianize Jordan, whose Jordanian character is in the process of reinforcement. I consider it a grave mistake, however, for Israel to present an historical evaluation about prospects for a ministate as a political demand. But I do think that such a state would not solve the Palestinian problem. It would be irredentist. It would not be able to satisfy the ambitions of the PLO leadership, which thrives on the conflict and has a vested interest in its continuation, not in its termination. I prefer the Hashemite solution. But leave it to the Palestinians and the Arabs to decide what they want.

It is one of the ironies of this conflict that Israel has tended to think that there is a possibility of reaching a settlement with the Palestinians in the West Bank, to think that peace will come gradually, incrementally, through the growth of good relations between Jews and Arabs living on the West Bank. That idea is irrelevant. People didn't understand that the Arabs in the West Bank are not an autonomous political factor, capable of reaching a settlement on their own. This misunderstanding had very harmful results because it prevented Israel from coming to grips with the real Palestinian problem—with the PLO. "To come to terms" with the West Bankers, as Dayan put it, is absurd. There is no possibility of reaching any settlement with the West Bank Arabs.

What should be the conditions for our withdrawal to the pre-1967 lines? I give first priority to an Arab change of heart, to an Arab expression of readiness to make peace in terms of finalizing the conflict. Until now I have not seen one phrase indicating such readiness. But change of heart, in itself, is not enough. It must be buttressed by practical arrangements to safeguard Israel's security. The chances that the Arabs are ready to finalize the con-

flict on the condition of our withdrawal are small. Though I am more liberal than self-styled doves, I consider it not 5 percent, but 1 to 10.

If the Arabs don't accept, then we may say this: since the Arabs don't want peace, we are not going to be guardians of the Arab territories as deposits forever. We are not Swiss bankers who hold deposits for a long time. We are in a good position to start producing facts, if they refuse to make peace.

EITAN: What is "producing facts"?

NAHUM: Producing facts means establishing Israeli settlements, and so on. I recognize the PLO. I consider the PLO, by the way, one of the most intellectual groups in the Middle East. Their sufferings have sensitized them to many problems. And it shapes the way they adapt their ideology, their practice, and their enmity toward Israel. I have for a long time believed that Israel should offer simultaneous recognition of legitimacy, but I am not sanguine at all that the PLO is ready to start such a dialogue. Yet if they refuse, it will shift the burden of proof on to them.

What are the weaknesses of my position? There are very cogent arguments against the policy of concessions. If Israel declares its readiness to withdraw and to let a Palestinian or a Palestinian-Jordanian state be established, the United States and others may take Israel at its word and exert pressure on it to withdraw—without an adequate Arab political *quid pro quo*. The interim agreement of September, 1975, is a case in point.

Furthermore, there are objective difficulties in making the security safeguards concrete and in making them into real assurances. Israel's concessions would be fragmented because they are divisible. A refusal to concede would be represented as petty narrow-mindedness and obstinacy. The demands from the Arab side are not so divisible. There is no symmetry here. For

Israel the loss of strategic assets is irreversible. It would be an exchange of real property that could not be recovered, for a promise to end the conflict—a promise that could be revoked. Moreover, the plurality of the Arab actors, the pressure of the extremists, the impossibility of solving all the items of contention—all these factors could impel the Arabs to reopen the conflict. They might not be able to resist the temptation while Israel has weakened itself by withdrawal. The Arabs themselves say they can make concessions because such concessions won't be permanent. Furthermore, internal difficulties of Arab society may drive them to external adventures. Arab society is seething with a desire for vengeance. Look at the cruelty in their internecine wars, the way they treated the Kurds, the way the Jordanians treated the Palestinians in Black September, the atrocities in the Lebanese civil war. All this does not augur well for a modicum of moderation with so deeply hated a neighbor as we are. A future Arab government may rescind on the obligation of its predecessor. Thus, opponents of concessions argue that Israel is better off if it sits tight and risks disapproval by world public opinion, even if it means being besieged, abandoned, and isolated. They argue that Israel should do its best to explain its case and its predicament. All this is better than being nice, affable, forthcoming, reasonable—and then perishing.

These are very strong arguments against my position. Still, I think that we are in a better position to debate and hold our ground when the problem is not withdrawal, yes or no, but the condition of the withdrawal. We can be much more obstinate and demanding on the conditions of the withdrawal than on the problem of principle.

MEIR: I want to clarify: 5 percent is a symbolic expression for the minimum, as is the red line idea. I didn't refer to the 1967 lines;

it might actually be a mistake to do so. If you use these borders in a tactical approach, and the Arabs say "yes," then you have to move to the 1967 lines exactly, without taking any red line, any minimum, into account. You have abandoned any possibility of even a minor strategic safeguard for our minimum needs—for a purely juridical, formal border.

NAHUM: You are fooling yourself if you think there is any chance whatsoever of the Arabs accepting other than the 1967 borders. They perhaps will be ready for minor changes, I don't know. But, for example, I don't believe that Egypt will make peace with Israel if we retain Yamit.* They made it very clear. I don't indulge in illusions. Either you want to make a proposition which can be accepted—a return to 1967—or otherwise there is no possibility of reaching an agreement.

MEIR: Even Rogers mentioned small changes.

NAHUM: I know, but he's not an Arab.

EITAN: Am I right in understanding that you are against the policy of step-by-step now?

NAHUM: I think step-by-step has exhausted itself, and I see danger in Geneva. But we have to make a liberal proposal, as I said. I am not sanguine that it will be accepted by the Arabs—I can't fool myself. At least it will improve our position, although I am alive to its dangers. It is very important for Israel not to clash with the *zeitgeist*—with the spirit of the age in the international political arena. This *zeitgeist* is what brought decolonization. To have the *zeitgeist* on our side, we must change our image in the most liberal fashion we can.

---

*A new Israeli town in North Sinai near the Gaza Strip, projected to be a regional center and regarded by Israeli authorities as a strategic buffer zone.

EITAN: How long should Israel wait until she is convinced about the final refusal of the Arabs to make peace, before starting to make facts in the areas?

NAHUM: I speak less about time than the principle. The process should be started with a declaration. We say: "We are ready to go back. But if you don't want to finalize the conflict, then that means that you are bent on vengeance, on war. And if you are, then we have only one consideration, and that is the strategic consideration." But I must emphasize that, in terms of Israel's strategy, I am against "going nuclear"—which was earlier referred to so cavalierly.

ZVI: Are you against annexation too?

NAHUM: I don't speak about annexation; mine is not an annexationist position.

HANAN: But you said we are not a bank.

NAHUM: I think that we will be in a much better posture to hold strategic positions if the Arabs don't want to finalize the conflict. Then we may produce strategic facts.

HANAN: Don't you realize that you would be very easily found out as trying to cheat the Arabs and the world?

NAHUM: In what way?

HANAN: Because you say: "I do not believe the Arabs will accept my offer." Then you say: "If they do not accept, we are going to establish facts." But you repeat all the time that they will not accept. And everyone knows it. And they will say, "Here are the Jews again trying to cheat the world." You are offering something that you know in advance they will not agree to. You put too high a price. This is what you do when you do not want to sell something. You know in advance they will never pay, so the reality is that you want to remain in the territories. So don't you have the slightest suspicion that someone will expose you as a cheat?

NAHUM: No. What I said about whether the Arabs will accept or not is a subjective belief of mine. It is outside of the objective proposition I am offering.

HANAN: But my question is, will not someone say, "He is trying to cheat"?

NAHUM: Why? I say I am ready. There may be Arabs who may say that. I don't deny it. For anything you do, however, there may be people who will try to describe it as if there are ulterior motives to it. I am convinced I value peace above anything. I am ready to pay very much for peace. I don't see another more lenient and more dovish gambit. So I want to start with this one and to pass the burden to them.

URI: You said that an erosion of the Arab position could come. When could it come?

NAHUM: Not overnight. I don't expect that. What I want to see is an intention to change. That is what is important. Peace is not an event, peace is a process. I want a sign that the process has begun.

URI: But how could it come?

NAHUM: How can the Arab position be changed? It seems to me that the erosion of the Arab position—let me call it the erosion of the "politicidal" attitude within the Arab position—will come only by impressing on the Arab public and governments the odium it will bring if they adhere to it—under whatever guise. What they do is always conceal this politicidal attitude in all kinds of verbal acrobatics—instead of saying that they want to destroy Israel, they say, "We want to liberate Palestine," or "We want a solution of the Palestinian problem."

The weakness of the Arab position is this politicidal attitude. They all show, in different degrees, uneasiness about it. They show hesitancy in avowing that politicide is the net outcome of the more elegant formulation of their objective.

You have to make the Arabs apologetic about their position against Israel and not confident about it, and that can only be achieved by condemning their position. One approach that some Israelis take says: We have to describe the Arab position as mild. Then it will be mild. That is believing the magic of a self-fulfilling prophecy. It is the philosophy of *New Outlook*, [a dovish, English-language Israeli journal] and I think it is counterproductive. To describe and give importance to Palestinian dissident views merely gives the Arabs an excuse to stick to their politicidal attitude. It seems to me a big mistake to treat the Palestinians as Saunders does—as if nobody knows what their objective is. That too only encourages them to adhere to their present position and their maximalist demands. An Israeli attitude which does not stress the politicidal factors, the barbarity which is in the Arab position—this attitude is the most damaging, that is why I am so critical of *New Outlook*.

EITAN: I want you to be clear. Someday when it is 100 percent certain that the Arabs do not want peace, then you are ready to establish facts in the administered territories. After 5, 10, 15 years, the facts would establish a new quality, a new face for the territories; they would become part and parcel of Israel—except for the political rights of the Arab population there. Is that right?

NAHUM: I am not for the annexation of the West Bank. I admire the Gush Emunim, but I think their enterprise is worthless, because they cannot change the Arab character of the area. The character of the area is decided by the people who live there. But if we need to have military presences and

positions outside the 1967 lines, then I'm prepared to set them up.

EITAN: Military posts?

NAHUM: Yes, to defend the area.

EITAN: But we know the settlements are not intended to defend. It is the other way around: they will actually need to be defended if war breaks out.

I would also like you to be more precise about this Jordanian-Palestinian context. You say it's not up to us to decide; let them decide. Put this in a concrete term of reference: a Geneva conference. According to the original arrangement, Israel has the right to veto new participants. If there is a consensus of the Arabs, maybe with the support of the United States, that a separate PLO delegation is to be invited, are you for it or against it? It's not just a question of whether we should be "sitting with murderers." More important, there is no doubt that if the PLO were to sit separately in Geneva, and if Israel agreed there to withdraw from part of the West Bank, then the PLO would take it.

NAHUM: Once we withdraw, it is not realistic to think that we are going to determine the nature of the regime there. It even implies contempt. I am ready for reciprocity, as I said, if the PLO recognizes the legitimacy of Israel. But I don't think they will do it. The illegitimacy of Israel is at the core of their ideology. People can shed what is peripheral in their ideology, but not what is central. Therefore, it's difficult for the PLO to do it. But if we offer them reciprocity, then we pass the burden of proof to them. We get rid of the Palestinian problem—with the stigma that it puts on Israel.

Dialogue Fragments

" ... Israel should declare readiness to withdraw to the pre-1967 borders."

"I consider the PLO, by the way, one of the most intellectual groups in the Middle East."

"I am ready for reciprocity ... if the PLO recognizes the legitimacy of Israel. But I don't think they will do it. The illegitimacy of Israel is at the core of their ideology. People can shed what is peripheral in their ideology, but not what is central."

"I am not for the annexation of the West Bank. I admire the Gush Emunim, but I think their enterprise is worthless, because they cannot change the Arab character of the area. The character of the area is decided by the people who live there."

—Nahum

"And if there are Arabs who seek an arrangement, a *modus vivendi* which would prevent a war and would leave the realization of their vision to future generations and to the historical process. I would call this leeway and would explore its potentialities."

"But I see a greater risk in the continuation of immobility. The problem with immobility is that it is likely to explode in your face."

"The option of a compromise based on the return of the territories should be kept open till hell freezes over. Because if we are responsible toward the next generation, we shouldn't do anything which would make it impossible for them to reach a compromise."

—Amir

"All this talk—that Israel must present the Arabs with a choice, either 'real peace' or nothing, is not the language of politics."

AMIR: Some participants have expressed empathy with the predicament of the Palestinian Arabs. Others have stated that they recognize the national rights of the Palestinians as a people seeking to have self-expression on their land, as a political community. These views I wholeheartedly support.

It has been said here that we should present our case, particularly in our relations to the United States, on the basis of its justice and moral validity. I suggest that justice and morality are indivisible and you cannot deny for others what you claim for yourself.

But this belief should not erode our position, which emanates from the predicament and rights of our own people. The unique historical course of the Jewish people is a solid foundation for the claim of statehood in Eretz Israel, and for faith in the future of the Jewish people on this land. I cannot accept the view heard here, which so lightheartedly writes off the viability of the Jewish people and prescribes assimilation. The awe-inspiring historical record of the Jewish people should be approached with greater caution, and credit should be given to the phenomenal ability of the Jewish people to preserve their identity and vitality for thousands of years.

If one accepts the validity of the claims of the two peoples and works on the assumption that they both may have a future in this land, then he is not free from answering the question, "How?" Even if it is next to impossible to visualize a peace agreement in the foreseeable future, one must be able to depict a picture of peaceful coexistence at some point. Because otherwise there is no future. As a target for our policies and a vision to guide our actions, we must have a concept of a situation in which there is a reasonably satisfactory meeting of the aspirations of the two peoples.

The more I turn the whole question in my mind and the more I listen to what is being said here—the more I am convinced that there is no escape from the conclusion that the only reasonable concept of a settlement is one based on partition. There are three million Israelis who are part of the Jewish people. There are about three million Palestinians who are part of the Arab nation. The aspirations of both groups are focused on historical Palestine. They must somehow be balanced. Each one wishes and has the right to maintain its tie to the largest circle to which it belongs. Jerusalem, I believe, should be shared—not necessarily on an equal basis, but proportionately to the historical importance of that city to each respective people.

These concepts should guide us in the long road ahead. They should inspire political initiatives, and should impose clear restrictions on our behavior in the territories. The option of implementing that compromise at some point in the future should not be closed. In other words—no Israeli settlements in the territories.

I believe that peace is a process, and that a concept of peace is the basis for policymaking. At this stage, I see the reduction of the level of the conflict as a concrete and realistic target for Israeli policy.

Between any two adversaries there may exist different levels of conflict. You can have a constant state of war. You can have sporadic wars. You can have tensions, with greater or lesser chances for the outbreak of war. To illustrate my point, I would like to turn back for a few moments to the history of the two basic periods of the Arab-Israeli conflict in the last twenty-eight years. I distinguish between the 1948 to 1967 period, and from 1967 on.

The first period was not, of course, a period of peaceful co-existence. The depth of Arab animosity was clear and no peace settlement with the Arabs was possible. There were border incidents and periods of tension. And there were wars—one all-out war roughly every decade. But those wars were not premeditated. They were the result of constellations of forces and circumstances which, against a background of basic animosity, produced escalation and confrontation. Perhaps those wars of 1956 and 1967 could even have been prevented, if checked at the early stages of escalation. The Israeli and Arab societies did not really mobilize all their resources for those wars. Active conflict with Israel was quite high on the list of Arab priorities but not always on the top of that list.

In the second period, the cycle of wars changed—to an outbreak every two or three years: After the 1967 war, there was the war of attrition in 1969 and 1970, and then there was the 1973 war. It is quite possible that in a year or two we shall have another war. This is a much more frequent cycle. In addition, the two societies now are mobilizing all their resources for the conflict—everything they can put into it. The conflict is of the highest priority in the Arab world. Since 1967 we have entered a race which is exhausting our resources and bringing us very close to the red line.

Why did things change in 1967? Evidently the territories had something to do with it. I suggest that for the Arabs if the *status quo* up to 1967 was one that could be described as unacceptable—after 1967 it became unbearable. The 1967 war, with its Israeli territorial gains, produced an Arab

determination to do actively everything within its power to terminate the occupation of parts of the sovereign territories belonging to Israel's neighbors, as well as the Israeli control of the whole of the land of Palestine. It may very well be that in retrospect—it still seems premature to draw conclusions—the war of 1967 will appear as the greatest disaster in the history of the state of Israel.

The Six Day War also created what were always described in Israel as the two preconditions for a settlement with the Arabs: First, that the Arabs become skeptical of their ability to destroy the state of Israel in any foreseeable future, and second, that the Israelis possess bargaining cards to be utilized for achieving a basic change in the relationship with the Arabs.

How did we utilize these assets? Bitan said that in 1967 we should have made a total proposal—all the territories in return for peace. And indeed, in 1967, the Israeli cabinet did make such an offer to Egypt. But we should remember that the Egyptians were to a large extent responsible for the Arab defeat in that war, and it would have been completely inconceivable for the Egyptians to make a separate peace with Israel. I think it still is inconceivable. But at certain points perhaps some progress in this direction could have been made or at least attempted. Unfortunately, when Sadat told [UN special representative for the Middle East] Gunnar Jarring, in February, 1971, that he was ready to sign a peace agreement with Israel, instead of exploring this avenue in order to achieve one of two results—either exposing Sadat as a fraud or making some substantial progress—we answered that we would not go back to the 1967 borders. And there were several other "noes" in our answer.

We have already discussed the opportunities for exploring the political potentiality of the Palestinian community in the West Bank. Some of us have said that such opportunities existed in 1967 and 1970. I say—1967, 1970, and 1972. I may be wrong, but the hard fact cannot be refuted: We did not try.

And, finally, there is the question of interim agreements. A good case can be made for the argument that we accepted in September, 1975, an agreement much inferior to what could have been achieved by a more flexible attitude to that option in February, 1971. And Dayan has recently expressed regrets on this account.*

Why is all this painful history relevant? Because one of the controversies around this table has been the question of "leeway." I put it to you that this history shows clearly the degree of leeway that Israeli diplomacy can have: Search actively for interim agreements, explore the possibilities of a comprehensive settlement, make progress with one section of Arab society in the territories. You can call it "some" leeway or "significant" leeway, call it 5 percent or 75 percent—in concrete terms this is the only scope for Israeli diplomacy.

Since 1973, the situation has not become more promising—I think that the war of Yom Kippur has somewhat reduced the chances of significant progress. Nevertheless, the war produced a few new factors which may, perhaps, counter-balance the erosion in Israel's bargaining power and work in a positive direction.

The argument that the Arabs will not accept any Israeli peace offer is really irrelevant to my approach, because I'm not speaking about peace but about a settlement within the range of what at least some Arabs may regard as legitimate. The Iraqis or the Libyans are against it, but at least some of the leading elements in Arab society are prone to this approach—those Arabs who may be described as relatively moderate.

This term, "moderate," should be explained, because there is much confusion about this whole notion of "Arab moderation"—whether it exists at all, and if it exists, what its nature is. In my view, there are really no ideological differences among Arabs on the basic conception of the state of Israel: they all agree that its creation was an act of injustice and it should be undone. There is, however, an important school of thought within Arab society which says: Israel, as a Jewish state, has no place in this region in the future, but this does not mean that the Arabs of this present generation are capable of destroying it or must undertake all the risks and sacrifices needed to achieve this objective within our time.

*Excerpts from Dov Goldstein, "The Government is Wrong—We Should Have Conducted Negotiations on the Partial Agreement Simultaneously with Egypt and Syria," March 21, 1975, from Ma'ariv in which Dayan answers a question as follows:

"In order to evaluate correctly Israel's mistake and the contribution of that mistake to the failure to achieve a partial agreement with Egypt long before the Yom Kippur war, I say that Israel should have been prepared to accept the existence of a reasonable number of Egyptian soldiers on the eastern bank of the canal in a way which wouldn't have in any way endangered the security of Israel. Israel should have been prepared to withdraw from the canal to a much longer distance than those 10 kilometers—approximately—for which she was ready.

"This would have made it possible to reach normalization of life by opening the canal and rehabilitating the canal towns. There are grounds for the supposition that such normalization would have created eventually a new reality in the South. Even if it is impossible to say for certain that the emergence of such a reality would have made the war impossible—it is possible that the Yom Kippur war wouldn't have broken out if it did. And it is possible that following the development of such normalization, more developments would have occurred which would have made the war more remote."

There are Arabs, and they are on the record, who say that every generation can set only a specific goal for itself. If this generation manages to contain Israel, to get back the territories and see the emergence of a Palestinian state on the West Bank and Gaza Strip—it is enough. Let the historical process take care of itself—the Zionist state will inevitably dissolve. Thus when Sadat is asked about real peace with Israel and answers: "Let's leave it to the next generation," it does not mean "let's leave the conclusion of peace to the next generation." It means let's leave the dissolution of the state of Israel for the future.

This is a kind of Arab attitude with which, if genuine, I can live. I am not happy about it. I condemn it morally. I have said earlier, and I put it conditionally, that some constraints in the Arab world might work in this direction. And if there are Arabs who seek an arrangement, a *modus vivendi* which would prevent a war and would leave the realization of their vision to future generations and to the historical process, then I would call that leeway and would explore its potentialities. There is no certainty about the solidity of this position among Arabs, and even if it is genuine today it may change tomorrow. But one should search for a system of checks and safety valves which would make the exploration of this leeway feasible.

Why is it so difficult for Israelis to see it in this light? We have had some indications of the answer to this question even in the course of these discussions. First, there is the fear which stems from the traumas of the Jewish people. There is an inherent, suspicious attitude which is justified on the basis of the Jewish historical experience. Second, there is the hypnotic effect of Arab ideology. Many people who are quite pragmatic in their thought become somehow intellectually paralyzed when they are confronted with the vicious texts expressing Arab animosity to Israel and are unable to discuss even questions which

belong to a different sphere—the level of practical politics.

Let me be clear on this subject. We all owe a debt to those scholars and experts who studied Arab anti-Israeli ideology and did much in order to disseminate it. They made a great contribution to the presentation of the Israeli case by making the world more knowledgeable about anti-Jewish themes in Arab literature, for example. But sometimes we paid the price for it. Often we have forgotten to distinguish between ideology and politics. The purpose of politics is not the reconciliation of divergent ideologies. When the Americans went to China, they did not seek to reconcile Chinese communism with the American way of life; they wanted to explore whether there existed certain overlapping interests which would make certain collaboration workable at that particular stage.

It's not a question of trust, either. Politics is the art of the possible. Frankly, I am not so eager, for example, to compel the PLO to change its National Covenant. I do not see this as a target. Of course, I would be very happy to see it disappear, but if we set conditions for negotiations with the Palestinians, I'm not sure that we should concentrate on this particular demand. It is very difficult to make a society change its ideology. I think we should deal with all Arabs who are ready to negotiate directly with Israel, to recognize Israel, and to express this recognition in practice. If they were to establish relations with Israel—I think this by itself would nullify the covenant. It was Disraeli who said in 1869: "Finality is not the language of politics." All this talk—that Israel must present the Arabs with a choice, either "real peace" or nothing—I think this is not the language of politics.

Let me return to the main issue of our discussions—the Palestinian-Jordanian-Israeli triangle. We should work for its solidification, for the establishment of a genuine triangle of three mutually recognized parties. It is on this basis that we should try to reach accommodations, arrangements, settlements—hopefully leading at some point to peaceful relations.

In this triangle, we have a Jordanian factor, which is definitely one of the most moderate factors in the Arab world. It has not belonged to the Arab radical front; it is not pro-Soviet. During most of the time, our relations with Jordan have seemed relatively tolerable. Collaboration with Jordan is also in harmony with our need to collaborate with the United States. Furthermore, we have even had a dialogue with the leadership of Jordan. Therefore, I wouldn't be so eager to get rid of "the little king." He has too many political assets for us. I feel very uneasy when I listen to people who so high-handedly express readiness to eliminate that factor from the Middle Eastern scene. You can eliminate him, you can help others eliminate him, but you must remember that when this happens, you will not know for whom the bell tolls. Hashemite Jordan can easily be replaced by a radical, pro-Soviet regime. It can be annexed by Syria. The negative developments which can emerge as a result of this are really alarming.

Second, we have the Palestinian factor. I agree that the Palestinian identity has crystallized only at a very late stage. National identities everywhere in the Fertile Crescent crystallized only after World War I, in some places earlier and in some places later. In the case of the Palestinians, the crucial stage appeared only after 1967 when, largely in protest against the Arab states and Arab regimes, the Palestinians asserted their particular identity. From some points of view, this identity is comparatively vague. But, as pointed out here, it is more powerful and more vital than that of other societies which have not had the same experiences.

I haven't met a single Arab in the territories and in Israel who says he is not a Palestinian. I have met many West Bankers who said they were not Jordanians, and Israeli-Arabs who resented the notion that they were Israelis. But none said he was not a Palestinian.

Therefore, we should include the Palestinian element if we search for a viable solution. We may use the Yariv formula— or any similar process for recognizing a responsible and genuine Palestinian leadership. It could emerge from the PLO, from outside the PLO, in a coalition with the PLO—it doesn't matter as long as it is a representative Palestinian delegation which comes to the negotiations with the intention of reaching a settlement with the state of Israel.

This concept of a triangle leads, of course, to the option of federation. I think that a Palestinian-Jordanian federation, on both sides of the Jordan River, having peaceful relations with Israel—would have many advantages. Above all, it is an Arab plan. The federation plan was conceived by King Hussein in 1972. Whether he did so in good faith or not is beside the point—it's an Arab plan; it's not a "Zionist conspiracy." It preserves the Jordanian framework as a reasonably safe barrier against Soviet or radical influences in the West Bank. It allows for self-expression for the Palestinians, who will be able to use their own flag and uphold the symbols of nationhood. Their region will not be a buffer zone, not a ministate. It will be part of a sovereign federation which will be viable economically and capable of absorbing and rehabilitating the refugees. Demilitarization will also be more feasible. As Dror said, you cannot demilitarize an independent third state, but you can do so with a small portion of a larger federal state. Finally, it would not contradict in any way the American interests in the region.

I'm not rigidly doctrinaire with regard to this solution. Many have pointed out rightly that we cannot really select for the Arabs a solution and work out its details as we like it. But on the other hand, I would not go to the other extreme of maintaining that we have no say in what happens just beyond our borders. This is not the rule of international relations. There are many cases in which the legitimate strategic interests of neighboring countries were mutually recognized and incorporated into the *status quo* on the two sides of the border.

Admittedly, my proposition has its weaknesses. It involves treading a very long road, and overcoming many obstacles—both Arab and Israeli. It also involves undertaking many risks, but here I must address myself to Pinhas's remarks about the risks of the negotiating process. The hidden assumption behind those remarks was that there is some safety, some security, in immobility, that as long as you don't do anything, everything will be all right, that the real dangers appear once you begin to negotiate. There is some substance to this argument—particularly if you assume that our negotiators are so weak-minded and weak-willed that once they start working on something, they will mess it up and yield to external pressures. But I see a greater risk in the continuation of immobility. The problem with immobility is that it is likely to explode in your face. This, to my mind, is precisely what happened in 1973. Up to 1973, we had had a period in which Israeli diplomacy regarded the very word "withdrawal" as taboo. Then the whole thing exploded. And now, I see a greater risk in remaining immobile, with our present borders, than I see in entering the negotiating process. Certainly I prefer a comprehensive settlement to interim agreements. But if a comprehensive settlement is at present out of the question, we should then pursue the art of the possible.

HANAN: You said that the government of Israel declared we would not go back to the 1967 borders. I maintain that behind this declaration there actually was readiness to return something like between 70 to 80 percent of the territories. When the Israeli government said we would not return, they meant we *would* return but with minor alterations.

AMIR: Well, this interpretation of minor alterations was never projected to the Arabs. Look at their reading of the Israeli situation—they hear that the Golan Heights is absolutely necessary for Israeli security; they see that we establish settlements along the cease-fire lines of the Golan Heights; they hear that East Jerusalem has been annexed; they hear that while Allon speaks of the Jordan Valley, others speak of the Gush Etzion, the West Bank's central ridge; they see us build settlements in Kiryat Arba, and in other places; they hear that Pit'hat Rafia is out of the question and Sharm el-Sheikh is out of the question; they hear us saying that we need a link between Sharm el-Sheikh and Elath. Can the Arabs read these as minor alterations?

ZVI: You said Sadat was part of an important school of thought in the Arab world that believes this generation need not risk everything against Israel. But don't you think he would come under future pressure from more extreme elements in the Arab world?

AMIR: I take the advice of Hanan. I do not trust the Arabs. I would not base any policy on confidence in Sadat's good intentions and his desire to renounce hostile policies. The only possibility we have is to work out arrangements in which there would be reasonable safeguards, guarantees, and checks and balances to make more difficult the outbreak of war and the violation of the agreements. If, at the same time, you manage to satisfy a reasonable number of legitimate Arab demands, you may create a situation in which the level of the conflict would become much lower.

I believe we must do everything possible to prevent war, because even if we win, we shall pay a very high price. I recognize the risks you pointed out, but I still prefer this way.

ZVI: You stated we couldn't make a separate peace agreement with Egypt, but then you said that we could have made some arrangement with the inhabitants of the West Bank, and that we could now do something toward Jordan-Palestinian federation. Are these statements compatible? Can Egypt be left out of such an arrangement? Especially, can Syria be left out, in light of the new axis between Syria and Jordan?

AMIR: We can try to make progress wherever and whenever it's possible. We must explore all the avenues simultaneously, without aiming at isolating one partner from the others.

ZVI: You spoke of the new cycle of war after 1967 because of our occupation of these territories. I agree. But don't you think that perhaps a more weighty factor was the growth of Arab power—oil as well as military power?

AMIR: No. The war of attrition, for example, was launched before they had the oil power. I believe that from their point of view our hold on the territories should not be allowed to solidify as the 1949 borders had solidified in the previous two decades.

URI: Do you agree with Shimon Peres's policy of offering the territories some kind of self-government? And if not, what should we do in the territories?

AMIR: This is a very theoretical question because there's very strong opposition in the West Bank to the proposal for local autonomy—for a number of reasons. The Arabs read Peres quite well. They know that he doesn't want to give up the West Bank. He's on record supporting the view that Israel cannot afford to withdraw from there. His proposal is a device to make a basically annexationist policy appear more liberal. So, why should they accept it?

What should be done in the meanwhile in the territories? Nothing. These are our bargaining cards. If we cannot make some progress towards a dialogue with the Palestinian Arabs—because of Rabat, the influence of the PLO, or whatever—then we should maintain those territories as a bargaining card for the next year, or for the end of the seventies, or for the eighties, or for whenever a bargain becomes feasible. By eliminating these cards we are hurting only ourselves. The option of a compromise based on the return of the territories should be kept open till hell freezes over. Because if we are responsible toward the next generation, we shouldn't do anything which would make it impossible for them to reach a compromise.

PINHAS: Do you see the model of the 1975 Sinai agreement as the prototype for the negotiating process in the future? Is this the way to explore the leeway? Actually isn't your most optimistic hope that we and the Arabs will return back to the cycle of wars every ten years, instead of every several years?

AMIR: I do not accept the 1975 agreement as a model. It is not a bilateral interim agreement. Basically, it is a triangle: we made concessions to the Egyptians, the Egyptians made promises to the Americans, and the Americans were very nice to us. This is exactly the kind of agreement which we shouldn't be interested in. I am definitely against the "salami scenario."

I admit that there is a risk that even a pragmatic leader who adopts a constructive approach may not have the resolution and the farsightedness to channel the process of negotiations toward those goals which I tried to outline.

As for going back to the cycle of war every ten years, I definitely prefer it to a cycle of war every two or three.

"Let the Arabs try us."

YAIR: I will start with Amir's pooh-poohing of ideology and his advice that we talk the language of politics. The last time that the world did this—against Hitler—it didn't work very well. The world didn't believe his ideological talk, and it led to terrible results. We, the Jews in Israel, have many good reasons to be worried, even frightened of the future. We have experienced much more than our share of troubles and tribulations. It is always appropriate to remind ourselves and all who care to hear, that we are the only nation on earth—there simply is no other—facing a brutal, inexorable threat of extermination.

We always stress that side of our life story. But let us not forget that there is also a heartening side. It might be a kind of Jewish happiness that we are specialists in. We, as a nation, have been through much worse times. As Churchill said, in quite desperate times, "It's not darker days we are facing, it's sterner days." The main difference for us, of course, is that we now have a place under the sun, our place. And we are not going to relinquish this right, this privilege. After a long period, we don't have to ask anybody permission to live here. And this place of ours, small as it is, is not just a synagogue in Haifa, as Sadat once suggested.

We can invite every Jew who wants to share this place with us. This is how I would define Zionism. It is a partial definition. I would not advise anybody to be so rash as Eitan—already closing the lid on the Jewish people. As Mark Twain once cabled after an obituary was mistakenly published by the AP, "The report of my death was premature." We are very far from liquidation. After four wars, and very few quiet days in between them—we are, I think, morally prepared for the future struggle. We do not delude ourselves about how terrible these struggles might be. We will face them not only for the sake of the state of Israel and the three million Jews living within its borders, but because this is the single way to keep the Jewish people in Israel and the Diaspora in existence. Without the rejuvenation which came about with the establishment of the state of Israel, it is doubtful whether Jews everywhere could brace themselves to stay in existence as a people for very long. Israel is still far from being a gem, far from fulfilling the spiritual hopes invested in her by the founding fathers. It even seems sometimes as only a pale carbon copy of the consumer society of the West, with an additional flavor of the Levant. But this is where the Jewish candle still burns. And in its twenty-eight years of noisy existence, more than in any generation of dispersal, Judaism has been strengthened, not weakened.

Today we are being bludgeoned with everything the Arabs can lay their hands on—ideologically and physically. This is nothing new. And it is not an aftermath of the Six Day War or of the Yom Kippur war. The only difference is Arab power, Arab confidence, and the almost enthusiastic applause of the outside world at their doings. The power and the applause have nothing to do with the measure of our rights or our justice. We are Jews. I have no persecution mania, but let's face it, we are a separate entity, and the Arabs are blessed with multitudes, with many lands, with geopolitical significance, and with natural wealth giving them a stranglehold over the world.

Our hold on Judea and Samaria is as good and as timely a pretext as any for the Arabs to repeat what they have been telling us for the last seventy years at least: be gone—and let us not set eyes on you anymore. It's not true that the conflict is about the lands conquered in the Six Day War and that we could effect a miraculous change of the Arab heart—a *volte face*—just by packing up and disappearing from the territories. We did not initiate the war. Does anybody still deny that the war was an opportunity seized upon by the Arabs to wipe us out, an opportunity which they had sought for so long?

The Arab intent to destroy Israel, not the borderline between the Jewish state and an Arab one, is what the conflict is all about. The conflict is about the most vital, the most fundamental matters: Will there be a Jewish state in Eretz Israel with sovereignty over its space and population? And can it maintain all sorts of connections with the Jews everywhere in the world at large? Yes or no? All answers from the Arabs—straight answers and camouflaged ones—are unanimous. They say, no.

There is no question about our deep historical feeling toward Judea and Samaria. There is also no doubt about the strategic importance of Golan and Sinai. Still, I don't think that the borders are the key question. The question of the borders is a judgment to be derived from specific conditions. I think we should negotiate with the Arabs about concessions and withdrawal. But let us do it only after we know, without the shadow of a doubt, where we are heading—whether toward the continued existence of Israel or toward its abolishment. For our continuing existence, as we define it, there is logic in making major concessions. But to hand over to the enemy who intends to crush you, the tools that will make his job easier, is bordering on madness.

I am for declaring outright that, for a limited period, we are ready to exchange the territories—all of them—for a real, full, complete, and lasting peace. But not for a semblance of it. It should be peace with the Palestinians and also at leas[t] front-line countries. Any o[ne] would be a sham and would ope[n] for later disaster.

Peace treaties should be completed [on both] sides, but Israel's withdrawal would [be] over a prolonged period. In the meantime, all hostilities of any kind, physical or verbal, would totally cease. Formal relations would not be postponed for the hereafter but should be established at a fixed time. There would be a specified time during which Israel would agree not to establish new settlements in the territories. When the time limit expired, if the offer were not taken, Israel would be free to reconsider its stand.

AMIR: How much time?

YAIR: A long period—a number of years. Not months; I mean years. Finally, it is desirable that the Russians should be a party to the arrangement.

What are the weaknesses of such a plan? First of all, it is far-reaching, and could be thought of as some kind of gimmick. I don't think it has to be so. It might be difficult to convince everybody, but it's not impossible. All parties should recognize one fact: the dangers to Israel are unlike the dangers to any other country in the region. It's one-sided. If the arrangements fail, there is no danger to anyone except Israel. No one else risks anything. Nevertheless, the Israeli public would ultimately support it. We all know that the biggest party in Israel, having an overwhelming majority, is the peace party. Let the Arabs try us.

The second weakness is that some in Israel feel that once you offer something you can't retract it. They will say that once you have agreed in principle to give up the territories, all that's left is the haggle about what Israel gets in return. In such a situation, the critics say, any Israeli stance against making more concessions will be condemned as intransigence.

I believe every one of us knows in his heart of hearts that even these generous

vith real sor-
nd I don't
ory, conces-
milar situa-
-heartedly,

'e owe it to
ght bring
ngth will
..aing. Let us
..ives by this act of grand con-
cession. We cannot go back to square one
without it.

The original sin was that Israel had men-
tal fatigue after 1973, and gave up a fun-
damental demand—a demand under-
standable by all—for direct negotiations.
We cannot return to it.

What if there is no peace? What then are
the alternatives? What about the Palestin-
ian problem? These people were the vic-
tims of the upheavals and wars that fol-
lowed the concerted aggression by Israel's
Arab neighbors in 1948 and 1967. Their
plight has inspired a great deal of sympathy
and encouraged their champions to argue
as if the Palestinians were the only
refugees in the world, as if something
placed their case above all other victims of
the massive ethnographic dislocation that
has afflicted many millions of people since
the Second World War. What is unique
about the Palestinians is not the merit of
their case, but the ruthlessness with which
their misfortune has been manipulated by
interested Arab governments and ambi-
tious politicians. The worst prejudices of
Islamic tradition were blended with the
crudest expressions of nationalism, par-
ticularly in the education of the young, to
keep the flames of hatred burning. It was
pointed out here, quite correctly I think,
that Palestinian nationalism is a very re-
cent phenomenon—paradoxically, born as
a response to Zionism and shaped by it.

But however recent the discovery of this
new national consciousness, the Palestin-
ians claim the heartland of Israel. And the
word is out that they will not give up until

they have their way. Israel must dis-
appear. In their more generous moments,
some Arab leaders say that the repentant
Israel might be allowed a shadowy exis-
tence in a much reduced form—as a kind of
Middle East Monaco. But most of them do
not accept even that. If the Arabs and the
Palestinians appear sometimes divided,
then let us remember that their principal
arguments rage about the best means to
achieve their coveted aim. The moderates
favor dismantling the Jewish state by
installments, while the hard-liners push
for an instant action to end everything
with one swift blow.

Nothing I have heard convinces me that
the PLO thinks otherwise. I don't know if
we here represent all the nuances of Israeli
public opinion, but I guess most of them.
Even by taking the views aired here, I
would risk saying that there is a common
understanding about what the PLO inten-
tions are—except maybe for some vague,
dissident voices, which are negligible in the
PLO.

The advent of oil power has had a pro-
found effect on the political conscience of
the Western world. Suddenly the case of
the Palestinians was accepted with greater
understanding. This is why the problem
became acute—not, as Amir said, because
of the 1967 war.

Until now the support which the Arab
cause received from the Soviet Union has
been balanced by the support Israel has
received from the United States. But an
evenhanded Western approach is bound to
shift the balance to the Arabs. The
resulting imbalance would give the Arab
governments such overwhelming confi-
dence that there will be no incentive left for
realistic peace negotiations.

The best course for peace is two-
pronged: to maintain the military and
diplomatic balance of power in the Middle
East, and to leave the whole issue of the
Palestinians at the bottom of the interna-
tional agenda. Only this course ensures the
lowering of the profile of the conflict, if

this is at all possible. And there might c[ome]
a point, which we can't see now, when [the]
Arabs will despair of achieving their go[al]
by force and will acquiesce in the existen[ce]
of Israel.

Some voices here have prophesied
doom if Israel does not succumb to the
most exorbitant demand of the Arabs.
Some pointed to Arab might, saying that
the qualitative and technological gap is narrowing. I beg to differ. We are hampered
mainly by external political reasons and
some internal political reasons—like the
lack of determined leadership. And we
don't allow ourselves the freedom of action
through which we could exert a not negligible influence over the Middle East situation. Even the freedom of action that was
ours before the Yom Kippur war is like a
dream to us now. Of course, if American
support is stopped and the Soviets and
others continue to support the Arab countries, then we are really in a fix. But that
has nothing to do with the myth of the
narrowing gap.

Eitan's enduring belief is in the milk of
human kindness. According to his gospel,
anti-Semitism died—unnoticed, presumably. And Zionism died with it. This is pure
futurology, as are his post-nationalist
cravings. Being not too far from Rome, let
me remind you that *homo homini lupus est* is
still the rule of the day. Just take a good
look around. And Amir's advice is that we
should talk the language of politics. But
when we regard what the other side is saying as political language, I find it very difficult to disregard their words and the way
they speak them. Remember what was said
by Moshen to *Die Zeit* and by Qaddoumi to
Newsweek.

Question to Moshen: "Aren't you going
to be content with a state that will be in
Judea and Samaria and the Gaza Strip?"
Answer: "Never. We want to restore for
ourselves every part of the land, every
field, every house that in the past was ours.
There is no power which will stop us from

Perhaps Israel's deficiencies are grea[t]
her sins many, but her existence i[s]
for the free world. Maybe an i[dea]
arrogance can go on s[ay]
the world can go on s[ay]
us. Maybe the need[s]
even this is rea[l]

AMIR: M[...]
tional [...]
th[...]

[...]
a[...]
A[...]
tw[...]
retu[rn ...] demo-
crati[c ...] to live in this so-
called [...] Israel without letting the
Palest[inia]ns return. If they choose the latter, they will surely die. And we will surely
win."

No wonder an Israeli Jew, who believes
in the ultimate victory of Israel—and victory for us is victory over terrifying odds—
believes it is a fight for existence. Yes, we
are greatly worried about what happened
to countries that have been abandoned. We
try sometimes to find historical analogies.
But they are not real analogies. Israel's case
is different not simply because of influence of the Jews in the United States, but
because Israel represents an idea, a belief in
the possibility of justice. I hope that many
people in the West, especially in the United
States, feel that Israel is an organic part of
Western civilization. If there is no hope for
Israel, there is no hope, ultimately, for
Western civilization. And the same goes, of
course, for the idea of liberty.

We Israelis are too immersed in the problems of day-to-day existence to keep
always in mind that Israel was not only
created as a solution to the Jewish plight
and a haven from persecution, pogroms
and insults, but also as a proof that history
is not just coincidence—to prove that
history has a direction and meaning.

and
is a test
a kind of
...usion. Perhaps
...sfactorily without
only in ourselves, but
...n to fight for existence.

question refers to the opera-
...ement in your exposition, in which
time factor is very important.
...houldn't there be a more symmetrical demand with regard to what the Arabs are
required to do? What you want to do is get
all the benefits immediately and give the
reciprocal concessions only piecemeal. If
we want the proposal to appear fair,
couldn't we have some balance between
these two things?

YAIR: If you were able to elaborate more
on what you mean by a symmetrical offer,
we could examine everything. But I don't
accept your premise. Because peace is a
benefit for both sides—it's not a benefit for
one side only. Both parties are getting
peace, and Israel is also vacating the territories gradually.

AMIR: You implied in your opening statement that I belittle ideology. There is
nothing farther from my mind. I consider
ideology extremely important. However,
what I said is that you cannot stop with ideology, that there is another dimension to
political behavior, namely practical politics.
The two are not mutually exclusive. If one
stresses practical arrangements, it does not
mean that he is disregarding completely
the importance of ideology.

YAIR: I might accept the second part of
what you say. Still, your exposition contained a very grave proposition. I return to
the analogy of Hitler. He was the laugh-
ingstock from 1923 almost to the war.
Nobody paid attention to what he said.

AMIR: But this is not an analogy. I am not
recommending that we pay no attention to

Arab ideology.

YAIR: There is more to it than that. Hitler
did what he did in Germany in the middle
of the Western world, where there is skep-
ticism and a high level of civilization. What
the Arabs are doing now is being done
where there are no safety valves like this.

AMIR: I agree with you on that.

MEIR: I want to come back to this point of
ideology and to your repeated analogy.
Because now you are not being hap-
hazard; you are really taking a stand. And if
you take that stand, then I cannot understand your position. Everybody knows
today—and one does not need to be a Hitler
specialist—that Hitler meant what he said.
People disregarded him, but today the logic
of the analysis working backwards is: One
should not have hesitated a moment to use
force in order to eradicate National Socialism and Hitler. One should have done it in
1933, the moment he arrived to power.
The Poles wanted to do it, but then the
French, as you know, refused, and it was
dragged on until 1939.

So now, if you make this comparison and
apply this analogy to our present situation, I really don't see how you can propose
your moratorium and your offer of territories in exchange for full peace. This is
madness. If you really conceive of the Arab
ideology in the same way as National
Socialism, you are playing the role of
Chamberlain. We at last have historical
experience now, so we can draw the conclusion in retrospect.

YAIR: I don't see the meaning of this question. Do you want me to say that as a result
of what we know about the situation we
should go to war?

MEIR: Or at least that we should make no
compromise whatsoever.

YAIR: I am more inclined to accept what
Nahum said this morning about the zeitgeist. This should guide us in our dealings

with everybody in the external world.

I also don't find your analogy valid. Because the difference between what happened then and what is happening now is that Hitler's opponents shut their eyes to the clear signs of what was going on. They believed what they wanted to believe. They deluded themselves. I don't think we are doing this now. We know exactly what they are saying and we draw conclusions from it. Still, I'm suggesting that we take a calculated risk. This is not Chamberlain. Chamberlain and the other powers sacrificed other nations' interests. We sacrifice our own interest—and that we are entitled always to do.

MEIR: I think you still don't read correctly the implications of your own position. You say Hitler—and ideologues like him—meant what he said. Next you compare it to the Arabs, and you said they too mean exactly what they say. There is absolutely no logical way to escape the conclusion that your proposal is of the utmost danger to Israel—actually a *non sequitur.* Because the Arabs mean it, and in the long run they will do it. And Hitler really meant it—that was the great mistake of the British. Never mind whether they sacrificed their own interests or those of others. If there is no discrepancy between the declarations and day-to-day policies of the Arabs then your moratorium is simply strengthening the Arabs, weakening Israel, and falling into the trap that some people here have mentioned.

YAIR: I don't think so: my proposal is not a *non sequitur,* because you cannot divide the parts of my suggestion. I stressed the dangers that my proposal can bring to Israel. Because I see grave dangers, I proposed several elements that will make it much more difficult for the Arabs to start the war again. There would be a prolonged period, during which safeguards would operate. Of course, all wars start from peace, so we cannot have a 100 per-

cent guarantee. But we have to take the plunge, knowing its dangers. I have not outlined a detailed plan here, but the concept is clear: if there is a long span of time with a complete absence of hostilities, and if they agree beforehand to several of our demands concerning what we mean by peace, then I think the danger to us will be largely diminished.

NAHUM: Your exposition prompts me to say that, at the end of this conference, we come down to two approaches. One is a head-on approach to the major problems; the other is the piecemeal, incremental, step-by-step approach proposed by Amir. His approach has great appeal, but he did not spell out its difficulties.

Once you leave the level of abstract discussion, it's very difficult to spell out the details or the probable results of an incremental approach. Such a process can bring good results if every small step adds to the previous one, and if there is continuity. But the danger that always frightens us is that we could find ourselves at the end of this process shorn of our major assets, the territories—and with the Arab position unchanged. So to sum it up, we have to use both approaches. To neglect either the overall approach to major problems or the piecemeal approach, and to separate them, means both will fail. The real problem is how to achieve a proper mix.

AMIR: I accept most of that. We must indeed combine the two approaches. I recognize the difficulty. I have been the only one here actually speaking in favor of partial agreements, and I presented the case as an advocate. I am aware of the fact that there are weaknesses in this approach and in fact pointed to some of them myself.

However, I must add something in a more reflective mood. We are all speaking about the risks of losing our assets. I wish to express some doubts, even though they are not fully crystallized in my mind. I am skeptical about the real value of these assets, considering the record of the last nine years. I am not so sure that the territories are the assets they appeared to be after 1967. I am not presenting a fully articulate thesis about this, I am merely stating my fear that, in a final reckoning, the territories may have turned out to be a liability.

APPENDICES

Appendix I: The Saunders Statement

The following statement was made at the request of the Special Subcommittee on Investigations of the House Committee on International Relations on November 12 by Harold H. Saunders, Deputy Assistant Secretary of State for Near Eastern and South Asian Affairs. It is reproduced here as it appeared in the Department of State's Bureau of Public Affairs Bulletin No. 8, November, 1975.

A just and durable peace in the Middle East is a central objective of the United States. Both President Ford and Secretary Kissinger have stated firmly on numerous occasions that the United States is determined to make every feasible effort to maintain the momentum of practical progress toward a peaceful settlement of the Arab-Israeli conflict.

We have also repeatedly stated that the legitimate interests of the Palestinian Arabs must be taken into account in the negotiation of an Arab-Israeli peace. In many ways, the Palestinian dimension of the Arab-Israeli conflict is the heart of that conflict. Final resolution of the problems arising from the partition of Palestine, the establishment of the State of Israel, and Arab opposition to those events will not be possible until agreement is reached defining a just and permanent status for the Arab peoples who consider themselves Palestinians.

The total number of Palestinian Arabs is estimated at a little more than 3 million. Of these, about 450,000 live in the area of Israel's pre-1967 borders; about 1 million are in the Israeli-occupied West Bank, East Jerusalem, and Gaza; something less than a million—about 900,000—are in Jordan; half a million are in Syria and Lebanon; and somewhat more than 200,000 or so are elsewhere, primarily in the gulf states.

Those in Israel are Israeli nationals. The great majority of those in the West Bank, East Jerusalem, and Jordan are Jordanian nationals. Palestinian refugees, who live outside of pre-1967 Israel and number 1.6 million, are eligible for food and/or services from the U.N. Relief and Works Agency [UNRWA]; more than 650,000 of these live in camps.

The problem of the Palestinians was initially dealt with essentially as one involving displaced persons. The United States and other nations responded to the immediate humanitarian task of caring for a large number of refugees and trying to provide them with some hope in life.

In later years, there has been considerable attention given to the programs of UNRWA that help not only to sustain those people's lives but to lift the young people out of the refugee camps and to train them and give them an opportunity to lead productive lives. Many have taken advantage of this opportunity, and an unusually large number of them have completed secondary and university education. One finds Palestinians occupying leading positions throughout the Arab world as professionals and skilled workers in all fields. The U.S. has provided some $620 million in assistance—about 62 percent of the total international support ($1 billion) for the Palestinian refugees over the past quarter of a century.

Today, however, we recognize that, in addition to meeting the human needs and responding to legitimate personal claims of the refugees, there is another interest that must be taken into account. It is a fact that many of the 3 million or so people who call themselves Palestinians today increasingly regard themselves as having their own identity as a people and desire a voice in determining their political status. As with any people in this situation, they have differences among themselves, but the Palestinians collectively are a political factor which must be dealt with if there is to be a peace between Israel and its neighbors.

The statement is often made in the Arab world that there will not be peace until the "rights of the Palestinians" are fulfilled, but there is no agreed definition of what is meant and a variety of viewpoints have been expressed on what the legitimate objectives of the Palestinians are.

• Some Palestinian elements hold to the objective of a binational secular state in the area of the former mandate of Palestine. Realization of this objective would mean the end of the present state of Israel—a member of the United Nations—and its submergence in some larger entity. Some would be willing to accept merely as a first step toward this goal the establishment of a Palestinian state comprising the West Bank of the Jordan River and Gaza.

• Other elements of Palestinian opinion appear willing to accept an independent Palestinian state comprising the West Bank and Gaza, based on acceptance of Israel's right to exist as an independent state within roughly its pre-1967 borders.

• Some Palestinians and other Arabs envisage as a possible solution a unification of the West Bank and Gaza with Jordan. A variation of this which has been suggested would be the reconstitution of the country as a federated state, with the West Bank becoming an autonomous Palestinian province.

• Still others, including many Israelis, feel that with the West Bank returned to Jordan, and with the resulting existence of two communities—Palestinian and Jordanian—within Jordan, opportunities would be created thereby for the Palestinians to find self-expression.

• In the case of a solution which would rejoin the West Bank to Jordan or a solution involving a West Bank-Gaza state, there would still arise the property claims of those Palestinians who before 1948 resided in areas that became the State of Israel. These claims have been acknowledged as a serious problem by the international community ever since the adoption by the United Nations of Resolution 194 on this subject in 1948, a resolution which the United Nations has repeatedly reaffirmed and which the United States has supported. A solution will be further complicated by the property claims against Arab states of the many Jews from those states who moved to Israel in its early years after achieving statehood.

• In addition to property claims, some believe they should have the option of returning to their original homes under any settlement.

• Other Arab leaders, while pressing the importance of Palestinian involvement in a settlement, have taken the position that the definition of Palestinian interests is something for the Palestinian people themselves to sort out, and the view has been expressed by responsible Arab leaders that realization of Palestinian rights need not be inconsistent with the existence of Israel.

No one, therefore, seems in a position today to say exactly what Palestinian objectives are. Even the Palestine Liberation Organization [PLO], which is recognized by the Arab League and the U.N. General Assembly as the representative of the Palestinian people, has been ambivalent. Officially and publicly, its objective is described as a binational secular state, but there are some indications that coexistence between separate Palestinian and Israeli states might be considered.

When there is greater precision about those objectives, there can be clearer understanding about how to relate them to negotiations. There is the aspect of the future of the West Bank and Gaza—how those areas are to be defined and how they are to be governed. There is the aspect of the relationship between Palestinians in the West Bank and Gaza to those Palestinians who are not living in those areas, in the context of a settlement.

What is needed as a first step is a diplomatic process which will help bring forth a reasonable definition of Palestinian interests—a position from which negotiations on a solution of the Palestinian aspects of the problem might begin. The issue is not whether Palestinian interests should be expressed in a final settlement, but how. There will be no peace unless an answer is found.

Another requirement is the development of a framework for negotiations—a statement of the objectives and the terms of reference. The framework for the negotiations that have taken place thus far and the agreements they have produced involving Israel, Syria, and Egypt has been provided by U.N. Security Council Resolutions 242 and 338. In accepting that framework, all of the parties to the negotiation have accepted that the objective of the negotiations is peace between them based on mutual recognition, territorial integrity, political independence, the right to live in peace within secure and recognized borders, and the resolution of the specific issues which comprise the Arab-Israeli conflict.

The major problem that must be resolved in establishing a framework for bringing issues of concern to the Palestinians into negotiation, therefore, is to find a common basis for the negotiation that Palestinians and Israelis can both accept. This could be achieved by common acceptance of the above-mentioned Security Council resolutions, although they do not deal with the political aspect of the Palestinian problem.

A particularly difficult aspect of the problem is the question of who negotiates for the Palestinians. It has been our belief that Jordan would be a logical negotiator for the Palestinian-related issues. The Rabat summit, however, recognized the Palestine Liberation Organization as the "sole legitimate representative of the Palestinian people."

The PLO was formed in 1964, when 400 delegates from Palestinian communities throughout the Arab world met in Jerusalem to create an organization to represent and speak for the Palestinian people. Its leadership was originally middle class and relatively conservative, but by 1969 control has passed into the hands of the Palestinian fedayeen, or commando, movement, which had existed since the mid-1950's but had come into prominence only after the 1967 war. The PLO became an umbrella organization for six separate fedayeen groups: Fatah; the Syrian-backed Saiqa; the Popular Democratic Front for the Liberation of Palestine [PFLP]; the General Command, a subgroup of the PFLP; and the Iraqi-backed Arab Liberation Front. Affiliated with the PLO are a number of "popular organizations"—labor and professional unions, student groups, women's groups, and so on. Fatah, the largest fedayeen group, also has a welfare apparatus to care for widows and orphans of deceased Fatah members.

However, the PLO does not accept the U.N. Security Council resolutions, does not recognize the existence of Israel, and has not stated its readiness to negotiate peace with Israel; Israel does not recognize the PLO or the idea of a separate Palestinian entity. Thus we do not at this point have the framework for a negotiation involving the PLO. We cannot envision or urge a negotiation between two parties as long as one professes to hold the objective of eliminating the other—rather than the objective of negotiating peace with it.

There is one other aspect to this problem. Elements of the PLO have used terrorism to gain attention for their cause. Some Americans as well as many Israelis and others have been killed by Palestinian terrorists. The international community cannot condone such practices, and it seems to us that there must be some assurance if Palestinians are drawn into the negotiating process that these practices will be curbed.

This is the problem which we now face. If the progress toward peace which has now begun is to continue, a solution to this question must be found. We have not devised an "American" solution, nor would it be it be appropriate for us to do so. This is the responsibility of the parties and the purpose of the negotiating process. But we have not closed our minds to any reasonable solution which can contribute to progress toward our overriding objective in the Middle East—an Arab-Israeli peace. The step-by-step approach to negotiations which we have pursued has been based partly on the understanding that issues in the Arab-Israeli conflict take time to mature. It is obvious that thinking on the Palestinian aspects of the problem must evolve on all sides. As it does, what is not possible today may become possible.

Our consultations on how to move the peace negotiations forward will recognize the need to deal with this subject. As Secretary Kissinger has said [October 7, 1975], "We are prepared to work with all the parties toward a solution of all the issues yet remaining—including the issue of the future of the Palestinians." We will do so because the issues of concern to the Palestinians are important in themselves and because the Arab governments participating in the negotiations have made clear that progress in the overall negotiations will depend in part on progress on issues of concern to the Palestinians. We are prepared to consider any reasonable proposal from any quarter, and we will expect other parties to the negotiation to be equally openminded.

Appendix II:
The Palestinian National Charter*

Decisions of the National Congress of the Palestine Liberation Organization held in Cairo from 1-17 July 1968. Reproduced here as it appeared in Basic Political Documents of the Armed Palestinian Resistance Movement, *edited and translated by Leita S. Kadi (Beirut: Palestine Liberation Organization Research Center, 1969).*

Article 1:   Palestine is the homeland of the Arab Palestinian people; it is an indivisible part of the Arab homeland, and the Palestinian people are an integral part of the Arab nation.

Article 2:   Palestine, with the boundaries it had during the British mandate, is an indivisible territorial unit.

Article 3:   The Palestinian Arab people possess the legal right to their homeland and have the right to determine their destiny after achieving the liberation of their country in accordance with their wishes and entirely of their own accord and will.

Article 4:   The Palestinian identity is a genuine, essential and inherent characteristic; it is transmitted from parent to children. The Zionist occupation and the dispersal of the Palestinian Arab people, through the disasters which befell them, do not make them lose their Palestinian identity and their membership of the Palestinian community, nor do they negate them.

Article 5:   The Palestinians are those Arab nationals who, until 1947, normally resided in Palestine regardless of whether they were evicted from it or have stayed there. Anyone born, after that date, of a Palestinian father—whether inside Palestine or outside it—is also a Palestinian.

Article 6:   The Jews who had normally resided in Palestine until the beginning of the Zionist invasion will be considered Palestinians.

Article 7:   That there is a Palestinian community and that it has material, spiritual and historical connection with Palestine are indisputable facts. It is a national duty to bring up individual Palestinians in an Arab revolutionary manner. All means of information and education must be adopted in order to acquaint the Palestinian with his country in the most profound manner, both spiritual and material, that is possible. He must be prepared for the armed struggle and ready to sacrifice his wealth and his life in order to win back his homeland and bring about its liberation.

* The participants refer to this document as the Palestinian National Covenant.

Article 8:   The phase in their history, through which the Palestinian people are now living, is that of national struggle for the liberation of Palestine. Thus the conflicts among the Palestinian national forces are secondary, and should be ended for the sake of the basic conflict that exists between the forces of Zionism and of imperialism on the one hand, and the Palestinian Arab people on the other. On this basis the Palestinian masses, regardless of whether they are residing in the national homeland and or in diaspora, constitute—both their organizations and the individuals—one national front working for the retrieval of Palestine and its liberation through armed struggle.

Article 9:   Armed struggle is the only way to liberate Palestine. Thus it is the overall strategy, not merely a tactical phase. The Palestinian Arab people assert their absolute determination and firm resolution to continue their armed struggle and to work for an armed popular revolution for the liberation of their country and their return to it. They also assert their right to normal life in Palestine and to exercise their right to self-determination and sovereignty over it.

Article 10:   Commando action constitutes the nucleus of the Palestinian popular liberation war. This requires its escalation, comprehensiveness and the mobilization of all the Palestinian popular and educational efforts and their organization and involvement in the armed Palestinian revolution. It also requires the achieving of the Palestinian people, and between the Palestinian people and the Arab masses so as to secure the continuation of the revolution, its escalation and victory.

Article 11:   The Palestinians will have three mottoes: national unity, national mobilization and liberation.

Article 12:   The Palestinian people believe in Arab unity. In order to contribute their share towards the attainment of that objective, however, they must, at the present stage of their struggle, safeguard their Palestinian identity and develop their consciousness of that identity, and oppose any plan that may dissolve or impair it.

Article 13:   Arab unity and the liberation of Palestine are two complementary objectives, the attainment of either of which facilitates the attainment of the other. Thus, Arab unity leads to the liberation of Palestine; the liberation of Palestine leads to Arab unity; and work towards the realization of one objective proceeds side by side with work towards the realization of the other.

Article 14:   The destiny of the Arab nation, and indeed Arab existence itself, depends upon the destiny of the Palestine cause. From this interdependence springs the Arab nation's pursuit of, and striving for, the liberation of Palestine. The people of Palestine play the role of the vanguard in the realization of this sacred national goal.

Article 15:   The liberation of Palestine, from an Arab viewpoint, is a national duty and it attempts to repel the Zionist and imperalist aggression against the Arab homeland, and aims at the elimination of Zionism in Palestine. Absolute responsibility for this falls upon the Arab nation—peoples and governments—with the Arab people of Palestine in the vanguard. Accordingly the Arab nation must mobilize all its military, human, moral and spiritual capabilities to participate actively with the Palestinian people in the liberation of Palestine. It must, particularly in the phase of the armed Palestinian revolution, offer and furnish the Palestinian people with all possible help, and material and human support, and make available to them the means and opportunities that will enable them to continue to carry out their leading role in the armed revolution, until they liberate their homeland.

Article 16:   The liberation of Palestine, from a spiritual point of view, will provide the Holy Land with an atmosphere of safety and tranquility, which in turn will safeguard the country's religious sanctuaries and guarantee freedom of worship and of visit to all, without discrimination of race, color, language, or religion. Accordingly, the people of Palestine look to all spiritual forces in the world for support.

Article 17:   The liberation of Palestine, from a human point of view, will restore to the Palestinian individual his dignity, pride and freedom. Accordingly the Palestinian Arab people look forward to the support of all those who believe in the dignity of man and his freedom in the world.

Article 18:   The liberation of Palestine, from an international point of view, is a defensive action necessitated by the demands of self-defense. Accordingly, the Palestinian people, desirous as they are of the friendship of all people, look to freedom-loving, justice-loving and peace-loving states for support in order to restore their legitimate rights in Palestine, to re-establish peace and security in the country, and to enable its people to exercise national sovereignty and freedom.

Article 19:   The partition of Palestine in 1947 and the establishment of the state of Israel are entirely illegal, regardless of the passage of time, because they were contrary to the will of the Palestinian people and to their natural right in their homeland, and inconsistent with the principles embodied in the Charter of the United Nations, particularly the right to self-determination.

Article 20:   The Balfour Declaration, the mandate for Palestine and everything that has been based upon them, are deemed null and void. Claims of historical or religious ties of Jews with Palestine are incompatible with the facts of history and the true conception of what constitutes statehood. Judaism, being a religion, is not an independent nationality. Nor do Jews constitute a single nation with an identity of its own; they are citizens of the Palestinian problem, or its internationalization.

Article 21:   The Arab Palestinian people, expressing themselves by the armed Palestinian revolution, reject all solutions which are substitutes for the total liberation of Palestine and reject all proposals aiming at the liquidation of the Palestinian problem, or its internationalization.

Article 22: Zionism is a political movement organically associated with international imperialism and antagonistic to all action for liberation and to progressive movements in the world. It is racist and fanatic in its nature, agressive, expansionist and colonial in its aims, and fascist in its methods. Israel is the instrument of the Zionist movement, and a geographical base for world imperialism placed strategically in the midst of the Arab homeland to combat the hopes of the Arab nation for liberation, unity and progress. Israel is a constant source of threat *vis-à-vis* peace in the Middle East and the whole world. Since the Liberation of Palestine will destroy the Zionist and imperialist presence and will contribute to the establishment of peace in the Middle East, the Palestinian people look for the support of all the progressive and peaceful forces and urge them all, irrespective of their affiliations and belief, to offer the Palestinian people all aid and support in their just struggle for the liberation of their homeland.

Article 23: The demands of security and peace, as well as the demands of right and justice, require all states to consider Zionism an illegitimate movement, to outlaw its existence, and to ban its operations, in order that friendly relations among peoples may be preserved, and the loyalty of citizens to their respective homelands safeguarded.

Article 24: The Palestinian people believe in the principles of justice, freedom, sovereignty, self-determination, human dignity, and in the right of all peoples to exercise them.

Article 25: For the realization of the goals of this Charter and its principles, the Palestine Liberation Organization will perform its role in the liberation of Palestine in accordance with the Constitution of this Organization.

Article 26: The Palestine Liberation Organization, representative of the Palestinian revolutionary forces, is responsible for the Palestinian Arab people's movement in its struggle—to retrieve its homeland, liberate and return to it and exercise the right to self-determination in it—in all military, political and financial fields and also for whatever may be required by the Palestine case on the inter-Arab and international levels.

Article 27: The Palestine Liberation Organization shall cooperate with all Arab states, each according to its potentialities; and will adopt a neutral policy among them in the light of the requirements of the war of liberation; and on this basis it shall not interfere in the internal affairs of any Arab state.

Article 28: The Palestinian Arab people assert the genuineness and independence of their national revolution and reject all forms of intervention, trusteeship and subordination.

Article 29: The Palestinian people possess the fundamental and genuine legal right to liberate and retrieve their homeland. The Palestinian people determine their attitude towards all states and forces on the basis of the stands they adopt *vis-à-vis* the Palestinian case and the extent of the support they offer to the Palestinian revolution to fulfill the aims of the Palestinian people.

Article 30:   Fighters and carriers of arms in the war of liberation are the nucleus of the popular army which will be the protective force for the gains of the Palestinian Arab people.

Article 31:   The Organization shall have a flag, an oath of allegiance and an anthem. All this shall be decided upon in accordance with a special regulation.

Article 32:   Regulations, which shall be known as the Constitution of the Palestine Liberation Organization, shall be annexed to this Charter. It shall lay down the manner in which the Organization, and its organs and institutions, shall be constituted; the respective competence of each; and the requirements of its obligations under the Charter.

Article 33:   This Charter shall not be amended save by (vote of) a majority of two-thirds of the total membership of the National Congress of the Palestine Liberation Organization (taken) at a special session convened for that purpose.

Appendix III: Allon Plan Documents

The following is an excerpt from The Allon Plan *by Yoram Cohen (Israel: Kibbutz Hameuhad, 1972), pages 171 to 176, translated from the original Hebrew.*

The following are the main points of the "Allon Plan" as presented in closed meeting at the time that the plan was submitted to the government:
   A. I propose that Israel insist that her eastern border must be the Jordan River and a line that bisects the Dead Sea down its length, and that the mandatory border in the Arava shall remain as it was before the Six Day War.
   B. To maintain stable defense on the one hand, and ensure the geostrategic completeness of the country on the other, we must annex to the state, as an inseparable part of its sovereign area, the following territories:

   1. A strip of between 10 to 15 kilometers in width along the length of the Jordan Rift Valley from the Beisan Valley to the north of the Dead Sea, while including a minimum of Arab population.
   2. A strip of a few kilometers wide, to be selected by the terrain, north of the Jerusalem-Dead Sea road, which will link up with the area north of the Atarot-Beit Horon-Latrun road, to include Latrun area.
   3. As for Mount Hebron and the Judean Desert, two possibilities must be con-

sidered: annexation of Mount Hebron with its population or, at least, the Judean Desert on the eastern approaches of Hebron down to the Dead Sea and the Negev.

4. To avoid including a large Arab population, the possibility must be considered of being satisfied with the Judean Desert, with minor border amendments such as the Etzion Bloc and southern Mount Hebron.

C. In those territories that I have mentioned, we should erect as soon as possible rural and urban settlements, and permanent army bases according to security needs.

D. Jewish urban residential developments should be built in East Jerusalem, in addition to rehabilitation and population of the Jewish Quarter in the Old City.

E. We must initiate contacts with leaders and personalities among the residents of the West Bank, in order to know their willingness, and encourage them, to set up an autonomous framework in the territories that will not be within Israeli sovereignty. The autonomous framework can be linked with Israel. Such a link can be expressed in joint economic frameworks, a mutual defense treaty, technical and scientific cooperation, cultural agreements and the finding of a joint solution for settlement of the refugees from Gaza in the West Bank.

F. Clearly the government will have to take the initiative in preparing a comprehensive long-term plan for the solution of the refugee problem, which is a painful one that can only be solved fully on the basis of regional cooperation with international assistance. Until the achievement of full cooperation, the government of Israel should go about the erection of a number of model settlements of refugees on the West Bank and perhaps also in Sinai. This is necessary for two reasons: to learn by experience, and to demonstrate goodwill and indicate our willingness to work for a constructive solution to the problem. It is necessary for reasons both humanitarian and political.

G. Israel must annex the Gaza Strip with its original population, that is to say those who lived there before 1948. As for the refugees who have not been absorbed for economic, social and other reasons, they should in my opinion be settled in the West Bank or El-Arish District at their option. The United Nations should continue to look after them, while Israel looks after all the regular needs of the permanent population. Of course the implementation of such a plan will demand time, and therefore, the Strip will not for the time being be annexed legally to Israel.

H. The delineation of precise border lines will of course be done after hearing the opinions of the chief-of-staff.

I. Similarly, we should establish—in my opinion—as soon as possible a supreme authority for handling of all the problems of the occupied territories and of the refugees, within the framework of the Prime Minister's Office.

And now, the main reasons for the Plan:

A. In favor of an immediate decision on the political future of the West Bank and Gaza Strip:

1. Non-determination of a position by the government of Israel does not mean that positions will not be adopted in other centers of power, friendly and hostile. From a political viewpoint, it is desirable that the policy makers of friendly

countries, and particularly of the United States, should know our intentions before they arrive at conclusions that might well not be in our favor. If differences of opinion between us and Washington are inevitable as regards the future of the territories that we now occupy, then it would be better that these should appear in the course of their appeal on our policy rather than as a result of our appeal against firm opinions on their side, lest considerations of prestige become involved. We must learn the lesson of the delayed decision, the lesson of the delay over the unification of Jerusalem. Had we decided on unification of the city days after its liberation, and had we carried out that unification shortly after the firing died down, then it is possible that such a wide front against that justified action would not have formed: the United States would not have seen itself as deceived; and the provocative act would not have taken place, at all times, on the eve of the vote in the Emergency Session of the United Nations.

It is within our power to no small degree to influence the decision-making process in Washington, London and other capitals in positive directions. Public opinion in the United States is largely on our side. The elections are far off for us in terms of having time to develop a more constant and complete activity; on the other hand, they are close enough that the competing parties, and particulary the candidates who will fight for the presidency will be compelled to take into account considerations of a largely sympathetic public opinon for Israel. It is also advisable to reach our decision before Washington and Moscow find a compromise that might, as can be expected, also be at our expense.

2. The ideological, psychological and political developments in the Arab population of the occupied territories also obliges us not to delay formulation of a policy as regards them and the territory on which they sit. They are slowly recovering from the trauma of their downfall; their disappointment with the leaders of the Arab countries is likely to blur gradually, and visions of driving Israel back to her previous border are likely to take the place of the despair that has been their lot in the first weeks since our victory. Moreover, having learned the lesson of those Arabs who collaborated in the Gaza Strip in 1956/57 and were abandoned by Israel in her withdrawal from the Sinai Peninsula and the Strip, only to be punished by the Egyptian authorities—the key men in the occupied territories are likely to shy away from cooperation with us as long as they are not convinced that we have a clear policy which will be carried out despite the anticipated difficulties in the international arena. How can they understand our policy when it is not clear to us?

3. From the standpoint of the government's prestige it is also desirable that we reach conclusions quickly. The Israeli public, with a healthy awareness, wants to know the intentions of the government. Meanwhile, the public is perplexed, and this does not add to our strength and unity, which we need so badly for the prolonged and difficult struggle that faces us.

4. The decisions taken on the annexation of Jerusalem alone, on the return of those refugees who so desire, and on abstention from creation of settlements in the territories beyond the pre-war frontiers of Israel—all are unavoidably interpreted in the world, in the Arab countries, among the populace of the territories, and by the Israeli public as if we are accepting, or at least willing to reconcile ourselves to renunciation of all the territories. This interpretation, if

it takes root in the interested parties, on a subject of such importance, might make life very difficult for us in the future. If we do wish to hold on to the territories, in one form or another, this will be viewed as a step far more rigid and surprising than it really is; and if a decision is taken to return the West Bank or a large part of it to the Hashemite kingdom, we will be in a weak bargaining position.

It seems to me, therefore, that we are already very late, and must not delay our decision any longer.

The following excerpts are from "Strategy of Peace," an address by Yigal Allon at the Hebrew University on June 3, 1973, translated from the original Hebrew. The address was published as a pamphlet by the Hebrew University in June, 1973.

Our eastern border is the most problematic, because this is where all the security, demographic and historic problems cluster in all their severity. Until the Six Day War this border was considered our "soft underbelly." As far as it is concerned, there are two possibilities: the first is to place the border on the mountain ridge of Judea and Samaria. Such a border would undoubtedly give us a firm and convenient defense disposition, but—it would mean bringing the decisive majority of the West Bank population into Israel proper, and the strategic profit would be surmounted by the demographic loss.

I would prefer the second possibility, in which our defense dispositions would be on the Jordan River, the Dead Sea and the barren hills of Samaria and the Judean Desert. On the other hand, this possibility relies on minimal "Latrun-type" amendments of the old armistice line—the "Green Line"—and leaves the dense Arab population of the West Bank to an Arab solution, while leaving them a sovereign corridor between Ramallah, Jericho and the Allenby Bridge. This deployment could stand up to a modern army, and is designed to protect the country not only against its immediate neighbors but also against the entire eastern expanse that stretches to the Persian Gulf and the Indian Ocean. And this becomes much more important now that the expanse is being equipped with a bounty of modern offensive weapons from various and conflicting sources. Such a deployment does afford Jerusalem and its satellites a hinterland against the threat of guerrilla warfare, and grants Israel settlement possibilities in territories that are almost totally uninhabited. And all this without any significant addition of Arab population.

There is no need to add that the areas on which we are prepared to compromise will be demilitarized in terms of all offensive weaponry and, thanks to our consolidation to the rear of the West Bank populace, their offensive potential will be neutralised.

Greater Jerusalem, with veteran and new Jewish residential areas around the city, must of course remain united under Israeli sovereignty, while the rights of all its inhabitants, no matter what their faith, are specifically guaranteed. Jerusalem was never an Arab capital, nor was it ever an Arab national center. It has never occupied for any nation or religion the place that it occupies in Jewish nationalism, history, faith and spiritual heritage.

However, there is and should be no ignoring the special bond of Islam, as of Christianity, to this city. In the framework of a peace treaty there is room to grant the Arab element that will be the party to the treaty a special religious status in the places holy to Islam. I stress a religious and not a political status. Though there is no surety, it seems to me that such a solution might break the stalemate.

In Sinai there is no demographic or historic problem, but first and foremost a major strategic problem. The Sinai peninsula can serve three military purposes: as a buffer zone between Egypt and Israel; as an invasion base into the Negev and central Israel; as a strategic trap for Egyptian forces.

Three times the Egyptians have tried to turn Sinai into an invasion base, and three times it has become a death trap for them. After three such experiences, our refusal to let the Egyptians turn it into an invasion platform yet again is only natural. Nevertheless, there is no chance of reaching a peace treaty with Egypt unless we agree to return the major part of the peninsula, while the remainder must stay in Israeli control. Moreover, the demilitarization of the Sinai peninsula, policed by joint Israeli-Egyptian teams, will increase the security of both sides.

There are four "weak links" in Sinai: 1. the historic invasion route along the coast, north through el-Arish and Gaza; 2. Nitzana–Quseima–Quantilla area; 3. Eilat area; 4. the Straits of Tiran.

And so, to improve our defensive disposition on our border with Egypt, Israel's control over reasonable defense areas in these four regions, and a territorial continuity between them—from Sharm el-Sheikh in the south to somewhere in the dunes between el-Arish and Rafiah on the Mediterranean coast to the north—must be guaranteed.

This control will permit us installation of an early warning system and electronic and aerial interception against aircraft on the one hand, and effective deployment for ground, air and sea counterattack in the case of another invasion attempt, on the other hand. Deployment for such an invasion will serve Israel as a *casus belli*. Without effective demilitarization of the peninsula, I would demand a deeper strategic depth.

Our control over Sharm el-Sheikh and the southern approaches of the Gulf of Eilat, will guarantee free navigation to all, and grant us a more convenient base to protect our maritime rights in the Bab el-Mandab Straits, at the southern approaches to the Red Sea. Israeli control over the approaches to the Gulf of Eilat and Egyptian control in parallel over the approaches to the Gulf of Suez, will create a mutual interdependence, for after all both sides will be interested in free navigation in both gulfs. Neither the historic bond nor ambitions for expansion of sovereignty are my motivations in wanting to hold these areas permanently. The needs of security obligate an unquestioned Israeli control of these strategic areas, so they should not again become the weak links that cause wars.

As for the Gaza Strip, it should not be returned to Egyptian rule. If the choice is between Israeli or Egyptian rule, then the Israeli is preferable. However, the demographic problem of the strip, which is mostly populated by refugees, is a troublesome one. And it is possible that, in looking for a solution that will give Jordan and the West Bank access to the Mediterranean, there will be room to consider turning Gaza into just such an outlet, with rights of traffic—but without a corridor.

Our firm hold on the Golan Heights—or at least a large part of them—and the Hermon Shoulder is most essential, not only to protect the Hule Valley settlements against salvoes of Syrian artillery, for after all we are erecting new settlements within Syrian artillery range. Our control over the heights is dictated in practice by Israel's overall strategic needs—because this is protection of our main water sources, of the Kinneret Basin and Upper and Lower Galilee.

Appendix IV: The Rabat Resolution

The Palestine Resolution of the Seventh Arab Summit Conference, Rabat, October 29, 1974. Reproduced here as it appeared in Journal of Palestine Studies *14 (1975).*

The Seventh Arab Summit Conference after exhaustive and detailed discussions conducted by their Majesties, Excellencies, and Highnesses, the Kings, Presidents and Amirs on the Arab situation in general and the Palestine problem in particular, within their national and international frameworks; and after hearing the statements submitted by His Majesty King Hussein, King of the Hashemite Kingdom of Jordan and His Excellency Brother Yasser Arafat, Chairman of the Palestine Liberation Organization, and after the statements of their Majesties and Excellencies the Kings and Presidents, in an atmosphere of candour and sincerity and full responsibility; and in view of the Arab leaders' appreciation of the joint national responsibility required of them at present for confronting aggression and performing duties of liberation, enjoined by the unity of the Arab cause and the unity of its struggle; and in view of the fact that all are aware of Zionist schemes still being made to eliminate the Palestinian existence and to obliterate the Palestinian national entity; and in view of the Arab leaders' belief in the necessity to frustrate these attempts and schemes and to counteract them by supporting and strengthening this Palestinian national entity, by providing all requirements to develop and increase its ability to ensure that the Palestinian people recover their rights in full; and by meeting responsibilities of close cooperation with its brothers within the framework of collective Arab commitment;

And in light of the victories achieved by Palestinian struggle in the confrontation with the Zionist enemy, at the Arab and international levels, at the United Nations, and of the obligation imposed thereby to continue joint Arab action to develop and increase the scope of these victories; and having received the views of all on all the above, and having succeeded in cooling the differences between brethren within the framework of consolidating Arab solidarity, the Seventh Arab Summit Conference resolves the following:

1. To affirm the right of the Palestinian people to self-determination and to return to their homeland;

2. To affirm the right of Palestinian people to establish an independent national authority under the command of the Palestine Liberation Organization, the sole legitimate representative of the Palestinian people in any Palestinian territory that is liberated;

3. To support the Palestine Liberation Organization in the exercise of its responsibility at the national and international levels within the framework of Arab commitment;

4. To call on the Hashemite Kingdom of Jordan, the Syrian Arab Republic, the Arab Republic of Egypt and the Palestine Liberation Organization to devise a formula for the regulation of relations between them in the light of these decisions so as to ensure their implementation;

5. That all the Arab states undertake to defend Palestinian national unity and not to interfere in the internal affairs of Palestinian action.

Appendix V:
Yasser Arafat's United Nations Speech

Statement by Yasser Arafat, 29th Session, United Nations General Assembly, November 13, 1974. Reproduced here as it appeared in the New York Times, *November 14, 1974.*

Mr. President, I thank you for having invited the Palestinian Liberation Organization to participate in this plenary session of the United Nations General Assembly. I am grateful to all those representatives of States of the United Nations who contributed to the decision to introduce the question of Palestine as a separate item of the agenda of this assembly. That decision made possible the Assembly's resolution inviting us to address it on the question of Palestine.

This is a very important occasion. The question of Palestine is being reexamined by the United Nations, and we consider that step to be a victory for the world organization as much as a victory for the cause of our people. It indicates anew that the United Nations of today is not the United Nations of the past, just as today's world is not yesterday's world. Today's United Nations represents 138 nations, a number that more clearly reflects the will of the international community. Thus today's United Nations is more nearly capable of implementing the principles embodied in its Charter and the Universal Declaration of Human Rights, as well as being more truly empowered to support causes of peace and justice.

Our peoples are now beginning to feel that change. Along with them, the peoples of Asia, Africa and Latin America also feel the change. As a result, the United Nations acquires greater esteem both in our people's view and in the view of other peoples. Our hope is thereby strengthened that the United Nations can contribute actively to the pursuit and triumph of the cause of peace, justice, freedom, and independence. Our resolve to build a new world is fortified—a world free of colonialism, imperialism, neocolonialism and racism in each of its instances, including Zionism.

Our world aspires to peace, justice, equality and freedom. It wishes that oppressed nations at present bent under the weight of imperialism might gain their freedom and their right to self-determination. It hopes to place the relations between nations on a basis of equality, peaceful coexistence, mutual respect for each other's internal affairs, secure national sovereignty, independence and territorial unity on the basis of justice and mutual benefit. This world resolves that the economic ties binding it together should be grounded in justice, parity and mutual interest. It aspires finally to direct its human resources against the scourge of poverty, famine, disease and natural calamity, toward the development of productive scientific and technical capabilities to enhance human wealth—all this in the hope of reducing the disparity between the developing and the developed countries. But all such aspirations cannot be realized in a world that is at present ruled over by tension, injustice, oppression, racial discrimination and exploitation, a world also threatened with unending economic disaster, war and crisis.

Great number of peoples, including those of Zimbabwe, Namibia, South Africa and Palestine, among many others, are still victims of oppression and violence. Their areas of the world are gripped by armed struggles provoked by imperialism and racial discrimination, both merely forms of aggression and terror. Those are instances of oppressed peoples compelled by intolerable circumstances into confrontation with such oppression. But wherever that confrontation occurs it is legitimate and just.

It is imperative that the international community should support these peoples in their struggles, in the furtherance of their rightful causes, in the attainment of their right to self-determination.

In Indo-China the peoples are still exposed to aggression. They remain subjected to conspiracies preventing them from the enjoyment of peace and the realization of their goals. Although people everywhere have welcomed the agreements of peace reached in Laos and South Viet-Nam, no one can say that genuine peace has been achieved, nor that those forces responsible in the first place for aggression have now desisted from their attacks on Viet-Nam. The same can be said of the present military aggression against the people of Cambodia. It is therefore incumbent on the international community to support these oppressed peoples, and also to condemn the oppressors for their designs against peace. Moreover, despite the positive stand taken by the Democratic Republic of Korea with regard to a peaceful, just solution of the Korean question, there is as yet no settlement of that question.

A few months ago the problem of Cyprus erupted violently before us. All peoples everywhere shared in the suffering of the Cypriots. We ask that the United Nations continue its efforts to reach a just solution in Cyprus, thereby sparing the Cypriots further war and ensuring peace and independence for them instead. Undoubtedly, however, consideration of the question of Cyprus belongs within that of Middle Eastern problems as well as of Mediterranean problems.

In their efforts to replace an outmoded but still dominant world economic system with a new, more logically rational one, the countries of Asia, Africa, and Latin America must nevertheless face implacable attacks on these efforts. These countries have expressed their views at the special session of the General Assembly on raw materials and development. Thus the plundering, the exploitation, the siphoning off of the wealth of impoverished peoples must be terminated forthwith. There must be no deterring of these peoples' efforts to develop and control their wealth. Furthermore, there is a grave necessity for arriving at fair prices for raw materials from these countries.

In addition, these countries continue to be hampered in the attainment of their primary objectives formulated at the Conference on the Law of the Sea in Caracas, at the Population Conference and at the Rome Food Conference. The United Nations should therefore bend every effort to achieve a radical alteration of the world economic system, making it possible for developing countries to develop. The United Nations must shoulder the responsibility for fighting inflation, now borne most heavily by the developing countries, especially the oil-producing countries. The United Nations must firmly condemn any threats made against these countries simply because they demand their just rights.

The world-wide armaments race shows no signs of abation. As a consequence, the entire world is threatened with the dispersion of its wealth and the utter waste of its energies. Armed violence is made more likely everywhere. We expect the United Nations to devote itself single-mindedly to curbing the unlimited acquisition of arms; to preventing even the possibility of nuclear destruction; to reducing the vast sums spent on military technology; to converting expenditure on war into projects for development, for increasing production, and for benefiting common humanity.

And still, the highest tension exists in our part of the world. There the Zionist entity cling tenaciously to occupied Arab territory; Zionism persists in the aggressions against us and our territory. New military preparations are feverishly being made. These anticipate another, fifth war of aggression to be launched against us. Such signs bear the closest possible watching, since there is a grave likelihood that this war would forebode nuclear destruction and cataclysmic annihilation.

The world is in need of tremendous efforts if its aspirations to peace, freedom, justice, equality and development are to be realized, if its struggle is to be victorious over colonialism, imperialism, neo-colonialism, and racism in all its forms, including Zionism. Only by such efforts can actual form be given to the aspirations of all peoples, including the aspirations of peoples whose States oppose such efforts. It is this road that leads to the fulfillment of those principles emphasized by the United Nations Charter and the Universal Declaration of Human Rights. Were the *status quo* simply to be maintained, however, the world would instead be exposed to prolonged armed conflict, in addition to economic, human and natural calamity.

Despite abiding world crises, despite even the gloomy powers of backwardness and disastrous wrong, we live in a time of glorious change. An old world order is crumbling before our eyes, as imperialism, colonialism, neo-colonialism and racism, the chief form of which is Zionism, ineluctably perish. We are privileged to be able to witness a great wave of history bearing peoples forward into a new world which they have created. In that world just causes will triumph. Of that we are confident.

The question of Palestine belongs to this perspective of emergence and struggle. Palestine is crucial amongst those just causes fought for unstintingly by masses labouring under imperialism and aggression. It cannot be, and is not, lost on me today, as I stand here before the General Assembly, that if I have been given the opportunity to address the General Assembly, so too must the opportunity be given to all liberation movements fighting against racism and imperialism. In their names, in the name of every human being struggling for freedom and self-determination, I call upon the General Assembly urgently to give their just causes the same full attention the General Assembly has so rightly given to our cause. Such recognition once made, there will be a secure foundation thereafter for the preservation of universal peace. For only with such peace will a new world order endure in which peoples can live free of oppression, fear, terror and the suppression of their rights. As I said earlier, this is the true perspective in which to set the question of Palestine. I shall now do so for the General Assembly, keeping firmly in mind both the perspective and the goal of a coming world order.

Even as today we address the General Assembly from what is before all else an international rostrum we are also expressing our faith in political and diplomatic struggle as complements, as enhancements of armed struggle. Furthermore we express our appreciation of the role the United Nations is capable of playing in settling problems of international scope. But this capability, I said a moment ago, became real only once the United Nations had accommodated itself to the living actuality of aspiring peoples, towards which an organization of so truly international a dimension owes unique obligations.

In addressing the General Assembly today our people proclaims its faith in the future, unencumbered either by past tragedies or present limitations. If, as we discuss the present, we enlist the past in our service, we do so only to light up our journey into the future alongside other movements of national liberation. If we return now to the historical roots of our cause we do so because present at this very moment in our midst are those, who, while they occupy our homes, as their cattle graze in our pastures, and as their hands pluck the fruit of our trees, claim at the same time that we are disembodied spirits, fictions without presence, without traditions or future. We speak of our roots also because until recently some people have regarded—and continued to regard—our problem as merely a problem of refugees. They have portrayed the Middle East Question as little more than a border dispute between the Arab states and the Zionist entity. They have imagined that our people claim rights not rightfully its own and fights neither with logic nor valid motive, with a simple wish only to disturb the peace and to terrorize wantonly. For there are amongst you—and here I refer to the United States of America and others like it—those who supply our enemy freely with planes and bombs and with every variety of murderous weapon. They take hostile positions against us, deliberately distorting the true essence of the problem. All this is done not only at our expense, but at the expense of the American people, and of the friendship we continue to hope can be cemented between us and this great people, whose history of struggle for the sake of freedom we honour and salute.

I cannot now forgo this opportunity to appeal from this rostrum directly to the American people, asking it to give its support to our heroic and fighting people. I ask it whole-heartedly to endorse right and justice, to recall George Washington to mind, heroic Washington whose purpose was his nation's freedom and independence, Abraham Lincoln, champion of the destitute and the wretched, and also Woodrow Wilson whose doctrine of Fourteen Points remains subscribed to and venerated by our people. I ask the American people whether the demonstrations of hostility and enmity taking place outside this great hall reflect the true intent of America's will? What, I ask you plainly, is the crime of the people of Palestine against the American People? Why do you fight us so? Does such unwarranted belligerence really serve your interests? Does it serve the interests of the American masses? No, definitely not. I can only hope that the American people will remember that their friendship with the whole Arab nation is too great, too abiding, and too rewarding for any such demonstration to harm it.

In any event, as our discussion of the question of Palestine focuses upon historical roots, we do so because we believe that any question now exercising the world's concern must be viewed radically, in the true root sense of that word, if a real solution is ever to be grasped. We propose this radical approach as an antidote to an approach to international issue that obscures historical origins behind ignorance, denial, and a slavish obeisance to the present.

The roots of the Palestinian question reach back into the closing years of the 19th century, in other words, to that period which we call the era of colonialism and settlement as we know it today. This is precisely the period during which Zionism as a scheme was born; its aim was the conquest of Palestine by European immigrants, just as settlers colonized, and indeed raided, most of Africa. This is the period during which, pouring forth out of the west, colonialism spread into the furthest reaches of Africa, Asia, and Latin America, building colonies, everywhere cruelly exploiting, oppressing, plundering the peoples of those three continents. This period persists into the present. Marked evidence of its totally reprehensible presence can be readily preceived in the racism practiced both in South Africa and in Palestine.

Just as colonialism and its demagogues dignified their conquests, their plunder and limitless attacks upon the natives of Africa with appeals to a "civilizing and modernizing" mission, so too did waves of Zionist immigrants disguise their purposes as they conquered Palestine. Just as colonialism as a system and colonialists as its instrument used religion, color, race and language to justify the African's exploitation and his cruel subjugation by terror and discrimination, so too were these methods employed as Palestine was usurped and its people hounded from the national homeland.

Just as colonialism heedlessly used the wretched, the poor, the exploited as mere inert matter with which to build and to carry out settler colonialism, so too were destitute, oppressed European Jews employed on behalf of world imperialism and the Zionist leadership. European Jews were transformed into the instruments of aggression; they became the elements of settler colonialism intimately allied to racial discriminations.

Zionist theology was utilized against our Palestinian people: the purpose was not only the establishment of Western-style settler colonialism but also the severing of Jews from their various homelands and subsequently their estrangement from their nations. Zionism is an ideology that is imperialist, colonialist, racist; it is profoundly reactionary and discriminatory; it is united with anti-Semitism in its retrograde tents and is, when all said and done, another side of the same base coin. For when what is proposed is that adherents of the Jewish faith, regardless of their national residence, should neither owe allegiance to their national residence nor live on equal footing with its other, non-Jewish citizens—when that is proposed we hear anti-Semitism being proposed. When it is proposed that the only solution for the Jewish problem is that Jews must alienate themselves from communities or nations of which they have been a historical part, when it is proposed that Jews solve the Jewish problem by immigrating to and forcibly settling the land of another people—when this occurs, exactly the same position is being advocated as the one urged by anti-Semites against Jews.

Thus, for instance, we can understand the close connection between Rhodes, who promoted settler colonialism in south-east Africa, and Herzl, who had settler colonialist designs upon Palestine. Having received a certificate of good settler colonialist conduct from Rhodes, Herzl then turned around and presented this Certificate to the British Government, hoping thus to secure a formal resolution supporting Zionist policy. In exchange, the Zionists promised Britain an imperialist base on Palestinian soil so that imperial interests could be safeguarded at one of their chief strategic points.

So the Zionist movement allied itself directly with world colonialism in a common raid on our land. Allow me now to present a selection of historical truths about this alliance.

The Jewish invasion of Palestine began in 1881. Before the first large wave of immigrants started arriving, Palestine had a population of half a million; most of the population was either Moslem or Christian, and only 20,000 were Jewish. Every segment of the population enjoyed the religious tolerance characteristic of our civilization.

Palestine was then a verdant land, inhabited mainly by an Arab people in the course of building its life and dynamically enriching its indigenous culture.

Between 1882 and 1917 the Zionist Movement settled approximately 50,000 European Jews in our homeland. To do that it resorted to trickery and deceit in order to implant them in our midst. Its success in getting Britain to issue the Balfour Declaration once again demonstrated the alliance between Zionism and imperialism. Furthermore, by promising to the Zionist movement what was not hers to give, Britain showed how oppressive was the rule of imperialism. As it was constituted then, the League of Nations abandoned our Arab people, and Wilson's pledges and promises came to nought. In the guise of a mandate, British imperialism was cruelly and directly imposed upon us. The mandate document issued by the League of Nations was to enable the Zionist invaders to consolidate their gains in our homeland.

In the wake of the Balfour Declaration and over a period of 30 years, the Zionist movement succeeded, in collaboration with its imperialist ally, in settling more European Jews on the land, thus usurping the properties of Palestinian Arabs.

By 1947 the number of Jews had reached 60,000; they owned about 6 per cent of Palestine arable land. The figure should be compared with the population of Palestine, which at that time was 1,250,000.

As a result of the collusion between the mandatory Power and the Zionist movement and with the support of some countries, this General Assembly early in its history approved a recommendation to partition our Palestinian homeland. This took place in an atmosphere poisoned with questionable actions and strong pressure. The General Assembly partitioned what it had no right to divide—an indivisible homeland. When we rejected that decision, our position corresponded to that of the natural mother who refused to permit King Solomon to cut her son in two when the unnatural mother claimed the child for herself and agreed to his dismemberment. Furthermore, even though the partition resolution granted the colonialist settlers 54 per cent of the land of Palestine, their dissatisfaction with the decision promoted them to wage a war of terror against civilian Arab population. They occupied 81 per cent of the total area of Palestine, uprooting a million

Arabs. Thus, they occupied 524 Arab towns and villages, of which they destroyed 385, completely obliterating them in the process. Having done so, they built their own settlements and colonies on the ruins of our farms and our groves. The roots of the Palestine question lie here. Its causes do not stem from any conflict between two religions or two nationalisms. Neither is it a border conflict between neighboring states. It is the cause of people deprived of its homeland, dispersed and uprooted, and living mostly in exile and in refugee camps.

With support from imperialist and colonialist powers, it managed to get itself accepted as a United Nations Member. It further succeeded in getting the Palestine Question deleted from the agenda of the United Nations and in deceiving world public opinion by presenting our cause as a problem of refugees in need either of charity from do-gooders, or settlement in a land not theirs.

Not satisfied with all this, the racist entity, founded on the imperialist-colonialist concept, turned itself into a base of imperialism and into an arsenal of weapons. This enabled it to assume its role of subjugating the Arab people and of committing aggression against them, in order to satisfy its ambitions for further expansion on Palestinian and other Arab lands. In addition to the many instances of aggression committed by this entity against the Arab States, it has launched two large scale wars, in 1956 and 1967, thus endangering world peace and security.

As a result of Zionist aggression in June 1967, the enemy occupied Egyptian Sinai as far as the Suez Canal. The enemy occupied Syria's Golan Heights, in addition to all Palestinian land west of the Jordan. All these developments have led to the creation in our area of what has come to be known as the "Middle East problem". The situation has been rendered more serious by the enemy's persistence in maintaining its unlawful occupation and in further consolidating it, thus establishing a beachhead for world imperialism's thrust against our Arab nation. All Security Council decisions and appeals to world public opinion for withdrawal from the lands occupied in June 1967 have been ignored. Despite all the peaceful efforts on the international level, the enemy has not been deterred from its expansionist policy. The only alternative open before our Arab nations, chiefly Egypt and Syria, was to expand exhaustive efforts in preparing forcefully to resist that barbarous armed invasion—and this in order to liberate Arab lands and to restore the rights of the Palestinian people, after all other peaceful means failed.

Under these circumstances, the fourth war broke out in October 1973, bringing home to the Zionist enemy the bankruptcy of its policy of occupation, expansion and its reliance on the concept of military might. Despite all this, the leaders of the Zionist entity are far from having learned any lesson from their experience. They are making preparations for the fifth war, resorting once more to the language of military superiority, aggression, terrorism, subjugation and, finally, always to war in their dealings with the Arabs.

It pains our people greatly to witness the propagation of the myth that its homeland was a desert until it was made to bloom by the toil of foreign settlers, that it was a land without a people, and that the colonialist entity caused no harm to any human being. No: such lies must be exposed from this rostrum, for the world must know that Palestine was the cradle of the most ancient cultures and civilizations. Its Arab people were engaged in farming and building, spreading culture throughout the land for thousands of years, setting an example in the practice of freedom of worship, acting as faithful guardians of the holy places of all religions. As a son of Jerusalem, I treasure for myself and my people beautiful memories and vivid images of the religious brotherhood that was the hallmark of our Holy City before it succumbed catastrophe. Our people continued to pursue this enlightened policy until the establishment of the State of Israel and their dispersion. This did not deter our people from pursuing their humanitarian role on Palestine soil. Nor will they permit their land to become a launching pad for aggression or a racist camp predicated on the destruction of civilization, culture, progress and peace. Our people cannot but maintain the heritage of their ancestors in resisting the invaders, in assuming the privileged task of defending their native land, their Arab nationhood, their culture and civilization, and in safeguarding the cradle of monotheistic religion.

By contrast, we need only to mention briefly some Israeli stands: its support of the Secret Army Organization in Algeria, its bolstering of the settler-colonialists in Africa—whether in the Congo, Angola, Mozambique, Zimbabwe, Azania or South Africa—and its backing of South Viet-Nam against the Viet-Namese revolution. In addition, one can mention Israel's continuing support of imperialists and racists everywhere, its obstructionist stand in the Committee of Twenty-Four, its refusal to cast its vote in support of independence for the African States, and its opposition to the demands of many Asian, African and Latin American nations, and several other States in the Conference on raw materials, population, the law of the sea, and food. All these facts offer further proof of the character of the enemy which has usurped our land. They justify the honorable struggle which we are waging against it. As we defend a vision of the future, our enemy upholds the myths of the past.

The enemy we face has a long record of hostility even towards the Jews themselves, for there is within the Zionist entity a built-in racism against Oriental Jews. While we were vociferously condemning the massacres of Jews under Nazi rule, Zionist leadership appeared more interested at that time in exploiting them as best it could in order to realize its goal of immigration into Palestine.

If the immigration of Jews to Palestine had had as its objective the goal of enaing them to live side by side with us, enjoying the same rights and assuming the same duties, we would have opened our doors to them, as far as our homeland's capacity for absorption permitted. Such was the case with the thousands of Armenians and Circassians who still live among us in equality as brethren and citizens. But that the goal of this immigration should be to usurp our homeland, disperse our people, and turn us into second-class-citizens—this is what no one can conceivably demand that we acquiesce in or submit to. Therefore, since its inception, our revolution has not been motivated by racial or religious factors. Its target has never been the Jew, as a person, but racist Zionism and undisguised aggression. In this sense, ours is also a revolution for the Jew, as a human being, as well. We are struggling so that Jews, Christians and Muslims may live in equality, enjoying the same rights and assuming the same duties, free from racial or religious discriminations.

We do distinguish between Judaism and Zionism. While we maintain our opposition to the colonialist Zionist movement, we respect the Jewish faith. Today, almost one century after the rise of the Zionist movement, we wish to warn of its increasing danger to the Jews of the world, to our Arab people and to world peace and security. For Zionism encourages the Jew to emigrate out of his homeland

and grants him an artificially-created nationality. The Zionists proceed with their terrorist activities even though these have proved ineffective. The phenomenon of constant emigration from Israel, which is bound to grow as the bastions of colonialism and racism in the world fall, is an example of the inevitability of the failure of such activities.

We urge the people and governments of the world to stand firm against Zionist attempts at encouraging world Jewry to emigrate from their countries and to usurp our land. We urge them as well firmly to oppose any discrimination against any human being, as to religion, race or color.

Why should our Arab Palestinian people pay the price of such discrimination in the world? Why should our people be responsible for the problems of Jewish immigration, if such problems exist in the minds of some people? Why do not the supporters of the problems open their own countries, which can absorb and help these immigrants?

Those who call us terrorists wish to prevent world public opinion from discovering the truth about us and from seeing the justice on our faces. They seek to hide the terrorism and tyranny of their acts, and our own posture of self-defense.

The difference between the revolutionary and the terrorist lies in the reason for which each fights. For whoever stands by a just cause and fights for the freedom and liberation of his land from the invaders, the settlers and the colonialists, cannot possibly be called terrorist, otherwise the American people in the struggle for liberation from the British colonialists would have been terrorists; the European resistance against the Nazis would be terrorism, the struggle of the Asian, African and Latin American peoples would also be terrorism, and many of you who are in this Assembly hall were considered terrorists. This is actually a just and proper struggle consecrated by the United Nations Charter and by the Universal Declaration of Human Rights. As to those who fight against the just causes, those who wage war to occupy, colonize and oppress other people, those are the terrorists. Those are the people whose actions should be condemned, who should be called war criminals: for the Justice of the cause determines the right to struggle.

Zionist terrorism which was waged against the Palestinian people to evict it from its country and usurp its land is registered in our official documents. Thousands of our people were assassinated in their villages and towns; tens of thousands of others were forced at gunpoint to leave their homes and the lands of their fathers. Time and time again our children, women and aged were evicted and had to wander in the deserts and climb mountains without any food or water. No one who in 1948 witnessed the catastrophe that befell the inhabitants of hundreds of villages and towns—in Jerusalem, Jaffa, Lydda, Ramle and Galilee—no one who has been a witness to that catastrophe will ever forget the experience, even though the mass blackout has succeeded in hiding these horrors as it has hidden the traces of 385 Palestinian villages and towns destroyed at the time and erased from the map. The destruction of 19,000 houses during the past seven years, which is equivalent to the complete destruction of 200 more Palestinian villages, and the great number of maimed as a result of the treatment they were subjected to in Israeli prisons, cannot be hidden by any blackout.

Their terrorism fed on hatred and this hatred was even directed against the olive tree in my country, which has been a proud symbol and which reminded them of the indigenous inhabitants of the land, a living reminder that the land is Palestinian. Thus they sought to destroy it. How can one describe the statement by Golda Meir which expressed her disquiet about "the Palestinian children born every day". They see in the Palestinian child, in the Palestinian tree, an enemy that should be exterminated. For tens of years Zionists have been harassing our people's cultural, political, social and artistic leaders, terrorizing them and assassinating them. They have stolen our cultural heritage, our popular folklore and have claimed it as theirs. Their terrorism even reached our sacred places in our beloved and peaceful Jerusalem. They have endeavoured to de-Arabize it and make it lose its Moslem and Christian character by evicting its inhabitants and annexing it.

I must mention the fire of the Aksa Mosque and the disfiguration of many of the monuments, which are both historic and religious in character. Jerusalem, with its religious history and its spiritual values, bears witness to the future. It is proof of our eternal presence, of our civilization, of our human values. It is therefore not surprising that under that sky these three religions shine in order to enlighten mankind so that it might express the tribulations and hopes of humanity, and that it might mark out the road of the future with its hopes.

The small number of Palestinian Arabs who were not uprooted by the Zionists in 1948 are at present refugees in their own homeland. Israeli law treats them as second-class citizens—and even as third-class citizens since Oriental Jews are second-class citizens—and they have been subject to all forms of racial discrimination and terrorism after confiscation of their land and property. They have been victims of bloody massacres such as that of Kfar Kassim, they have been expelled from their villages and denied the right to return, as in the case of the inhabitants of Ikrit and Kfar-Birim. For 26 years, our population has been living under martial law and was denied the freedom of movement without prior permission from the Israeli military governor, this at a time when an Israeli law was promulgated granting citizenship to any Jew anywhere who wanted to emigrate to our homeland. Moreover, another Israeli law stipulated that Palestinians who were not present in their villages or towns at the time of the occupation were not entitled to Israeli citizenship.

The record of Israeli rulers is replete with acts of terror perpetrated on those of our people who remained under occupation in Sinai and the Golan Heights. The criminal bombardment of the Bahr-al-Bakar School and the Abou Zaabal factory are but two such unforgettable acts of terrorism. The total destruction of the Syrian city of Kuneitra is yet another tangible instance of systematic terrorism. If a record of Zionist terrorism in South Lebanon were to be compiled, the enormity of its acts would shock even the most hardened: piracy, bombardments, scorched-earth, destruction of hundreds of homes, eviction of civilians and the kidnapping of Lebanese citizens. This clearly constitutes a violation of Lebanese sovereignty and is in preparation for the diversion of the Litani River waters.

Need one remind this Assembly of the numerous resolutions adopted by it condemning Israeli aggressions committed against Arab countries, Israeli violations of human rights and the articles of the Geneva Conventions, as well as the resolutions pertaining to the annexation of the city of Jerusalem and its restoration to its former status?

The only description for these acts is that they are acts of barbarism and terrorism. And yet, the Zionist racists and colonialists have the temerity to describe the just struggle of our people as terror. Could there be a more flagrant distortion of truth than this? We ask those who usurped our land, who are committing murderous acts of terrorism against our people and are practicing racial discrimination more extensively than the racists of South Africa, we ask them to keep in mind the United Nations General Assembly resolution that called for the one-year suspension of the membership of the Government of South Africa from the United Nations. Such is the inevitable fate of every racist country that adopts the law of the jungle, usurps the homeland of others and persists in oppression.

For the past 30 years, our people have had to struggle against British occupation and Zionist invasion both of which had one intention, namely the usurpation of our land. Six major revolts and tens of popular uprisings were staged to foil these attempts, so that our homeland might remain ours. Over 30,000 martyrs, the equivalent in comparative terms of 6 million Americans, died in the process.

When the majority of the Palestinian people was uprooted from its homeland in 1948, the Palestinian struggle for self determination continued under the most difficult conditions. We tried every possible means to continue our political struggle to attain our national rights, but to no avail. Meanwhile we had to struggle for sheer existence. Even in exile we educated our children. This was all a part of trying to survive.

The Palestinian people produced thousands of physicians, lawyers, teachers and scientists who actively participated in the development of the Arab countries bordering on their usurped homeland. They utilized their income to assist the young and aged amongst their people who remained in the refugee camps. They educated their younger sisters and brothers, supported their parents and cared for their children. All along, the Palestinian dreamt of return. Neither the Palestinian's allegiance to Palestine nor his determination to return waned; nothing could persuade him to relinquish his Palestinian identity or to forsake his homeland. The passage of time did not make him forget, as some hoped he would. When our people lost faith in the international community which persisted in ignoring its rights and when it became obvious that the Palestinians would not recuperate one inch of Palestine through exclusively political means, our people had no choice but to resort to armed struggle. Into that struggle it poured its material and human resources. We bravely faced the most vicious acts of Israeli terrorism which were aimed at diverting our struggle and arresting it.

In the past 10 years of our struggle, thousands of martyrs and twice as many wounded, maimed and imprisoned were offered in sacrifice, all in an effort to resist the imminent threat of liquidation, to regain our right to self determination and our undisputed right to return to our homeland. With the utmost dignity and the most admirable revolutionary spirit, our Palestinian people has not lost its spirit in Israeli prisons and concentration camps or when faced with all forms of harassment and intimidation. It struggles for sheer existence and it continues to strive to preserve the Arab character of its land. Thus it resists oppression, tyranny and terrorism in their ugliest forms.

It is through our popular armed struggle that our political leadership and our national institutions finally crystallized and a national liberation movement, comprising all the Palestinian factions, organizations, and capabilities, materialized in the Palestine Liberation Organization.

Through our militant Palestine national liberation movement, our people's struggle matured and grew enough to accommodate political and social struggle in addition to armed struggle. The Palestine Liberation Organization was a major factor in creating a new Palestinian individual, qualified to shape the future of our Palestine, not merely content with mobilizing the Palestinians for the challenge of the present.

The Palestine Liberation Organization can be proud of having a large number of cultural and educational activities, even while engaged in armed struggle, and at a time when it faced increasingly vicious blows of Zionist terrorism. We established institutes for scientific research, agricultural development and social welfare, as well as centres for the revival of our culture heritage and the preservation of our folklore. Many Palestinian poets, artists and writers have enriched Arab culture in particular, and world culture generally. Their profoundly humane works have won the admiration of all those familiar with them. In contrast to that, our enemy has been systematically destroying our culture and disseminating racist, imperialist ideologies; in short, everything that impedes progress, justice, democracy and peace.

The Palestine Liberation Organization has earned its legitimacy because of the sacrifice inherent in its pioneering role, and also because of its dedicated leadership of the struggle. It has also been granted this legitimacy by the Palestinian masses, which in harmony with it have chosen it to lead the struggle according to its directives. The Palestine Liberation Organization has also gained its legitimacy by representing every faction, union or group as well as every Palestinian talent, either in the National Council or in people's institutions. This legitimacy was further strengthened by the support of the entire Arab nation, and it was consecrated during the last Arab Summit Conference, which reiterated the right of the Palestine Liberation Organization, in its capacity as the sole representative of the Palestinian people, to establish an independent national State on all liberated Palestinian territory.

Moreover, the Palestine Liberation Organization's legitimacy was intensified as a result of fraternal support given by other liberation movements and by friendly, like-minded nations that stood by our side, encouraging and aiding us in our struggle to secure our national rights.

Here I must also warmly convey the gratitude of our revolutionary fighters and that of our people to the non-aligned countries, the socialist countries, the Islamic countries, the African countries and friendly European countries, as well as all our other friends in Asia, Africa and Latin America.

The Palestine Liberation Organization represents the Palestinian people, legitimately and uniquely. Because of this, the Palestine Liberation Organization expresses the wishes and hopes of its people. Because of this, too, it brings these very wishes and hopes before you, urging you not to shirk a momentous historic responsibility towards our just cause.

For many years now, our people has been exposed to the ravages of war, destruction and dispersion. It has paid in the blood of its sons that which cannot ever be compensated. It has borne the burdens of occupation, dispersion, eviction and terror more uninterruptedly than any other people. And yet all this has made our people neither vindictive nor vengeful. Nor has it caused us to resort to the racism of our enemies. Nor have we lost the true method by which friend and foe are distinguished.

For we deplore all those crimes committed against the Jews, we also deplore all the real discriminations suffered by them because of their faith.

I am a rebel and freedom is my cause. I know well that many of you present here today once stood in exactly the same resistance position as I now occupy and from which I must fight. You once had to convert dreams into reality by your struggle. Therefore you must now share my dream. I think this is exactly why I can ask you now to help, as together we bring out our dream into a bright reality, our common dream for a peaceful future in Palestine's sacred land.

As he stood in an Israeli military court, the Jewish revolutionary, Ahud Adif, said: "I am no terrorist; I believe that a democratic State should exist on this land." Adif now languishes in a Zionist prison among his co-believers. To him and his colleagues I send my heartfelt good wishes.

And before those same courts there stands today a brave prince of the church, Bishop Capucci. Lifting his fingers to form the same victory sign used by our freedom-fighters, he said: "What I have done, I have done that all men may live on this land of peace in peace." This princely priest will doubtless share Adif's grim fate. To him we send our salutations and greetings.

Why therefore should I not dream and hope? For is not revolution the making real of dreams and hopes? So let us work together that my dream may be fulfilled, that I may return with my people out of exile, there in Palestine to live with this Jewish freedom-fighter and his partners, with this Arab priest and his brothers, in one democratic State where Christian, Jew and Moslem live in justice, equality, fraternity and progress.

Is this not a noble dream worthy of my struggle alongside all lovers of freedom everywhere? For the most admirable dimension of this dream is that it is Palestinian, a dream from out of the land of peace, the land of martyrdom and heroism, and the land of history, too.

Let us remember that the Jews of Europe and the United States have been known to lead the struggles for secularism and the separation of Church and State. They have also been to fight against discrimination on religious grounds. How can they then refuse this humane paradigm for the Holy Land? How then can they continue to support the most fanatic, discriminatory and closed of nations in its policy?

In my formal capacity as Chairman of the Palestine Liberation Organization and leader of the Palestinian revolution I proclaim before you that when we speak of our common hopes for the Palestine of tomorrow we include in our perspective all Jews now living in Palestine who choose to live with us there in peace and without discrimination.

In my formal capacity as Chairman of the Palestine Liberation Organization and leader of the Palestinian revolution I call upon Jews to turn away one by one from the illusory promises made to them by Zionist ideology and Israeli leadership. They are offering Jews perpetual bloodshed, endless war and continuous thralldom.

We invite them to emerge from their moral isolation into a more open realm of free choice, far from their present leadership's efforts to implant in them a Masada complex.

We offer them the most generous solution, that we might live together in a framework of just peace in our democratic Palestine.

In my formal capacity as Chairman of the Palestine Liberation Organization, I announce here that we do not wish one drop of either Arab or Jewish blood to be shed, neither do we delight in the continuation of killing, which would end once a just peace, based on our people's rights, hopes and aspirations had been finally established.

In my formal capacity as Chairman of the Palestine Liberation Organization and leader of the Palestinian Revolution I appeal to you to accompany our people in its struggle to attain its right to self-determination. This right is consecrated in the United Nations Charter and has been repeatedly confirmed in resolutions adopted by this august body since the drafting of the Charter. I appeal to you, further, to aid our people's return to its homeland from an involuntary exile imposed upon it by force of arms, by tyranny, by oppression, so that we may regain our property, our land, and thereafter live in our national homeland, free and sovereign, enjoying all the privileges of nationhood. Only then can Palestinian creativity be concentrated on the service of humanity. Only then will our Jerusalem resume its historic role as a peaceful shrine for all religions.

I appeal to you to enable our people to establish national independent sovereignty over its own land.

Today I have come bearing an olive branch and a freedom-fighter's gun. Do not let the olive branch fall from my hand. I repeat: do not let the olive branch fall from my hand.

War flares up in Palestine, and yet it is in Palestine that peace will be born.

Appendix VI:
Decision of the Palestinian National Council

"Political Programme for the Present Stage of the Palestine Liberation Organization Drawn up by the Palestinian National Council, Cairo, June 9, 1974." Reproduced here as it appeared in Journal of Palestine Studies 12 (1974).

The Palestinian National Council:

On the basis of the Palestinian National Charter and the Political Programme drawn up at the Eleventh Session, held from January 6-12, 1973; and from its belief that it is impossible for a permanent and just peace to be established in the area unless our Palestinian people recover all their national rights and, first and foremost, their rights to return and to self-determination on the whole of the soil of their homeland; and in the light of a study of the new political circumstances that have come into existence in the period between the Council's last and present sessions, resolves the following:

1. To reaffirm the Palestine Liberation Organization's previous attitude to Resolution 242, which obliterates the national rights of our people and deals with the cause of our people as a problem of refugees. The Council therefore refuses to have anything to do with this resolution at any level, Arab or international, including the Geneva Conference.

2. The Liberation Organization will employ all means, and first and foremost armed struggle, to liberate Palestinian territory and to establish the independent

combatant national authority for the people over every part of Palestinian territory that is liberated. This will require further changes being effected in the balance of power in favour of our people and their struggle.

3. The Liberation Organization will struggle against any proposal for a Palestinian entity the price of which is recognition, peace, secure frontiers, renunciation of national rights and the deprival of our people of their right to return and their right to self-determination on the soil of their homeland.

4. Any step taken towards liberation is a step towards the realization of the Liberation Organization's strategy of establishing the democratic Palestinian state specified in the resolutions of previous Palestinian National Councils.

5. Struggle along with the Jordanian national forces to establish a Jordanian-Palestinian national front whose aim will be to set up in Jordan a democratic national authority in close contact with the Palestinian entity that is established through the struggle.

6. The Liberation Organization will struggle to establish unity in struggle between the two peoples and between all the forces of the Arab liberation movement that are in agreement on this programme.

7. In the light of this programme, the Liberation Organization will struggle to strengthen national unity and to raise it to the level where it will be able to perform its national duties and tasks.

8. Once it is established, the Palestinian national authority will strive to achieve a union of the confrontation countries, with the aim of completing the liberation of all Palestinian territory, and as a step along the road to comprehensive Arab unity.

9. The Liberation Organization will strive to strengthen its solidarity with the socialist countries, and with forces of liberation and progress throughout the world, with the aim of frustrating all the schemes of Zionism, reaction and imperialism.

10. In the light of this programme the leadership of the revolution will determine the tactics which will serve and make possible the realization of these objectives.

The Executive Committee of the Palestine Liberation Organization will make every effort to implement this programme, and should a situation arise affecting the destiny and the future of the Palestinian people, the National Assembly will be convened in extraordinary session.

Appendix VII:
"A Palestinian Strategy for Peaceful Co-existence," by Said Hammami

Said Hammami is the London Representative of the Palestine Liberation Organization. This speech is reproduced here as it appeared in Middle East International 45 (March 1975).

"I have come bearing an olive branch and a freedom-fighter's gun. Do not let the olive branch fall from my hand." *Yasser Arafat, at the UN General Assembly, November 13, 1974.*

We Palestinians believe that the creation of the State of Israel was a grave political error, one which has done grievous harm to the interests of all concerned—the world community, the Great Powers, the Jewish people themselves and, of course, our own Palestinian people. But it was not merely an error, it was also a crime. A crime perpetrated against the natural, fundamental and inalienable rights of the Palestinians. There is really no need to argue this. The facts speak clearly for themselves to anyone who listens with an open mind. And it seems to me that now at last—though far too late—the reality of this error and this crime is fairly well recognised and accepted throughout the world, as the UN debate on Palestine in November 1974 clearly shows—except of course among those whose minds are closed to any facts or arguments which do not suit the demands of political Zionism.

I say "political" Zionism because it is this that has caused all the trouble in Palestine. With the original objective of providing a refuge for those Jews genuinely in need of one, we Palestinians had no quarrel. It was only our apprehension that this concept was to be distorted into a political dominion at our expense—an apprehension which was to be so tragically justified by events—that led us to oppose the Zionist colonisation of our homeland and the violence with which it was forced upon us.

Holding as we do this view of the creation of Israel, it is entirely natural that we should wish and hope that one day this interloper state will disappear from the scene in the Middle East. Most of us believe that some day, sooner or later, Israel, as it exists today—a racist, exclusive Zionist State—will indeed disappear. We will rejoice when that happens, but we would prefer it to happen peacefully and by mutual agreement, rather than amid violence and recrimination. Meanwhile we will do whatever is in our power to further that happy day—a happy day not only for ourselves and our Arab brothers and for the world at large, but also for the Jewish people throughout the world and, not least, for the poor benighted citizens of Israel who have been so corrupted and misled by their Zionist rulers. Everybody will be better off when this racist, colonialist anachronism has gone.

This does *not* mean that we, the Palestinians of my generation, are determined to "drive into the sea" the Jews now living in Israel. That is a myth propagated by Israel and the World Zionist Movement in order to reinvoke the spectre of genocide and to excite world sympathy for Israel and world antipathy towards Palestinians.

As Yasser Arafat stated in his speech at the UN, we believe that all Jews who are living in Israel must have the right to remain there. And in principle, we are prepared to accept that Jews living abroad who are really in need of a refuge and a new home should continue to be permitted to come and settle in Palestine. There was never any objection on our part to the immigration of such *bona fide* refugees until political Zionism sought to make use of them as the advance guard for the establishment of a settler state. But in practice we would maintain that on grounds of justice and relative need the "ingathering" of *our* exiles, the Palestine refugees, ought to take priority.

We make no apology for our opposition to the Zionist State as it exists today. We have every right and every reason to oppose it and we shall continue to do so, so long as it retains its present Zionist structure and denies to the indigenous Palestinians the rights it confers automatically on Jewish immigrants from anywhere else in the world. Let there be no doubt about this. Whatever settlement may emerge from Geneva or elsewhere will continue to be criticised and condemned by Palestinians so long as it envisages the continued existence of a racialist state in Israel open to Jews from all over the world but closed to its original Arab inhabitants.

Now, before anyone runs away with the idea that what I am saying is confirmation of Israeli and Zionist allegations about the hopeless intransigence of the Palestinians and their determination to wreck the present hopes of peace in the Middle East, I would like to observe that it is by no means unheard-of for a government or a country or a people to have to live with a state of affairs of which it does not approve, while continuing to declare its opposition to that state of affairs and its determination to do what it can to change it. The world cannot expect us to approve the maintenance of the present Zionist state of Israel. But we recognize that we may have to live with it for the time being until "insha'allah", a better basis for coexistence emerges between our people and the Jewish people now settled in our land.

If it is right for Western democracies to look forward to a day when white supremacy in South Africa and Rhodesia will be replaced by a form of democratic rule under which white, black and coloured people belonging to those countries will live together in peace and as equals, it is just as legitimate for us Palestinians to look forward to a day when Zionist supremacy in Israel will be replaced by a democratic system in which Jews, Moslems and Christians belonging to this land will live together in peace and equality. If we continue to proclaim this as our aim we are *not* sabotaging peace (as the Israeli Government would have everyone believe) anymore than the British Government and indeed the United Nations are sabotaging peace when they call for an end to white racialist rule in Rhodesia.

Israeli and Zionist propaganda habitually and, I believe, deliberately, confuses principles and practice in this matter and tries to convince the world that, because all Palestinians condemn in principle the Zionist state of Israel (as they all undoubtedly do), therefore they are all committed to its destruction by violence and force. Palestinian leaders may speak, as Yasser Arafat did at New York, of "living together in a framework of just peace" and of not wishing "one drop of either Arab or Jewish blood to be shed". But whatever they say is ignored or brushed aside. For Israeli Zionist propagandists it is enough that we are opposed to political Zionism and its manifestation in Israel; that must mean that we are hell bent on its overthrow by violence and conflict and know no other way of achieving our end. But of course the one proposition does not necessarily follow from the other—though the *non sequitur* may not be obvious to Israelis, who have more reason than most to fear the truth of the adage that "those who live by the sword shall die by the sword."

To turn now from principle to practice and method, I must first deal with the vexed question of Palestinian "terrorism", as it is usually called in the Western news media, or, as I would prefer to call it, "counter-terrorism" since it is in fact the product of and response to the state terrorism which Israel has pursued towards the Palestinians since the Zionist state was first established by violence and terror in 1948.

I am myself a man of peace and I deplore violence in political affairs, particularly when it involves innocent people who are not a party to the conflict. But by the normal and accepted standards of patriotic duty I do not believe that anyone can justly condemn Palestinians for taking up arms against Israeli oppression. One may disagree with their choice of targets and may reject the violence of some of their actions. But in principle they have every bit as much justification for resorting to armed struggle against the oppressors of their people and the occupiers of their country as had the Maquis in France during World War II. Indeed, Israel's prolonged cruelty towards the Palestinians and violation of their rights, coupled with the international community's lamentable failure over so many years to put right the wrongs done to the Palestinians, afford a special justification for the Palestinians to resort to armed struggle. What else were they to do?

As a practical matter, it is often said by Western observers that the Palestinian militants are harming their own cause by their acts of violence, and there is obviously some truth in this in so far as these acts may turn world opinion against them and lose the Palestinians sympathy among their fellow-men. But against this two questions may be put. First, is there any evidence to show that the Palestinians have anything positive to gain from the sympathy of a world which showed itself so indifferent to their plight during the years before they took up arms on any significant scale? What practical value has sympathy, in the face of Israeli intransigence and Zionist manipulation of the news media? And second, is there not ample evidence that it was only when the Palestinians resorted to armed struggle that the rest of the world began taking them seriously? Seven years ago, when the Security Council adopted its famous Resolution 242, the only mention it made of the Palestinians and their rights was a reference to the need to achieve "a just settlement of the refugee problem". Can anyone doubt that, if the Resolution were being adopted today, it would make much more specific reference to the Palestinians not as refugees but as people possessing their won national rights?

However, having now won a hearing from world opinion (primarily, I believe, as a result of militant action), the practical question for our Palestinian leadership in the context of possible peace negotiations is whether a continuation of the armed struggle against Israel is the most *effective* method to be pursued. In particular, if we assume that a probable outcome of any peace settlement is likely to be the establishment of some kind of Palestinian state on territory recovered from Israel, it seems to me that a very necessary and useful subject for discussion is whether we may then hope to pursue our unaltered, ultimate aim of a "state in partnership" covering the whole area of Israel/Palestine by non-violent and evolutionary means rather than by a continuation of armed struggle.

At the outset, let me admit at once that, even if such a strategy were adopted, it might well not be possible to rule out entirely continued sporadic acts of violence by individuals driven to desperation by continued injustice on the part of Israel under Zionist leadership. I am afraid that this is the penalty which Israel and the Israelis must be prepared to put up with for having taken another people's birthright and having imposed their state on another people's ancestral land. But the possibility, even the likelihood, of occasional acts of violence by individuals ought not, I suggest, to discourage us from trying to follow a non-violent, evolutionary Palestinian approach to a tolerable form of co-existence between Israeli Jews and Palestinian Arabs, following on the establishment of a limited or partial peace settlement.

Basically, the question for the Palestinians is whether they can afford to pursue a wait-and-see policy in the expectation that sooner or later, the Zionist structure of Israel is bound to disintegrate and give way to some more permanent and more acceptable form of co-existence. This is a speculative field of discussion and no one can be dogmatic about how the future may develop. But let me outline a possible projection of the future if a Palestinian state were established on a part of the Palestinian homeland and if the Palestinian leadership then decided to pursue an evolutionary strategy towards its ultimate goal of a "state in partnership".

Our *first* task would then be to secure a massive injection of external aid for the economic and social development of the Palestinian State with a view to putting it, in time, on an equal footing with Israel in terms of industrial, technological and educational progress. I have no doubt that ample funds for an intensive programme of development would be readily forthcoming from the Arab World and also, I would hope, from the international community at large.

An essential aspect of this programme of development would be the creation of employment opportunities within the Palestine State with a view to maximizing its capacity to support population. For our second task would be to promote the progressive "ingathering" of the Palestinian exiles now living in diaspora and their rehabilitation on their own soil.

Thirdly, we could aim to open and maintain a continuous and developing dialogue with any elements within Israel who were prepared to meet and talk with Palestinians regarding the form of a mutually acceptable co-existence which might in time be developed between two peoples living in the country to which they both lay claim. We have our own ideas on this subject of course, but we would approach the dialogue with open minds, ready to listen to what Israelis have to suggest as well as to put forward our own suggestions.

To promote confidence and a frank and realistic exchange of ideas consideration could be given to the maintenance of open frontiers between Israel and the Palestinian State and to permitting, even encouraging, a mutual interpenetration of commerce, industry and cultural activities. Within reasonable limits and having regard to the need to provide for the ingathering of the exiled Palestinians, one need not even exclude the idea of allowing Israeli Jews to live in the Palestinian state (not, of course, in paramilitary settlements, like the existing *nahals*, but as peaceful private individuals prepared to live in harmony with their neighbours) provided they accepted Palestinian citizenship and provided a corresponding concession were made to enable Palestinians to go and live in Israel. In the Middle East of today, these ideas may sound like a dream. But this is the Palestine of tomorrow which the Palestinians dream of, as Yasser Arafat said at the UN.

All of this will take time and must depend on the maintenance of effective security for the infant Palestinian State. This is a real problem. We have heard so much in the past of Israel's need for security, but to us Palestinians and to other Arabs living in the countries adjacent to Israel this seems like putting the boot on the wrong foot. We believe, on the basis of our experience over the past twenty-seven years, that we are more in need of protection against Israel than Israel is of protection against the Arabs. I know that Western opinion has difficulty in believing this, but the truth is—and this is attested to by international peace-keepers like General E.L.M. Burns and General Carl von Horn, as well as by Israelis themselves—that it has suited the book of Israel's leaders in the past to have conditions of instability prevailing on her borders so that these could be exploited from time to time to provide pretexts for renewed war and renewed opportunities of expansion. If a limited settlement is to survive and gain time for the two peoples to learn to live together at peace and in mutual tolerance, the first necessity is to provide the most cast-iron safeguards possible against a Ben Gurion or a Moshe Dayan or an Arik Sharon contriving in future to manufacture a new crisis and a new conflict to upset the settlement if peace seems to be working to the disadvantage of Zionism in Israel. That will be the real risk once a settlement is reached. For our part, we Palestinians would be prepared to accept and indeed press for the most stringent and effective international safeguards *provided* they were directed not less at Israel than at the new Palestinian state and Israel's other Arab neighbours.

It will not be easy—indeed I would say it is virtually impossible—for Zionist Israel, penned back within the 1967 borders and shorn of its dynamic expansionism, to live in peace with its neighbours and still to survive. Once those conditions have been established, either Israel will have to burst out of them and resume its aggressive role or it will have to change internally and shed its Zionist character. I hope the latter will take place and that is why I have placed such stress on the needs for safeguards against renewed aggression and expansionism by Israel.

Consider what is likely to happen within Israel if a settlement emerges in Geneva which includes the establishment of a Palestinian state and which can be stabilised by the introduction of really effective safeguards against future breaches of the peace.

Up to now, the momentum of Zionism has been maintained by the fear of insecurity, by antisemitism (real or alleged), by threats of genocide and extermination and so on. Once stability and peace are ensured the momentum will be lost and the whole idea of political Zionism will lose much of its appeal both for Jews living in Israel and for their supporters outside. In these circumstances there is bound to be a falling-off in the massive flow of external aid into Israel. Even with this aid, Israel has not found it easy to survive and has had constantly to importune its patient supporters for more. Without it, Israel is certainly not viable and would be quite unable to support the highly artificial level of economic activity which it has had in the past. As before the 1967 war, unemployment and severe balance-of-payments problems are likely to coincide. The level of taxation, already extremely burdensome, will have to be raised even higher. Again as before 1967, it is likely that the rate of emigration will sharply increase and more than offset any new immigration. (The Israeli authorities publish no figures for emigration from Israel, but reliable sources indicate that it is already almost as large as today's much reduced level of immigration). Meanwhile, as a necessary part of the settlement, Israel will have had to withdraw from her 1967 conquests and to accept back at least a substantial number of the Palestinian inhabitants uprooted in 1947 and 1948. This will mark the end of an era for the Israelis, the end of a heady, intoxicating adventure in which their leaders have taught them to expect continuous success.

Already a growing number of Israelis are alive to the need for a new and more constructive attitude towards the Palestinians; they are aware that, without it, the sands are beginning to run out for them. As a result a new wind is blowing within Israel, a wind of truth and disillusionment. The conjunction of all these factors will drive all sensible, thoughtful people within Israel to re-appraise their country's future and its capacity to survive as an exclusive Zionist enclave—or "ghetto"—in the Arab World.

Meanwhile also, the Palestinians will be sitting on the borders of Israel in our own Palestinian state with its embassies in Washington and London, Paris and Moscow, and its representatives seated (as they should have been long ago) in the United Nations. With the rising power of the Arab World behind us, we shall be watching and waiting, developing our human and material resources, gathering strength and drawing in our dispersed people with all their rich talents of industry, intellect and adaptability. And we shall be offering to anyone who cares to listen in Israel the chance to sit down and talk with us like sensible human beings about our future, on the basis not of conflict but of peaceful and mutually advantageous co-existence. We hope that it will be possible before long to work out a form of co-existence which will enable the two peoples to live together within a reunited Palestine, while maintaining through cantonal arrangements and a constitutional division of legislative and administrative powers the distinctive character of each.

Not in our lifetime? Perhaps—though once the process of change begins within Israel it may proceed faster than anyone thinks. But in any case we Palestinians can afford to wait. We have learned to be patient through many painful years. Time, as well as justice, is on our side. And perhaps power also, in the fullness of time. One day men will be reading in their history books about the episode of Zionist Israel and looking back on it, will see that it was, after all, only a passing aberration in the course of history in the Middle East.

Appendix VIII:
King Hussein's Federation Proposal

An address by King Hussein to Jordanian and Palestinian dignitaries on March 15, 1972, concerning the basic principles of a plan to establish a United Arab kingdom of Palestine and Jordan. Reproduced here as it appears in The Arab-Israeli Conflict, *edited by John Norton Moore (Princeton, New Jersey: Princeton University Press [for the American Society of International Law], 1974).*

My dear brethren,
Dear Citizens,

It gives me great pleasure to meet with you today and to talk to you and to the nation about the affairs of the present, the past, its experiences and our aspirations and hopes for the future.

The establishment of the state of Jordan in 1921 was the most important step taken in the life of the Arab Revolution after the plot against it by its allies in the first World War was discovered. With the issue of the Balfour Declaration in 1917, the formation of the State of Jordan gained a new dimension, in that it made it possible to exclude the land east of the Jordan River from the application of the Declaration and thus save it from the Zionist schemes of that period.

In 1948 when the Arab armies entered into Palestine, the smallest among them was the "Jordan army"; yet it was able to save that part of Palestine which extends from Jenin in the north to Hebron in the south and from the Jordan River in the east to a point lying not more than 15 kilometers from the sea-shore in the west. The Jordan army was also able to save Jerusalem—the Holy Old City—in its entirety and other areas outside the city wall to the north, south and east, all of which came to be known later as Arab Jerusalem. That area which came to be known as the "West Bank" was all that remained to the Arabs from the whole of Palestine together with the narrow area now called the "Gaza strip."

After a brief period of temporary administration, the leaders of the West Bank, and a selected group of leaders and notables, representing the Arabs of Palestine who had left their homes in the occupied territories, found the union with the East Bank was a national demand and a guarantee in the face of the constantly expanding Israeli dangers. They therefore, called for two historic conferences, the first of which convened in Jericho on 1.12.1948 and the second in Nablus on 28.12.1948. Representatives of all sections of the population including leaders and men of thought, young and old, labourers and farmers, all, attended the two conferences. Resolutions were adopted requesting His Majesty King Abdallah ibn Al-Hussein to take immediate steps to unite the two Banks into a single state under his leadership. His Majesty responded to the appeal of the nation and ordered that constitutional and practical steps be taken to realize this important national desire, which steps included that elections be held to choose legal representatives of the people of the West Bank to sit in Parliament. On April 24, 1950 the new parliament representing both Banks with its senators and deputies, held a historic session in which the first real step in contemporary Arab history was taken on the road to unity, which the Arab Revolt proclaimed on the dawn of its inception. This was achieved by the declaration of the union of the two Banks and by their fusion into one dependent Arab state with a democratic parliamentary monarchy to be known as the Hashemite Kingdom of Jordan.

The union sailed in seas which were neither calm nor smooth. There were many underhanded currents stirred up by external hands attempting to create tempests in the face of the ship to force it slowly towards the rocks. But the awareness of the people in both Banks, their firm belief in the unity of their land and their recognition of the dangers lurking behind the frontiers, were the basic guarantee for the safety of the union and for its salvation from all the evils that beset it.

Foremost among the realities which the union of both Banks evolved day after day was that those living therein are one people, not two peoples. This reality became first clear when the Ansars (the supporters)—the inhabitants of the East Bank—welcomed their brethren, the Muhajereen (the Emmigrants)—the refugees from the territories of Palestine in 1948—and shared with them the loaf of bread, the roof and both sweetness and bitterness of life. This fact of life was emphasized and deepened by every step the government took and was clearly reflected in everyone of its institutions: In the armed forces, in the ministries and the various government departments, this reality became clear, also in all sectors of life: be it economic, agricultural or social .... The day came when it was impossible for anybody to distinguish between one from the West and one from the East, unlike the way a Palestinian is distinguished from a non-Palestinian in other parts of the Arab World.

The unity of blood and destiny between the people of both Banks reached its summit in 1967 when the sons of both Banks stood on the soil of the West Bank as they did for over twenty years, kneading its sacred soil with their common blood. But the struggle was stronger than their power and circumstances were bigger than their courage. And the catastrophe occurred.

In the midst of this sea of suffering created by the June calamity the aims of the Jordan government in that period which followed the war, were summed up in two aims: the brave stand in the face of continuous and unceasing aggression aginst the East Bank, and the strong determination to liberate the occupied land and free our kin and brethren in the West Bank. All our efforts were directed to achieve both these goals in an atmosphere of confidence that the Arab States would support Jordan in its calamity, and with unlimited trust that the unity of Arab destiny had become a deeply rooted reality in the conscience of the whole Arab nation, a reality which cannot be shaken by regional interest however great and which cannot be reached by plans and intentions however underhanded.

And suddenly, Jordan found itself facing a new catastrophe, which if allowed to befall the country, would have resulted in the loss of the East Bank, and would have laid the stage for a final liquidation of the Palestinian case and forever. The forces setting this calamity had mobilized many elements to serve their purpose. Many other elements also fell into the nets of these forces. Many of these elements claimed the Palestinian identity of the sacred cause and thus played their roles under the guise of that name. The contradictions and conflicting currents prevailing in the world found their way into the ranks of these elements.

It was only natural that Jordan should rise up to confront the impending tragedy. The challenge was met by the stand of the unique combination of its people: the Muhajereen and the Ansars. This evil subversion was shattered on the rock of the firm national unity, as it was disintegrated by the awareness of the new man, born in 1950 who grew and flourished in the challenges which he had to face during the past twenty years.

During all that period, and specially after the June war in 1967 or even before it, the leadership of Jordan was thinking about the future of the state and was planning for it. The leadership based its thinking on its faith in the message of Jordan, which message found its roots in the great Arab Revolution and its confidence in the man living on both sides of the river and his ability to play his role in serving its message and its aims.

The manner in which the fulfillment of the Palestinian cause was viewed, carried in its folds, the far reaching scope of the Arab-Israeli conflict. Palestine had always been the first goal of Zionist plans. The people of Palestine were its first victims, and were to be followed by the people of both Banks. Even if Zionist expansionism was to end at some limit, Zionist interest would only rest by keeping the Arab world weak and disunited in order to be able to safeguard its territorial gains forever. Because the opposite camp stands as one united force, it thus becomes incumbent on all Arabs to stand united also. Even more, unity in itself is not sufficient unless it comprises a real understanding encompassing all modern methods and aspects of modern development.

Jordan has always understood the magnitude of the tragedy that befell the Palestinians. After the Zionist plot had dispersed them, in 1948 no country, Arab or non-Arab, offered the Palestinians what Jordan gave them in the way of honourable life and decent living. In Jordan, and under the auspices of the union of both Banks, the genuine Palestinian community was found among the overwhelming majority of the people who live in both Banks, and in it the Palestinian found the appropriate framework in which to live and move as well as the real starting point for the will of liberation and all its hopes.

The Palestinians had existed hundreds of years before 1948 and continue to exist since 1948. But the events which started to prevail throughout the Arab World and all the forces and currents which manipulate them started to overlook these facts and to ignore them in conformity with the state of indecision which our nation is undergoing since years. This artificial status was given further impetus by the various conferences, plots and attacks, we have been seeing and hearing of. It was as if the Palestinian was intended to dissociate himself from his national identity and to place himself in a small separate flask which could easily be destroyed at any moment. Surely, this appeared to be another plot being hatched in the long chain of plots against the people of Palestine and the whole of the Arab nation.

These suspicious movements were not directed only to the minority of the Palestinians living outside both Banks, but were also aimed at the majority here in the hope of forcing the people of the West Bank into a state which would separate them from all that surrounds them. If some of the powers that encourages these currents do not conceal their desire to abandon their responsibilities toward the Palestine cause and the Palestinian people, by pushing them into separation, yet its brilliance however attractive it may seem to them, should not conceal from us the danger of their reaching a situation which would make them an easy prey to Israel's unlimited greed. These suspicious movements try to make the Jordan rule appear as attempting to seek gains and benefits. They try to find their way into our unity in an attempt to weaken it and create doubts about it. Attempts are also being made to exploit some people's desire to obtain material gains to the extent of pushing them to play their roles to attain their ultimate vicious end.

The Israeli occupation of the West Bank and other Arab territories dear to us has managed to continue due to the disintegration of the Arab front, the lack of coordination, the struggle to establish opposing axes and camps, the abandonment of the essence of the Palestine cause and its needs, the concentration on talking in the name of the Palestine cause in place of consorted action, as well as the attempt by certain groups to attain power through internal strife. All this also led to deepen the suffering of the Palestine people and to push them into a state of utter confusion and loss. The talk about municipal elections in the West Bank is merely an example of such a tragedy which certain quarters are trying to exploit to their own interests.

And yet, Jordan has never ceased to call for a united front needing mobilization and coordination of efforts. Jordan has never hesitated to stretch its hand with all sincerity to all its Arab brethren in its belief in the unity of our cause and our destiny and future. Jordan did not spare any effort towards liberation, although the above realities in the Arab world retarded it. Yet the serious planning for the future of the state went on, as well the events and positions taken against this country have failed to weaken our belief in the imperativeness of our final victory in liberating the land and the people. This belief is based not only in our faith in the justice of our cause, but is also based on our faith in our country and people on both Banks of the river and in our nation as a whole.

Thus, it was decided to move with the state into a new stage based in its essence on liberation, its concept reflecting the aspiration of our people and embodying their belief in the unity of our nation and their sense of belonging to it. In addition to all that it is based on the absolute determination to regain the legitimate rights of the Palestinian people, and is directed to place them in a position which will enable them to regain and safeguard these rights.

This was the pledge we made to give our people the right of self-determination. It is our answer to all those who chose to doubt that pledge and void it from its essence. Today that pledge will find its way to every citizen in this country and to every individual in this nation and in the world. It is now expanding to exceed the limits of words in order to face every possibility of disunity and to embody all national aims and goals.

We wish to declare that planning for the new phase has come as a result of continuous meetings, discussions and consultations which were held with the representatives and leaders of both Banks. There was unanimous consensus that the main shape of the new phase should include the best and most developed concept of a modern democratic state. In addition to that, it will help to create a new society built by a new man to become the driving force which will put us on the way to victory, progress, unity, freedom and a better life.

We are pleased to announce that the basic principles of the proposed plan are:
1. The Hashemite Kingdom of Jordan shall become a United Arab Kingdom, and shall be thus named.
2. The United Arab Kingdom shall consist of two regions:
   A. The Region of Palestine, and shall consist of the West Bank and any other Palestinian territories to be liberated and where the population opts to join it.
   B. The Region of Jordan, and shall consist of the East Bank.
3. Amman shall be the central capital of the Kingdom and at the same time shall be the capital of the Region of Jordan.
4. Jerusalem shall become the capital of the Region of Palestine.
5. The King shall be the Head of the State and shall assume the central executive authority assisted by a Central Council of Ministers. The central legislative authority shall be vested in the King and in the National Assembly whose members shall be elected by direct and secret ballot. It shall have an equal number of members from each of the two regions.
6. The Central Judicial Authority shall be vested in a "Supreme Central Court."
7. The Kingdom shall have a single Armed Forces and its Supreme Commander shall be the King.
8. The responsibilities of the Central Executive Power shall be confined to matters relating to the Kingdom as a sovereign international entity insuring the safety of the union, its stability and development.
9. The Executive Power in each region shall be vested in a Governor General from the Region and in a Regional Council of Ministers also from the Region.
10. The Legislative Power in each Region shall be vested in "People's Council"

which shall be elected by direct secret ballot. This Council shall elect the Governor General.

11. The Legislative Power in each Region shall be vested in the courts of the region and nobody shall have any authority over it.

12. The Executive Power in each Region shall be responsible for all its matters with the exception of such matters as the constitution requires to be the responsibility of the Central Executive Power.

It is obvious that the implementation of this proposed plan will require the necessary constitutional steps and Parliament shall be asked to draw up the new constitution of the country.

This new phase to which we look will guarantee the rearrangement of the "Jordan-Palestinian home" in a manner that will insure for it additional innate strength and thus the ability to achieve our hopes and aspirations. This plan will strengthen the joint fabric of both Banks and will satisfy the requirements of their unity and brotherhood and shall lead to deepen the sense of responsibility in the individual in both regions of the Kingdom, to best serve our cause without prejudicing any of the acquired rights of any citizen of Palestinian origin in the Region of Jordan or any citizen of Jordanian origin in the Region of Palestine. For this plan collects but does not disperse; it strengthens but does not weaken; and it unifies but does not disintergrate. It does not allow any changes in the gains that our citizens have acquired as a result of twenty years of union. Any attempt to cast doubt on all this will be tantamount to treason against the unity of the Kingdom and against the cause, the nation and the homeland. The citizen in our country has passed such experience and has achieved a level of awareness and ability which qualify him to cope with coming responsibilities with greater confidence and determination.

If ability is a bliss which should grow to become man's responsibility toward himself and toward others, if his awareness is a weapon to be used for his own good and that of others, then the time has come for our man to stand face to face with his responsibilities, to discharge them with honesty and practice them with courage and honour.

Thus, the above formula becomes a title for a new page, brilliant and firmly believing in the history of this country. Every citizen has his role and his duties. As to the armed forces, which have marched right from the beginning under the banner of the great Arab Revolution, that included and will forever include among its ranks the best elements from among the sons of both Banks, these armed forces will remain ready to receive more of our sons from both Banks, based on the highest level of efficiency, ability and organization, it shall always be open to welcome any one who wishes to serve our nation and our cause with absolute loyalty to the eternal goals of our nation.

This Arab country is the home of the cause, just as it is from the Arabs and for the Arabs. Its record of sacrifice for our nation and our cause is full and well known. Its pages were inscribed by the blood of its gallant armed forces and its free people. The more the positions taken against it, change into more positive brotherly assistance and support, the easier it will be for it to continue its glorious march of sacrifices, with more ability and hope, until it regains for our nation its rights and attains victory.

This Arab Country is the country of all, Jordanians and Palestinians alike.

When we say Palestinian we mean every Palestinian be he in the East or West of this great world on condition that he should be loyal to Palestine and should belong to Palestine. Our call is for every citizen in this country to rise and play his role and shoulder his responsibilities in this new phase, it is also addressed to every Palestinian outside Jordan to answer the call of duty, far from appearances and free from ailments and diversion and to proceed and join his kin and brethren along a single path based on this message, united in one front, clear in the aims, so that all should cooperate to reach the goals of liberation and to build up the structure to which we all aspire.

"GOD WILL AID THOSE WHO AID HIS CAUSE."

Appendix IX: The Rogers Plan

"A Lasting Peace in the Middle East: An American View," an address by Secretary of State William P. Rogers on December 9, 1969. Reproduced here as it appears in The Arab-Israeli Conflict, *edited by John Norton Moore (Princeton, New Jersey: Princeton University Press [for the American Society of International Law], 1974.*

I am very happy to be with you this evening and be a part of this impressive conference. The Galaxy Conference represents one of the largest and most significant efforts in the Nation's history to further the goals of all phases of adult and continuing education.

The State Department, as you know, has an active interest in this subject. It is our belief that foreign policy issues should be more broadly understood and considered. As you know, we are making a good many efforts toward providing continuing education in the foreign affairs field. I am happy tonight to join so many staunch allies in those endeavors.

In the hope that I may further that cause I want to talk to you tonight about a foreign policy matter which is of great concern to our nation.

U.S. POLICY IN THE MIDDLE EAST

I am going to speak tonight about the situation in the Middle East. I want to refer to the policy of the United States as it relates to that situation in the hope that there may be a better understanding of that policy and the reasons for it.

Following the third Arab-Israeli war in 20 years, there was an upsurge of hope that a lasting peace could be achieved. That hope has unfortunately not been realized. There is no area of the world today that is more important, because it could easily again be the source of another serious conflagration.

When this administration took office, one of our first actions in foreign affairs was to examine carefully the entire situation in the Middle East. It was obvious that a continuation of the unresolved conflict there would be extremely dangerous, that the parties to the conflict alone would not be able to overcome their legacy of suspicion to achieve a political settlement, and that international efforts to help needed support.

The United States decided it had a responsibility to play a direct role in seeking a solution.

Thus, we accepted a suggestion put forward both by the French Government and the Secretary General of the United Nations. We agreed that the major powers—the United States, the Soviet Union, the United Kingdom, and France—should cooperate to assist the Secretary General's representative, Ambassador Jarring, in working out a settlement in accordance with the resolution of the Security Council of the United Nations of November 1967. We also decided to consult directly with the Soviet Union, hoping to achieve as wide an area of agreement as possible between us.

These decisions were made in full recognition of the following important factors:

First, we knew that nations not directly involved could not make a durable peace for the peoples and governments involved. Peace rests with the parties to the conflict. The efforts of major powers can help, they can provide a catalyst, they can stimulate the parties to talk, they can encourage, they can help define a realistic framework for agreement; but an agreement among other powers cannot be a substitute for agreement among the parties themselves.

Second, we knew that a durable peace must meet the legitimate concerns of both sides.

Third, we were clear that the only framework for a negotiated settlement was one in accordance with the entire text of the U.N. Security Council resolution. That resolution was agreed upon after long and arduous negotiations; it is carefully balanced; it provides the basis for a just and lasting peace—a final settlement—not merely an interlude between wars.

Fourth, we believe that a protracted period of no war, no peace, recurrent violence, and spreading chaos would serve the interests of no nation, in or out of the Middle East.

U.S.-SOVIET DISCUSSIONS

For 8 months we have pursued these consultations in four-power talks at the United Nations and in bilateral discussions with the Soviet Union.

In our talks with the Soviets we have proceeded in the belief that the stakes are so high that we have a responsibility to determine whether we can achieve parallel views which would encourage the parties to work out a stable and equitable solution. We are under no illusions; we are fully conscious of past difficulties and present realities. Our talks with the Soviets have brought a measure of understanding, but very substantial differences remain. We regret that the Soviets have delayed in responding to new formulations submitted to them on October 28. However, we will continue to discuss these problems with the Soviet Union as long as there is any realistic hope that such discussions might further the cause of peace.

The substance of the talks that we have had with the Soviet Union has been conveyed to the interested parties through diplomatic channels. This process has served to highlight the main roadblocks to the initiation of useful negotiations among the parties.

On the one hand, the Arab leaders fear that Israel is not in fact prepared to withdraw from Arab territory occupied in the 1967 war.

On the other hand, Israeli leaders fear that the Arab states are not in fact prepared to live in peace with Israel.

Each side can cite from its viewpoint considerable evidence to support its fears. Each side has permitted its attention to be focused solidly and to some extent solely on these fears.

What can the United States do to help overcome these roadblocks?

Our policy is and will continue to be a *balanced* one.

We have friendly ties with both Arabs and Israelis. To call for Israeli withdrawal as envisaged in the U.N. resolution without achieving agreement on peace would be partisan toward the Arabs. To call on the Arabs to accept peace without Israeli withdrawal would be partisan toward Israel. Therefore, our policy is to encourage the Arabs to accept a permanent peace based on a binding agreement and to urge the Israelis to withdraw from occupied territory when their territorial integrity is assured as envisaged by the Security Council resolution.

BASIC ELEMENTS OF U.N. RESOLUTION

In an effort to broaden the scope of discussion we have recently resumed four-power negotiations at the United Nations.

Let me outline our policy on various elements of the Security Council Resolution. The basic and related issues might be described as peace, security, withdrawal, and territory.

Peace Between the Parties

The resolution of the Security Council makes clear that the goal is the establishment of a state of peace between the parties instead of the state of belligerency which has characterized relations for over 20 years. We believe the conditions and obligations of peace must be defined in specific terms. For example, navigation rights in the Suez Canal and in the Strait of Tiran should be spelled out. Respect for sovereignty and obligations of the parties to each other must be made specific.

But peace, of course, involves much more than this. It is also a matter of the attitudes and intentions of the parties. Are they ready to coexist with one another? Can a live-and-let-live attitude replace suspicion, mistrust, and hate? A peace agreement between the parties must be based on clear and stated intentions and a willingness to bring about basic changes in the attitudes and conditions which are characteristic of the Middle East today.

Security

A lasting peace must be sustained by a sense of security on both sides. To this end, as envisaged in the Security Council resolution, there should be demilitarized zones and related security arrangements more reliable than those which existed in the area in the past. The parties themselves, with Ambassador Jarring's help, are in the best position to work out the nature and the details of such security arrangements. It is, after all, their interests which are at stake and their territory which is involved. They must live with the results.

Withdrawal and Territory

The Security Council resolution endorses the principle of the nonacquisition of territory by war and calls for withdrawal of Israeli armed forces from territories occupied in the 1967 war. We support this part of the resolution, including withdrawal, just as we do its other elements.

The boundaries from which the 1967 war began were established in the 1949 armistice agreements and have defined the areas of national jurisdiction in the Middle East for 20 years. Those boundaries were armistice lines, not final political borders. The rights, claims, and positions of the parties in an ultimate peaceful settlement were reserved by the armistice agreements.

The Security Council resolution neither endorses nor precludes these armistice lines as the definitive political boundaries. However, it calls for withdrawal from occupied territories, the nonacquisition of territory by war, and the establishment of secure and recognized boundaries.

We believe that while recognized boundaries must be established and agreed upon by the parties, any changes in the preexisting lines should not reflect the weight of conquest and should be confined to insubstantial alterations required for mutual security. We do not support expansionism. We believe troops must be withdrawn as the resolution provides. We support Israel's security and the security of the Arab states as well. We are for a lasting peace that requires security for both.

ISSUES OF REFUGEES AND JERUSALEM

By emphasizing the key issues of peace, security, withdrawal, and territory, I do not want to leave the impression that other issues are not equally important. Two in particular deserve special mention: the questions of refugees and of Jerusalem.

There can be no lasting peace without a just settlement of the problem of those Palestinians whom the wars of 1948 and 1967 have made homeless. This human dimension of the Arab-Israeli conflict has been of special concern to the United States for over 20 years. During this period the United States has contributed about $500 million for the support and education of the Palestine refugees. We are prepared to contribute generously along with others to solve this problem. We believe its just settlement must take into account the desires and aspirations of the refugees and the legitimate concerns of the governments in the area.

The problem posed by the refugees will become increasingly serious if their future is not resolved. There is a new consciousness among the young Palestinians who have grown up since 1948 which needs to be channeled away from bitterness and frustration toward hope and justice.

The question of the future status of Jerusalem, because it touches deep emotional, historical, and religious wellsprings, is particulary complicated. We have made clear repeatedly in the past two and a half years that we cannot accept unilateral actions by any party to decide the final status of the city. We believe its status can be determined only through the agreement of the parties concerned, which in practical terms means primarily the Governments of Israel and Jordan, taking into account the interests of other countries in the area and the international community. We do, however, support certain principles which we believe would provide an equitable framework for a Jerusalem settlement.

Specifically, we believe Jerusalem should be a unified city within which there would no longer be restrictions on the movement of persons and goods. There should be open access to the unified city for persons of all faiths and nationalities. Arrangements for the administration of the unified city should take into account the interests of all its inhabitants and of the Jewish, Islamic, and Christian communities. And there should be roles for both Israel and Jordan in the civic, economic, and religious life of the city.

It is our hope that agreement on the key issues of peace, security, withdrawal, and territory will create a climate in which these questions of refugees and of Jerusalem, as well as other aspects of the conflict, can be resolved as part of the overall settlement.

FORMULAS FOR U.A.R.-ISRAEL ASPECT OF SETTLEMENT

During the first weeks of the current United Nations General Assembly the efforts to move matters toward a settlement entered a particularly intensive phase. Those efforts continue today.

I have already referred to our talks with the Soviet Union. In connection with those talks there have been allegations that we have been seeking to divide the Arab states by urging the U.A.R. to make a separate peace. These allegations are false. It is a fact that we and the Soviets have been concentrating on the questions of a settlement between Israel and the United Arab Republic. We have been doing this in the full understanding on both our parts that, before there can be a settlement of the Arab-Israeli conflict, there must be agreement between the parties on other aspects of the settlement—not only those related to the United Arab Republic but also those related to Jordan and other states which accept the Security Council resolution of November 1967.

We started with the Israeli-United Arab Republic aspect because of its inherent importance for future stability in the area and because one must start somewhere.

We are also ready to pursue the Jordanian aspect of a settlement; in fact the four powers in New York have begun such discussions. Let me make it perfectly clear that the U.S. position is that implementation of the overall settlement would begin only after complete agreement had been reached on related aspects of the problem.

In our recent meetings with the Soviets we have discussed some new formulas in an attempt to find common positions. They consist of three principal elements:

First, there should be a binding commitment by Israel and the United Arab Republic to peace with each other, with all the specific obligations of peace spelled out, including the obligation to prevent hostile acts orginating from their respective territories.

Second, the detailed provisions of peace relating to security safeguards on the ground should be worked out between the parties, under Ambassador Jarring's auspices, utilizing the procedures followed in negotiating the armistice agreements under Ralph Bunche in 1949 at Rhodes. This formula has been previously used with success in negotiations between the parties on Middle Eastern problems. A principal objective of the four-power talks, we believe, should be to help Ambassador Jarring engage the parties in a negotiating process under the Rhodes formula.

So far as a settlement between Israel and the United Arab Republic goes, these safeguards relate primarily to the area of Sharm al-Shaykh controlling access to the Gulf of Aqaba, the need for demilitarized zones as foreseen in the Security Council resolution, and final arrangements in the Gaza Strip.

Third, in the context of peace and agreement on specific security safeguards, withdrawal of Israeli forces from Egyptian territory would be required.

Such an approach directly addresses the principal national concerns of both Israel and the U.A.R. It would require the U.A.R. to agree to a binding and specific commitment to peace. It would require withdrawal of Israeli armed forces from U.A.R. territory to the international border between Israel [or Mandated Palestine] and Egypt which has been in existence for over a half century. It would also require the parties themselves to negotiate the practical security arrangements to safeguard the peace.

We believe that this approach is *balanced* and fair.

U.S. INTERESTS IN THE AREA

We remain interested in good relations with all states in the area. Whenever and wherever Arab states which have broken off diplomatic relations with the United States are prepared to restore them, we shall respond in the same spirit.

Meanwhile, we will not be deterred from continuing to pursue the paths of patient diplomacy in our search for peace in the Middle East. We will not shrink from advocating necessary compromises, even though they may and probably will be unpalatable to both sides. We remain prepared to work with others—in the area and throughout the world—so long as they sincerely seek the end we seek; a just and lasting peace.

Appendix X:
Biographies of the Participants

Each of the participants was asked to write his own biography. These biographies appear below as written.

JOSEPH BEN SHLOMO was born in Poland in 1930 and emigrated to Palestine with his parents in 1933. He remembers his childhood and adolescence as a life shadowed by perpetual anxiety—from 1936 to 1939, the attacks and massacres of the Jewish population in Palestine by the Arabs; and from 1939 to 1945, fears as the Germans approached the borders of Palestine. His father's large family and part of his mother's had been exterminated in the Holocaust. In his high school years, he was a member of the youth group of the Haganah. All this, and above all the non-stop continuity of wars with the Arabs from 1947 to 1973, formed the basic experience of a Jew and Israeli: a deeply rooted conviction that if the Jews are not strong enough, Israel will become a second Auschwitz. Ben Shlomo has studied modern philosophy, philosophy of religion and Jewish mysticism at the Hebrew University and Oxford. He has written on these subjects and now teaches at the Hebrew University and the University of Tel Aviv. Until 1968 Ben Shlomo was ready for far-reaching concessions to the Arabs. Since then his conviction has grown that each and every Israeli concession will only strengthen Arab motivation to destroy Israel, a conviction coupled with the belief that the Christian world will not behave any differently than it did in the past.

SAUL FRIEDLANDER was born in Prague in 1932, and became a citizen of Israel in 1948. After studying political science and history in Paris, in America (Harvard), and Geneva, he received his Ph.D. in political science from the University of Geneva. Since 1964 he has taught history and international relations at the Graduate Institute of International Studies in Geneva. From 1963 to 1975 he was chairman of the Department of International Relations and head of the Institute of International Relations at the Hebrew University, Jerusalem. Friedlander now is professor of history at Tel Aviv University, as well as at the Institute in Geneva. He is the author of a number of books on national-socialism, the Jewish Holocaust during World War II, and the Arab-Israeli conflict, including *Pius the XII and the Third Reich, Kurt Gerstein, Prelude to Downfall: Hitler and the United States,* and with Mahmoud Hussein, *Arabs and Israelis: A Dialogue.* Friedlander's most recent book is *Histoire et Psychoanalyse.* On the issue of the Israeli-Arab conflict, Friedlander strongly favors a posture of great flexibility and readiness for compromise, including readiness on Israel's side to negotiate not only with the Arab states but with the Palestinians as well.

YEHOSHOFAT HARKABI was born in 1921 in Haifa. He studied philosophy, Arabic literature and history at the Hebrew University. He served in the Haganah and in the Jewish Brigade of the British Army during World War II. His graduate studies were continued after the war; he was one of twenty-five young men trained as the nucleus of the Foreign Service for the coming Jewish state. He returned to the Haganah service during the War of Independence, served in the Israeli Army, and was a member of the military mission that negotiated the armistice with Egypt. As secretary to the minister of foreign affairs, he later participated in Israel's secret direct negotiations with King Abdullah in Jordan. He became deputy chief of intelligence in 1950, spent a year in further study in Paris in 1954-1955, and next returned to Israel as chief of intelligence. He held this position during the Sinai campaign in 1956 and was promoted to major general. After ending his tenure in 1959, he studied at Harvard University. Following service as deputy director general of the prime minister's office, he worked between 1963-1968 for the Ministry of Defense and earned his Ph.D. from the Hebrew University. Since 1968 he has taught at the Hebrew University in the Department of International Relations and Middle Eastern Studies. During 1974-1975 he was on loan to the Ministry of Defense as assistant to the minister for strategic policy. His publications include, among others: *Nuclear War and Nuclear Peace, Arab Attitudes Toward Israel,* and *Palestinians and Israel.*

YEHUDA LITANI was born in Jerusalem in 1943. He completed a program of Oriental studies in high school, and he continued his Arabic language training during his military service. He served in the army until 1964, and he later studied the history of the Middle East at the Hebrew University in Jerusalem. In 1968 he began working in the Israeli television network, and he covered for the news department developments among the Israeli Arabs and in the territories of the West Bank and the Gaza Strip. His responsibility for these same subjects continued afterwards, when he worked for Israeli Radio Broadcasting. In 1971-1972, he served as the spokesman at the military headquarters for Judea and Samaria, and in this position he had an opportunity to observe the policies and activities of the military government in the Israeli-held territories. Since 1972 he has worked as the correspondent of the daily newspaper *Ha'aretz*, reporting on the West Bank, the Gaza Strip, and East Jerusalem.

MOSHE MA'OZ became interested in the Palestinian Arabs as a boy living in a section of Tel Aviv, where he was born near the Arab town of Jaffa. Through contacts with Arab neighbors, he acquired his first knowledge of Arabic, which he later studied at high school in Tel Aviv. In 1955, at the age of twenty, he began his study of Middle East history and Arabic language and literature at the Hebrew University, Jerusalem. His undergraduate and graduate studies concentrated on the modern history of the Arabs in Syria, Lebanon, and Palestine. In 1966 Ma'oz obtained his doctorate from Oxford University, having done research at St. Antony's, and he was then invited as a lecturer in the newly-established Department of Middle East History at Tel Aviv University. He moved to the Hebrew University in 1968 and since then has taught in the Department of History of Islamic Countries. He became chairman of that department in 1970, and in 1971 was elected as chairman of the Institute of Asian and African Studies for a term of four years. As an associate professor, he has been, since 1975, the director of the Harry S Truman Research Institute at the Hebrew University. He has authored or edited the following books: *Ottoman Reform in Syria and Palestine*, *Modern Syria*, *Studies on Palestine During the Ottoman Period*, and *Palestinian Arab Politics*. He has published many scholarly articles and in recent years has written on the Middle East for the Israeli daily Newspapers *Ha'aretz* and *Ma'ariv*. Ma'oz has periodically participated in the work of government ministries on Arab affairs.

EHUD OLMERT was born in 1945 and was brought up in a village near Haifa, where he had a chance to be in contact with Arab citizens of Israel who live in that area. He graduated from the Hebrew University in Jerusalem, having studied psychology, philosophy, and law. He is now a practicing lawyer. He has had experience as a military correspondent for the Israeli military media, and during the Yom Kippur war he was a correspondent with Gen. Ariel Sharon's forces. In 1973, at the age of twenty-eight, he was elected to the Knesset, and he is presently the youngest member of parliament in Israel. Olmert is a member of the La'am faction in the Likud Bloc and of the Likud Secretariat. In the Knesset he serves on the Law and Constitution Committee, the Knesset Committee, and the Sports Committee. During his several years in the parliament, he has attracted widespread publicity for his extensive campaign in investigating and exposing crime rackets and extortion in Israel. This work has led him to the poorer living quarters of Jerusalem and Tel Aviv, where he has learned first-hand the varied social problems of local communities. Currently he is engaged in an intensive effort to influence the Israeli government to adopt new approaches and policies in dealing with these issues.

YEHOSHUA PORATH was until recently the head of the Department of History of Islamic Countries, at the Hebrew University, Jerusalem, from which he had graduated. Since 1968 he has been the editor of *Ha-Mizrah He-Hadash* (The New East), the quarterly of the Israel Oriental Society. His spheres of teaching and research cover social, cultural and political histories of the Middle East in general and the Fertile Crescent in particular. He has written various scholarly articles and is the author of two books: *The Emergence of the Palestinian-Arab National Movement, 1918-1929,* and *From Riots to Rebellion, The Palestinian-Arab National Movement, 1929-1939.*

DANNY RUBINSTEIN was born in Jerusalem in 1937, where he grew up. He served in the army between 1955 and 1958 and then lived for a short time on a kibbutz. He later concentrated on sociology and Oriental studies at the Hebrew University in Jerusalem, and he studied Arabic, a language he first learned during childhood alongside Arab neighbors in Jerusalem. Against the background of his academic studies of Arab language and history his practical exposure came after the Six Day War, as he became further acquainted in Jerusalem with Arabs, their culture and their way of life. Since the 1967 war, he has worked for the daily newspaper *Davar,* as its correspondent for Arab affairs in both the occupied territories and in Israel. He also is conducting research into the problems and life of the Arabs.

ZE'EV SCHIFF was born in 1932 in France but has lived most of his life in Israel. He was raised in Tel Aviv, and he studied history and Middle East affairs at Tel Aviv University. He is now the military affairs commentator for the *Ha'aretz* daily and is a member of the paper's editorial board. His years of close contact with the Israeli Defense Forces and national security problems has brought him into contact not only with daily details of the Middle East conflict, but also with its broader issues. In his journalistic work, Schiff covered the Vietnam War in 1966 and has toured NATO installations. His writings include *La Guerre Israelo-Arabe,* a book published in France about the Six Day War; *Fedayeen: Guerrillas Against Israel; Wings Over Suez,* an account of the war of attrition; *A History of the Israeli Army;* and *October Earthquake: Yom Kippur, 1973,* for which he was awarded the Sokolow prize, Israel's highest journalism accolade. His most recent book is *A Lexicon of Israeli Security,* the most comprehensive compendium of its kind now available.

DAVID SHAHAM was born in Poland in 1923 and arrived in Palestine at the age of one year. He was educated in Tel Aviv and graduated from Tel Aviv University with a law degree. He also studied one year at the Dramatic Workshop of the New School of Social Research in New York. A kibbutz member, he was an active member in the Hashomer Hatzair Youth Movement, on whose behalf he spent three years in an educational capacity in Los Angeles and New York. He has published eight books, including novels and short stories, and he established and for three and a half years edited *OT,* the Israel Labour Party's weekly paper. He is currently an editor of *New Outlook,* an independent Middle East monthly magazine published in English in Israel and with international circulation. He contributes regularly to the Hebrew language daily *Yediot Ahronot* and to the weekly supplement of the daily *Al Hamishmar-Hotam.* Since 1967 he has been active in various peace organizations and has expressed his views in hundreds of articles in Hebrew and English. He headed a prosperous private advertising agency, selling his interest in it some six years ago. He also serves as a general editor of the Hebrew edition of the *Youth Britannica*, currently being prepared for publication under contract with the *Encyclopedia Britannica*. And he plays chamber music (violin) to relax from it all.

MOSHE SHAMIR was born in Safed, Eretz Israel, in 1921 and grew up in Tel Aviv. As a member of the Hashomer Hatzair (Young Watchmen), a pioneering Zionist-Socialist movement, he lived on a kibbutz from 1940 to 1947, joined the Haganah and served after 1943 in the Palmach. In 1948 his first novel, *He Walked in the Fields,* became the first original play to be performed in the state of Israel. His later novels were published in many editions and translations, and he also wrote short stories, essays, and books for children and youth. His political autobiographical book is *My Life with Ishmael.* Fifteen of his plays have been performed in Israel and other countries, some of which were performed in movies and on television. A member of the editorial board of the daily newspaper *Ma'ariv,* he is also a columnist and editor of that paper's literary supplement. He has been awarded major literary prizes and has lectured at universities in Israel, the United States, and England. After the Six Day War, he was one of the founders of the Land of Israel Movement. Between 1969 and 1971 he was head of the *aliyah* office of the Jewish Agency in London. He is chairman of the Central Council of La'am, a component of the Likud Bloc, and a member of the Likud executive committee.

SHIMON SHAMIR was born in Rumania in 1933 and came to Palestine in 1940. He studied at the Hebrew University of Jerusalem, receiving his B.A. in Middle Eastern history and Arabic; and he completed his Ph.D. in Oriental studies at Princeton University. After several years of teaching at the Hebrew University, he was invited in 1966 to develop a Middle Eastern studies program for the newly-founded Tel Aviv University. He instituted there the Department of Middle Eastern and African History, which he headed until 1971 and in which he is a professor of modern Middle Eastern history. He also established within Tel Aviv University the Shiloah Center for Middle Eastern and African Studies—the leading Israeli research center in this field—which he directed until 1973 and in which he is active as a senior research associate. He also serves as the head of the Graduate School of History, which includes all the regional research centers of the university. He has published works on the modern history of the Arabs—particularly on Ottoman Syria and Palestine, contemporary Egypt, and intellectual trends and ideologies; he also has conducted interdisciplinary research on Palestinian society. He appears frequently in the Israeli media—TV, radio and press—as a political analyst, and has conducted a number of lecture-tours in the United States and other countries. He has participated extensively in the Israeli public debate, advocating political initiatives for breaking the deadlock in the Middle East and making progress toward a compromise settlement with the Arabs—including the Palestinians.

OHAD ZMORA was born in 1933 in Tel Aviv, Eretz Israel. His career has included service in the army as a military correspondent, the study of Hebrew literature and philosophy at the Hebrew University in Jerusalem, and work as a journalist on several newspapers after 1956. He has been the managing editor of *Davar*, and he is now the editor of *Davar-Hashavua* weekly magazine, for which he writes occasionally on political matters. For several years, he also was the Israeli correspondent of the Danish newspaper *Politiken*. After having been a member of the Mapai wing of the Labour Party, he became active in 1965 in Ben Gurion's new party, Rafi, which split from Mapai. Zmora again joined the Labour Party when it was reorganized in 1968. In addition to his newspaper responsibilities, he is literary editor of Zmora, Bitan and Modan Publishing House.

Appendix XI: Reference Maps

The British Mandate for Palestine, 1922-1948

The Peel Commission Partition Plan, July, 1937

The United Nations Partition Plan, 1947

The Mideast, 1949-1967

The Mideast at the Close of the 1967 War

Disengagement Accords After the 1973 War

The Allon Plan

Israeli Population Settlements

Jerusalem's Holy Places in the Old City

Israeli Extension of Jerusalem Municipal Boundaries

The British Mandate for Palestine, 1922-48

MEDITERRANEAN SEA

LEBANON

SYRIA

Haifa

Jordan River

Tel Aviv
Jaffa

Amman

Jerusalem

Gaza

Dead Sea

Port Said

Suez Canal

Cairo

EGYPT

TRANS-
JORDAN

Suez

SINAI PENINSULA

Gulf of Suez

Gulf of Aqaba

| | MANDATE

SAUDI ARABIA

Red Sea

MILES

0   25   50

The Peel Commission Partition Plan, July, 1937

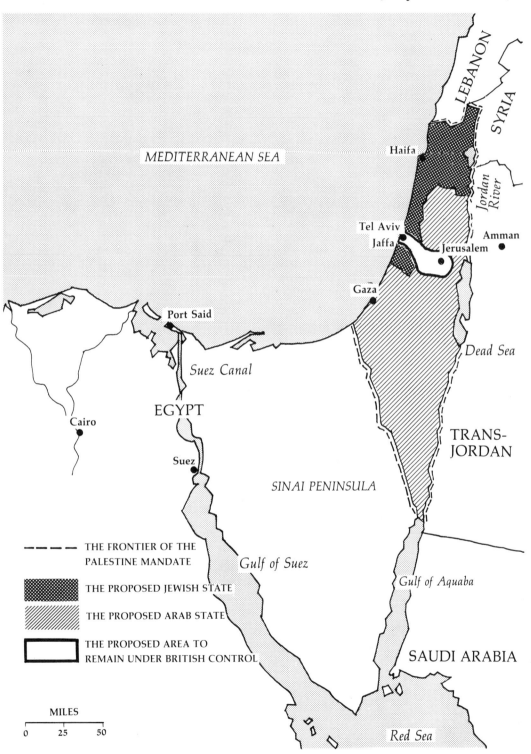

LEBANON

SYRIA

MEDITERRANEAN SEA

Haifa

Jordan River

Tel Aviv

Jaffa

Amman

Jerusalem

Gaza

Dead Sea

Port Said

Suez Canal

EGYPT

TRANS-
JORDAN

Cairo

Suez

SINAI PENINSULA

- - - - THE FRONTIER OF THE
PALESTINE MANDATE

THE PROPOSED JEWISH STATE

THE PROPOSED ARAB STATE

THE PROPOSED AREA TO
REMAIN UNDER BRITISH CONTROL

Gulf of Suez

Gulf of Aquaba

SAUDI ARABIA

MILES

0   25   50

Red Sea

The United Nations Partition Plan, 1947

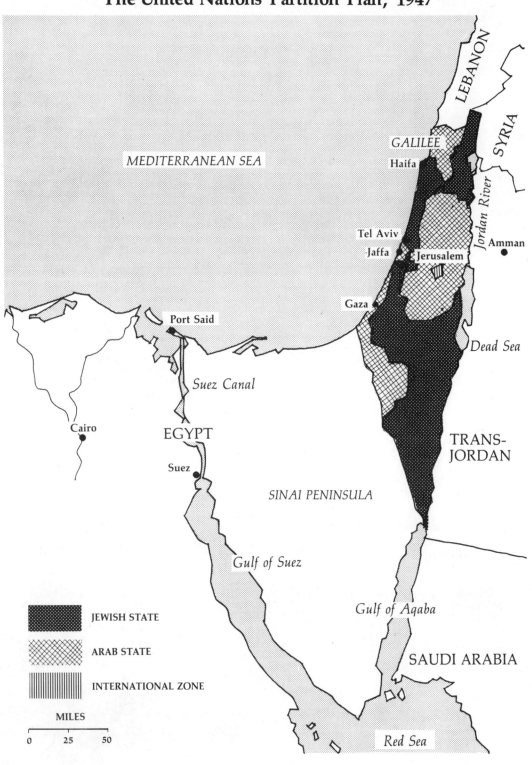

LEBANON

SYRIA

MEDITERRANEAN SEA

GALILEE

Haifa

Jordan River

Amman

Tel Aviv

Jaffa

Jerusalem

Gaza

Dead Sea

Port Said

Suez Canal

Cairo

EGYPT

Suez

SINAI PENINSULA

TRANS-
JORDAN

Gulf of Suez

Gulf of Aqaba

SAUDI ARABIA

JEWISH STATE

ARAB STATE

INTERNATIONAL ZONE

MILES

0   25   50

Red Sea

The Mideast, 1949-67

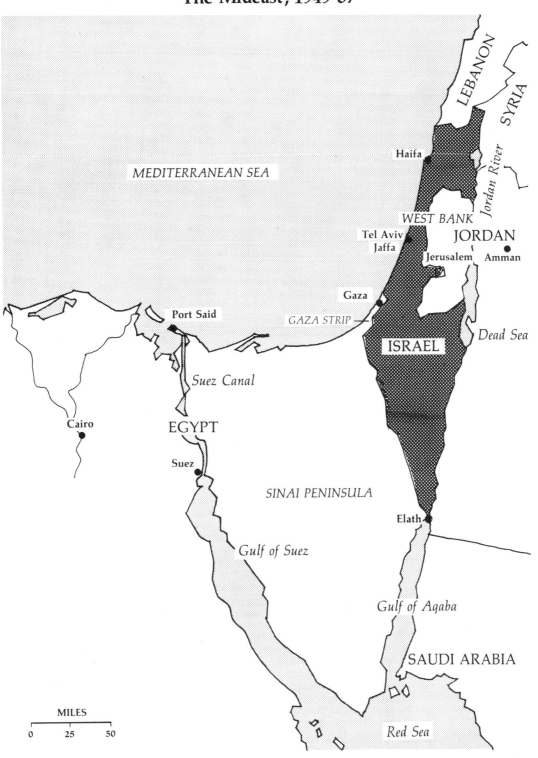

LEBANON

SYRIA

MEDITERRANEAN SEA

Haifa

Jordan River

WEST BANK

Tel Aviv
Jaffa

JORDAN

Jerusalem   Amman

Gaza

GAZA STRIP —

ISRAEL

Dead Sea

Port Said

Suez Canal

Cairo

EGYPT

Suez

SINAI PENINSULA

Elath

Gulf of Suez

Gulf of Aqaba

SAUDI ARABIA

MILES

0   25   50

Red Sea

The Mideast at the Close of the 1967 War

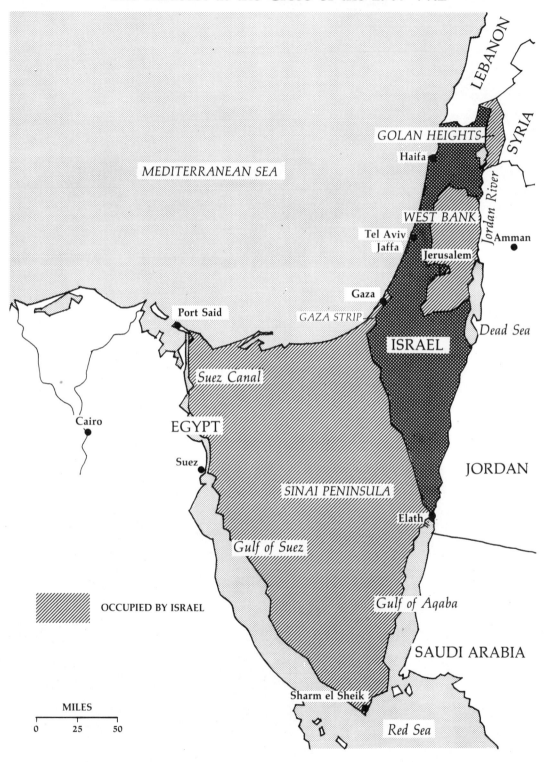

LEBANON

SYRIA

MEDITERRANEAN SEA

GOLAN HEIGHTS

Haifa

Jordan River

WEST BANK

Tel Aviv
Jaffa

Amman

Jerusalem

Gaza

GAZA STRIP

Dead Sea

ISRAEL

Port Said

Suez Canal

Cairo

EGYPT

Suez

JORDAN

SINAI PENINSULA

Elath

Gulf of Suez

Gulf of Aqaba

OCCUPIED BY ISRAEL

SAUDI ARABIA

Sharm el Sheik

Red Sea

MILES

0   25   50

Disengagement Accords After the 1973 War

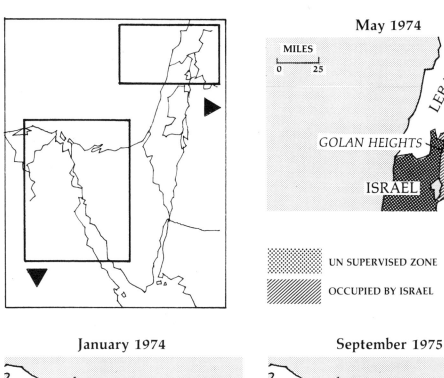

May 1974

MILES

0 25

LEBANON

GOLAN HEIGHTS

SYRIA

ISRAEL

:::::::: UN SUPERVISED ZONE

///////// OCCUPIED BY ISRAEL

January 1974

Port Said

Suez Canal

SINAI PENINSULA

Cairo

Suez

EGYPT

MILES

0 25

Abu Rudeis

Gulf of Suez

September 1975

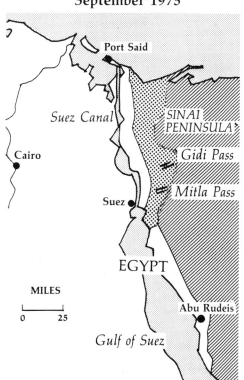

Port Said

Suez Canal

SINAI PENINSULA

Gidi Pass

Mitla Pass

Cairo

Suez

EGYPT

MILES

0 25

Abu Rudeis

Gulf of Suez

The Allon Plan

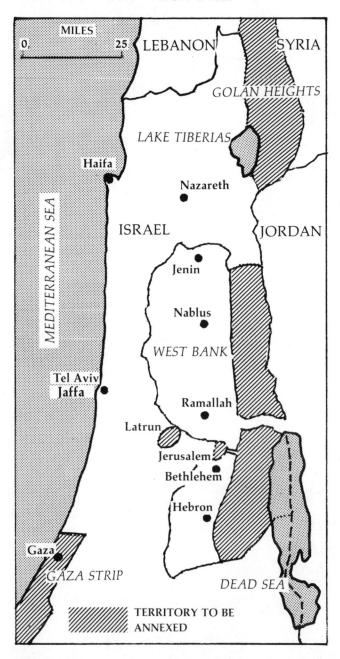

MILES
0, 25

LEBANON · SYRIA

GOLAN HEIGHTS

LAKE TIBERIAS

Haifa ●

Nazareth ●

ISRAEL

JORDAN

MEDITERRANEAN SEA

Jenin ●

Nablus ●

WEST BANK

Tel Aviv
Jaffa ●

Ramallah ●

Latrun

Jerusalem ●
Bethlehem ●

Hebron ●

Gaza ●

GAZA STRIP

DEAD SEA

TERRITORY TO BE
ANNEXED

Map designations, key and shading adapted in simplified form from Ze'ev Schiff and Eitan Haber, *Israel Army and Defence: A Dictionary* (Tel Aviv: Zmora Bitan Modan, 1976), pp. 45-46.

Israeli Population Settlements

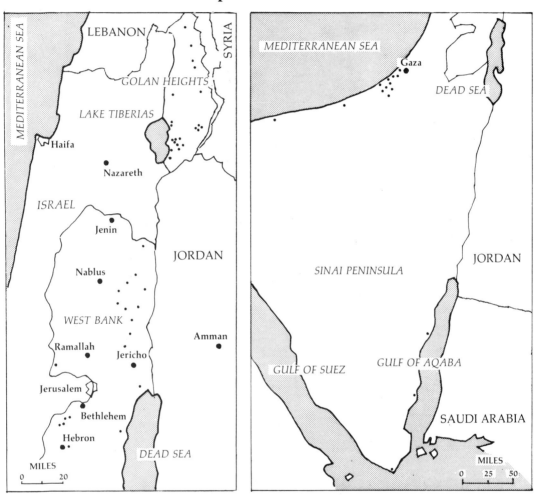

Location and number of settlements based on Ze'ev Schiff and Eitan Haber, *Israel Army and Defence: A Dictionary* (Tel Aviv: Zmora Bitan Modan, 1976), p. 164. For reference purposes, the outline of the West Bank has been added to the original map.

Jerusalem's Holy Places in the Old City

1. Church of the Holy Sepulcher
2. Church of St. Veronica
3. Mosque of Omar
4. Church of the Redeemer
5. Church of St. John the Baptist
6. The Citadel (Herod's Palace)
7. Christ Church
8. Church of St. Mark
9. Church of St. Anne
10. Solomon's Throne
11. Dome of the Rock
12. Wailing Wall
13. Islamic Museum
14. Aksa Mosque
15. Cathedral of St. James

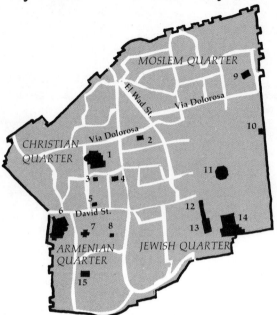

Israeli Extension of Jerusalem Municipal Boundaries

————————	ISRAEL'S BOUNDARY BEFORE 1967
—·—·—·—·—	ISRAELI MUNICIPAL LIMITS FOR THE CITY BEFORE 1967
··················	JORDANIAN MUNICIPAL LIMITS FOR THE CITY BEFORE 1967
— — — — —	ISRAELI MUNICIPAL LIMITS FOR THE CITY AFTER 1967

Note: In the 1949 Armistice
Agreement, Mount Scopus was
designated an Israeli enclave

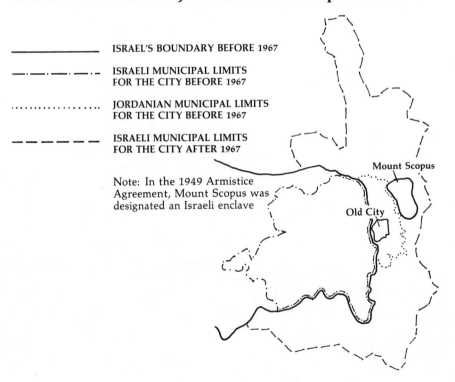